Cognitive Developmental Change

Cognitive Developmental Change makes an original contribution to the fields of developmental, cognitive and educational science by bringing together a uniquely diverse range of perspectives for analysing the dynamics of change. Connecting traditional Piagetian, information processing, and psychometric approaches with newer frameworks and tools for the assessment and analysis of developmental change, it provides the reader with a cutting-edge account of the latest theory and research. The contributors, all internationally respected experts, were asked when writing to consider three main aspects of cognitive change: its object (What changes in the mind during development?), its nature (How does change occur?) and its causes (Why does change occur? Or, what are the internal and external factors responsible for cognitive change?). As a result chapters cover key theories of cognitive change, the factors that affect change, including neurological, emotional and socio-cultural factors, and the latest methods for measuring and modelling change.

ANDREAS DEMETRIOU is Professor of Psychology and Dean of the School of Social Sciences and Sciences of Education, University of Cyprus. He is on the editorial board of several leading journals and has published over 120 books, book chapters and journal articles in the areas of cognitive development and education.

ATHANASSIOS RAFTOPOULOS is Associate Professor of Epistemology and Cognitive Science in the Department of Psychology, University of Cyprus. He has published extensively on the foundations of cognition, research methods and conceptual change.

Cambridge Studies in Cognitive and Perceptual Development

Series Editors
GIYOO HATANO
University of the Air, Chiba, Japan
KURT W. FISCHER
Harvard University, USA

Advisory Board
Gavin Bremner, *Lancaster University, UK*
Patricia M. Greenfield, *University of California, Los Angeles, USA*
Paul Harris, *Harvard University, USA*
Daniel Stern, *University of Geneva, Switzerland*
Esther Thelen, *Indiana University, USA*

The aim of this series is to provide a scholarly forum for current theoretical and empirical issues in cognitive and perceptual development. As the twenty-first century begins, the field is no longer dominated by monolithic theories. Contemporary explanations build on the combined influences of biological, cultural, contextual and ecological factors in well-defined research domains. In the field of cognitive development, cultural and situational factors are widely recognized as influencing the emergence and forms of reasoning in children. In perceptual development, the field has moved beyond the opposition of 'innate' and 'acquired' to suggest a continuous role for perception in the acquisition of knowledge. These approaches and issues will all be reflected in the series, which will also address such important research themes as the indissociable link between perception and action in the developing motor system, the relationship between perceptual and cognitive development and modern ideas on the development of the brain, the significance of developmental processes themselves, dynamic systems theory and contemporary work in the psychodynamic tradition, especially as it relates to the foundations of self-knowledge.

Titles published in the series

1. Jacqueline Nadel and George Butterworth, *Imitation in Infancy*
2. Margaret Harris and Giyoo Hatano, *Learning to Read and Write: A Cross-Linguistic Perspective*
3. Michael Siegal and Candida Peterson, *Children's Understanding of Biology and Health*
4. Paul Light and Karen Littleton, *Social Processes in Children's Learning*
5. Antonio M. Battro, *Half a Brain is Enough: The Story of Nico*
6. Andrew N. Meltzoff and Wolfgang Prinz, *The Imitative Mind: Development, Evolution and Brain Bases*
7. Nira Granott and Jim Parziale, *Microdevelopment: Transition Processes in Development and Learning*
8. Edited by Heidi Keller, Ype H. Poortinga and Axel Schölmerich, *Between Culture and Biology: Perspectives on Ontogenetic Development*
9. Nobuo Masataka, *The Onset of Language*

Cognitive Developmental Change

Theories, Models and Measurement

Edited by

Andreas Demetriou and Athanassios Raftopoulos

PUBLISHED BY THE PRESS SYNDICATE OF THE UNIVERSITY OF CAMBRIDGE
The Pitt Building, Trumpington Street, Cambridge, United Kingdom

CAMBRIDGE UNIVERSITY PRESS
The Edinburgh Building, Cambridge, CB2 2RU, UK
40 West 20th Street, New York, NY 10011–4211, USA
477 Williamstown Road, Port Melbourne, VIC 3207, Australia
Ruiz de Alarcón 13, 28014 Madrid, Spain
Dock House, The Waterfront, Cape Town 8001, South Africa

http://www.cambridge.org

First published 2004

Printed in the United Kingdom at the University Press, Cambridge

Typeface Times 10/12 pt.   *System* LaTeX 2_ε [TB]

A catalogue record for this book is available from the British Library

Library of Congress cataloguing in publication data
Cognitive developmental change : theories, models and measurement / edited by
Andreas Demetriou and Athanassios Raftopoulos.
   p.   cm. – (Cambridge studies in cognitive and perceptual development)
Includes bibliographical references and index.
ISBN 0 521 82579 2
1. Cognition in children – Congresses.   I. Demetriou, Andreas.   II. Raftopoulos,
Athanassios.   III. Cambridge studies in cognitive perceptual development.
BF723.C5C6343   2004   155.4′13 – dc22   2004045498

ISBN 0 521 82579 2 hardback

*Dedicated to the memory
of Robbie Case,
a great developmentalist*

Contents

List of contributors   *page* xi
Preface and acknowledgements   xiii

Introduction: the what, how and why of developmental
change: the emergence of a new paradigm   1
ANDREAS DEMETRIOU AND ATHANASSIOS
RAFTOPOULOS

1 Mind, intelligence and development: a cognitive,
   differential and developmental theory of intelligence   21
   ANDREAS DEMETRIOU

2 Types of cognitive change: a dynamical, connectionist
   account   74
   ATHANASSIOS RAFTOPOULOS AND
   CONSTANTINOS P. CONSTANTINOU

3 Developmental patterns in proportional reasoning   118
   HAN VAN DER MAAS, BRENDA JANSEN AND
   MAARTJE RAIJMAKERS

4 Building general knowledge and skill: cognition and
   microdevelopment in science learning   157
   MARC SCHWARTZ AND KURT W. FISCHER

5 Cognitive change as strategy change   186
   JOKE TORBEYNS, LAURENCE ARNAUD, PATRICK
   LEMAIRE AND LIEVEN VERSCHAFFEL

6 The emergence of mind in the emotional brain   217
   MARC D. LEWIS

7 Practices of quantification from a socio-cultural
   perspective   241
   GEOFFREY B. SAXE

8 Contributions of central conceptual structure theory to
   education   264
   SHARON GRIFFIN

9 Accelerating the development of general cognitive
   processing   296
   PHILIP ADEY

10 Dealing with change: manifestations, measurements
   and methods   318
   ELENA L. GRIGORENKO AND PAUL A. O'KEEFE

11 Dynamic modelling of cognitive development: time,
   situatedness and variability   354
   PAUL VAN GEERT

12 Modelling individual differences in change through latent
   variable growth and mixture growth modelling: basic
   principles and empirical examples   379
   JAN-ERIC GUSTAFSSON

   Index   403

Contributors

Philip Adey King's College London, UK

Laurence Arnaud LPC-CNRS and Université de Provence, France

Constantinos P. Constantinou Department of Education, University of Cyprus, Cyprus

Andreas Demetriou Department of Psychology, University of Cyprus, Cyprus

Kurt W. Fischer Graduate School of Education, Harvard University, USA

Sharon Griffin Department of Education, Clark University, USA

Elena L. Grigorenko Department of Psychology, PACE Center, Yale University, USA

Jan-Eric Gustafsson Department of Education, Göteborg University, Sweden

Brenda Jansen Department of Psychology, University of Amsterdam, The Netherlands

Patrick Lemaire LPC-CNRS and Université de Provence, France

Marc D. Lewis Ontario Institute for Studies in Education, University of Toronto, Canada

Paul A. O'Keefe Department of Psychology, PACE Center, Yale University, USA

Athanassios Raftopoulos Department of Psychology, University of Cyprus, Cyprus

Maartje Raijmakers Department of Psychology, University of Amsterdam

Geoffrey B. Saxe Department of Psychology, University of California, Berkeley, USA

Marc Schwartz Graduate School of Education, Harvard University, USA

Joke Torbeyns Catholic University of Leuven, Center for Instructional Psychology and Technology, Belgium

Han van der Maas Department of Psychology, University of Amsterdam, The Netherlands

Paul van Geert Department of Psychology, University of Groningen, The Netherlands

Leaven Verschaffel Catholic University of Leuven, Center for Instructional Psychology and Technology, Leuven

Preface and acknowledgements

Most of the chapters included in this volume have first been presented at two conference symposia, one organized for the Biennial Meeting of the Society for Research in Child Development that took place in Minneapolis in April 2001 and the other organized for the Xth European Conference on Developmental Psychology that took place in Uppsala, Sweden, in August 2001. Both of these symposia focused on the nature of cognitive developmental change from a number of different perspectives and were dedicated to the memory of the late Robbie Case who died suddenly a year earlier in Toronto. As organizers of these symposia and editors of this volume we are grateful to all of our contributors for their participation in this project, and for their cooperation in the long and cumbersome process of the editing of the chapters in their present form. We are also grateful to the University of Cyprus for the financial support that made possible both our participation in the two symposia above and the preparation of the volume itself.

The book is dedicated to the memory of Robbie Case, an inspired, original, and deep developmental thinker whose work has widened our understanding of cognitive development and has opened new conceptual and methodological roads in developmental cognitive science. His untimely death at the age of fifty-six deprived the field of an incisive forward looking mind at the peak of his personal and epistemic maturity and his family and friends of his warm and always enriching presence. We hope that this volume constitutes a step forward on the roads that Robbie opened for all of us.

Introduction
The what, how and why of developmental change: the emergence of a new paradigm

Andreas Demetriou and Athanassios Raftopoulos

This book presents current theory and research on cognitive change. Chapter authors were invited to discuss cognitive change from the perspective of its three main aspects. Its object (*what* changes in the mind during development?), its nature (*how* does change occur?), and its causes (*why* does change occur, or, in other words, what are the factors, internal and external, that are responsible for cognitive change?). Obviously, these are both old and fundamental questions and all theories of development attempted to answer one or more of them. Piaget was the first to provide a full set of answers to all three of these questions. His answer to these questions can rather easily be summarized as follows: operational structures (what?) change through reflecting abstraction, which organizes the results of assimilation and accommodation (how?), because of maturation, cultural influences, and self-organization (why?) (Piaget 1970, 2001). The rate of change during the course from birth to maturity varies systematically, accelerating and slowing down at different phases, so that cognitive development appears to be stage-like. In a sense, this summary of Piaget's theory is also an accurate summary of the present volume. If this had been the whole story it would have been nice because our task of writing an introduction to the book would have finished here. Fortunately, for the field at least, this is not the whole story. We have come a long way since Piaget in our knowledge about all three aspects of change and therefore an introduction is indeed needed.

Naturally, the twelve chapters included in the book overlap to a large extent, because they are driven by the same three questions noted above. However, the answers and emphasis differ, depending upon each chapter's particular epistemological assumptions, the aspects of the mind it focuses on, and the methods employed. Overall, the book involves three sections. Chapters in the first section present, or emanate from, current models of cognitive development, with an emphasis on change itself. The chapters of (1) Demetriou, (2) Raftopoulos, (3) van der Maas, Jansen and Raijmakers, (4) Schwartz and Fischer, and (5) Torbeyns, Arnaud, Lemaire and Verchaffel belong to this set. These chapters focus more on the *what* or *how* of change and leave the *why* question in the background. Chapters in the second section focus on the methods or factors that induce or cause cognitive change. This section contains chapters by (6) Lewis,

(7) Saxe, (8) Griffin, and (9) Adey. Naturally, these chapters focus on the *how* and *why* questions and leave the *what* question in the background. Finally, the chapters in the third section focus on methods, mainly statistical and technical, that can be used to capture, demonstrate, specify and model change. These are the chapters by (10) Grigorenko and O'Keefe, (11) van Geert, and (12) Gustafsson. These chapters are more related to the *what* and *how* rather than the *why* question.

In this introduction, we will attempt to integrate the answers given to the three questions in all chapters into a common framework. The aim of the discussion is to set the scene but also to facilitate the reader to move beyond the particulars of each chapter by pinpointing the common underlying assumptions about cognitive developmental change that dominate current research and theorizing. In the pages below we will first try to specify the general trends that run through the whole volume in regard to the general conceptions of cognitive change. Then we will summarize and discuss each of the various chapters belonging to the three sets mentioned above. Finally, in the concluding section we will integrate the answers given by all chapters to our three guiding questions.

From the classical to the dynamic conception of cognitive change: the emergence of a new paradigm

All the chapters in this book show that modern cognitive and developmental psychology are shifting away from classical approaches to studying developmental phenomena to a more dynamic approach. The classical approach is based on the standard conception of the cognizer as one who receives inputs from the environment, builds internal representations of relevant aspects of the environment, processes these representations, and based on the outcome of this process acts on the environment transforming it. The cognizer and the environment form a system consisting of two independent entities that interact.

Cognizers have stored concepts and have competencies that allow them to interact with the environment. These competencies can be measured by means of various experiments; the subject matter of developmental psychology is the study of changes in these competencies. Thus, it is assumed that the subjects in an experiment have a salient competence that psychological experiments are designed to examine and measure. Of course, various factors, including measurement error, can intervene in the course of the experiment and affect the performance, which thus deviates from the true score that would have been achieved had the subject had the opportunity to display her competence unperturbed by other external factors. Thus, what the experiments actually measure is the performance not the competence of the subject. The extraneous factors that intervene bear no information on the studied phenomenon, and, in this sense, they distort the measurement. The only way to make a true measure of the competence, the salient capability of the subject, is to filter out the extraneous influences, that is, to remove the variability and reduce the data to their average. This is the guiding principle of the statistical methods employed by developmental psychologists in the classical tradition.

According to the emerging approach, cognizers do not simply receive input from the environment, store representations, process them, and output some action. This picture reflects not the way the mind operates, but the way we employ abstract symbolic structures. Instead, cognizers form a whole with the environment and dynamically interact with it. Cognizer and environment form an entangled or intertwined, soft-assembled, system. The problem-space and the opportunities for exploitation it offers become part and parcel of the processing procedure, and, in that sense, the mind transcends its biological confines and extends itself into the world, which it uses as a tool, to its own benefit. This means that the sequential order between input, processing and output relaxes and cedes its place to a kind of an 'action loop' ('an intricate and iterated dance in which "pure thought" leads to actions which in turn change or simplify the problems confronting "pure thought"' (Clark 1997, 36)) in which the relations among input, processing, and output become much more intricate and interrelated to be adequately described as a serial process.

In this sense, the strategies employed by the mind incorporate operations upon the world 'as an intrinsic part of the problem-solving activity' (Clark 1997, 67). The world no longer functions as a mnemonic repository in which we store information, but as the space on which we act, build external representations and systematically transform in ways that facilitate the mind in its tasks. Understanding cognition this way means that one has to abandon the view of the mind as an entity that is isolated from the world that builds and processes internal representations of the world, in favour of a conception of the mind as an entity embedded in the world. The mind so conceived, continuously and systematically uses external representations, thereby always remaining directly interleaved with the world.

Given the view of the environment as an extension of the mind and as an entangled part of the inseparable whole organism-and-environment, the behaviour of an organism can be properly understood only in a specific context. The context becomes a part of the problem-solving activity, and it is not just the space within which problem solving takes place. This is the contextualist or situated approach to cognition. According to this approach, a concept is no longer a static object in the mind, but an 'object' in the extended mind/brain-environment system. Since what transpires in this system is a loop of mutual actions, it is more proper to view concepts as processes that occur over relatively short time spans and that involve an interplay between the properties of the organism and the properties of the context.

If concepts are processes assembled on the basis of organismic and environmental components that form an interactive loop, the concept is necessarily characterized by a certain variation. Thus, each time a concept is being assembled when the cognizer engages in a problem solving activity within a specific context, the performance in the relevant task is by its nature variable and dependent upon the specific context. Since time is an intrinsic variable in dynamic phenomena, the context can never be the same, even if the same task is repeated over and over again within the same controlled experimental conditions; repetition by itself makes a difference. The variability and fluctuation in measurements are not due to extraneous factors that are irrelevant to the task; they are inherent characteristics of the phenomenon.

General models of cognitive change

The chapter by Demetriou presents his theory of the architecture and development of the mind. The theory attempts to identify and distinguish the modules and abilities involved in the mind, specify their functional common constraints, explicate their real time functioning, and, finally, map their developmental course and explain how and why they change with age. Thus, this theory describes, first, general processing potentials (such as speed of processing, attention, working memory), general problem solving processes (such as goal setting, planning, self-monitoring and self-regulation), and specialized capacity spheres (that is, those underlying the understanding of different types of relations in the environment, such as quantitative, causal, spatial, categorical reasoning, etc.). Then, it describes the developmental course of each of these processes and tries to explicate when, how, and why change occurs. Moreover, it involves premises concerned with individual differences in cognitive organization, functioning and development.

According to this theory, each of the processes involved is a developmental explanandum in itself. That is, any theory of development must explicitly describe and explicate the development of each of the processes mentioned above throughout life. However, it is also assumed that the development of each of the various processes depends, more or less, on the status and development of one or more of the other processes. Therefore, understanding the dynamic relations between processes is both a sine qua non condition for understanding the development of each individual process and an explanandum in itself. In this direction, the theory offers descriptions of the development of each process and a dynamic systems framework aiming to capture the contribution of each process to the development of the rest. Specifically, it is shown that general processing and representational constraints set general upper limits for each of the specialized problem solving and understanding capabilities of successive phases of development. A considerable part of change in the specialized processes (circa 30 per cent) is due to changes in the general processing capacities. However, for change to occur and stabilize in the specialized processes, special domain-relevant experience and practice is needed. If this is not available, general potentials may eventually remain unformed or unrealized. Thus, in their turn, the domain-specific capabilities determine, to a considerable extent, how much of the general processing and representational potentials are realized.

Growth and dynamic systems modelling are used to pinpoint these reciprocal interactions. This modelling suggests that the tighter is the interaction between processes the more stable and spurt-like or stage-like it is. Moreover, it also shows that there are systematic individual differences in the tightness of the interactions between processes, which, in turn, result in corresponding differences in the rate and stability of individual development. These differences are reflected in differences in classical measures of intelligence, suggesting that the dynamics of individual cognitive development determine, to a considerable extent, how much of one's abilities are put to efficient use relative to others.

The chapter by Raftopoulos aims to answer the question of how does change of present processes and abilities into more advanced processes and abilities occur within a dynamic context? The chapter attempts to explicate, in terms of a combination of connectionist and dynamic systems modelling, how and why change may occur in a cognitive system that involves the generalized and specialized processes described in Demetriou's theory. According to Raftopoulos, cognitive change results from external pressures on the system, which tries to accommodate them by transforming, combining, re-combining, refining and abandoning concepts and skills already possessed.

Since the terms 'concepts' and 'skills' are understood in the dynamical sense described above, the notion of attractor (the dynamical equivalent a prototype concept) and of basin of attraction (the dynamical equivalent of variations of this prototype) is introduced to capture better their dynamical significance, and cognitive change is described as a trajectory on the activational landscape of a dynamical network. The idea that change is to be modelled by means of transitions in the state space of a dynamic system is at the heart of dynamical theories of cognition. Raftopoulos argues that dynamic connectionism can account for the processes of change at the conceptual level by (a) explaining how these are implemented by means of changes in the landscape of the activation space of a network, that is, by change in the relations between attractors and basins of attraction, and (b) by proposing some well-defined neural network mechanisms that can account for these changes.

Raftopoulos focuses his discussion on the class of networks that may change their structure (add or delete units and/or change connectivity patterns) while they learn, in order to increase their representational power. However, there is the possibility that certain neural networks can and do increase their expressive power without changing their structure. Under certain circumstances, small changes in synaptic weights can cause a real phase transition. More specifically, dynamical theory provides an explanation of how qualitatively new modes may emerge, not as a result of structural changes in the network, but because of the internal function of a self-organizing system (Raijmakers 1997). In this case, it seems that only a single general mechanism of change needs to be posited, that of continuous and gradual small changes in the connection weights of a network.

The non-linear dynamics of a system can result in more expressively powerful structures by means of self-organization and of the non-linear dynamic governing the activation functions of their processing units. Such transitions from a lower to a higher level of complexity, when the control parameters of a system transcend a threshold and critical mass effects occur, abound in dynamical theory (Elman 1995; Kelso 1995; Thelen and Smith 1994). From these studies, a common thread emerges. The internal synergies of the coupled systems that interact and the underlying non-linear dynamics may result in phase transitions and in the emergence of qualitatively new, more complex, modes: 'Certain preferred collective states of the system are depicted as synergetic wholes that can be brought forth (but not programmed) by the action of some control parameter', Clark (1997, 473). These changes are manifest in a discontinuous, stage-like, increase of the level of performance of the system, that is, in dramatic changes in the output (behaviour). These transitions correspond to the state transitions of dynamical systems. In these cases, the values of control parameters change continuously and the changes may be arbitrarily small, and yet, they lead to an increase in the expressive power (measured as computational complexity) of a system.

In their chapter, Han van der Maas, Brenda Jansen and Maartje Raijmakers focus on the mechanics of transition to higher levels of understanding. They take the common balance as their domain of understanding and Siegler's rule system as a description of the sequence of successive levels of understanding the relations between the factors (i.e. weights and distances) involved. According to this system, understanding of these relations moves across a sequence of four main levels of increasing complexity such that higher levels integrate more fully the relations between the various dimensions involved (i.e. number of weights and distances from the fulcrum on the two sides of the balance). Van der Maas et al. examine the details of phase transitions across these levels and they show that the transition across some levels (from level I to level II) is a genuine phase transition that exhibits most of the catastrophe flags, and hence it is a discontinuous, stage-like transition. Variability and fluctuation in performance figures notably in their account. Subjects are easily perturbed when transition is likely to occur, and thus their performance is very sensitive to context effects.

The classical Rule Assessment Methodology (RAM) that Siegler applied to the problem of the balance scale detects only rules that are known a priori, as a result of a task analysis. According to this method, tasks of increasing complexity are constructed to map a succession of mental rules, supposedly applied by the thinker, so that each task can be solved by the application of one and only one rule of the hierarchy. Solving a particular task automatically allocates the thinker to the rule supposedly represented by the task. However, the authors argue, the child may use unobserved rules, which the RAM fails to detect. These 'hidden' rules play the role of latent properties, which correspond to the concept of a latent variable in Latent Class Analysis. A latent variable is the factor that acts as a common cause underlying the phenomena under study and which accounts for the observed pattern of association between the manifest variables. The unobserved latent property of proportional reasoning, for instance, determines the behaviour of a person's manifest indicators, her performance on the balance scale problem, for instance.

The application of latent class analysis reveals the existence of unobserved rules in the development of the understanding of balance scale tasks (such as the compensation rule and the buggy rule), that did not appear in Siegler's and others' accounts. Moreover, the latent classes reflect the structure in the observed data, unlike the rule classification of RAM and the connectionist analyses of the balance scale by McClelland (1995) and arise independently from the rules postulated in a theory. The analysis of the rules and their use, and the study of the phase transition from Rule I to Rule II, lead the authors to propose a restricted, overlapping waves model instead of the standard overlapping waves model of Siegler (1996), to describe the development of problem solving on the balance scale task. The model includes both waves that overlap to a great extent and waves that hardly overlap (hence its designation as 'restricted'). The former reflect the continuous aspects of the development of a given individual in the balance scale task, and the latter its stage-like discontinuous aspects. Rule I and Rule II, for instance, are non-overlapping waves, hence the discontinuous development from Rule I to Rule II. The use of catastrophe theory, finally, enables the authors to explain rather than assume the abruptness that characterizes certain developmental phenomena. Moreover, this analysis is embedded in the context of Anderson's ACT-R theory (Anderson and Lebiere 1998), which specifies the capacity constraints, the general problem solving mechanisms, and the task-specific concepts required by each rule. Obviously, this approach brings this chapter close to the work presented in this volume by Demetriou, Torbeyns et al., Griffin and Adey.

Variation of understanding over time and the development of specific tools for describing how people use groping and adaptation to build new knowledge is the subject-matter of Mark Schwartz and Kurt Fischer's chapter. They employ the microdevelopmental method and their aim is two-fold: (a) to explore understanding and variations in understanding over time as subjects confront new problems, and (b) to demonstrate how skills-analysis can account for the specific trajectories that students move through, when they reach more complex understanding of the parameters and their interrelations involved in these tasks. The microdevelopmental method ensures that, unlike what happens in most developmental frameworks that study long-term changes, change and understanding is studied under the perspective of short-term building of components for specific tasks. More specifically, they examine in detail the process of building understanding in two tasks, namely, building bridges and electrical circuits. Since the skill levels that individuals will construct are intricately associated with, and depend upon, changes in context and individual state, understanding is a dynamic situated process.

The performance in the tasks examined and the processes that lead to it are ordered developmentally along Fischer's (1980) systems of levels and tiers. The notion of functional level contradistinguished with the optimal level, and the notion of developmental range, prominently figure in their account. The functional level refers to the best the individual can do in the context of a specific task without support from her environment. The optimal level refers to the best the individual čan do in the context of a specific task with support from her environment. An individual's developmental range is the interval between her optimal and functional levels. These notions emphasize the role of the learning environment, in its general sense, upon performance in a task and highlight its dynamical situational aspect.

It is worthwhile to note that the authors notice stages of regression; when subjects encounter a novel problem they regress in their strategies; that is, they use more primitive skills than those already included in their cognitive repertoire. The explanation of this phenomenon is that the subjects use the more primitive skills and not their more sophisticated ones in order to familiarize themselves with the new domain. One might attempt to explain this further by arguing that the subjects attempt to capture first the simpler regularities of the domain (let us call them first-order regularities) and then proceed to build more complex understanding based on these first-order regularities. In order to do that, though, they must use those skills from their cognitive repertoire that are better tuned to understanding the more basic, and hence less complex aspects of the phenomena: these are the less sophisticated skills.

The analysis of the task involving electric circuits nicely demonstrates this effect. This way, the more basic skills put in use in a new domain may be coordinated differently, and new more complex skills that suit better this specific domain may be developed. This would justify the authors' claim that 'microdevelopment is the process of recovering and reorganizing skills when confronting novel problems in order to construct new skills that are needed to meet the demands of the new problem' (Schwartz and Fischer, this volume).

The theme of cognitive variability as an important feature of human cognition throughout life is at the center of the contribution of Joke Torbeyns, Laurence Arnaud, Patrick Lemaire and Leaven Verschaffel. Cognitive variability means that several strategies can be used successfully either from the same subject on different occurrences of the same task, or from different subjects performing the same task. Torbeyns et al. discuss first various theoretical issues related to the information-processing approach to cognitive development with the emphasis being on Siegler's models. They also present and compare two research methods, to wit, the microgenetic and the choice/no choice method. Then, they apply these two methods to studying change in toddlers' strategy use in problem solving and change in children and adults' strategy characteristics in the domain of computational estimates.

Their conclusion is that cognitive variability is the norm and that the choice of strategies may be either progressive (the strategies adopted are more and more effective), or regressive (a subject who solves a task by using an effective strategy may for various reasons subsequently adopt a less effective or ineffective strategy). Strategy choice depends upon four factors: the problem features, the characteristics of the strategy, the situational constraints, and the individual differences. The main claim is that information processing approaches show that cognitive development should not be construed as a succession of modes of thinking, but as involving several modes of thinking coexisting and competing. Both progression and regression in the effectiveness of adopted strategies are therefore expected and indeed observed. Cognitive development proceeds gradually, with continuous changes in the repertoire of available strategies, their frequency, efficiency and adaptiveness.

The information processing tradition radically departs from the dynamic tradition discussed above, especially in the analogy that it draws of the mind as a serial computer that performs computations on symbols. However, despite this, Torbeyns et al. reach the same conclusion with regard to variability and fluctuation as van Geert, van der Maas et al. and Raftopoulos, namely, that variability and fluctuation are intrinsic to the phenomena under study and not the results of extraneous factors independent to the phenomenon.

Thus, variability and fluctuation in performance and thereby progression and regression is an emerging property of the natural dynamics of a system that is soft-assembled from constituents that interact in complex ways to form a complex system, which includes the immediate environment (recall that, according to Torbeyns et al. the strategy choice depends upon the problem features, the characteristics of the strategy, the situational constraints, and the individual differences). From this perspective, progress and regress are the result of the non-linear interactions of the subparts of the complex system. Neither of them can be explained solely in terms of the transformations of the developing organism's states; their roots lie in the interlocking of multiple context-dependent processes, both internal and external to the organism.

If we focus on each phase of development in its own sake and examine the developing person as a system, which is part of a wider system (its own environment), then development appears only positively. People function at multiple levels concurrently and thus there are various indicators for different aspects of growth of a given system. Hence, focusing on one indicator of the system may show regress when in fact massive positive changes have occurred. For instance, disappearance of stepping movements in the period three to seven months is accompanied by large positive changes in the development of the body and its control by the brain. Wrong use of words (e.g., the word horse to denote a shoe) coincides with a large expansion of vocabulary. Looking for an object at the wrong place in the A-not-B arrangement is accompanied by an expansion in memory capacity (Gershkoff-Stowe and Thelen in press).

Inducing and causing cognitive change: from description and explanation to practice

The four chapters in the second section present work that aims either to explain or induce cognitive change in reference to broad biological or socio-cultural causal factors. The first chapter, contributed by Marc Lewis, brings the dynamic approach from the organization of functional mental units to the organization of the brain itself and the interpretation of the relations between cognition and emotion. Lewis agrees with dynamic systems theorists (Thelen and Smith 1994) that what develops are cognitive and perceptual coherence, and how they develop is through the mechanism of selection of functional forms, of 'what works'. However, he points out that this account tells us only half of the story because it does not explain the why of development. That is, it does not explain why some forms work better than other forms. He suggests that emotions are responsible for the selection of forms that work because they index events that have acquired significance within the particular environments of family, community, culture and niche. That is, the emotional system is organized to guide attention, action, and thought according to what is proficient and useful, and this is how cognitive abilities emerge systematically in the service of functionality. Thus, Lewis elaborates on how emotion guides neural self-organization (1) in real-time cognitive processes, (2) along the path of cognitive development, and, finally, (3) along unique developmental pathways referred to as personality styles.

Lewis discusses the four levels in which the brain is organized, that is, the brain stem (a set of nuclei for programmed responses to internal and external events), the diencephalons (the thalamus and hypothalamus that process and route sensory input, providing a more detailed picture of the world), the limbic system (the hippocampus and amygdala that are responsible for fitting responses to the learned aspects of situations, holding memory of those situations and the actions they require, and motivating behaviour) and the cortex, which is the locus of what we normally call cognition, perception and attention.

In the past it was believed that higher levels dominated over and controlled the functioning of lower levels. However, we now know that the downward flow of control and modulation is reciprocated by an upward flow of motivational arousal. The brain stem and diencephalon fuel the limbic system with excitation and arousal, locking in behavioural activation and inhibition systems, and they also fuel the cortex with chemicals that recruit its activities to ancient mammalian and even reptilian goals. Primitive agendas and requirements thus flow up the neural axes from its most primitive roots at the same time as executive attention, planning, and knowledge subordinate each lower level by the activities of the cortex. It is the reciprocity of these upward and downward flows that links cognition with motivation. Thus, cognition is based on the two-way synchronization of all brain systems that intertwines understanding and problem solving with motivation and even individual differences in regard to them.

Lewis demonstrates this twofold developmental causation with two related examples. The first is the emergence of inhibitory control or executive control, at about the age of four. The brain region held responsible for this acquisition is the anterior cingulate cortex, an attentional system that is considered important for self-regulation and error monitoring. Yet, despite, its 'cognitive' function, the anterior cingulate is an extension of the 'emotional' limbic system to which it is directly connected. The second example is the emergence of individual attentional and cognitive biases, an important constituent of personality formation, driven by preoccupations with those aspects of the world that are motivationally relevant to each individual. A key executive function of mind emerges when the anterior cingulate becomes entrained, over and over again, with problematic situations, such that its *function* is the function of regulating negative emotion. Thus, the anterior cingulate instantiates a level of attention, control and consciousness, but its mode of operation is shaped by its motivational origins. These two examples demonstrate the emotional basis of emergent neural patterns that underpin executive control and individual differences in early cognitive development.

The chapter by Geoffrey Saxe bears a big difference from the previous chapter and an impressive similarity to it. It is clearly different in that it focuses on socio-cultural factors as a source of cognitive change. Thus, it moves from the material substrate of individual functioning and development to its collective and historical frame. At the same time, this chapter is impressively similar to Lewis's chapter (to all of the other chapters, for that matter), in so far as it defines the mind as a system inexorably interleaved with the wider context in which it functions and develops. Saxe takes quantification practices as an illustrative case for the effects of related socio-cultural practices on understanding and cognitive change. Quantification practices refer 'to socially patterned ways in which individuals draw upon cultural forms (like number words, rulers, charts, and geometrical shapes) to construct and accomplish mathematical goals in everyday activities'. In particular, he studies candy selling by children on the streets in Brazil. This practice, like any other practice that is culturally and historically formulated and sustained, is a complex system where 'the interconnected actions of sellers, clerks, customers, all working with cultural forms like currency, candy, and written representations of prices, create and re-create a pattern of social organization that endures'. This system enables children to construct and use procedures for the estimation and processing of complex proportional relations between buying prices, selling prices, and quantities involving very large numbers that are normally out of the reach of primary school children. This is due to the fact that the cultural practices of quantification provide an integrated and user-friendly representational system that enables the child to grasp the relations between the various quantitative scales involved and mentally and actually move from the one to the other. In this system, microgenesis, ontogenesis and sociogenesis are well concerted with each other. In fact, Saxe and his colleagues test this culturally rich system of inducing quantification in actual classrooms and he finds that it does work more than more traditional practices.

Thus, in answering the 'how' question, Saxe suggests that collective practices and activities are important, because they are rich in task-relevant meaning that is transparent to the children so that they can function as bridges between the target mathematical notions, the particular task to be mastered, and the child's currently available notions and skills. In fact, these practices and activities may be seen as the mechanisms themselves that transform a present state of understanding into a more advanced one. In answering the 'why' question, Saxe suggests that cognitively relevant cultural practices work because they are at one and the same time optimally demanding and they provide a historically refined context that can sustain motivation for involvement. That is, they are not too difficult for the child so that they do not cause aversion and at the same time they have obvious social, cultural and historical value.

The two chapters following present large-scale intervention programs that aimed to boost and accelerate cognitive development. In her chapter, Sharon Griffin elaborates on the educational aspects of the theory of the late Robbie Case. In its latest version, this theory analyses the mind in a way that is very similar to the analysis offered by Demetriou. That is, it is proposed that there are central constraints, defined in terms of processing efficiency and working memory, which determine the complexity of problems that can be represented and solved, and a set of central conceptual structures underlying concepts and problem solving skills in different domains. Both the general constraints and the central conceptual structures coincide considerably with the general processing and representation potentials and the capacity spheres described by Demetriou. In fact, Case and Demetriou started a research project aiming at the integration of the two theories (Case et al. 2001) but Robbie's untimely death brought this project to a halt.

According to this theory, change in central conceptual structures is made possible by changes in working memory, which in their turn, are largely determined by biological factors, such as neuronal myelinization. However, to be implemented, these changes require both active exploration of the domain concerned by the developing person and/or social interaction that will provide relevant information and/or models. These factors enable the construction of new units of thought through the progressive elaboration and differentiation of old units or their hierarchical integration into more complex units. Griffin presents a program of research that uses this developmental model as a basis for intervention aiming to boost the development of underprivileged children in the domain of mathematical thinking. This program proved very successful because it is guided by a detailed specification of both the developmental sequences in regard to the domain of interest and the mechanisms of transition across the levels of the sequence. Thus, the teacher knows what to attempt to attain at particular times for particular children, how to structure relevant activities that map the normal course of ascension, and how to measure any progress attained. Griffin presents results showing that this program is highly successful, indicating that a valid cognitive developmental theory is a good practical tool that can guide educational applications.

In the next chapter, Adey presents a large intervention program that he has developed with Michael Shayer. This program is broader and more eclectic than the program described by Griffin because it draws on a number of general theories of development to formulate its intervention target and tools. Specifically, it draws (i) on classical Piagetian theory for the specification of the general mechanism of change, which is equilibration, and also for the specification target concepts and skills; (ii) on Vygotskian notions, such as the notions of social construction as a means of change and the zone of proximal development, for the specification of intervention goals that are optimal for particular children as a means for implementing equilibration; and (iii) on neo-Piagetian concepts, such as metacognition, for the specification of problem solving strategies and skills that must be imparted to the children.

In addition to these three main pillars of intervention, as they call them, they also offer two more pragmatic pillars, 'concrete preparation' and 'bridging'. The former aims to familiarize children with concepts and materials in a given domain and it is very similar to Case's exploration. Bridging aims to generalize the results of intervention to new concepts and domains and is a means for ensuring transfer. This method is very effective in terms of accelerating and boosting development in the target domains and also development in very remote domains related to general school performance. According to Adey, what the method accomplishes is to enable children to explore relations and connections between the concepts and skills of interest and build new concepts and skills. In fact, Adey goes as far as to state that intelligence may to a large extent be 'connectivity'. He proposes that the basic means of connectivity is directed chunking, a mechanism known to generate connections. In answering the why question Adey invokes the general potentials that are maturationally determined, and are associated with different phases of development.

Capturing, measuring and modelling change

The last three chapters focus on methods for capturing, measuring and modelling change. The first of these chapters, by Grigorenko and O'Keefe, is a general overview of the methods that can be used to study different forms of change. The chapter discusses, first, various types of growth models. Among these various types of growth are classical learning curves, such as S-shaped learning curves, saltatory growth and stepwise growth, which are discussed in many of the other chapters in this volume. Second, it elaborates on various measurement approaches that have been developed to quantify different types of growth, occurring naturally or as a result of intervention. Specifically, it discusses the strengths and weaknesses of conventional approaches to measuring change by means of simple change scores (gain scores), as estimated through the pre- to post-test difference scores, regression approaches, and repeated measures analyses of variance. Also, it briefly introduces modern approaches to change quantification. These approaches are subdivided into two groups. The first group has been developed to measure change under the assumption of continuity (e.g. the multidimensional Rasch-family model for learning and change and the mixed-population Rasch model). The second group has been developed to measure change under the assumption of discontinuity and it is similar to the approach espoused by van Geert and van der Maas and colleagues in this volume.

In the next chapter, van Geert, one of the major proponents of dynamic systems theory as a paradigm for developmental science, elaborates on the fundamental differences between the classical psychonomic and psychometric models of human cognition and the dynamic systems model. In the classical models, people are supposed to *have* concepts or abilities, which can be demonstrated and thus measured under appropriate circumstances. Thus, according to these models, statistical indexes, such as means, are thought to represent the 'actual' state concepts or abilities 'possessed' and variability around the mean is considered as measurement error caused by random variations either within persons or in the environments where the measurements are taken. In classical psychological models, persons are segregated from not only the environment but also, to a large extent, time. From the perspective of the dynamic systems approach, concepts or abilities are processes inexorably intertwined with the current context in which they happen, rather than fixed (and thus definable) entities of any kind that simply interact with the environment. Thus, environmental variations and time do matter strongly, because they are part of these processes. By implication, variability and fluctuation in performance and thereby regression are emerging properties of the natural dynamics of a system that is soft-assembled from constituents that interact non-linearly to form a complex system, which includes the immediate environment. From this perspective, progress and regress are the result of the non-linear interactions of the subparts of the complex system. Thus, any attempt to reduce data to averages destroys an important ingredient of the phenomenon and undermines its understanding. New statistical techniques should be developed to allow the systematic study of the variations and fluctuation. Van Geert proposes several methods capable of providing data congruent with this paradigm. In short, data must represent both modal tendencies and ranges and they must be collected densely enough and for as long as is needed to reveal the transformations of interest in the process of interest. Obviously, many of the chapters that appear in this volume (the chapters by Demetriou, Raftopoulos, van der Maas et al., Schwartz and Fischer and Lewis) present work that was conceived, executed, and tested according to the paradigm and methods advocated by van Geert.

The last chapter by Jan-Eric Gustafsson is in many ways complementary to the chapter by van Geert. It presents an approach and methods for the study of change that originated from a paradigm that is very different from the paradigm underlying van Geert's dynamic systems approach. Specifically, Gustafsson's chapter originates from the tradition of the psychology of individual differences and it discusses methods that can be used to uncover individual differences in growth. These methods are among the most robust modern methods that the psychologist has at her disposal to study cognitive change as such as well as changes in the relations between psychological processes or traits. They are a class of methods that evolved from confirmatory factor analysis and structural equations modelling in order to capture patterns of change while at the same time taking into account individual differences in ability at different points in time.

Admittedly, for a long time, researchers refrained from studying individual differences in growth because of serious methodological problems, such as unreliable difference scores and a negative correlation between initial status and change. Recently, however, new tools have been developed within the framework of latent variable modelling, which not only solve such methodological problems, but also contribute new powerful methods for studying correlates, antecedents and consequences of individual differences in change. In these models, latent variables are used to represent parameters such as intercept, slope, and curvature of a growth function (which stand for initial state, the rate, and the form of change, respectively, of the process of interest). Instead of estimating individual values of these parameters, parameters describing the distribution of individual values (i.e. mean and variance) are estimated in a random coefficient modelling approach. Because the parameters of the growth function are represented as latent variables, these may be related as dependent or independent variables to other latent or manifest variables in a general structural equation model. In Gustafsson's chapter, the basic principles of latent variable growth modelling are presented, and the methodology is illustrated in models of data from repeated test-taking of the Swedish Scholastic Aptitude Test.

It must be stressed that this class of methods, if applied together with dynamic systems modelling, may enable the researcher to specify simultaneously both the dynamics of change in either individual processes or in constellations of processes and the possible existence of systematic individual differences in these dynamics. Demetriou, in his chapter, presents a study in which these methods were jointly applied showing that different groups of people, well specified in terms of their characteristics, grow cognitively in systematically different ways. That is, some grow more smoothly and in a more stable way and others grow more erratically and in unstable ways, depending upon the particular combination of background processes such as processing efficiency and working memory.

Conclusions

The chapters prepared for this volume suggest that, in the field of cognitive development, science grows in much the same way as its subject matter, the human mind. There is both continuity relevant to the concerns and notions of the past and sharp changes in approaches, methods, and general modelling styles adopted. In so far as the 'what' of cognitive development is concerned, all researchers who contributed chapters in this volume are still concerned with the development of all kinds of notions that were of interest to Piaget himself and the first researchers of intelligence. Reasoning and problem solving as such and the notions and concepts of mathematics, science, and the social world are still at the foreground and these are well represented in this volume. All chapters are somehow related to these concerns. Processing efficiency in its various aspects, such as speed of processing, working memory, and control, which were imported in cognitive development from the information processing tradition that flourished in the 1950s and the 1960s, is already a stable and integral part of research and theorizing about the 'what' of cognitive change. The chapters by Demetriou, van der Maas et al., Griffin and Adey are related to these issues. Concerns about the neural and emotional bases of cognitive development are already part, although much less integrally, of the concerns of cognitive developmental researchers. The chapter by Raftopoulos brings artificial networks in the understanding of cognitive change and Lewis brings neuroscience and emotions. Self-understanding and consciousness are also important topics in the cognitive science of today, certainly more than the extent to which they are represented in the present volume. Demetriou, Torbeyns and Adey discuss issues related to these topics. We can foresee that in the coming years, concerns about the neural, the emotional, and the consciousness aspects of cognitive change will come to the foreground and that the more classical topics, such as the development of mathematical or scientific understanding, will be re-examined from the perspective of these new concerns.

How does change occur? Usually, in developmental science, this question is understood in two complementary ways. The first is concerned with the mechanics and mechanisms of change. That is, how a mental unit (for example, a concept, skill, representation, strategy, rule, operation, schema) is transformed or reshaped into a mental unit that is different from the previous one in one or more respects. If answered from the point of view of mechanics, the emphasis is on changes in the nature of the mental unit under question or in its composition (e.g. qualitative transformation of the unit, incorporation of a new component, or rearrangement of the relations between its components). If answered from the point of view of mechanisms, the emphasis is on the processes, procedures, or routines that implement the transformation. An analogy from biological developmental in regard to the differences between the mechanics and the mechanisms of change would be the mapping of the bodily transformations that lead from a child to an adolescent during puberty (the mechanics of the transformation) and the mapping of the hormonal influences that drive these transformations (the mechanisms of change). The second is concerned with the pace or rate of change. That is, how fast is the transformation of the unit under question and how long does it take to complete? Examination of change from this point of view usually aims to specify if change is smooth and continuous or abrupt and discontinuous.

Obviously, these approaches, although clearly distinct, are complementary to each other. Mechanics specify the internal nature of change, mechanisms are the effectors of change, and rate specifies the phenomenology of change in relation to time. All of the chapters presented in this volume are related to one or more of these aspects of change. Demetriou, van der Maas et al., Schwartz and Fischer, Torbeyns et al., Griffin and Adey either present or make use of detailed maps of the course of transformation of a variety of domains of thought and processes from early childhood to adulthood that speak about the mechanics of change in different domains. Internal processes, such as meta-representation, representational flexibility, and metacognition (Demetriou, Torbeyns et al., Adey), cognitive-behavioural processes, such as problem solving and exploration (Griffin), and external processes, such as socio-cultural scaffolding (Saxe, Adey), are powerful mechanisms of change that drive and guide the mechanics of conceptual and ability transformation. Moreover, using dynamic systems modelling, all chapters somehow specify the rate of change of most of these domains, showing that overall it is logistic in nature. In other words, it is slower at the beginning and the end than in its middle regions (Demetriou) but, if examined microscopically through microgenetic methods, it may temporarily involve regressions, returns, and spurts which reflect the underlying transformations and re-combinations before they stabilize.

Raftopoulos analyses the mechanics in detail in terms of dynamic connectionism and shows how different forms of change simply result from differences in the strength of connections between the components of the units of interest, their connections to other units and/or the introduction of new hidden units. Differences in the mechanics of change are reflected in differences in the rate or form of change as this is reflected in the models presented by van der Maas et al. and Torbeyns et al. That is, some kinds of re-arrangements in the relations of components result in fast and radical transformations of the units under question and other re-arrangements result in slower and smoother kinds of changes. The advances in methods of studying and modelling developmental changes that are reflected in this book (see Demetriou, van der Maas, Raftopoulos, van Geert and Gustafsson for examples of these methods) may one day show the fractal nature of cognitive developmental formations and the catastrophic nature of their change as in other realms of nature. That is, the same basic formations and patterns of change repeat themselves on different levels of organization and we only need the right methods to uncover and describe them.

Why does cognitive change occur? At a global level, the answer emanating from the volume as a whole is very Piagetian: because human minds are open systems that interact with a variable environment. Environmental variability necessitates adaptations (or re-equilibrations) in mental structures in order to cope with the new and the unexpected. So environmental variability is the main cause of cognitive change. Why does it take so long to reach relative efficiency and thereby stability, that is, adult levels? Biologically oriented scholars would ascribe cognitive change to the brain, the mind's organ. They would argue that cognitive change is patterned on the time course needed by the brain to unravel its material potentials and build the representations and operations necessary to capture and deal with the systematicity and the variability of the world. Obviously, this sounds like a strong reductionist explanation of cognitive change, because it seems to ascribe changes in the mind to changes in the brain. Indeed, this was the position espoused by the information processing models of cognitive development, such as the models proposed by Case, Halford and Pascual-Leone, which took measures of processing efficiency as an index of the representational and operational possibilities of the brain. Socio-culturally oriented scholars emphasized the social, cultural, and historical factors of change and argued that it is mainly due to internal constraints of knowledge structure as they exist in the culture. Thus, development, from this point of view, maps the time needed by culture to impart its structure to the growing individual. The socio-cultural approach is no less reductionist than the biological approach, although the two go in opposite directions. The chapters presented in this volume suggest that neither direction is right in itself. Cognitive change is a dynamic process in which all participating components cause changes of the one or the other kind to the one or the other degree to the other components. Changes in processing potentials do cause changes in thinking but these latter changes reflect back and affect the condition of processing potentials (Demetriou). The brain does posit constraints on what can be abstracted from the environment but it is also continually moulded by the environment so that brain structures reflect somehow the history of the subject's relations with the environment. In fact, the importance of environmental messages that shape the person's motivational frames directing thinking is marked by the environment on related brain structures (Lewis). Moreover, socio-cultural means and tools do cause change, but this is mediated and moderated by both biological and functional constraints that are characteristic of the given time (Saxe, Griffin, Adey) and these constraints usually differ systematically across individuals (Gustafsson). Overall, the causation of cognitive change resides in the relations between the factors involved rather than in any one of them alone. This is what we have to study in the years to come.

REFERENCES

Anderson, J. R. and Lebiere, C. (1998). *The atomic components of thought*. Mahwah, NJ: Lawrence Erlbaum Associates, Inc.

Case, R., Demetriou A., Platsidou, M. and Kazi, S. (2001). Integrating concepts and tests of intelligence from the differential and the developmental traditions. *Intelligence, 29*, 307–36.

Clark, A. (1997). Being there: putting brain, body, and world together again. Cambridge, MA: The MIT Press.

Elman, J. L. (1995). Language as a dynamic system. In R. F. Port and T. van Gelder (eds.) *Mind as motion: exploration in the dynamics of cognition*. Cambridge, MA: The MIT Press.

Fischer, K. W. (1980). A theory of cognitive development: the control and construction of hierarchies of skills. *Psychological Review, 87*, 477–531.

Gershkoff-Stowe, L. and Thelen, E. (in press). U-shaped changes in behavior: a dynamic systems perspective. *The Journal of Cognition and Development*.

Kelso, S. (1995). *Dynamic patterns: the self organization of brain and behavior.* Cambridge, MA: The MIT Press.

McClelland, J. L. (1995). A connectionist perspective on knowledge and development. In T. J. Simon and G. S. Halford (eds.) *Developing cognitive competence*, Hillsdale, NJ: Lawrence Erlbaum.

Piaget, J. (1970). Piaget's theory. In P. H. Mussen (ed.) *Carmichael's handbook of child development* (pp. 703–32). New York: Wiley.

  (2001). *Studies in reflecting abstraction.* Sussex, UK: Psychology Press.

Siegler, R. S. (1996). *Emerging minds.* Oxford: Oxford University Press.

Thelen, E. and Smith, L. (1994). *A dynamic system approach to the development of cognition and action.* Cambridge, MA: The MIT Press.

1   Mind, intelligence and development: a cognitive, differential and developmental theory of intelligence

Andreas Demetriou

Since the end of the nineteenth century, three fields of psychology have attempted to understand the human mind: cognitive, differential and developmental psychology. Each of these fields was and still is driven by different epistemological assumptions regarding the nature of the human mind, has adopted different priorities in regard to the aspects of the mind to be studied, and has used different methods for the investigation of the phenomena of interest.

Specifically, cognitive psychology focused primarily on the more dynamic aspects of mental functioning to explain how information from the environment is recorded, represented, stored and processed for the purpose of understanding, problem solving and decision making in real time. Thus, the primary aim of research and theory in this field was to model the flow and processing of information in the mind. In general, according to this tradition, the human mind is an information processing system operating under limited representational and processing resources. Therefore, three aspects of the mind are of utmost importance in this tradition: representational capacity, control of processing and efficiency. Change in the information processing tradition is conceived as increasing automatization of performance on a given task. This is equivalent to saying that, with experience and practice, the control of performance shifts from the monitoring and regulation of central control processes to the forces underlying the dynamic organization of task-specific performance and the inter-connection of the components involved in this performance with the task-relevant environmental stimuli (Broadbent 1971; Logan and Gordon 2001; Posner and Boies 1971).

Differential psychology aimed primarily to measure and explain individual differences in mental abilities. In the differential tradition the mind is conceived as an ability system that enables individuals to acquire knowledge and skills and use them as efficiently as possible to meet challenges and solve problems posed by the environment. Cognitive entities are phenomenologically and

The present version of the chapter profited considerably from the comments of Karin Bakracevic, Iriana Diakidoy, Han van der Maas and Michael Shayer. Special thanks are due to Costas Christou and Nicos Mousoulides for their help in the preparation of the figures included in this chapter.

globally specified on the basis of correlations and internal mechanisms are assumed rather than analysed in this approach. Moreover, how an individual performs relative to other individuals is more important for the specification of an individual's ability rather than how the individual tackles a problem. This field has been very successful in uncovering a number of stable dimensions of ability and cognitive functioning that can be used to measure and compare individuals. Specifically, in this tradition, there is growing agreement that intelligence is a three-level hierarchical system. This hierarchy involves general intelligence, or *g*, a set of broad abilities, such as spatial, verbal, and mathematical reasoning, and a variety of narrow abilities within *g* or within each of the broad abilities mentioned above (Carroll 1993; Gustafsson and Undheim 1996; Jensen 1998). In this tradition, stability is considered to dominate over change. It is well known that IQ is considered as a more or less stable characteristic or trait of the individual. That is, it is accepted that an individual's IQ does not change appreciably for most of his life (Deary, Whalley, Lemmon, Crawford, and Starr 2000).

Finally, developmental psychology focused primarily on the development of mental functions in order to specify both their quality and form at different phases of life and the causes and mechanisms underlying their transformation with growth. Thus, this field modelled the stages and the dynamics of the development of mental functions. In the developmental tradition, the mind is a knowing and understanding system par excellence. It is driven by the need to understand the underlying structure and the functioning of the world. This is considered possible because development drives the individual to build increasingly complex and abstract mental structures that make accessible more complex and less familiar aspects of the world. Thus, internal mechanisms for concept formation and change and problem solving are of utmost importance in this approach. These mechanisms are conceived as logically sound systems whose organization and functional properties define the kind of understanding and problem solving that is possible at successive phases of life. Change in this tradition is considered as transformation in both the kind of representations that can be constructed about the world and the organization of the processes and operations that can be brought to bear on representations. With development, representations become more accurate and the operations that can be applied on them become more intricately and stably inter-related. As a result, the aspects of the world that can be understood and the quality of problems that can be solved changes systematically (Piaget 1970, 2001).

Divisions or specializations in science in general reflect the limitations of knowledge and method and the dominant concerns of a particular historical and cultural era rather than actual characteristics of the phenomena of interest. Thus, despite its complexity and sophistication, the human mind is a single integrated and well orchestrated system, which needs not respect the divisions of labour in psychological science as specified above. We believe that the time is ripe for an integration of the basic findings, assumptions and postulates of the three fields into an overarching model of the human mind that would be able to accommodate, at one and the same time, the basic intellectual functions and processes and their organization, their real time operation as an integrated system, the factors underlying their change and development, both microscopically and macroscopically and finally, the factors underlying intra- and inter-individual differences in regard to the attainment, operation and development of these functions and processes. Previous attempts at integration focused only on two of the three fields, such as the cognitive and the psychometric (Deary 2000a; Sternberg 1985), the cognitive and the developmental (Case 1985; Pascual-Leone 1970), or the developmental and psychometric (Demetriou and Efklides 1985; Demetriou et al. 1993). However, all three must be integrated, if a general theory of intelligence and mind is to become possible.

This is the aim of the present chapter. That is, in this chapter we will summarize a model that attempts to integrate the three traditions into a comprehensive description of the architecture and development of the human mind. Thus, from the point of view of the questions guiding the present volume, I will attempt to specify (a) *what* are the main functions and dimensions involved in the mind and what is their condition at different phases of development, (b) *why* these dimensions and functions change with age, that is what are the causal factors that underlie their change, and (c) *how* they change with age, that is how they are transformed with growth into higher levels of functioning. These issues will be discussed in this order in the pages following.

The architecture of the human mind

There is an increasing consensus that intelligence is a hierarchical and multidimensional edifice that involves both general-purpose and specialized processes and abilities. Understanding, learning or performance on any task, at a particular point in time, is a mixture of these two types of processes.

General processes

The general processes revolve around a strong directive-executive function (DEF) that is responsible for setting and pursuing mental and behavioural goals until they are attained. The constructs serving DEF are usually analysed and studied from three different perspectives, that is, (i) their efficiency, (ii) their capacity, and (iii) the fundamental operations that they involve.

Processing efficiency

Processing efficiency refers to how well the person executes the processes activated in the service of DEF at a given moment. Technically speaking, processing efficiency refers to the ability to focus on, encode and operate on goal-relevant information and inhibit or resist goal-irrelevant information until the current mental or behavioural goal is attained. Thus, selective attention is the functional manifestation of processing efficiency. Ideally, processing is considered to be efficient when it is completed without mistakes and unnecessary mental operations that would result in excessive mental effort.

A common measure of efficiency is *speed of processing*. Speed of processing refers to the time needed to identify a unit of information or execute a given mental act. Because executive control is an integral part of information processing, measures of speed of processing vary widely from very simple, where the person must recognize a simple stimulus (such as a letter, geometrical figure, or colour) under optimum conditions without any interference, to complex conditions, where the person must identify a target stimulus among other interfering stimuli and/or inhibit response to all but the target stimulus (e.g. choose a letter among others according to a particular rule). In these conditions, speed of processing is usually defined as the time between the presentation of a target stimulus and the emission of the required response from the person. Traditionally, the faster an individual can recognize a stimulus or execute a mental act, ignoring irrelevant information, if required, the more mentally efficient he is thought to be. Naturally, speed of processing increases as a function of the amount of information that must be attended to and processed. That is, the more the information to be integrated or the more the responses to be coordinated the more is the time required (Deary 2000b).

Processing capacity

Processing capacity is defined as the maximum amount of information and mental acts that the mind can efficiently activate simultaneously under the direction of DEF. In the current psychological literature, working memory is regarded as the functional manifestation of processing capacity. It is generally accepted that working memory involves both central executive processes (to be specified below) and modality-specific storage that specializes in the representation of different types of information. Baddeley's (1990, 1993) model is exemplary for this type of architecture of working memory. According to this model, working memory involves two general systems, the central executive system and the episodic buffer, and two specialized storage buffers, one specializing in the storage of phonological and one specializing in the storage of visuo/spatial information.

In spatial terms, the central executive is actually the locus of the executive operations involved in DEF. That is, the central executive is an attentional control system that is responsible for strategy selection, monitoring and coordination of the operation of the two specialized storage systems, and the coordination of information in working memory with information in long-term memory. The episodic buffer is 'a temporary storage system capable of holding information from the slave systems of working memory and long-term memory in some form of multimodal code. It is assumed to be controlled by the central executive, and to allow access through conscious awareness. As such, the mechanism is assumed to represent an approach to the binding problem, that is, the problem of how information from different sources is combined to create the perception of a single coherent episode' (Baddeley and Hitch 2000, 135).

The phonological loop involves a short-term phonological buffer and a subvocal rehearsal loop. The first stores verbal information as encountered. Information in this buffer decays rapidly. The second counteracts this decay by refreshing memory traces through rehearsal guided by DEF. The faster the rehearsal the more the information that can be held in the phonological loop. The visuo-spatial sketchpad is responsible for the retention and manipulation of visual or spatial information. The specialized systems draw upon partially different resources. As a result, each is amenable to interference from system-specific information that does not affect the other system. That is, the phonological loop is affected by interference from verbal but not visuo-spatial information; the visuo-spatial sketchpad is affected by visuo-spatial but not verbal information (Shah and Miyake 1996). However, these systems are interrelated in the episodic buffer and information from one can be translated into the code of the other through rehearsal guided by DEF. Other specialized buffers associated with other senses, such as smell and touch, may also be present.

Directive-executive control processes

These processes involve five basic components: (i) a feedforward or directive function which sets the mind's current goals; (ii) a planning function that proactively constructs a road map of the steps to be made in the pursuit of the goal; (iii) a comparator or regulatory function which regularly effects comparisons between the present state of the system and the goal; (iv) a negative feedback control function which registers discrepancies between the present state and the goal and suggests corrective actions; and (v) an evaluation function which enables the system to evaluate each step's processing demands vis-à-vis the available structural possibilities and necessary skills and strategies of the system so as to make decisions about the value of continuing or terminating the endeavour and evaluate the final outcome achieved. These processes operate recursively, so that goals and subgoals may be renewed according to every moment's evaluation of the system's distance from its ultimate objective. These regulatory functions operate under the current structural constraints of the system that define the system's current maximum potentials discussed above (Demetriou 2000; Demetriou and Efklides 1989; Demetriou and Kazi 2001).

Consciousness is an integral part of DEF. That is, the very process of setting mental goals, planning their attainment, monitoring action vis-à-vis both the goals and the plans, and regulating real or mental action requires a system that can remember and review and therefore know itself. Therefore, conscious awareness and all ensuing functions, such as a self-concept (that is, awareness of one's own mental characteristics, functions, and mental states) and a theory of mind (that is, awareness of others' mental functions and states), are part of the very construction of the system. This postulate bears a very important implication for the general theory of the mind because it suggests that intelligence and personality are directly linked (Demetriou 2003; in press; Demetriou and Kazi 2001; Demetriou, Kyriakides and Avraamidou 2003). However, we will not embark on this issue in this chapter.

Specialized processes

Specialized processes refer to mental operations and problem-solving skills that are suitable for the handling (i.e. the comparison, combination, transformation), of different types of information, relations and problems. Unfortunately, there is not as yet any consensus about what constitutes a domain of thought because there are no commonly acceptable criteria for the delimitation of domains. Thus, the specification of domains varies with tradition or line of research.

Criteria and general architecture of domains

We propose that to qualify for the status of a domain of thought, a block of mental operations must satisfy the following criteria. First, it must serve an identifiable *special function or purpose* vis-à-vis the organism's adaptational needs. Second, it must be responsible for the representation and processing of a particular *type of relations* between environmental entities. In fact, the special function of the system is to enable the organism to deal with a particular type of environmental relations. Third, it must involve *specialized operations and processes* that are appropriate for the representation and processing of the type of relations concerned. In a sense, the operations and processes of a domain of thought are the mental analogues of the type of relations concerned. Fourth, it must be *biased to a particular symbol system* that is more appropriate than other symbol systems to represent the type of relations concerned and facilitate the execution of the operations concerned.

The domains may be analysed into three main types of components. Specifically, each domain involves (i) core processes, (ii) rules, mental operations and processing skills and (iii) knowledge and beliefs. Core processes are special kinds of mental processes within each system. That is, they are very fundamental processes that ground each of the domains into its respective environmental realm. Therefore, these processes are obviously the result of our evolution as a species, and may somehow characterize the cognitive functioning of other species as well. During development, core processes are the first manifestations of the systems, and these are predominantly action and perception bound. If a minimum set of conditions is present in the input, they are activated and provide an interpretation of the input, which is consistent with their organization.

The operations, rules, and principles of the second level refer to systems of mental (or, frequently, real) actions that are used intentionally to deal with information and relations in each of the domains. From the point of view of development, core processes constitute the starting points for the construction of operations, rules and knowledge included in each of the domains. That is, at the initial phases of development, operations, rules and knowledge arise through interactions between the core processes and the corresponding domain of the environment. Then they are differentiated and reconstructed as a result of their own interaction with the environment and with each other.

Finally, each system involves knowledge of the reality domain with which it is affiliated, that is, knowledge accumulating over the years as a result of the interactions between a particular system and its respective domain of reality. Conceptual and belief systems pertaining to the physical, the biological, psychological and the social world are found at this level of the organization of the various systems.

From the point of view of differential psychology, operations and rules, together with the operations involved in DEF, constitute the basis of fluid intelligence and knowledge and beliefs are the basis of crystallized intelligence (Carroll 1993; Cattell 1971; Gustafsson and Undheim 1996). From the point of view of developmental psychology, operations and rules constitute what Piaget called 'operative intelligence', whereas knowledge and beliefs are part of empirical knowledge (Piaget 1970). From the point of view of cognitive psychology, processes, rules and operations constitute the basis of procedural and episodic cognition and knowledge and beliefs constitute the basis of declarative cognition (Anderson 1983). Piaget (1970) and the neo-Piagetians (Case 1985; Pascual-Leone 1988) focused on the development of operations and rules. The conceptual change movement, which was very strong in the psychology of cognitive development in the decade of the 1980s, focused primarily on the change of knowledge and beliefs (Carey 1985).

The domains

Our research has uncovered the following six domains of thought that satisfy the criteria summarized above: the domains of categorical, quantitative, spatial, causal, verbal, and social thought (Demetriou 1998a, 1998b, 2000; Demetriou and Efklides 1985, 1989; Demetriou, Efklides and Platsidou 1993; Demetriou, Efklides, Papadaki, Papantoniou, and Economou 1993; Demetriou, Pachaury, Metallidou, and Kazi 1996; Demetriou, Platsidou, Efklides, Metallidou, and Shayer 1991; Demetriou and Kazi 2001; Kargopoulos and Demetriou 1998;

Shayer, Demetriou, and Prevez 1988). Clearly, the domains of verbal, spatial, and quantitative thought satisfy all four criteria discussed above. That is, each has a special function, it is addressed to a special type of relations in the environment, it involves characteristic operations and rules that can be easily discerned from those of the others and it is biased to a different symbol system (language, mental images, mathematical notation, respectively). It is to be stressed that these domains are recognized as distinct by all theories and traditions. That is, they are some of the broad domains of thought uncovered by psychometric research (Carroll 1993; Gustafsson and Undheim 1996; Jensen 1998). Moreover, in cognitive psychology, these three domains exist as almost autonomous domains of specialization in research and theorizing. Research and theory on verbal and syllogistic reasoning (Rips 1994), spatial thought and mental imagery (Kosslyn 1980), and mathematical thought (Hart 1981) are so separate from each other that one can speak of different fields in cognitive psychology. This obviously reflects the functional and representational differences between these three domains. The other three domains (i.e. categorical, causal, and social reasoning) clearly satisfy the first three criteria (i.e. function, type of relations, and mental operations) but not the fourth (that is, there is no symbol system distinctly associated with each of them).

It is clear, however, that in factor analysis all six domains do come out as distinct factors (Case 1992; Case, Demetriou, Platsidou and Kazi 2001; Demetriou and Kyriakides in press; Demetriou, Kyriakides and Avraamidou 2003). Figure 1.1 presents the results of confirmatory factor analysis showing that five of the domains come out as independent factors and that there is a second-order factor that stands for the general processes described above (Demetriou et al. in press). Moreover, it must be noted that an analysis of these five systems from the point of view of their logical composition suggests that each operates according to its own logical principles (Kargopoulos and Demetriou 1998). Finally, Case's (1992) recent analysis of central conceptual structures, which, by and large, coincide with most of the domains analysed here, suggests that each of them involves its own semantic networks for the representation of domain-specific information and relevant actions and operations from the part of person. These logical and semantic differences between the domains suggest that they are cognitively distinct from each other in addition to being dimensions of systematic individual differences, as suggested by their factorial autonomy. Therefore, it is clear that the psychometric methods of classical and modern confirmatory factor analysis that capture dimensions of individual differences converge with the cognitive methods of logical and semantic analysis that capture the formal and mental composition of cognitive domains. In the pages below we will not discuss the domain of social thought, due to space considerations.

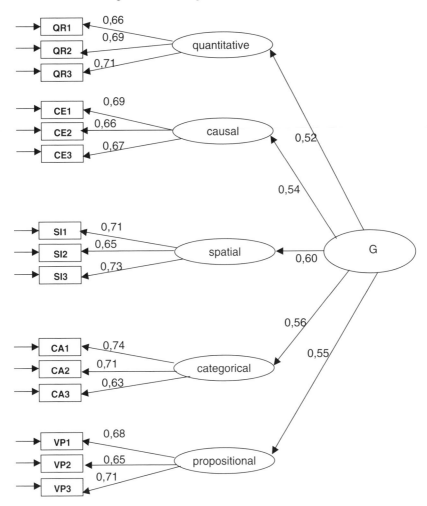

Figure 1.1. The general structure of the mind as specified by confirmatory factor modelling.
Note: The symbols QR, CE, SI, CA, and VP stand for quantitative-relational, causal-experimental, spatial-imaginal, categorical-analytical and verbal-propositional abilities.

Categorical reasoning

The primary function of categorical reasoning is to enable the person to identify information that is important for the task at hand and reduce unnecessary complexity so as to facilitate future information selection needs. Thus, categorical reasoning specializes in the handling of similarities and differences between objects. Processes related to the recognition of conspecifics (i.e. recognition of the members of the same species), such as the infant's preference for the human face as contrasted to other objects, or categorical perception according to colour, are examples of the core elements involved in this system. At the second level of organization, it involves operations enabling the person to spot and process similarities and differences between objects. For example, it involves classification skills and strategies enabling the individual to construct categories and operate on them. Our conceptions and misconceptions about the world, such as the concepts that we have about physical phenomena, living beings in general, or different types of persons, constitute the third level of organization in this system.

Quantitative reasoning

All elements of reality can potentially undergo quantitative transformations. Things aggregate or separate so that they increase, decrease, split or multiply in space or time for many different reasons. Subitization is an example of the core processes involved in this system. Subitization refers to our ability to specify the numerosity of small sets (smaller than three or four elements) by simply looking at them. At the second level of organization, quantitative reasoning involves operations enabling the thinker to deal with the various quantitative transformations mentioned above. Prominent among these operations are counting, pointing, bringing in and removing and sharing, and their internalized mental counterparts, that is the four arithmetic operations. The third level of the organization of this system involves all kinds of factual knowledge about the quantitative aspects of the world. Examples include knowledge about time reading, money values and rules underlying everyday transactions, and numerical knowledge, such as the multiplication tables.

Spatial reasoning

Spatial reasoning enables thinking about objects and episodes as such and orientation in space. Therefore, in this domain, spatial relations within (the composition and structure of objects) and between objects (relative distances, directions, and orientations) acquire prominence because they are crucial in the representation of objects themselves, their location in space, and of the space that surrounds them, as such. Formation of mental images and processes, such as perception of size, depth, and orientation of objects, are examples of this system's core processes. To be able to represent them, operate on them, and move between them, the thinker needs operations, such as mental rotation or direction tracking and reckoning, which honour these relations, thereby enabling the thinker to visualize objects and space from the perspective needed so as to be able to recognize and locate them and efficiently move between or to them. Mental images, mental maps and scripts about objects, locations, scenes, or layouts stored in memory belong to the third level of the organization of this system (Kosslyn 1980).

Causal reasoning

Objects and people are very often dynamically related, sometimes functioning as the cause of changes and other times as the recipients of causal effects. Causal reasoning enables the grasp of dynamic interactions between objects or persons. Perception of fundamental causal relationships, such as when there is direct transfer of energy from one object to another (e.g. we push something to move it), are examples of the core processes involved in this system. At the second level of organization, causal reasoning involves operations enabling the thinker to manipulate and represent causal relations. Prominent among these are trial and error manipulations aiming to uncover the causal role of objects. Isolation of variables (or systematic experimentation) is a more elaborate process employed to manipulate systematically dynamic causal relations. Knowledge related to the 'why' and 'how' of things pertains to the third level of the organization of this system. Our understanding of the reasons underlying physical and social events as well as their procedural aspects comes from the functioning of the operations mentioned above and constitute our ready-made attributions about the dynamic aspects of the world (Demetriou et al. 1993; Demetriou, Efklides et al. 1993).

Verbal reasoning

In so far as function is concerned, verbal reasoning facilitates interaction between persons, and it is used as a guide to action. Core processes in this system underlie the ability, which is present from infancy, to use the grammatical and syntactical structures of language (e.g. '*if* this *then* that', '*either* this *or* that') in order to infer the relations between the events or situations mentioned in a sequence of sentences (Braine 1990; Demetriou 1998b). At the second level of organization, operations and processes in this domain are primarily directed to the truth and validity relations between verbal statements so that the person may judge the accuracy of the information received, decipher deception, etc. Two types of skills are used to attain these aims. First, there are grammatical and syntactical skills enabling the individual to interpret and interrelate the components in verbal statements so that information may be abstracted in goal-relevant, meaningful, and coherent ways. Second, there are skills enabling one to differentiate the contextual from the formal elements in a series of statements and operate on the latter. For example, focusing on such verbs as 'is' or 'belongs to', or connectives such as 'and', 'if', and 'or', directs thinking to the relationships between the statements, rather than simply the statements themselves. These processes, the second in particular, enable one to grasp the basic logical relations of conjunction ('. . . and . . . and . . .'), disjunction ('either . . . or'), implication ('if . . . then'), etc. (Efklides, Demetriou and Metallidou 1994). Explicit knowledge about grammar and syntax and explicit knowledge about logical reasoning belong to the third level of the organization of this system.

Directions and forms of development across processes and systems

Each of the constructs discussed above as well as its relations with the other constructs changes with age. Therefore, any overarching theory would first have to specify the developmental direction and form of each of these constructs. That is, it would have to specify where each of these constructs goes and what its characteristics are at successive phases of life. Moreover, this theory would have to specify the developmental dynamics of the systems as a whole. That is, how changes in any of these constructs are related to changes in the other constructs along with age. The discussion below will focus on these two aspects of development. Specifically, we will first describe the general form of development that seems able to describe growth in all of these processes. Then we will sketch the development of each the various systems. Finally, we will elaborate on their dynamic relations.

The general forms of development

Recently, van Geert (1994, this volume) suggested that the language and methods of dynamic systems theory must be adopted for the specification of change in cognitive processes and their inter-relations. According to van Geert, the fundamental assumptions of dynamic systems theory are compatible with the fundamental assumptions of cognitive developmental theory. Thus, employing these methods may reveal the actual form and dynamics of development of different cognitive functions more successfully than it has been possible by other more classical methods used until now. According to the basic assumption of dynamic systems theory, any kind of change is logistic when it occurs under limited resources. Obviously, this is precisely the assumption of cognitive developmental theory, because in cognitive development and functioning, change and learning always occur under limited resources. Thus, van Geert proposed that change in all of the constructs discussed here may be described by a logistic function.

In general, logistic growth is non-linear and it follows an S-shaped pattern of changes. That is, change is rather slow at the beginning but it gradually accelerates until to attain a certain momentum. When this momentum is attained change becomes very fast and it remains so until to approach the end-state of the process or ability under consideration. After a certain point rather close to the end-state, the rate of change decelerates continuously until it becomes difficult to notice. The general idea underlying this model is that change is autocatalytic and that it occurs under limited resources. That is, the change itself produces further change and in so doing it exhausts the resources fuelling the process. Thus, change consumes the resources available for it, thereby slowing its rate after the resources remaining fall below a certain level. (Demetriou et al. 2002, 99)

Technically speaking, the model implies that any ability A, at any moment in time, has a specific level or magnitude, A_t, and is growing from the one state to the next until it reaches its final end-state, which is conceived to function as A's carrying capacity, that is the force pulling the capacity to change. The model assumes that development is, partly, time-dependent and iterative. That is, at each time t, the present A depends on the previous levels of A. The process depends also on a growth rate r, which may be specified in reference to the difference between the states of A at two successive points in time. This parameter is the autocatalytic factor that causes A at time t to grow and attain a new level $A + 1$ at time $t + 1$. Thus, if we know the present level of an ability at time t, its carrying capacity and its growth rate we can iteratively specify its condition at a succession of times $t + 1$, $t + 2$, $t + 3$, etc. The growth rate may be a fixed integer, which is individually defined only in reference to the process or ability under consideration. However, the growth rate may also be a composition of several abilities A_2, A_3, etc., as will be shown in the next section. An idealized model of logistic development from birth to early adulthood would appear as shown in Figure 1.2. That is, there are successive cycles of logistic development such that when the command of one type of information becomes complete then another type begins to develop and so on. We will show below that this model is able to describe the development of different aspects of processing efficiency, working memory, and different domains of thinking. Dawson and her colleagues (Dawson, Xie and Wilson 2003) found this model able to describe the development of social understanding and moral reasoning.

The development of general processes

The development of processing efficiency

Processing efficiency can be measured in various ways. The complexity of measures may vary from very simple (such as the time needed to recognize a familiar stimulus, for example name a colour, a geometrical figure, a letter or a word) to quite complex (such as to recognize a stimulus presented among other distractive stimuli or emit a particular response previously paired with each of a set of stimuli). Thus, absolute values for processing efficiency in general or speed of processing in particular are not of primary developmental interest, because they vary extensively with the complexity of the stimuli presented or the response required. What is of developmental interest is the form of change as a

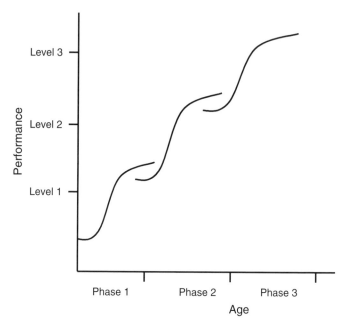

Figure 1.2. The general model of logistic growth.

function of age. Hale and Fry (2000) and Kail (1991) presented ample evidence that processing speed changes uniformly with age, in an exponential fashion, across a wide variety of different types of information and task complexities, such as mental rotation, memory search, name retrieval, visual search, mental addition, figural matrices and geometric analyses. That is, change of speed of processing is fast at the beginning (i.e. from early to middle childhood) and it decelerates systematically (from early adolescence onwards) until it attains its maximum in early adulthood. This pattern of change is presented in Figure 1.3a.

According to Kail (1991), what is common between the different tasks is the child's cycle time, that is, the time needed to execute each step or mental operation in the sequence of operations needed to attain a goal. Thus, any speed difference between a child and an adult solving the same task is due to the fact that the child's cycle times are longer than those of the adult. As cycle times decrease, processing becomes faster until it reaches its maximum.

In line with these findings, our research showed that processing speed changes logistically with age across a wide variety of Stroop-like tasks, systematically varying in symbolic medium (verbal, numerical, and figural) and complexity, ranging from very simple, such as to recognize familiar colour words written in the same ink colour (e.g., the word RED written in red ink) to very complex (e.g., to recognize Chinese ideographs constructed of other ideographs differing in meaning, form and pronunciation from the target ideograph). In fact, tasks requiring the person to select and respond to one attribute of the stimulus among other interfering attributes, such as the Stroop-like tasks, are considered measures of selective attention and control of processing (Demetriou et al. 1993, 2002, 2003).

It needs to be noted here that the exponential changes specified by Kail in regard to the development of processing speed are part of the general logistic function described above, because exponential change also defines development as a function of a present state, an end-state, and a change or decay parameter. The main difference between exponential and logistic growth is that the first examines each ability separately and it ignores the initial and final parts of the development of the process under consideration. Moreover, it must also be noted that the precise relation of a construct with age is a function of the type of information being examined. Specifically, Kail's exponential functions describe changes in speed of processing of symbol-like information, such as letters, number digits, words or geometrical figures, which are appropriate for persons from middle childhood onwards. Examining processing speed in regard to other types of information, which are more appropriate for other periods of life, such as the human face at infancy, would obviously show that the logistic function repeats itself in infancy in regard to this infancy-relevant information.

The development of processing capacity

There is no general agreement as to how processing capacity is to be defined. As already discussed above, many researchers, based on Baddeley's (1993) model, conceive of processing capacity as a working memory system that involves a central executive that is responsible for orchestrating storage, transformation, and retrieval of information, and modality-specific storage buffers, such as phonological and visuo-spatial storage, that are responsible for holding active different types of information. Under this paradigm, measures of capacity vary depending upon the component or the combination of components addressed. That is, at the one extreme, some researchers try to measure the capacity of the storage buffers purified from executive processes, as much as this is possible (Baddeley 1993; Pascual-Leone 1970). At the other extreme, others try to measure the capacity of the central executive (Cowan 1999; Engle 2002). The general pattern of development may be summarized as follows.

First, there is general agreement that the capacity of all components of working memory (i.e. executive processes, phonological, and visual storage) increases with age. In fact, the development of all three components seems to follow the same pattern of change and to be able to be described by a logistic curve which is very similar to the exponential curve that describes the change of processing efficiency (see below). This pattern of change of the three components of working memory is illustrated in Figure 1.3b.

Second, there seems to be an inverse trade-off between the central executive and the storage buffers, so that the higher the involvement of executive processes the less is the manifest capacity of the modality-specific buffers. This is so because the executive operations themselves consume part of the available processing recourses. However, with age, executive operations and information are chunked into integrated units. As a result, with development, the person can store increasingly more complex units of information. For instance, primary school age children can remember single numbers whereas adolescents can store the products of operations applied on numbers (Case 1985).

To account for this evidence, we proposed the functional shift model (Demetriou et al. 1993). This model presumes that when the mental units of a given level reach a maximum degree of complexity, the system tends to reorganize these units at a higher level of representation or integration so as to make them more manageable. Having created a new mental unit, the system prefers to work with this rather than the previous units due to its functional advantages. It is important to remember this tendency in the development of working memory because later we will show that working memory and thinking are inseparably interwoven.

The development of DEF

DEF enables humans to set goals, plan the steps for their attainment in advance, implement these steps, and evaluate ongoing actions or productions relevant to the goal or current sub-goal in order to introduce adjustments to plans and actions, if needed. In the first year of life, goal setting may be seen as part of sensorimotor means–ends sequences of behaviour, where goals are equivalent to desirable objects or events that the infant wants to obtain or restore. By the end of the second year, these desires are explicitly represented as goals associated with action plans, as, for instance, is the sequence of actions for retrieving an object that was somehow lost from sight. After this age, the development of DEF may be described as a process increasingly enabling the person to inhibit reaction to stimuli, if needed, and flexibly alternate between actions according to a preconceived plan.

Research into speeded performance that explicitly requires the inhibition of response and therefore taps executive control shows that the development of the mechanisms underlying control is, at least in part, independent from general activation mechanisms, and they are well established by early adolescence. Specifically, Williams, Ponesse, Schachar, Logan, and Tannock (1999) applied the stop-signal procedure to map changes in the person's ability to activate

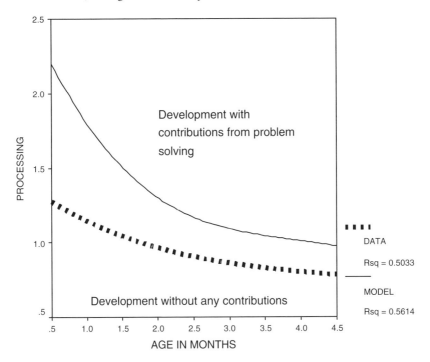

Figure 1.3a. Development of different processes according to dynamic systems modelling assuming presence or absence of interaction between processes.

and inhibit responses. According to this procedure, the individual is instructed to emit a particular response to a given 'go' stimulus (e.g. press a particular button when a particular stimulus appears, such as a letter or figure) and to refrain from emitting this response if, in the meantime, another 'stop' stimulus is presented (e.g. a particular sound). Williams et al. (1999) tested subjects from six to eighty-one years of age and found, in agreement with the development of speed of processing as depicted above, that speed of response to the go signal changes throughout childhood followed by marked slowing throughout adulthood. In contrast, speed of stopping becomes faster throughout childhood (until about the age of twelve years) with very little change in adulthood. In line with these findings, Band, van der Molen, Overtoom, and Verbaten (2000) have recently shown that a global response control mechanism underlying non-selective inhibition (that is, the ability to inhibit all bending responses if a given message shows up) is established by the age of five years. However, selective inhibition (that is, the ability to selectively inhibit different responses according to a variety of messages) continues to develop beyond childhood.

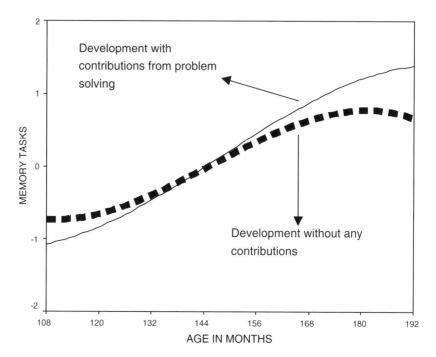

Figure 1.3b.

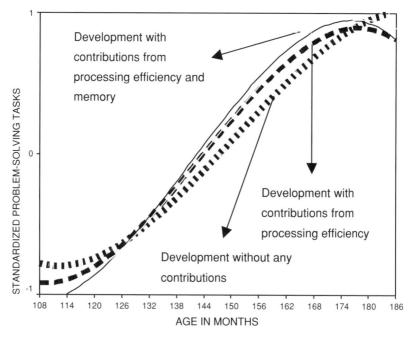

Figure 1.3c.

Studies directly focusing on the development of executive control are in line with these findings. According to the findings of Zelazo and his colleagues (Frye, Zelazo and Burack 1998; Zelazo and Frye 1998), children up to the age of three years can represent only a single goal and they cannot shift from one goal to another according to a certain rule. One of the tasks used by these researchers is the dimensional-change card sort. This task examines children's ability to represent a goal to direct ongoing activity and to shift from the one goal to the other. In this task, children are shown two target cards, each associated with a sorting tray. They are also shown a series of test cards and their task is to sort them into the appropriate sorting tray according to a certain rule that specifies the dimension according to which sorting is to be effected. For instance, the rule may be 'Put the blue ones here; put the red one here.' Then, after sorting several cards according to this rule, they are asked to sort the cards according to a second rule that specifies that sorting is to be effected according to another dimension. For instance, 'Put the flowers here; put the cars here.' In this task, two-year-old children can operate with only a single rule (e.g. 'If it is red, it goes here'). By the age of three, children can operate with a rule that specifies two levels (e.g. 'If it is red, it goes here, if it is blue it goes here'). However, children younger than five years of age cannot shift to another rule; instead, they persist in doing the sorting according to the first rule that was given to them. According to Zelazo and Frye (1998), to be able to shift from the one rule to the other, the child must be able to integrate the rules into a higher-order rule that specifies when each of the two lower-order rules is to be used. For instance, in the example of dimensional-change card sort described above, this rule might be as follows: 'If we were playing colour, then if it is red it goes here and if it is blue it goes here, but if we were playing shape, then if it is a red car it goes here and if it is a blue flower it goes here').

According to Zelazo and Frye, the rules that specify the goal for a particular sequence of actual or mental actions aimed to solve a problem is a conscious process where there is awareness of the rules as plans for action. In fact, several authors argue that the development of executive control as specified here is closely related to the development of the child's theory of mind, that is the child's understanding that other people have mental states that function as causes of their behaviour (Perner and Lang 1999; Frye, Zelazo and Burack 1998). The experimental paradigm used to study children's understanding of this aspect of the mind is rather simple. For instance, the experimenter places a candy in box A in front of both the child and an assistant. The assistant then leaves the room and the experimenter moves the candy from box A to box B. The assistant returns and the child is asked to indicate in which box the assistant will look for the candy. Box A corresponds to the assistant's representation of the candy's location; box B corresponds to the child's representation of the present place of the candy. Tasks designed according to this paradigm have come to be known as the *false belief tasks*. Children who indicate location A are obviously able to understand that the representation of a given situation depends on available information and that a person's behaviour stems from his own representation. Children who indicate position B are obviously unwilling to recognize that others may represent a situation differently than they themselves will represent it. Many studies have shown that three-year-old children cannot solve this kind of task, whereas four-year-old children can, suggesting that three-year-olds do not have a theory of mind whereas four-year-olds have.

According to Frye et al. (1998), to have a theory of mind implies an ability to build a rule hierarchy that specifies each person's representations of a situation and the action ensuing from each of these representations. This rule hierarchy might be as follows: 'People act according to what they know; what people know comes from what they see; I saw both, the candy placed in box A and then in box B. He saw candy placed only in box A. Thus, he will look for it in box A.' Obviously, this rule is very similar to the double rule above enabling five-year-olds to shift across dimensions in the dimensional-change card sort. Indeed, recent research by Andrews, Halford, Bunch, Bowden and Jones (2003) suggests strongly that the attainment of theory of mind does require the ability to build rule hierarchies involving two rules with two levels each. In turn, according to Perner and Lang, 'better understanding of one's own mind provides better insights into how to exert self control, and the exercise of self control is one of the main grounds for building such an understanding' (Perner and Lang 1999, 343). Thus, it seems that the development of DEF is closely linked to the development of self-awareness, as assumed in the previous section concerned with the architecture of the mind.

During the primary school years executive control becomes differentiated and planful, thereby making action plans available to the thinker. That is, planfulness integrates under an overarching plan the main goals and objectives, the subgoals, and the strategies and actions needed to attain goals and subgoals, and a time plan that specifies when strategies and actions are to be applied. So defined, planfulness is not present before the age of about nine years. In her classic study of the development of visual scanning strategies, Vurpilot (1968) showed that children younger than this age do not formulate a plan that would allow them to compare systematically and exhaustively two houses in order to find out if they are entirely similar or if they differ in some characteristics. In fact, many of Piaget's classic formal operational tasks (Inhelder and Piaget 1958) may be considered as tests of planfulness, because they require actions according to a preconceived complex and hierarchical action plan.

The proper operation of DEF depends on the evaluative functions that provide on-line and final information about the success or failure of the action plan applied. Without this function, DEF may be less accurate than needed or it may misdirect the thinker relative to the problem at hand. Despite its importance, it is only recently that researchers started to study the development of cognitive self-evaluation as part of a general system of the mind that underlies intellectual performance and understanding. In our laboratory, we study self-evaluation of cognitive performance from the age of three years to maturity (Demetriou and Efklides 1989; Demetriou and Kazi 2001; Kazi 2002). The general pattern of development is rather easily described. Specifically, it seems that self-evaluation develops in a recycling fashion, which involved three major cycles: 3–7, 8–12, and 13–18. That is, within each phase of development, self-evaluation and self-awareness about the relevant mental operations is very low and inaccurate at the beginning and it tends to increase and become more accurate with development until the end of the phase. Entering the next phase resets self-evaluation of cognitive outcomes and self-awareness about the cognitive processes involved to zero, from where it gradually takes off again with the development of the new phase-specific problem-solving operations and skills. This pattern of change in self-awareness indicates that the thinker needs time and experience to acquire knowledge and sensitivity to the condition of the operations and processes of the new phase.

It must be noted, however, that these developmental trends in self-evaluation and self-awareness coexist with large individual differences in the accuracy of self-evaluations and self-awareness. In fact, these individual differences are systematic in that persons performing low relative to their age mates are more likely to be inaccurate in both their self-evaluation and self-awareness. Thus, it seems that there is a vicious developmental cycle involving intellectual achievement and self-evaluation and self-awareness such that if the one is low and slow in development the other also tends to be low and to develop slowly. In this case, self-improvement is not possible, because the thinker is not aware of his limitations so as to take measures to remove them.

The development of specialized thought domains

The development of the various domains is associated with changes in all three components involved in them, that is, core processes, mental operations and rules, and knowledge and beliefs. Because of space considerations, the discussion here will focus primarily on the development of rules and mental operations in each of the domains and it draws from the findings of our earlier research (Demetriou et al. 1993, 1991, 1996, 2002, 2003; Demetriou and Kyriakides, in press; Shayer et al. 1988). The aim is to highlight both the similarities and differences in the development of the various domains in order to explicate why and how they occur. Also, here we will outline the changes that take place from the age of two years to adulthood. It is emphasized, however, that all systems are considered present from birth and that they develop systematically from birth onwards, when language and other arbitrary forms of representation make their appearance. Moreover, we will not discuss the development of the social domain. Table 1.1 summarizes the development of the five domains to be discussed here.

Table 1.1. *The modal characteristics of the five environment-oriented systems during development.*

Age	Qualitative-analytical	Quantitative-relational	Causal-experimental	Spatial-imaginal	Verbal-propositional
3–4	Proto-categories. Classifications are based on phenomenal criteria. Categorical inference is based on the transformation of observed characteristics into a conclusion (i.e., 'He is a "doctor" because he has a stethoscope').	Proto-quantitative schemes. Understanding of the effects of fundamental quantitative acts, such as addition or removal of elements from a set of things. Understanding of the basic principles of counting, e.g. that each number name corresponds to one set only.	Proto-causal schemes. Causal sequences can be differentiated from random sequences on the basis of the structure of events in space and time. Experimentation is based on 'trial and error' as no preconceived hypothesis is present.	Global mental images. These may be very accurate but their different parts cannot be mentally manipulated independently of each other.	Primary reasoning, i.e. automatic use or understanding of propositions in everyday speech.
5–6	A criterion may be preselected and applied in order to specify the identity of objects and their similarity relations (e.g. colour, shape etc.) This criterion may be used to classify things on the basis of having or not having this attribute. Class inclusion relations based on natural kinds may be understood.	Coordination of proto-quantitative schemes. The 'increase-decrease scheme' is, for example, coordinated with the basic principles of counting. This generates a first understanding of number conservation.	Coordination of proto-causal schemes. This enables accurate descriptions of causal sequences. The child may search for the cause of an event (e.g. why a toy does not work) by testing (usually persistently and inflexibly) some idea directly suggested by the apparent aspects of the event.	Pictures can now be analysed in their parts. Spatial dimensions are constructed and spatial operations, such as mental rotation, can be effected.	Propositions can be distinguished from each other and organized in order to suggest a given conclusion. Permission rules are now understood (if you do X, then you can do Y).

7–8	Analytical strategies are intentionally and systematically applied. As a result, logical multiplication is possible. This yields novel categories and classes.	Appearance of proper mathematical concepts, such as cardinal and ordinal number, which integrate different proto-quantitative schemes. This enables the child to dimensionalize reality, and, thus, conceive of properties, such as, quantity, length, weight, area, etc.	'Proto-theories', i.e. integrated views about the phenomena of the social and physical world. These are geared in personal experience and they are not taken as models to be tested.	'Fluent' mental imagery, that is spatial and imaginal operations, can be skilfully applied in order to analyse and transform mental images or representations of space	Inference is explicitly applied. A series of premises can be connected and the conclusion can be deduced, if the logical relations suggested by the premises are real.
9–10	Analysis and logical multiplication can be applied on non-familiar material.	Simple mathematical relations can be processed, even when they are symbolically represented (e.g., equations, such as $8?3 = 5$ or $a + 5 = 8$, can be solved).	'Proto-theories' become theories in action, i.e. it is understood that they may not be valid and may be falsified by reality. The testing of these theories is, however, occasional and fragmentary and is guided by each next happening rather than by a preconstructed plan.	Representation of very complex realities. The new and the unfamiliar cannot yet be imaginally constructed.	Logical necessity appears as a functional aspect of reasoning.
11–12	Analysis and logical multiplication is first applied on the goals of analysis as such rather than on the objects of analysis. As a result, children become able to differentiate between goal-relevant and goal-irrelevant information, focus on the first, and ignore the latter.	Quantitative reality is represented as a complex set of relations. Proportional reasoning (understanding of relations between relations) appears. Simple symbolic representations can, moreover, be coordinated in order to specify a general quantity (e.g. equations, such as $x = y + 3$, can be solved when y is specified.	Suppositions, i.e., alternative conceptions about causal relations begin to appear. This generates systematic combinatorial thought. The isolation-of-variables strategy can now be applied, when a hypothesis to be tested is presented. Under this condition, the supposed causal factor is systematically varied and one or two other factors are held constant.	The imaginal representation of the non-real starts to become possible.	Premises are conceived as expressions of the possible. Thus, reasoning can be applied in order to test the logical validity of the formal relations between propositions independently of their content. This approach is now applied on 'easy relations', such as conjunction and disjunction.

(cont.)

Table 1.1. (*cont.*)

Age	Qualitative-analytical	Quantitative-relational	Causal-experimental	Spatial-imaginal	Verbal-propositional
13–14	Analysis and classification proceeds strategically. It can thus process very complex problems which involve systems of relevant and irrelevant information.	Proportionality can be applied on counter-intuitive relations. Moreover, complex symbolic expressions can now be coordinated in order to specify a quantity (e.g., x can be specified if $x = y + z$ and $x + y + z = 30$).	Clear hypotheses can now be formulated and experiments can be designed to test them. There may not be a complete match between hypotheses and experiments.	There is originality in how the familiar and the non-familiar can be represented.	The previous approach can be applied on more complex relations, such as implication.
15–16	Classes about dynamical relations or about continuous variables on top of attribute variables.	Quantitative dimensions are fully generalized and the concept of a variable is established. It is, thus, understood that a variable can be symbolized in a number of ways, which can be specified in reference to other representations (e.g. it is understood that the equation $a + b + c = a + x + c$ is valid if $b = x$).	Hypotheses, experimental manipulations, and results of manipulations can be integrated into models.	Personal worlds of imagery may be constructed. Aesthetic criteria may be very important	Reasoning on reasoning as such starts to become possible.

Note: The table is based on Table 4.2, Demetriou et al. 2003.

Protorepresentations

At the age of two to three years, children handle representations that are taken as single undifferentiated blocks that stand for familiar objects or concepts and have a transparent relation to them. As a result, relations at this early phase of development are not constructed as such but are intuitively 'read out', so to speak, from the representational block. In the domain of categorical thought, relations in protocategories, for instance, are part of a representational ensemble that includes characteristics and actions (he is a doctor because he wears a blouse and examines patients with a stethoscope). Likewise, 'proto-quantitative schemes' (Resnick, Bill and Lesgold 1992) can solve simple mathematical tasks that require judgement on the basis of absolute criteria (e.g. 'few', 'many', 'a lot') or comparisons on the basis of a single dimension (e.g. 'less', 'more', etc.) (see Case, 1992; Gelman and Gallistel 1978). Protocausal schemes are episodic representations that preserve the structure of events in time. Thus, children at this phase 'read' causality from dominant sequences of events in time and have no systematic method for dissociating and manipulating different parts of these sequences in order to distinguish causal from apparent relationships. Instead, trial-and-error is the dominant means for examining cause–effect relationships at this age. In the domain of visuo-spatial reasoning children can hold accurate images of objects or events. However, these are represented as global and undifferentiated visual mental images that can be scanned by the mind's eye but their different parts cannot be mentally manipulated independently of each other. Finally, propositional reasoning at this phase is automatic in that inferences are based on undifferentiated blocks of prose rather than on propositions. That is, when they speak, two- to three-year-old children correctly use most of the connectives and conditionals involved in inference schemas, such as *and*, *but*, *or*, *because*, and *if* and they can understand their meaning if they are embedded in permission schemas (e.g. 'if you want to play outside you must put your coat coat on') (Harris and Nunez 1996). However, at this phase, children think about the actual elements mentioned in the premises and they cannot differentiate premises and conclusions. Thus, they run into trouble when their factual knowledge is in conflict with the information given in the premises (for example, they refuse to accept that the argument following is correct: birds fly, dogs are birds, therefore dogs fly).

Dual representations

At about the age of three to four children start to differentiate representations and thus to operate on two of them at the same time. When this is possible, children start to build concepts in the various environment-oriented domains (there must be at least two representations to conceive of a class, a quantity, a cause–effect relation, a spatial relation, such as 'above', or make an inference, respectively) (Case 1985; Fischer 1980; Demetriou 1998b). Moreover, they start to understand the multifaceted nature of the world, as indicated by their understanding of the appearance–reality distinction (because they can represent an object in its present and in an earlier condition) (Flavell, Green and Flavell 1995), and their acquisition of a theory of mind (because they can understand that the same thing can be represented differently by two persons) (Wellman 1990). In fact, dual representations are needed for understanding the representational nature of symbols themselves, because in order to use a symbol one must represent both the object to be represented and the symbol itself (de Loache, Miller, and Pieroutsakos 1998).

Integrated representations

At about the age of five to six years representations or operations on representations are integrated with each other. The result is that proto-concepts evolve into dimensions and operations become ensembles that can be planned in advance. Thus, in the domain of categorical thought, systematic classification starts to be possible, because a criterion may be preselected and applied in order to specify the identity of objects and their similarity relations (e.g. colour, shape etc.). This criterion may be used to classify things on the basis of having or not having the attributes specified by the criterion. Thus, class inclusion relations based on natural kinds can be understood, indicating that semantic networks can already be analysed systematically. In the domain of quantitative thinking, the coordination of proto-quantitative schemes leads to actual quantitative judgements and estimations. For example they coordinate the 'increase–decrease scheme' mentioned above with basic counting skills, thereby acquiring a first understanding of number conservation. Numerical operations in action can also be applied and tagged to symbols (Griffin, this volume). In a similar manner, in the causal domain, proto-causal schemes are coordinated with each other. This enables accurate descriptions of causal sequences. Moreover, the preschool child may now search for the cause of an event (e.g. why a toy does not work) by testing (usually persistently and inflexibly) some idea directly by trial and error. In the visuo-spatial domain, children at this phase can retain accurate and detailed visual images of objects or episodes, which they can analyse in their parts. As a result, they construct dimensions along which they can systematically operate on an image. For instance, they can execute mental rotations. In the verbal propositional domain, propositions can be distinguished from each other and organized for the sake of drawing conclusions from them. Thus, at this phase, they can draw the conclusion suggested by the two premises following: 'If there is either a cow or goat, then there is a pear. There is a cow. Therefore, there is a pear.' In other words, children at this stage are explicitly aware of the inferential process that connects premises and conclusions into coherent arguments, and are sensitive to logical necessity. Thus, permission rules are now understood (if you do X, then you can do Y) (Harris and Nunez 1996).

Systems of representations

In the next phase, at the age of seven to nine years, the representations and mental operations constructed above are integrated into systems that can be revised at will. As a result, thinking becomes analytical and fluid. In the domain of categorical thinking, analytical strategies are intentionally and systematically applied. As a result, logical multiplication is possible. This yields novel categories and classes. In the domain of quantitative reasoning proper, mathematical concepts, such as cardinal and ordinal number, integrating different proto-quantitative schemes, make their appearance. This enables the child to dimensionalize reality, and, thus, conceive of properties, such as quantity, length, weight, area, etc. As a result, simple mathematical relations can be processed, even when they are symbolically represented (e.g. equations, such as $8 ? 3 = 5$ and $a + 5 = 8$, can be solved). In the domain of causal reasoning, 'proto-theories' become theories in action, i.e. it is understood that they may not be valid and may be falsified by reality. The testing of these theories is, however, occasional and fragmentary and is guided by each next happening rather than by a preconstructed testing plan. In the domain of spatial reasoning, very complex realities can be imagined and mental actions on them foreseen. In the domain of verbal-propositional reasoning, logical necessity appears as a functional aspect of reasoning.

Transcendent representations

Representations at the age of about ten to twelve years are quite complex relative to the representations of the previous phase, because they can integrate multiple non-overly obvious dimensions. That is, in all domains, two dimensions with at least two levels each can be represented and operated on. In the domain of categorical thought, two independent dimensions (life – living vs. non-living beings – and movement – moving on earth and flying) can be operated on so that all possible cross-classifications and their logical relations (e.g. class inclusion) can be fully grasped, when they are not counteracted by relevant experience. In the domain of quantitative reasoning, proportionality becomes possible initially as an ability to grasp proportional relations that appear obvious (e.g. problems involving numbers which are multiples of one another, such as 2/4 and 4/8). In the domain of causal thought, suppositions, i.e. alternative conceptions about causal relations, begin to appear. This generates systematic combinatorial thought. The isolation-of-variables strategy can now be applied, when a hypothesis to be tested is presented. Under this condition, the supposed causal factor is systematically varied and one or two other factors are held constant. In the domain of spatial thought, mental images can be operated on along two dimensions, in order to be somehow transformed in its characteristics (e.g. a paper punched in a particular way) and mentally rotated along a given direction (e.g. the paper is unfolded in a particular way). In the domain of propositional thought, pre-adolescents start to be able to grasp the logical aspects of propositions and thus extract their logical relations even when they conflict with the actual content of them, as in the example given above. However, at this initial level, thought still lacks the flexibility to explicitly differentiate the formal from the informational aspects of an argument so as to systematically construct all logical implications of the propositions involved. In general, at this level, representations are still relatively undifferentiated and experience-dependent, despite their relative complexity.

Foresighted representations

At the next level, at about thirteen to fourteen years of age, thinking starts to become emancipated from intuitive supports, thereby becoming able to operate strategically on complex problems that require systematic differentiation of relevant from irrelevant information and integration of relevant information according to the current goal. This indicates an explicit understanding that the solution resides in the relations between the components of the problem. As such, this understanding provides a holistic approach to problems, which enables the thinker to conceive of and explore alternative possible solutions and test them against each other until the best one is selected. This approach to problems enables the thinker both to reduce the problem load when complexity is the major obstacle to solution by appropriately partitioning the goal and operational complexity in manageable subgoal stucks or fill in gaps in information through inter-relating other well defined information. The only limitation at this level is that each of the dimensions and structures to be integrated is explicitly defined.

Thus, at this level categorical thinking is emancipated from intuitive supports and it can operate strategically on very complex problems involving systems of relevant and irrelevant information. Moreover, they can construct the second pair of verbal analogies when they are given their first pair (e.g. if given the pair 'bed: sleep' they say 'table: eating'), which indicates a flexibility in elaborating semantic relations between concepts. Quantitative thinking can grasp counterintuitive proportional relations (e.g. the child can specify which of the two ratios, 4/5 or 7/8, is bigger) and solve algebraic problems where the unknown can be specified in reference to other given numbers (specify m given that $m = 3n + 1$ and $n = 4$). In the domain of spatial thought, adolescents can construct mental images by projecting from a number of dimensions. For example, they can conceive the three-dimensional object that will result from the rotation of letters such as P around its vertical axis. This indicates that their imaginal capacity is flexible enough to compose mental images according to a goal. In the domain of causal thought, adolescents start to be able to envisage alternative hypotheses about the possible effect of the factor under consideration, introduce relevant manipulations to test each of them, and eventually choose between them to find the one best fitting to the combination between the relevant pieces of evidence. Thus, at this level, the isolation of variables strategy is systematically applied and different types of causal relations (necessary and sufficient or necessary and non-sufficient) can be matched with relevant evidence. Propositional reasoning becomes robust enough to be able to integrate propositions into consistent logical sequences and grasp their implications, once there are no misleading cues. That is, problems addressed to transitivity relations (e.g. p is q, q is r $=> p$ is r), modus ponens (i.e. $p \cdot q, p => q$), and denying the consequent (i.e. $p \vee q, -q => p$) can now be solved.

Implicit representations

At the next level, at about the age of fifteen to sixteen years, the limitation that the components to be integrated are well defined is removed. As a result, adolescents at this level become able to integrate implicitly related structures. In categorical thought, adolescents can now grasp the relations between rules defining different sets of data. Thus, they can, for instance, decipher the most complex of the matrices involved in Raven-like tests that require the thinker to grasp the underlying rules by analysing each of the figures involved in relation to the other figures along two or more dimensions. In quantitative thought, the thinker can now solve problems that require algebraic reasoning proper. For example, they can now specify the value of x when it is known that $x = y + z$ and $x + y + z = 20$ (i.e. 10) or when the equation $L + M + N = L + P + N$ is valid (i.e. when $M = P$). These problems require an abstract conception of number such that it leads to the understanding that any number can be expressed by alternative symbols and that symbols can be reciprocally defined in reference to each other, depending upon the particular relation that connects them. Likewise, the spatial items scaling at this level requires an ability to conceive of the components of an image in relation to its other components or in relation to external systems of reference. Thus, thought fluidity in approach is the foremost characteristic of this level. In the causal domain, adolescents can design rather complex experiments where they have to hold several factors constant at once or match hypothesis with evidence in order to interpret the role of the factor they examine. All of these items require the person to grasp transformations on the basis of the relations between items. In propositional reasoning, they can now transform premises (for example by negating them) and inter-relate the results of these transformations until their logically necessary conclusion is specified.

Principled representations

At the next level, at the age of sixteen to seventeen, adolescents start to be able to integrate relations at multiple levels and conceive of the underlying principles that interconnect them. For example, in categorical reasoning, they can grasp third-order analogical relations such as those involved in the following analogy: {(tail : fish :: feed : mammals) :::: [movement]} :::: {(propeller : ship :: wheels : car) :::: [transportation]}. These relations, to be conceived, must somehow be purified from their category-specific or level-specific characteristics and inter-connected via the common property that runs through them both horizontally and vertically, that is within and across levels. This formalization enables the adolescents, for the first time, to acquire an epistemological awareness of the value of empirical evidence relative to a causal model of reality. That is, they start to understand that a single negative piece of evidence is enough to falsify a model that was built on a series of positive evidence generated by experiments, and deductively derived conclusions. This ability culminates, in the early college years, in the ability to conceive and specify all formal relations involved in propositional arguments. For example, they can now understand logical fallacies such as the fallacy of confirming the consequent (that is, they understand that if p and $-q$ is valid, and $-q$ is observed, no conclusion can be drawn about the state of p (that is, that p also occurs) because p may be due to reasons other than the occurrence of $-q$). This understanding indicates that they are able to understand how exactly each proposition constrains the condition of the other propositions in an argument and specify the whole web of logical relations.

The nature of development in the domains

The summary of the development of the various domains attempted above suggests clearly that there indeed are general developmental trends running through all domains. These trends can be described in reference to three dimensions: the nature of representations, complexity of representations and mental operations and flexibility in handling them.

The most important aspect in the development of representation is probably the relation between representations and reality. That is, with age, representations tend to become increasingly dissimilar or differentiated from their referents. Thus, they appear to be increasingly arbitrary in so far as their physical resemblance to their referents is concerned. As a result, their meaning is semantically constructed through their inter-relation or association with other representations already in place. The development from representational embeddedness and transparency to representational detachment and arbitrariness is continuous from birth to maturity, although at some phases change is more obvious and drastic than at other phases.

The successive levels are systematically ordered so that the operations and representations in each next level include and integrate the operations and representations of the previous level into a higher-order structure. Therefore, each next level is hierarchically more complex than the preceding level. For this reason, the sequences described conform to the specifications of the general theory of hierarchical complexity (Commons, Trudeau, Stein, Richards, and Krause 1998; Dawson and Gabrielian 2003) and to the prescriptions of Item Response Theory for valid task hierarchies, as tested (Demetriou and Kyriakides, in press) through the Rasch (1980) and the Saltus (Wilson 1989) model. In the section following we will show that the ascension along this hierarchy is, partly, due to expansion of the capacity of the general systems, of the mind.

It needs to be stressed, however, that the developmental analysis attempted above suggests that there is something more than sheer expansion in complexity in the development of thought. Specifically, the road from intuitively facilitated problems at the age of three to formal models at the age of eighteen implies changes along the dimension of representational flexibility. That is, these changes imply that, with development, thinkers become better able to view each of the components of a problem separately from each other and reconstruct their relations at will, according to the plans or goals of a particular moment. This representational flexibility provides computational flexibility, because it enables the person to compute alternative tentative solutions and then select the one best fitting to the accepted goal or model of the moment. In fact, the analysis attempted above indicated that changes along this dimension of representational flexibility may be as important in intellectual development as changes along the dimension of informational complexity.

We are reminded, for instance, that once a principle related to a particular kind of problem is grasped and the relevant strategy is available, differences in complexity between tasks do not matter very much. For example, at the first level of transcendent representations adolescents grasp the basic principles underlying the relations between numbers. Thus, they can solve simple equations where either a number (e.g. $8 - a = 5$) or an operation (e.g. $8 * 3 = 5$) is missing. When these principles are consolidated, at the next level, informational complexity is not a major problem. Adolescents can solve problems where 2, 3 or 4 operations are missing (e.g. $8 * 3 \# 2 = 10$). This implies that differences in complexity do not matter very much, if the nature of problems can be identified and the representational flexibility that is necessary to plan the attack on them is available. Under this condition, the thinker is able to formulate strategies for the reduction of informational load and generate the alternative conceptions needed to specify all dimensions involved in the problem space. Thus, differences between items scaling at different levels may be related to both differences in their complexity and in the representational flexibility needed to construct the necessary relations.

The dimension of representational flexibility may be one of the crucial dimensions underlying individual differences in intelligence. In other words, it may be the case that general cognitive developmental changes in reasoning, that is within person changes in mental age, come from changes in the general potentiation factors, such as processing efficiency and general self-monitoring and self-regulation strategies. That is, changes in these factors enhance the person's ability to construct more complex and abstract concepts and deal with more complex problems. However, individual differences at each age level, that is differences in IQ, come from differences in representational flexibility which enable the thinker to make strategy shifts as required by particular problems and circumstances. That is, differences in representational flexibility underlie individual differences in the kind of problems that may be solved despite their similarities in informational complexity. More flexible individuals can construct more refined concepts that are better tuned to the nuances of the environment and produce more original and problem-geared solutions to problems.

Moreover, attention needs to be drawn to the possible differences between the precise organization of mental operations and representations across the various domains or in the rate of progression along each of the domain-specific sequences described above. Specifically, the very existence of the domains suggests that the general sequences described above do not imply a complete equivalence in the complexity or the organization of concepts and operations across the various domain-specific systems described by the theory. In fact, the analysis above suggests that it is difficult to find fully equivalent formations for the concepts or problems that can be represented and dealt with across the various environment-oriented systems at the same age. This is due to the fact that the mental operations and representations that are particular to each environment-oriented system are themselves different. That is, the nature of representations (e.g. contrast, for instance, the subjective character and the similarity of mental images to the objects they represent with the phenomenally arbitrary but socially defined meaning of words), rules (e.g. contrast, for instance, the logical necessity underlying mathematical rules and syllogistic reasoning with the reality-dependent constraints underlying spatial relations), and versatility (variations of rules that are logically necessary are much more constrained than variations of rules that have a subjective character, such as imagery, as this is reflected in the differences between mathematics and the visual arts par excellence) varies across domains. Therefore, differences in development across domains are to be expected and depend upon both experience in and disposition to each of them that provide access and facility in the peculiarities of the representations and rules of each domain. The growth curves for three of the domains provide strong support to this conclusion. It can be seen in Figure 1.4 that the growth curves of the domains of categorical

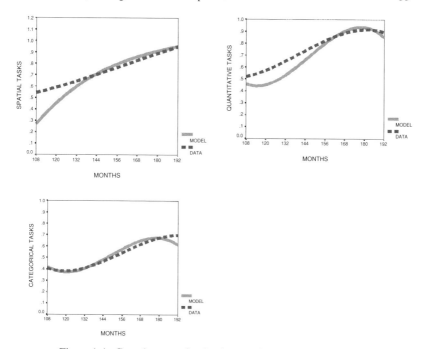

Figure 1.4. Growth curves for the three problem-solving domains.

and quantitative thought, although logistic in both cases, differ in developmental rate (the curve of quantitative thought indicates faster development). The growth curve of spatial thought is quadratic, indicating that developmental change in this domain is governed by different dynamics as compared to the other two domains.

Dynamic relations between processes and systems

The relations between the general and the specialized processes are complex and bi-directional. Specifically, on the one hand, general processes set the limits for the construction, the operation, and the development of the domain-specific systems. The general forms and directions of development discussed above reflect, to a large extent, the state and condition of these limits. On the other hand, specialized processes provide the frame and raw material for the functioning of general processes. Thus, the consolidation of the general processes and variations from the general forms reflect differences between the specialized processes. In this section we will discuss in some detail the dynamic relations between the various processes and present relevant empirical evidence.

Bottom-up dynamics

The models of the effects of general processes on specialized processes adopt a reductionist or bottom-up approach. That is, they assume that lower-level and thus more general processes constrain the condition of more complex and thus more specialized processes. According to this approach, processing efficiency constrains the condition of working memory and thinking, and working memory constrains the condition of thinking. In general, these models ascribe age changes in the quality of intelligence to changes in efficiency and working memory (developmental models) and individual differences in intelligence to individual differences in these general processes (differential models). How are these effects explained?

Salthouse (1996) proposed two mechanisms to account for the effects exerted by processing efficiency on more complex functions, the limited time mechanism and the simultaneity mechanism. According to the first mechanism, when processing speed is slower than the demand of a given task, performance is degraded because there is competition between the currently executed operations and the operations of the immediate past. That is, 'the time to perform later operations is greatly restricted when large proportions of the available time is occupied by the execution of early operations' (Salthouse 1996, 404), with the result that processing always lacks behind current needs. According to the second mechanism, 'products of early processing may be lost by the time that later processing is completed. To the extent this is the case, relevant information may no longer be available when it is needed' (Salthouse 1996, 405). Thus, the operation of higher-level mental functions, such as working memory or reasoning, may be impaired due to lack of critical information.

In regard to the working memory–thinking relations, the common assumption is that thinking is positively related to working memory capacity because enhanced working memory increases the connections and associations that can be grasped or built either between the units of the newly encountered information or between this information and information already stored in long-term memory. Thus, the larger the capacity of working memory the more complex are the concepts that can be grasped or the problems that can be solved.

However, it must be emphasized that there is no consensus as to the exact role of the various lower-level processes in the functioning and development of higher-level processes. In the psychometric literature, some scholars emphasize the role of processing efficiency in intellectual functioning and individual differences in regard to it. For instance, Jensen (1998) and Deary (2000a) believe that speed of processing is the most important factor in the definition of g, because speed reflects the quality of the brain to process information. However, Stankov and Roberts (1997) showed that the importance of speed of processing is not due to speed itself but to the fact that speeded tasks require selective attention. Under this perspective, directed attention is the crucial factor. These findings go in line with other findings that executive control seems to be the primary factor in individual differences in *g* or in fluid intelligence (Engle 2002). Other scholars emphasize the role of working memory. That is, Hale and Fry (2000) and Kyllonen and Christal (1990) presented evidence showing that working memory is much more closely related to fluid intelligence or general intelligence (Miller and Vernon 1992) than speed of processing.

This discrepancy in evidence and interpretation is also present in the developmental literature. Kail and Salthouse (Kail 1991; Kail and Salthouse 1994; Salthouse 1996) believe that speed of processing is the crucial factor in developmental changes in general intelligence. Others believe that changes in inhibition as such, which reflects the state of executive control processes, are the factors of primary importance in cognitive development (Bjorklund and Harnishfeger 1995; Dempster 1991, 1992; Harnishfeger 1995). Finally, the class of models which are known as the *neo-Piagetian models* of cognitive development (Case 1985, 1992; Halford 1993; Pascual-Leone 1970, 1988) maintain that working memory capacity is the causal factor in cognitive development. Obviously, the integrative theory to come will be able to explicate the phenomena of interest only when the role of each of the processes will be clarified.

Recent advances in structural equation modelling and dynamic systems modelling help specify with high precision the direction, size and nature of these interactions. Our recent research (Demetriou et al. 2002) suggests that bottom-up effects operate in a cascade fashion. That is, more fundamental processes are embedded in more complex processes in such a way that each process that resides one level higher in the mental hierarchy involves all lower level processes plus characteristics which are particular to it. Figure 1.5 illustrates this cascade relation between the various processes. This figure summarizes the results of a longitudinal study that covered the age span eight to sixteen years of age. In this study, participants (who were eight, ten and twelve years old at first testing) were tested three times (separated by one-year intervals) on tasks addressed to speed of processing, control of processing, executive, phonological and visual memory, and quantitative, spatial and propositional reasoning. This cascade model was tested separately on the performance attained by the whole sample at each testing wave, in order to examine how the relations between the various constructs are affected by development. Moreover, the model was tested on the performance attained on processing efficiency (i.e., speed and control of processing) at the first testing wave, on memory tasks (i.e., executive, phonological, and visuo-spatial memory) at the second testing wave, and on the cognitive tasks (i.e. spatial, quantitative and verbal reasoning) at the third testing wave. This last model is obviously a very robust test of the relations of interest because it involves measures of the different structures and

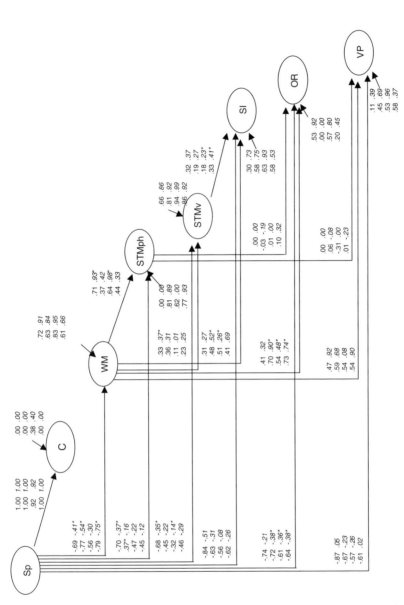

Figure 1.5. Model of the structural relations between factors across the three testing waves (Sp = speed of processing, C = control of processing, WM = working memory, STMph = short-term memory–phonological, STMv = short-term memory–verbal, SI = spatial imaginal system, QR = qualitative-relational system, VP = verbal-propositional system). *Note:* The second column of coefficients stand for the models fitted after removing the effect of age.

levels of the mind examined at different points in time. The four coefficients associated with each structural relation tested in the model shown in Figure 1.5 correspond to the four tests of the model described here.

It can be seen that speed of processing is the most fundamental factor and its condition determines fully the condition of control of processing so that the faster a person is in processing the more efficient this person is in control of processing. Technically speaking, processing speed under conditions where control is needed, such as when one must recognize the ink colour (e.g. blue) of a colour word with a different meaning (e.g. the word 'red'), can be fully predicted from processing speed under facilitating conditions, such as simply reading words. It needs to be noted that this finding concurs with Stankov and Roberts (1997) who point out that speed of processing tasks are indexes of controlled attention processes. Because of the complete covariation of the two measures of processing efficiency, in the other relations involved in the model only speed is used. Specifically, it can be seen that speed of processing is strongly associated with the central executive in working memory so that the faster the persons are the more able they appear to cope with information that must be stored in and recalled from working memory. In turn, both speed and executive processes in memory are associated with the capacity of the two modality-specific short-term storage buffers. Finally, the condition of all of these processes is additively associated with the functioning of the specialized domains of thinking. That is, about 60–65 per cent, or more, of the variance of specialized domains of reasoning, such as quantitative, spatial, and verbal reasoning, is accounted for by the various components of processing efficiency and processing capacity.

There are three aspects of the model shown in Figure 1.5 that require special mention. First, it is noticeable that two of the various processes, that is speed of processing and executive processes in working memory, emerge as the two pivotal constructs in this cascade of relations. That is, each largely determines the condition of other constructs in their own system (that is speed determines the condition of control in processing efficiency and executive processes determine the condition of the specialized storage buffers in working memory) and the two of them together are the most fundamental predictors of the various domains of thinking. This is suggested by the fact that these two constructs account for almost all of the variance accounted for in each of the specialized thinking domains. According to Demetriou et al. (2002) these two predictors of thinking 'are complementary manifestations of the same underlying construct: guided processing under time constraints' (p. 70). In other words, a very large part of the variance in specialized domains of thinking (two thirds or more) is accounted for by DEF processes enabling the thinker to stay focused, encode information, and respond to it, or organize it in working memory so as to be maximally storable, usable, and retrievable.

Second, the exact contribution of these fundamental processes to the functioning of the domains varies from the one domain to the other. For instance, on the one hand, the contribution of executive processes of working memory to the functioning of quantitative reasoning is considerably stronger than their contribution to the functioning of spatial or propositional reasoning. On the other hand, the contribution of visuo/spatial storage as such to the operation of spatial reasoning (11 per cent of the variance) is considerably larger than the contribution of phonological storage to the functioning of quantitative or propositional reasoning. Third, a considerable amount of variance in each of the domains (the remaining third) cannot be accounted for by these fundamental processes. Obviously, this is related to the particularities of each domain, such as the command of domain-specific operations and processes, of domain-appropriate symbol systems, and knowledge about the problem-specific entities involved. The theorist must be sensitive to these differences in the composition of domains because they may explain, as we have shown above, the dynamics of their real time functioning and learning, their development and individual differences in regard to them.

Top-down dynamics

Researchers espousing a conceptual change approach have documented that changes in knowledge and expertise within a domain may influence the functioning of reasoning processes or domain-free processes, such as those underlying working memory (Carey 1985; Chi 1976; Schneider 2002). In cognitivist terms, this is tantamount to saying that changes in declarative knowledge result in changes in procedural knowledge. In psychometric terms, it would be tantamount to saying that changes in crystallized intelligence result in changes in fluid intelligence or *g*. In our terms, this is equivalent to saying that changes in the third level of organization of the thought domains (i.e. knowledge and beliefs) cause changes in their second level of organization (i.e. operations and rules). Dynamic systems modelling allows the researcher to test these dynamic interactions between constructs residing at different levels of the mental architecture by integrating into the equation expressing the development of each construct effects contributed from other constructs. Specifically, this kind of modelling allows the investigator to integrate into the equation, in addition to the autocatalytic or self-development growth factor, change factors from other constructs in order to specify how change in the construct of interest would be shaped.

Figure 1.3 shows the development of processing efficiency, working memory, and problem solving under the assumption that each of them draws only upon itself in development or that they receive influences from the other constructs. Specifically, in the first case, the growth curve represents the assumption that growth occurs only under autocatalytic effects or that development is fuelled only by the carrying capacity of the process under question. In the second case, the model assumes that, in addition to the autocatalytic effects, there are contributions to each process coming from dynamic state and change dynamics of the other processes. Thus, in this later case, autocatalytic effects and effects from other processes add up into a dynamic system involving all interacting processes. The mathematics of these models are fully presented in Demetriou et al. (2002).

It can be seen that the development of processing efficiency and working memory (Figure 1.3a and Figure 1.3b, respectively) is faster when they receive effects from problem solving than when they are supposed to capitalize only on their own capacity for development. Specifically, the curves of development for these two constructs are steeper, reflecting faster progression towards the end state, when effects from problem solving are assumed as compared to the curves reflecting the development of each of them alone. This means that changes in problem solving function as a mediator for the improvement of memory and processing efficiency, at least up to the point of the asymptote. In other words, top-down effects are also present.

Figure 1.3c shows a number of alternative models where different combinations of factors are assumed to affect the development of problem solving. It can be seen that when problem solving is assumed to draw only upon itself, development is slower than when it receives influences from only one of the two potentiation factors (i.e. speed of processing). Moreover, development is considerably faster when it receives influences from both of the two potentiation factors (i.e. speed of processing and working memory) than when it receives effects from one or none of them. It is also highly interesting that the contributions of each of these two potentiation factors to the growth of problem solving are different in their initiation and termination, due to their differences in growth rate. When both effects are present, the curve takes off and levels off considerably earlier than any of these two.

Mental structure, development and individual differences

The discussion has so far focused on general organizational and developmental patterns. In this section we shall focus on individual differences in both the organization of processes and their development. The main aim is to specify the role of the various processes in the functioning and development of other processes and their contribution to the formation of different types of developers.

Developmental and differential factors

In the previous section we maintained that the various processes interact dynamically both during on-line functioning and during development so that the present state or changes in any of them can influence the state and functioning of the others or cause changes in them. In particular, our structural and dynamic systems modelling suggested that there are both bottom-up and top-down influences, such that hierarchically lower-level, more general, processes provide or open possibilities for the functioning and development of hierarchically higher-level, more specialized, processes, and these provide the frame and means for the full use of these general processes, thereby ensuring stability and flexibility in their functioning. Two issues need to be clarified in regard to the role of each process vis-à-vis the functioning of the others. First, we need to specify if the role of each process remains stable or undergoes changes with development. Second, we need to specify what is the exact role of each process in the functioning and change of other processes. We tried to answer these questions in the longitudinal study described above. The model shown in Figure 1.5 highlights our findings in regard to both issues.

In so far as the first issue is concerned, it can be seen that the relations between speed of processing and the various components of working memory or the three domains of reasoning tend to decrease from the one testing wave to the next. Interestingly, the relations between working memory and reasoning remain generally stable. This pattern of relations indicates that, with development, the role of speed of processing in regard to the functioning of other processes becomes weaker whereas the role of working memory remains stable. Thus, it seems that, on the one hand, with development, factors other than processing efficiency acquire prominence in the construction and functioning of memory-specific or domain-specific reasoning skills and operations. On the other hand, the stability of the relations between working memory and the three reasoning domains indicates that working memory is somehow an integral part of reasoning so that it cannot be detached from it. This finding is fully in line with the functional shift model in the development of working memory proposed by Demetriou et al. (1993) and summarized above. That is, the change of the complexity of the unit of information that can be held in working memory with development indicates that working memory co-evolves with thinking so that mental units in these two aspects of the mind cannot be dissociated.

The coefficients shown in italics in Figure 1.5 provide further information about the role of these two potentiation factors vis-à-vis the functioning and development of reasoning. Specifically, these coefficients reflect the relations between the various factors after removing the possible effects of age on these relations. Technically speaking, to remove the effects of age from these relations, each of the various variables was regressed on the age of the subjects at the first testing wave. This manipulation purifies the various between-factor relations from possible cohort and individual differences at the start, thereby providing the possibility to test the effects of sheer growth on these relations.

It can be seen that this manipulation results in a weakening of the relation between processing efficiency and each of the reasoning domains (coefficients dropped from circa 0.6 to circa 0.3 or less) while the relation between working memory and these domains was not affected (it remained circa 0.5) or it even increased.

These findings suggest that processing efficiency covaries closely with age, whereas working memory does not. In turn, this pattern suggests that these two potentiation factors have a different role in the development and functioning of the specialized domains of reasoning. That is, processing efficiency is a strong developmental factor and working memory is a strong differential factor in regard to these domains. In other words, developmental changes in processing efficiency open new possibilities both for working memory itself and for the various domains of reasoning. The realization of these possibilities into actual memory strategies and domain-specific skills, processes and operations depends on many factors, such as personal interests, environmental and social opportunities etc. However, how many of these possibilities are realized in working memory as such does affect the construction of domain-specific thinking and problem-solving skills. In other words, for each level of processing efficiency there is a range of levels of working memory, and individual differences in the precise level of working memory persons have attained underlie individual differences in how and how much of the processing potentials available at a given age will be implemented in domain-specific thinking skills and concepts. Therefore, the present findings seem to clarify that processing efficiency is the developmental factor and working memory is the differential factor in regard to the development of thinking.

How is this web of relations to be explained developmentally? Given that processing efficiency is the fundamental factor for both WM and thinking, one must assume that for each level L_{wm} of WM, there is a minimum level L_{preff} of processing efficiency. In a similar manner, for each level L_{th} of thinking there is a particular combination $L_{wm,preff}$ of processing efficiency and WM. However, attaining the level L_{preff} of processing efficiency that is necessary for the level L_{wm} of WM or attaining the combination $L_{wm,preff}$ of processing efficiency and WM that is necessary for a level L_{th} of thinking does not imply that these possible levels are going to be attained automatically. That is, these necessary levels simply open the possibility for the attainment of their corresponding possible levels. To have them attained, however, other factors must be satisfied. Specifically, the attainment of the working memory that is possible, given the present processing efficiency, requires the strategies and skills needed for the organization, storage and retrieval of information up to the level L_{preff} of the given processing efficiency. In a similar manner, the attainment of the possible level of thinking in each of the various domains requires the domain-specific reasoning and problem-solving skills, operations and strategies that correspond

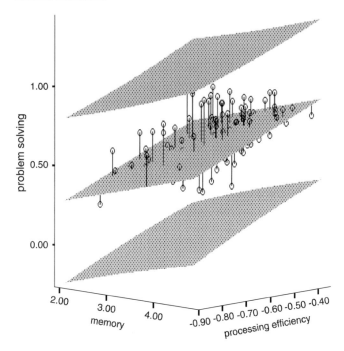

Figure 1.6. Development of problem solving as a function of processing efficiency and working memory development.

to the combination $L_{wm,preff}$ of processing efficiency and WM. However, the construction of these strategies and skills requires relevant experience and practice. Moreover, it is plausible to assume that the more the minimum of the necessary levels L_{preff} and $L_{wm,preff}$ is exceeded the easier it becomes to build their corresponding levels L_{wm} and L_{th}, respectively. In fact, one of the reasons for acceleration of development after a certain point within each developmental phase postulated by the logistic model of growth is the excess in the available resources that goes within each level in parallel with the construction of the necessary skills, operations and strategies. Figure 1.6 illustrates these relations between the three fundamental aspects of the mind.

Different types of developers

The dynamic intertwining of the various dimensions of intelligence discussed above suggests that variations in any of them may affect the functional and developmental state and dynamics of the mind as a whole. For instance, minor differences in processing efficiency or working memory may cause large differences in the efficiency of functioning or the rate and stability of development in the various domains of reasoning specified above. In other words, differences in the combinations of the underlying potentiation factors of thought may cause large phenotypical variations of the reasoning processes that depend on them and these variations in reasoning may, in their turn, influence the further development of these underlying potentiation factors. That is, there may be different types of thinkers and developers that reflect the underlying dynamic organization of the processes that define intelligence.

To examine this possibility, we applied mixture growth modelling on the performance of the subjects involved in our longitudinal study. This method enables the developmental researcher to specify if there are different classes in a sample of persons, depending on the combinations of the dimensions involved in the analysis. Indeed, this analysis uncovered four classes of persons. The first class included normal developers. That is, this class included the children performing lowest in all three abilities but who showed the largest gains as a result of development in all three abilities. The second class included children whose eventual attainment was lower than what is justified by their processing efficiency. Specifically, children in this class were fast processors but their memory and problem-solving attainment was comparatively lower in both initial state and degree of change compared to children in the other classes. It is noted that almost all of these children belonged to the two older cohorts, suggesting that they were already late in transforming their processing capabilities into actual problem-solving abilities. Children in the third and the fourth class were practically identical in processing efficiency but they differed in memory and problem solving. That is, children in class 3 were higher in memory and lower in problem solving than children in class 4. However, they developed less than children in class 4 in both memory and problem solving.

Moreover, in addition to the differences between the four classes in the rate of development, there were interesting differences in the stability of their problem-solving attainments. That is, the development of reasoning in classes 1 and 4 was very stable, as indicated by the fact that performance improved and remained stable from one testing wave to the next across the various reasoning tasks. In contrast, performance in classes 2 and 3 was rather unstable, especially in terms of the most difficult items. That is, performance at a next testing wave was lower than performance on a subsequent wave on many reasoning tasks. We ascribed this instability to the fact that working memory was not as advanced as needed to enable the persons in these classes to sustain their reasoning achievements into levels corresponding to their processing possibilities as indicated by the condition of their processing efficiency. This interpretation is in line with the claim advanced above that working memory operates as a factor of individual differences in regard to reasoning whereas processing efficiency operates as

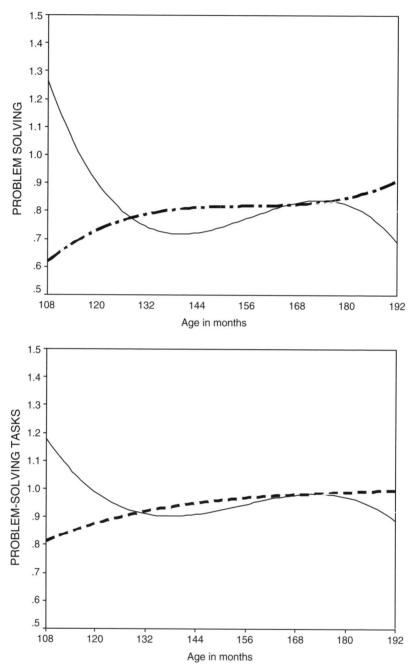

Figure 1.7a and b. Development of problem solving in stable (dashed lines) and unstable (solid lines) developers under the assumption of no effects from processing efficiency and working memory (panel A) and the presence of these effects (panel B).

a developmental factor that opens developmental possibilities but it does not ensure their actualization.

The differences in the dynamics of development of different classes of developers are nicely illustrated in Figure 1.7. This figure shows the developmental curves for (a) of one the classes of stable developers (i.e. class 4) and (b) for the two classes of unstable developers combined (i.e. classes 2 and 3). Panel A of Figure 1.7 shows the logistic growth of each class in regard to problem solving independently of any effects from the other factors and panel B of Figure 1.7 shows the same model under the assumption that problem solving receives effects from processing efficiency and working memory. It is clear in both panels that development in the class of stable developers is always moving upwards whereas in the group of unstable developers it wavers up and down. Moreover, it is also clear that stable developers (panel B) are the most efficient in transforming the contributions of processing efficiency and working memory into stable problem-solving attainments.

The discussion above about the dynamic relations between different processes has explained how each system can function as a cause of change in another system. It is plausible to assume that different types of change are effected via different mechanisms, i.e. there are mechanisms which transfer changes (a) across the hierarchical levels of the mental architecture, (b) within hierarchical levels, that is, from one domain to the other, and (c) from one component to the other within a given domain. These mechanisms need not be discussed here as the chapter by Raftopoulos (this volume) is dedicated to them (see also Demetriou and Raftopoulos 1999; Demetriou, Raftopoulos, and Kargopoulos 1999).

Conclusions

This chapter aimed to integrate findings and postulates from cognitive, differential, and developmental models of the human mind into an overarching model that would be able at one and the same time to describe and explain the architecture of the mind, its development, and individual differences in regard to both architecture and development. As such, the model is based on studies specifically designed to empirically substantiate it. It is hoped that the chapter shows that such a model, even if still far from completeness, is feasible. At a descriptive level, the constructs of the three approaches are complementary to each other. At an explanatory level, this chapter shows that constructs from one approach may be invoked as explanatory factors for the condition and change of constructs in the other approaches. In this concluding section we will try to highlight this interweaving of the three approaches in the model summarized here.

In so far as architecture is concerned, it seems clear that both general and specialized capabilities and processes do exist and they are organized hierarchically so that more complex and specialized processes include more simple or general processes. This type of architecture, which is the culmination of more than a century of psychometric research (Carroll 1993; Gustafsson and Undheim 1996; Jensen 1998), is largely consistent with findings in both the cognitive and the developmental approach (Case et al. 2001; Demetriou et al. 2002). Specifically, a large part of what is defined as *g* in psychometric theory (that is, the factors that are responsible for the fact that all mental tests correlate positively with each other) can be reduced to mechanisms underlying processing efficiency, processing capacity, and directive-executive control, which have been the primary target of research and theory in cognitive psychology. In fact, these very mechanisms seem able to explain, to a considerable extent, the state of understanding and problem solving at successive age levels, which is the object of developmental psychology and individual differences in regard to it. It is highly interesting that some of these general processes – processing efficiency and DEF – were found to be the factors explaining the development of working memory and thinking whereas working memory itself was found to be the factor explaining individual differences in thinking.

In this common model, the definition of intelligence boils down to a simple function. The more mentally efficient (that is, the faster and more focused on goal), capable (that is, the more information one can hold in mind at a given moment), planful and foresighted (that is, the more clearly one can specify one's goals and plan how to achieve them), and flexible (that is, the more one can introduce variations in the concepts and mental operations one already possesses) a person is, the more intelligent (both in regard to other individuals and in regard to a general developmental hierarchy) this person will prove to be. In other words, excelling and developing in understanding, learning, reasoning, and problem solving is, to a considerable extent, a function of increase in mental efficiency, capacity, planfulness and flexibility. In psychometric terms, this is tantamount to saying that differences in the processes associated with *g* cause differences in general inferential and reasoning mechanisms. In developmental terms, this is tantamount to saying that changes in the processes underlying *g* result in the qualitative transformation of the general structures of thought underlying understanding and reasoning at successive ages so that more complex and less familiar problems can be solved and more abstract concepts can be constructed. This is so because the missing links in the abstract or unfamiliar problems and concepts can be constructed ad hoc or introduced by the thinker from other realms or from the thinker's past.

Thus, the specification of the combinations between (1) efficiency (in terms of a standard metric of processing speed), (2) DEF (in terms of a standard metric of goal formation, planning and feedback management), (3) working memory (in terms of a standard metric of storage management and capacity), (4) flexibility (in terms of a standard metric of variation initiation and handling), and (5) operations and rules in each of the specialized domains for each of the successive years of life would transform the concept of mental age from a descriptive construct into an explanatory construct able to highlight *what possibilities* exist and *how* and *why* they are implemented into actual performance. Therefore, future research would have to associate the successive years of mental age with the various sequences and combinations specified here so that each of them has full meaning for both the theorist and the practitioner in regard to *what* can be done by children and *how* at different mental ages. Moreover, this association will help to bring developmental theory to real life because information about a person's IQ would inform one about two aspects of the person's present condition. First, how far this person he has progressed relative to his age on the ladder of different abilities and how well he has mastered the abilities associated with his age. Admittedly, IQ in its present form is rather silent in regard to the dynamics of change and learning and in regard to the cognitive flexibility that characterizes the individual at a given age. Thus, IQ tests must be enriched in the direction of the model presented here in order to be able to speak about these dimensions of intellectual functioning and development.

In so far as change is concerned, the three traditions also seem to melt into this overarching model. Specifically, on the one hand, transition mechanisms specified by developmental theory are useful for differential theory, because they highlight why and how change in mental age occurs. On the other hand, mechanisms of change as specified in the cognitive theory, which underlie the automatization of performance, highlight how newly acquired developmental structures in a given phase get established and consolidated, thereby preparing the way for the transition to the next phase of development. Moreover, both kinds of mechanisms of change explain individual differences in IQ because they underlie changes in mental age. On the other hand, it also seems possible that knowing an individual's IQ (primarily g) would be useful as a predictor of the rate of change that is possible, for this individual, from the point of view of the cognitive theory (i.e. how fast this individual can automatize skills and processes relative to a new task) and developmental theory (i.e. what is this individual's rate of progression across the stage hierarchy?).

The differentiation of development across domains is an integral part of the organization and functioning of the human mind. This is so because in each of the domains there are constraints directly coming from the particularities in the mental operations, the representations and the skills that characterize each of the domains. That is, performance within and across persons may vary even if general processes are kept constant, because the dynamics of functioning and development differs across domains and the mastering of this dynamics depends on both special domain-specific disposition and domain-specific experience.

Domain-specific disposition is a multiplier of general potentials. If domain-specific disposition falls short of general potentials in a given domain, obviously attainment in this domain will prove to fall below the level of general potentials. For instance, visuo-spatial ability will fall below general potentials in the blind, even if general potentials are very high. If it is high, such as a special proclivity in visualization, visuo-spatial ability will exceed the level expected on the basis of the condition of general potentials. Domain-specific experience is needed to give the chance to the developing person to customize, so to speak, the general possibilities and processes to the particularities and constraints of each of the domains. Obviously, practice to the extreme in a domain will elevate this domain to the upper limit of general potentials. Overall, the particular combination of general potentials, domain-specific disposition, and domain-specific experience determines the momentum, the stability, and the direction of development in the individual.

It is hoped that this chapter suggests clearly that neither Gardner-like theories (e.g. Gardner 1983), which postulate the existence of autonomous multiple intelligences, nor Jensen-like theories (e.g. Jensen 1998), which stress the primacy of general processes, do justice to the complexity of the human mind. The human mind involves both general and specialized abilities, each of which functions as a dimension of intra- and inter-individual differences during both on-line functioning and developmental time. That is, general processes are everywhere but they can never be seen alone and specialized domains are the interface through which the mind interleaves with the different realms of the world, but they involve general processes as part of their construction and they need them for their functioning and development. Developmental dynamics provide the melting pot where general and specialized processes get integrated and refined into world-relevant systems of understanding and action. Thus cognitive, differential and developmental considerations are of utmost importance for the understanding and improvement of the functioning of the mind. At the same time, as Saxe (this volume) shows, social, cultural and historical influences set the frame in which the cognitive, differential and developmental dynamics operate.

REFERENCES

Anderson, J. R. (1983). *The architecture of cognition*. Cambridge, MA: Harvard University Press.
Andrews, G., Halford, G. S., Bunch, K. M., Bowden, D. and Jones, T. (2003). Theory of mind and relational complexity. *Child Development, 74*, 1476–99.
Baddeley, A. D. (1990). *Human memory: theory and practice*. Hillsdale, NJ: Erlbaum.
   (1993). Working memory or working attention? In A. D. Baddeley and L. Weiskrantz (eds.) *Attention, selection, awareness, and control. A tribute to Donald Broadbent* (pp. 152–70). Oxford: Clarendon Press.

Baddeley, A. D. and Hitch, G. H. (2000). Development of working memory: should the Pascual-Leone and the Baddeley and Hitch models be merged? *Journal of Experimental and Child Psychology, 77*, 128–37.

Band, G. P. H., van der Molen, M. W., Overtoom, C. C. E. and Verbaten, M. N. (2000). The ability to activate and inhibit speeded responses: Separate developmental trends. *Journal of Experimental Child Psychology, 75*, 263–90.

Bjorklund, D. F. and Harnishfeger, K. K. (1995). The evolution of inhibition mechanisms and their role in human cognition and behavior. In F. N. Dempster and C. J. Brainerd (eds.) *Interference and inhibition in cognition* (pp. 141–73). New York: Academic Press.

Braine, M. D. S. (1990). The 'natural logic' approach to reasoning. In W. F. Overton (ed.) *Reasoning, necessity, and logic: developmental perspectives* (pp. 133–57). Hillsdale, NJ: Erlbaum.

Broadbent, D. E. (1971). *Decision and stress*. New York: Academic Press.

Carey, S. (1985). *Conceptual change in childhood*. Cambridge, MA: MIT Press.

Carroll, J. B. (1993). *Human cognitive abilities: a survey of factor-analytic studies*. New York: Cambridge University Press.

Case, R. (1985). *Intellectual development. Birth to adulthood*. New York: Academic Press.

(1992). *The mind's staircase: exploring the conceptual underpinnings of children's thought and knowledge*. Hillsdale, NJ: Erlbaum.

(1992). The role of the frontal lobes in the regulation of cognitive development. *Brain and Cognition, 20*, 51–73.

Case, R., Demetriou, A., Platsidou, M. and Kazi, S. (2001). Integrating concepts and tests of intelligence from the differential and the developmental traditions. *Intelligence, 29*, 307–36.

Cattell, R. B. (1971). *Abilities: their structure, growth, and action*. Boston: Houghton Mifflin.

Chi, M. T. H. (1976). Short-term memory limitations in children: capacity or processing deficits? *Memory and Cognition, 23*, 266–81.

Commons, M. L., Trudeau, E. J., Stein, S. A., Richards, F. A. and Krause, S. R. (1998). Hierarchical complexity of tasks shows the existence of developmental stages. *Developmental Review, 18*, 237–78.

Cowan, N. (1999). An embedded-processes model of working memory. In A. Miyake and P. Shah (eds.) *Models of working memory: mechanisms of active maintenance and executive control* (pp. 62–101). Cambridge: Cambridge University Press.

Dawson, T. L., Xie, Y. Y. and Wilson, M. (2003). Domain-general and domain-specific developmental assessments: do they measure the same thing? *Cognitive Development, 18*, 61–78.

Deary, I. J. (2000a). *Looking down on human intelligence*. Oxford: Oxford University Press.

(2000b). Simple information processing and intelligence. In R. J. Sternberg (ed.) *Handbook of intelligence* (pp. 267–84). Cambridge: Cambridge University Press.

Deary, I. J., Whalley, L. J., Lemmon, H., Starr, J. S. and Crawford, J. R. (2000). The stability of individual differences in mental ability from childhood to old age: follow-up of the Scottish Mental Survey. *Intelligence, 28*, 49–55.

de Loache, J. S., Miller, K. F. and Pierroutsakos, S. L. (1998). Reasoning and problem solving. In D. Kuhn and R. Siegler (eds.) W. Damon (series ed.) *Handbook of Child Psychology (5th ed.): Vol. 2: Cognition, perception and language*
(pp. 801–50). New York: Wiley.

Demetriou, A. (1998a). Nooplasis: 10 + 1 postulates about the formation of mind.
*Learning and Instruction. The Journal of the European Association for Research
on Learning and Instruction, 8*, 271–87.

  (1998b). Cognitive development. In A. Demetriou, W. Doise, K. F. M. van Lieshout
(eds.) *Life-span developmental psychology* (pp. 179–269). London: Wiley.

  (2000). Organization and development of self-understanding and self-regulation:
toward a general theory. In M. Boekaerts, P. R. Pintrich and M. Zeidner (eds.)
Handbook of self-regulation (pp. 209–51). Academic Press.

  (2003). Self-formations: toward a life-span model of the developing mind and self.
Journal of Adult Development, 17, 151–71.

  (in press). Unity and modularity in the mind and the self. Towards a general theory.
In Chandler, M., Lalonde, C. and Lightfoot, C. (eds.) *Changing conceptions of
psychological life*. Mahwah, NJ: Lawrence Erlbaum and Associates.

Demetriou, A., Christou, C., Spanoudis, G. and Platsidou, M. (2002). The development
of mental processing: efficiency, working memory, and thinking. *Monographs of
the Society for Research in Child Development, 67* (serial no. 268).

Demetriou, A. and Efklides, A. (1985). Structure and sequence of formal and postformal
thought: general patterns and individual differences. *Child Development, 56*, 1062–
91.

  (1989). The person's conception of the structures of developing intellect: early adolescence to middle age. *Genetic, Social, and General Psychology Monographs,
115*, 371–423.

Demetriou, A., Efklides, A. and Platsidou, M. (1993). The architecture and dynamics
of developing mind: Experiential structuralism as a frame for unifying cognitive
developmental theories. *Monographs of the Society for Research in Child Development, 58* (5–6, serial no. 234).

Demetriou, A., Efklides, A., Papadaki, M., Papantoniou, A. and Economou, A. (1993).
The structure and development of causal-experimental thought. *Developmental
Psychology, 29*, 480–97.

Demetriou, A. and Kazi, S. (2001). *Unity and modularity in the mind and the self:
studies on the relationships between self-awareness, personality, and intellectual
development from childhood to adolescence*. London: Routledge.

Demetriou, A. and Kyriakides, L. (in press). A Rasch-measurement model analysis of
cognitive developmental sequences: validating a comprehensive theory of cognitive development. *British Journal of Educational Psychology*.

Demetriou, A., Kyriakides, L. and Avraamidou, C. (2003). The missing link in the
relations between intelligence and personality. *Journal of Research in Personality,
37*, 547–81.

Demetriou, A., Pachaury, A., Metallidou, Y. and Kazi, S. (1996). Universals and speci-
ficities in the structure and development of quantitative-relational thought: a cross-
cultural study in Greece and India. *International Journal of Behavioral Development, 19*, 255–90.

Demetriou, A., Platsidou, M., Efklides, A., Metallidou, Y. and Shayer, M. (1991). Structure and sequence of the quantitative-relational abilities and processing potential from childhood and adolescence. *Learning and Instruction: The Journal of the European Association for Research on Learning and Instruction, 1*, 19–44.

Demetriou, A. and Raftopoulos, A. (1999). Modeling the developing mind: from structure to change. *Developmental Review, 19*, 319–68.

Demetriou, A., Raftopoulos, A. and Kargopoulos, P. (1999). Interactions, computations, and experience: interleaved springboards of cognitive emergence, *Developmental Review, 19*, 389–414.

Dempster, F. N. (1991). Inhibitory processes: a neglected dimension of intelligence. *Intelligence, 15*, 157–73.

(1992). The rise and fall of the inhibitory mechanism: toward a unified theory of cognitive development and aging. *Developmental Review, 12*, 45–75.

Efklides, A., Demetriou, A. and Metallidou, A. (1994). The structure and development of propositional reasoning ability. In A. Demetriou and A. Efklides (eds.) *Mind, intelligence, and reasoning: structure and development* (pp. 151–72). Amsterdam: Elsevier.

Engle, R. W. (2002). Working memory capacity as executive attention. *Current Directions in Psychological Science, 11*, 19–23.

Fischer, K. W. (1980). A theory of cognitive development: the control and construction of hierarchies of skills. *Psychological Review, 87*, 477–531.

Flavell, J. H., Green, F. L. and Flavell, E. R. (1986). Development of knowledge about the appearance-reality distinction. *Monographs of the Society for Research in Child Development, 51* (1, serial no. 212).

(1995). Young children's knowledge about thinking. *Monographs of the Society for Research in Child Development, 60* (1, serial no. 243).

Fry, A. F. and Hale, S. (1996). Processing speed, working memory, and fluid intelligence: evidence for a developmental cascade. *Psychological Science, 7*, 237–41.

Frye, D., Zelazo, P. D. and Burack, J. A. (1998). Cognitive complexity and control: I. Theory of mind in typical and atypical development. *Current Directions in Psychological Science, 7*, 116–21.

Gardner, H. (1983). *Frames of mind. The theory of multiple intelligences.* New York: Basic Books.

Gelman, R. and Gallistel, R. (1978). *The child's understanding of number.* Cambridge, MA: Harvard University Press.

Gustafsson, J. E. and Undheim, J. O. (1996). Individual differences in cognitive functions. In D. C. Berliner, and R. C. Calfee (eds.) *Handbook of educational psychology* (pp. 186–242). New York: Macmillan.

Hale, S. and Fry, A. F. (2000). Relationships among processing speed, working memory, and fluid intelligence in children, *Biological Psychology, 54*, 1–34.

Halford, G. S. (1993). *Children's understanding: the development of mental models.* Hillsdale, NJ: Erlbaum.

Harnishfeger, K. K. (1995). The development of cognitive inhibition: theories, definitions, and research evidence. In F. N. Dempster and C. J. Brainerd (eds.) *Interference and inhibition in cognition* (pp. 175–204). New York: Academic Press.

Harris, P. L. and Nunez, M. (1996). Understanding permission rules by preschool children. *Child Development, 67,* 1572–91.

Hart, K. M. (1981). *Children's understanding of mathematics: 11–16.* London: John Murray.

Inhelder, B. and Piaget, J. (1958). *The growth of logical thinking from childhood to adolescence.* London: Routledge.

Jensen, A. R. (1998). *The G factor: the science of mental ability.* New York: Praeger.

Kail, R. (1991). Developmental functions for speed of processing during childhood and adolescence. *Psychological Bulletin, 109,* 490–501.

Kail, R. and Park, Y. (1994). Processing time, articulation time and memory span. *Journal of Experimental Child Psychology, 57,* 281–91.

Kail, R. and Salthouse, T. A. (1994). Processing speed as a mental capacity. *Acta Psychologica, 86,* 199–225.

Kargopoulos, P. and Demetriou, A. (1998). What, why, and whence logic? A response to the commentators. *New Ideas in Psychology, 16,* 125–39.

Kazi, S. (2002). 'Structure and development of hypercognitive abilities from 3 to 8 years of age'. Thessaloniki: Aristotle University Press (PhD Thesis).

Kosslyn, S. M. (1980). *Image and mind.* Cambridge, MA: Harvard University Press.

Kyllonen, P. and Christal, R. E. (1990). Reasoning ability is (little more than) working-memory capacity? *Intelligence, 14,* 389–433.

Logan, G. D. and Gordon, R. D. (2001). Executive control of visual attention in dual-task situations. *Psychological Review, 108,* 393–434.

Lohman, D. F. (2000). Complex information processing and intelligence. In R. J. Sternberg (ed.) *Handbook of Intelligence* (pp. 285–340). Cambridge: Cambridge University Press.

Miller, L. T. and Vernon, P. A. (1992). The general factor in short-term memory, intelligence, and reaction time, *Intelligence, 16,* 5–29.

Newell, A. and Simon, H. (1972). *Human problem solving.* Englewood Cliffs, NJ: Prentice-Hall.

Pascual-Leone, J. (1970). A mathematical model for the transition rule in Piaget's developmental stages. *Acta Psychologica, 32,* 301–45.

(1988). Organismic processes for neo-Piagetian theories: A dialectical causal account of cognitive development. In A. Demetriou (ed.) *The neo-Piagetian theories of cognitive development: toward an integration* (pp. 25–64). Amsterdam: North-Holland.

Perner, J. and Lang, B. (1999). Development of theory of mind and executive control. *Trends in Cognitive Science, 3,* 337–44.

Perner, J., Lang, B., and Kloo, D. (2002). Theory of mind and self-control: More than a common problem of implication. *Child Development, 73,* 752–67.

Piaget, J. (1970). Piaget's theory. In P. H. Mussen (ed.) *Carmichael's handbook of child development* (pp. 703–32). New York: Wiley.

(2001). *Studies in reflecting abstraction.* London: Psychology Press.

Posner, M. I. and Boies, S. J. (1971). Components of attention. *Psychological Review 78,* 391–408.

Rasch, G. (1980). *Probabilistic models for some intelligence and attainment tests.* Chicago: University of Chicago Press.

Resnick, L. B., Bill, V. and Lesgold, S. (1992). Developing thinking abilities in arithmetic class. In A. Demetriou, M. Shayer, and A. Efklides (eds.) *Neo-Piagetian
theories of cognitive development* (pp. 210–30). London: Routledge.

Rips, L. J. (1994). *The psychology of proof: deductive reasoning in human thinking.*
Cambridge, MA: The MIT Press.

Salthouse, T. A. (1996). The processing-speed theory of adult age differences in cognition. *Psychological Review, 103,* 403–28.

Schneider, W. (2002). Memory development in childhood. In U. Goswami (ed.)
Blackwell handbook of childhood cognitive development (pp. 236–56). London:
Blackwell.

Shah, P. and Miyake, A. (1996). The separability of working memory resources for spatial thinking and language processing: an individual differences approach. *Journal
of Experimental Psychology: General, 125,* 4–27.

Shayer, M., Demetriou, A. and Pervez, M. (1988). The structure and scaling of concrete
operational thought: three studies in four countries. *Genetic, Social, and General
Psychology Monographs, 114,* 307–76.

Spearman, C. (1904). 'General intelligence' objectively determined and measured.
American Journal of Psychology, 15, 201–93.

Stankov, L. and Roberts, R. (1997). Mental speed is not the 'basic' process of intelligence. *Personality and Individual Differences, 22,* 69–84.

Sternberg, R. J. (1985). *Beyond IQ. A triarchic theory of human intelligence.* New York:
Cambridge University Press.

Thelen, E. and Smith, L. B. (1994). *A dynamic systems approach to the development of
perception and action.* Cambridge, MA: MIT Press.

van Geert, P. (1991). A dynamic systems model of cognitive and language growth.
Psychological Review, 99, 395–417.

　(1994). *Dynamic systems development: change between complexity and chaos.* Hemel
Hempstead: Harvester Wheatsheaf.

Vurpilot, E. (1998). The development of scanning strategies and their relation to visual
differentiation. *Journal of Experimental Child Psychology, 6,* 632–50.

William, H. M. (1990). *The child's theory of mind.* Cambridge, MA: MIT Press.

Williams, B. R., Ponesse, J. S., Schachar, R. J., Logan, G. D. and Tannock, R. (1999).
Development of inhibitory control across the life span. *Developmental Psychology,
35,* 205–13.

Wilson, M. (1989). Saltus: a psychometric model of discontinuity in cognitive development. *Psychological Bulletin, 105* (2), 276–89.

Zelazo, P. R. (1998). McGraw and the development of unaided walking. *Developmental
Review, 18,* 449–71.

Zelazo, P. R. and Frye, D. (1998). Cognitive complexity and control: II. The development
of executive function in childhood. *Current Directions in Psychological Science,
7,* 121–6.

2   Types of cognitive change: a dynamical, connectionist account

Athanassios Raftopoulos and Constantinos P. Constantinou

In this chapter we offer a dynamical account of types of conceptual change both at the cognitive and the mathematical level. Our aim is to show that some classes of neural models can implement the types of change that we have proposed elsewhere. First, we introduce certain types of change that purport to account for the kinds of conceptual change observed in human development. These types are first described at the cognitive level. In the second part of the chapter, we discuss the mathematical/representational level realizations of the cognitive level representations and we claim that the latter can be depicted as points in the system's activational landscape. The concepts of attractors and basins of attraction are introduced and their role is discussed. Our guide in developing our account is the dynamical connectionist theory. In the third part of the chapter we offer a dynamical account of the types of change and we claim that, at this level, conceptual change can be modelled as a process of modification, appearance and disappearance of attractors and/or basins of attraction that shape the system's landscape. Finally, we discuss the kinds of mechanisms at the representational level that could produce the types of change observed at the cognitive level and modelled by means of dynamic connectionism.

Levels in the analysis of the mechanisms of change

Conceptual change can be accounted for at various levels of explanation. We distinguish here the *cognitive*, the *representational* and the level of the *functional architecture*. The first is a semantic or knowledge level. The second is the level of symbolic structure. The third level constitutes the mechanisms that implement behaviour (Pylyshyn 1984). Our stratification is based on and modifies Marr's (1982) distinction between the *computational*, the *algorithmic* and the *implementational* level of analysis of cognitive systems. The modification was deemed necessary because we would like to reserve the term 'computation' for other purposes, and we prefer the term 'representational' to 'algorithmic', since there are accounts of cognition that deny the algorithmic nature of mental operations.

At the cognitive level, one can discuss cognitive operations that apply to information-processing content (such as addition and subtraction), operations that apply to conceptual structures as wholes, such as differentiation or coalescence (Carey 1985, 1992; Chi 1992), or conceptual combination, generalization and hypothesis formation (Thagard 1992). This level addresses the issue of the functions computed by the information processing system. Change can be addressed from the viewpoint of the organization of mental structures in forming conceptual systems, and of the restructuring of this organization, due to conceptual changes (Thagard 1992; Chi 1992). Finally, one can explain change at this cognitive level using the tools of dynamic systems theory (Thelen and Smith 1994; Kelso 1995).

At the representational level one can examine the algorithmic processes that realize conceptual change at the cognitive level by transforming representations, such as Newell and Simon's (1972) 'problem behaviour graph'. This is a problem-solving method in production systems, in which a problem-solving activity is conducted by applying production rules within a data-base in a predetermined strategic fashion (progressive deepening of search). The whole process is constrained by certain short-term memory restrictions. This level addresses the dynamics of change. In the connectionist approach to modelling cognition one can study the dynamical processes cast in terms of dynamics system theories, or the changes in the connection weights and network structure (Elman et al. 1996; Schultz et al. 1995; Plunkett and Sinha 1992). Finally, at the implementational level, one can attack the problem of the neural mechanisms that subserve change.

The review of the various perspectives through which one can examine conceptual change allowed us to view some of the theories of change that were proposed relatively recently. Though these accounts have shed light on the types of change at the cognitive and the representational level, they are constrained by certain shortcomings, such as: (a) disregarding certain forms of change; (b) studying the structure but not the dynamics of change; (c) focusing on the dynamics but having very little to say about changes in information-processing content; (d) following Marr in accepting the autonomy of levels of explanation and discussing change exclusively at the cognitive level, thereby ignoring representational issues; and (e) discussing change at the representational level ignoring the way the processes at the representational level give rise to complex representations and 'generate behaviour and patterns that take on functionality within itself, without reference to an *a posteriori* analysis by an external observer'(Crutchfield 1998, 635).

In this chapter, we will discuss a theory of types of cognitive change that purports to take up the different levels at which change can be addressed, while avoiding the aforementioned shortcomings. Our aim is to show how certain classes of neural networks could implement the types of change that have been proposed elsewhere by Demetriou and Raftopoulos (1999). In the first part we sketch the general theory within the context of which we try to model change. In the second part of the chapter, we will summarize the types of change, as they are presented in Demetriou and Raftopoulos (1999a), we will critically assess them and stipulate additional types. In the third part of the chapter, we will deal with the dynamics of change, relying on the dynamical interpretation of connectionist networks to explore possible means of modelling the stipulated types. Finally, in the last part we discuss the kinds of mechanisms, which, within the context of dynamical connectionism, could (a) produce the types of change stipulated in the preceding parts, and (b) account for the transformations in the neural networks that could model these types of change.

To that end, we (a) employ actual neural networks whose behaviour as they learn can be viewed as falling under the heading of one or the other of our kinds of change; and (b) describe the behaviour at the dynamical level that neural networks should exhibit if they are to implement some of the most complex kinds of change. If successful, we will have shown that neural networks can implement our types, and we will have put forth the sketch of an account that takes up both structural and dynamical elements of change. It should be stressed at this juncture that we do not intend the implementations with neural networks to provide any kind of support for a specific theory of change. Neither do we intend the neural network implementations to show that the Demetriou and Raftopoulos theory is more adequate than other theories. By considering the dynamics of change under the perspective of neural modelling we hope to amend some of the lacunas of previous theories of change. In fact, our chapter may be viewed as an exercise in the direction of developing this field so that future work can be more fruitful, concentrated and of course, robust.

Theoretical background

Demetriou and Raftopoulos (1999) argue for a theory of conceptual change that addresses the issue of how a learning system makes the transition from one state to another. The basic assumption underlying this theory is the claim that any adequate theory of cognitive change needs to satisfy the following four requirements.

First, it requires a theory about cognitive architecture. In other words, to be able to account for change, a theory must first be able to specify what is changing. Second, it requires a theory of developmental sequences and functions. That is, it should specify (a) the successive developmental forms of the units of interest (e.g. concepts or relations) from a less to a more mature or complete state and (b) the relationship of the sequence of interest with age. This latter part is the descriptive aspect of a general theory of change, which illustrates what is generated by the change. Third, it requires a theory about the types of change at all levels of description, and a theory of the mechanisms, that is, the processes at each level, that bring changes about. It needs to specify how change occurs. In other words, it needs to specify how new forms come out of the old ones and what types of operations facilitate the transition. Finally, it requires a theory of developmental causes; it should aim to specify what makes progression along the sequences mentioned above possible. In other words, it needs to specify why change occurs.

The theory tries to meet some of these requirements and needs to be extended to take up some others. On the positive side, it has, first, a detailed model of the cognitive architecture which specifies what systems are involved in the mind and how these systems are organized (Demetriou, Efklides, and Platsidou 1993; Demetriou this volume). It suffices to note here that the theory assumes that the mind is organized in three main levels. The first includes environment-oriented domain-specific systems that specialize in the representation of and interaction with particular types of relations in the environment. The specific systems are succinctly described by Demetriou in this volume.

The second level includes self-oriented monitoring and representation processes that build maps of the environment-oriented systems. These maps are used to guide problem solving and decision making during off-line problem solving (Demetriou and Kazi 2001).

These two knowing levels of the mind (the cognitive and the hypercognitive levels) operate and interact with each other under the constraints of the processing potentials available at a given age. Speed of processing, control of processing and working memory are the functions that define these potentials. These constraints may be taken as a third level in the organization of the mind.

Second, the theory of conceptual change offers a detailed map of the development of each of the systems involved in each of the levels of mind specified above (Demetriou 1998; Demetriou et al. 1993; Demetriou and Valanides 1998).

Third, the theory provides a detailed analysis of the types of change that are observed both in cognitive development and during learning and attempts to explain how change occurs within and across systems and levels (Demetriou and Raftopoulos 1999).

The theory also offers a model of developmental causes, by attempting to specify why change occurs. Thus, the theory specifies the factors that may activate the types of change. In addition, pertaining to the mechanisms of change, our theory has to offer at the cognitive level (a) the standard Piagetian mechanisms of assimilation, accommodation and equilibration, and (b) a sketch of two hypercognitive mechanisms that complement the standard Piagetian mechanisms. Thus, it needs to be expanded to account for the mechanisms that implement the types of change described here, at the representational level. This will be attempted in the last part of the chapter.

The theory posits that, to develop, a system (a) must regularly come under conditions which cause inefficient or erroneous operation vis-à-vis its current goals; (b) needs sources furnishing examples of the 'currently best' representations of the situation and the most efficient course of action; (c) needs a right-or-wrong marking device which can capture the deviations between the alternatives and direct the selection of the currently best solution.

Revisions and extensions to the theory

Since the theory has been published, several lines of criticism have been formulated. The original version of the theory did not usefully account for several types of change, in that it did not offer an adequate account of the dynamics of change. In the next section of this chapter, we will examine the different lines of criticism, we will restate some aspects of the theory and we will make some revisions that will formulate a better model of the types of cognitive change. Thus, we will briefly present the types of change as they appear in Demetriou and Raftopoulos (1999), assess, and revise them. Our aim is to show that the new types can account for some of the kinds of conceptual change in child development, and that, being at a more general level, can unify existing theories of conceptual change. This section focuses on the structural aspect of change, that is, on the content of the structures that are being changed and of the new structures. Then, in another section we will address the dynamical aspects of change at the representational level and attempt to analyse strong and weak change.

A cognitive account of the mechanisms of change

Five types of conceptual change were previously identified at the cognitive level (Demetriou and Raftopoulos 1999): 'bridging', 'interweaving', 'fusion', 'differentiation', and 'refinement'.

Bridging was conceived as a type of cognitive change that characterizes the construction of a new mental structure by means of a combination of existing structures that belong to different environment-oriented systems (EOS). It was assumed that the component structures used in the construction are retained unmodified and could be independently evoked under the appropriate environmental stimuli. An example of bridging would be the use of graphical representations, developed in the spatial domain, to express categorical or covariation relations, belonging to the qualitative or the quantitative domain, respectively. This new capability broadens the scope of the problems that the organism can represent and process. We think now that the condition that the two bridged structures should belong to different EOS is unnecessarily restrictive, because there are many cases in which structures from the same domain are combined to produce a new structure. As an example, think of the formation of the concept 'striped apple' from bridging the concepts 'apple' and 'stripedness'.

An example of this type of change comes from neural network simulations of learning how to read (Plaut and Shallice 1993; Plaut et al. 1996; Plaut 1999). These simulations show that the network learns to pronounce non-words by combining its knowledge regarding the pronunciation of words it has learned during its training. It learns to pronounce the non-word 'dy', for example, by combining its knowledge of the pronunciation of 'd' and 'y', in words such as 'do' and 'by'. The combination leaves unaffected the pronunciations of 'd' and 'y', which can obviously be used separately in different circumstances. Thus, we extend 'bridging' to include cases like these.

A different kind of bridging occurs when the structures 'social' and 'lie' are bridged (Lakoff 1987) to form the structure 'social lie'. In the bridged structure 'social lie' the former structure cancels one of the background conditions of the latter. A prototypical lie presupposes that the person who intends to deceive does that if and only if she does not intend to be helpful. But when one utters a social lie trying to be polite, one does not intend not to help. In this case, the content of the resulting structure is not merely the sum of the contents of the constituents.

Consider now the emergence of the metaphor 'more is up'. Recurrent co-occurrence of patterns in experience in which an increase in quantity is accompanied by an increase in height lead to the conflation of the quantitative concept 'more' and of the spatial concept 'up'. In this case recurrent experiential correlations across domains reinforce the neural connections among the relevant neural structures. The bearing of the spatial concept of 'up', and perhaps of other spatial-relational concepts, upon the quantitative domain structures the latter. Once this 'conflation' has been established, 'more' usually activates 'up'. This 'conceptual blending' goes further than mere addition of content. The target domain acquires new structure and inherits new inferential schemes.

The case of the mapping from the domain of wave mechanics upon the domain of the phenomena of light and the resulting formation of the structure 'light wave' offers an additional example. 'Wave' and 'light' existed before, as independent well-formed structures, and the mapping blends them. But after the formation of the construct 'light wave' the constituent structure 'light'

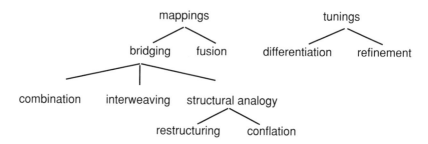

cognitive mechanisms of change

Figure 2.1. The taxonomy of the mechanisms of change.

undergoes a profound restructuring, and when used again is not the same structure as before (Wosilait et al. 1999).

Following Johnson (1981), we will coin the type of cognitive change implemented by simple association that is strengthened through recurrent concurrence 'conflation'. The type of conceptual change exemplified in the construction of the 'light wave' will be called 'restructuring'. In the case of the conflation of the spatial with the quantitative domain, learning by simple association explains the phenomenon, since the surface structure of the two domains suffices to establish the relation. The mapping from wave mechanics to the domain of light phenomena requires a more complicated learning mechanism; the restructuring of one domain on the basis of transfer from another presupposes the discovery of more abstract structure that applies to both domains, despite their surface differences. Thus, the cognizer has to undertake a more active role, and construct knowledge rather than simply relying on experiential connections to establish this knowledge.

In view of the above, we propose the following reorganization of the scheme of cognitive types of change (Figure 2.1). There are two categories of types of change. *Mappings*, in which structures are mapped, and *Tunings*, which include ways of modifying a structure. *Mappings* contain *Bridging* and *Fusion*. *Tunings* contain *Differentiation* and *Refinement*.

The condition of the original theory that the bridged structures remain unaltered after bridging is relaxed, so that modifications in these structures even when used separately are allowed. Thus, *Bridging* becomes a class of three types of change, namely, *Combination*, *Interweaving* and *Structural Analogy*. Bridging becomes somewhat equivalent to Fauconnier's (1997) 'conceptual blending'. The unifying feature of this class is that (a) two or more existing structures are brought together to bear on each other and form a more complex structure, and (b) after bridging the constituent structures retain their functional autonomy, even though they may have been modified.

The blended structures in *Bridging* may remain unaltered and the resulting structure(s) may either retain the characteristics of the constituent structures (striped apple), or some of the characteristics of one component may be overridden by the other (social lie). In this case, the type of change is *Combination*. Alternatively, the blended structures may undergo modification, as happens in *Interweaving* and *Structural Analogy*.

The integration of previously unrelated mental units for the sake of the construction of a new mental unit may engender a preference for the use of the new unit and an ensuing reduction in the isolated use of the units involved in the integration, although these units may still be available to the thinker. We propose the term *Interweaving* to denote the type of change, which is characterized by the blending of units involved and the modification of their probability of use in favour of the new unit. For example, the interweaving of hypothesis formation with the isolation-of-variables ability within the causal-experimental EOS will result in the model construction ability. Although each of the two specialized integral abilities may be present in itself, the model construction ability will dominate the other abilities.

Finally, the last type of change in the class of *Bridging* is *Structural Analogy*, which itself contains two types of change, namely, *Restructuring* and *Conflation*, that we defined above.

The next type of change in the class of mappings is *Fusion*. This is differentiated from bridging in that the mapped structures do not retain their relative autonomy after the mapping; instead, they fuse to one of the existing structures, or form a new structure. The construction of new mental structures within the same domain frequently results in the disappearance of the structures involved in the construction from the cognitive repertory. An example would be the integration of the concept of number succession with verbal counting. Once this construction is established, it is improbable that thoughts about number succession can be effected without activation of the number name sequence or that this sequence can be free from a representation of the succession of numbers. Another example would be the fusion of retrieval and counting strategies, which are involved in simple operations of addition and subtraction performed by children aged four to six. After fusion, around the ages of six to seven, the predominant strategy is retrieval by rote memory (Siegler 1986). This type also accounts for the kind of change exemplified in the concept of motion. Aristotle's distinction between violent and natural motions collapses, generating a single concept, Galileo's concept of motion (this is Carey's 1985 'coalescence').

The other main category of changes do not rely on any mappings but, instead, on the modification of a structure. In this class, which we call *Tuning*, one encounters two types, *Differentiation* and *Refinement*. Development frequently derives from an improvement in the accuracy of the functioning of an available mental structure, which usually implies either a better focusing of the structure on the target elements or a better mapping of the possible variations of the structure onto the relevant target elements. This type of change is called *Differentiation*. Consider the concept of 'degree of heaviness'. Research (Smith et al. 1985) shows that children construct and retain until at least their twelfth year a notion of heaviness that incorporates the adult's notions of 'weight' and 'density' in a unified whole. They account for all relevant phenomena by activating this undifferentiated compound concept of weight/density, which children use as a 'degree of heaviness'. As a result, children show intrusion of the adult concept of weight on judgements that adults would base on density. The concept of degree of heaviness eventually elicits contradictions (such as in the case of sinking and floating) and the resulting cognitive conflicts lead to the differentiation of this concept into the concepts of 'weight' and 'density'.

Another example of differentiation is the formation of the grammatical structures in language acquisition. The young child has initially no knowledge of grammatical structure and is producing sentences by rote memorization with no special roles assigned to the constituent parts. During the acquisition of syntax her mental space devoted to language becomes increasingly differentiated, as the child learns structures, such as 'verb', 'subject', 'object', that play different roles in language.

Refinement's function is the rejection of elements of a mental structure that are found irrelevant or redundant (elimination). An example of elimination is the rejection of quantity judgments on the basis of spatial criteria once the quantity-relevant structure is established. The increasing schematization of operations in all mental organizations, which is a basic characteristic of both grand scale cognitive development and the acquisition of expertise (Chi, Glaser, and Rees 1982), may largely be ascribed to refinement. Refinement is involved when a newly constructed structure gets elaborated, as it is being applied to its salient domain. This process leads to the abandonment of redundant elements of the structure and the elimination of incoherent parts. The history of science is full of examples of this kind of elaboration and refinement. As such, refinement is usually a follow-up to the other types of change.

The postulated types of conceptual change bear on structures as wholes and not just on their contents. Thus, they transcend and subsume mere cognitive operations, such as addition. This opens the road to a theory of change that encompasses previous accounts, which were based either on information-processing content transformations or on the reorganizations of mental structures within conceptual systems. Thus, our theory encompasses Carey's types of cognitive change, to wit coalescence, differentiation, and concept reanalysis, and also takes up Thagard's (1992) and Chi's (1992) reorganizations of conceptual systems.[1]

The representational level: a dynamical account of conceptual change

We think that an adequate explanation of that behaviour must invoke a mixed-level explanation of behaviour at all three levels. Thus, a theory of change must be able to show how the cognitive structures involved at the cognitive level (that is, those entities that are the constituent elements of the system's computations) are instantiated as properties of dynamical systems. It must also provide an account of how the system's computations occur.

The reason is that different systems can perform the same computations in different ways. An analysis restricted to the cognitive level misses important differences between the information processing systems.[2] This is not to deny, of course, the significance of the cognitive account. First, without it, one would not know how to interpret the system's actions, since the representational account is restricted only to the formal properties of the representational vehicles that carry information. Second, the analysis at the representational level is usually guided, at least in top-down views of functional analysis, by the preceding analysis at the cognitive level. Thus, our account of the dynamics of change relies heavily upon the analysis of the types of change performed at the cognitive level.

Here, we discuss the way representations can be modelled as properties of cognitive systems. At this level one examines the mathematical/formal implementation of the cognitive level. We examine the way cognitive states are represented and how they are transformed and processed by means of operations performed on data structures purely on the basis of either formal properties (for algorithmic models of cognition) or geometrical properties (for dynamical models).

---

[1] Thus, Thagard's *differentiation* (which is defined differently from our term) and *decomposition* fall within our *differentiation*, and his *coalescence* is our *fusion*. Branch jumping can result from *restructuring* (X-rays are reclassified as instances of light), from *fusion* (rest is deemed to be a kind of motion in Galileo's theory of motion) and so forth. This takes up Thagard's *reorganizations*. *Addition* and *deletion* can be the result of any of our mechanisms, as they affect the content of the structures involved in the change. Finally, *hierarchy redefinition* can be the result of a combination of, say, *restructuring* and *refinement*, the point being that these two mechanisms may engender a new theory redefining some theoretical terms.

[2] For a detailed discussion of the limitations of purely cognitive, as well as representational, accounts see Dawson 1998.

These transformations can be either algorithmic (determined by means of a set of rules that apply to discrete static symbols that are the representations of the system) or dynamical (determined by means of mathematical relations that apply to continuous variables and specify their interrelations and evolution in time). This is why we call these processes mathematical-state transitions; they describe the way the system moves between points in its state-space. We propose to address the issue of the mathematical implementation of change from the perspective of connectionist theory interpreted in a dynamical way. Thus, we are going to assume that a cognitive system is associated with a dynamical system physically realized by a neural network.

Neural networks as dynamical systems

Recent studies in the cognitive neurosciences show clearly that the physical brain is a complex system of interconnected neurones that interact by conducting electricity and releasing neurotransmitters. Research also shows those parts of neurones process signal in non-linear ways (Quartz and Sejnowski 1997). Neurones are organized in modules, large-scale units consisting of tens or hundreds of thousands of neurones. Neurones within modules may be connected through feedback loops. Modules also interact through feedback loops that allow signals to be transmitted among modules back and forth. These are the *re-entrant connections* among neurones in the brain.

The term is owed to Edelman and accounts for the interconnections between neurones. The function of re-entrant mappings is to carry out perceptual categorization dynamically by mapping the activities between two independent networks which 'must work simultaneously in response to a stimulus and then interact by reentry to provide some abstract higher-order linkage of their representation' (Edelman 1987, 61). These networks, construed as brain maps, are connected by massively parallel and reciprocal connections. The monkey's visual system, for instance, seems to consist of over thirty different maps that are linked to each other by reciprocal and parallel connections (Edelman 1992). The re-entry connections map the activity of any system onto the others and reciprocally, by allowing the transmission of information in all directions.

Feedback loops introduce iterative processes in the brain and they allow context and history to affect signal processing. This is so because the signal that reaches a neurone or a module is added to the signal that re-enters the neurone or the module through the re-entrant connections from other neurones or modules. Let us call these other neurones 'context neurones'. Context neurones or modules may process other aspects of the incoming signal and inform the neurone or module for the results of their processing, rendering thus the processing at that site sensitive to context. Alternatively, they may process part of the input signal that has first passed from our neurone or module (first pass). Thus, upon receiving the signal from the context neurones, the neurone or module processes the external input along with its own previous activation state, which may have eventually been modified by the processing in the context units themselves. Thus, the context in which the input occurs, as well as the history of the previous activations of the neurone or module that does the processing, affects each step in the processing.

Iteration, sensitivity to context and history, and interdependence of the components of a system are signs of complex dynamical systems. In such systems, the dynamics of a system can result in more expressively powerful structures by means of self-organization, and of the non-linear dynamic governing the activation functions of their processing units. Such transitions from a lower to a higher level of complexity abound in dynamical theories of cognitive and motor processes (Elman 1995; Kelso 1995; Kunnen and Bosma 2000).

In connectionism the re-entrant connections assume the form of 'context units', or clean-up units (Elman 1990), and they constitute the working memory of the system. They receive input from the hidden units of a network and output to these same hidden units. Their role is to feed back to the hidden units the results of the processing of the input to the system by the same hidden units. Consequently, the hidden units simultaneously receive and process the external input along with their own previous activation state. The input is presented sequentially part by part (word by word in the case of Elman's simulations) to the input units. When a part of the input has been fed to the network, the input units are activated and activate the hidden units. The activation of the hidden units is fed to the context units, which are activated in their turn. This activation is fed back to the hidden units, which in this way receive not only the activations coming from the input units that receive the next part of the input, but those of the context units as well. Thus, in each cycle, the hidden units are made aware, as it were, of their activations in the previous cycle.

Thus, the context units constitute the working memory of the network, in the sense that they, by receiving input from the hidden units, 'store' the results of each processing cycle. These results are 'retrieved' for reprocessing and interaction with other processing cycles, by means of the context units' output to the hidden units. This way each new word of the input sentence is processed in the context of all preceding words, a context that is provided by the 'context units'. Restricting initially the feedback from the context to the hidden units, and then gradually increasing it, models the increase in working memory.

The restriction of the feedback is effectuated after a number of words have been presented as input to the network. The training is partitioned into five phases in which the feedback is randomly eliminated after a specific number of words. In *phase 1* the feedback is eliminated after every third or fourth word. In each subsequent phase the number of the word after which the feedback is eliminated increases by one. Thus, in *phase 4* the feedback is eliminated after the sixth or seventh word. At the final phase, *phase 5*, full feedback is allowed. In each phase, the system can process only those sentences, or fragments of sentences, whose structure is visible in the word-number-window that is determined by the number of words after which the feedback is eliminated.

After a word has been fed to the network (cycle 1) the context units 'store' the activation values of the hidden units. When the next word (cycle 2) is presented the stored information is fed back to the hidden units, and the new activation values are again stored in the context unit. This process is repeated until the words in the sentence are exhausted. Now, if the word-number-window is narrow (let us say the number is three to four words), then the context units can store information to feed it back to the hidden units for only three or four cycles. In the fourth or fifth cycle the context units do not provide any further information to the hidden units (the feedback is eliminated). When the hidden units receive the input from the fourth or fifth word they do not 'recall' the results of their previous processing, since the context units do not feed them with their past activation values. As the word-window widens, the number of cycles in which the hidden units 'recall' their last activation increases. As the amount of feedback increases, therefore, the number of input–output cycles after which the content of the context units is still fed back to the hidden units increases, allowing the system to process more complex cases. This growth in the number of cycles has the same effects as the growth of the working memory span, and can be used to model the latter. This procedure results in a system, which starts with a limited memory, which is gradually growing.

Thus, it is reasonable to assume that the brain/mind plus environment system forms a complex dynamical whole structure, and that recurrent neural networks with non-linear activation functions of their units (the Sigmoid activation function, for instance) capture this dynamic non-linear character. Henceforth, as stated above, we are going to assume that a cognitive system is associated with a dynamical system physically realized by a neural network.

Recurrent neural networks (Elman 1990), cascade correlation networks (Shultz et al. 1995) and Hopfield nets, with distributed representations and continuous activation levels, can naturally be construed in a dynamical way. That is, they can be described by means of the evolution of the activation values of their units over time. In order to be able to model growth and avoid various problems plugging lifelong learning in neural networks (mainly catastrophic interference), one needs to consider a special class of networks, namely adaptive or generative networks. These networks can modify their structure during learning by adding or deleting nodes and can change their learning rates.

The number of units making up the network determines the number of dimensions of the state-space associated with the system. Their activation values constitute the actual position in the state-space of the system. Adding an axis with a quantity that is time-dependent, such as energy, yields the phase-space of the system. Both in state- and phase-space, one can represent all the possible states that a system can take in time. Hence, in the connectionist account, the states of a cognitive system are depicted by the sets of activation values of the units that distributively encode these states. The set of activation values is a vector whose tip defines a specific point in the state-space. Hence, a point in the state-space realizes a specific cognitive state of the system with a certain content, and thus this point is called a content-realizing point (Horgan and Tienson 1996).

These activation values are the variables of the dynamical system and their temporal variation constitutes the internal dynamics of the system, which defines the internal structure of the system. In addition to the state-space of a system, an external control space is also defined. This space constitutes the external structure of the system, and contains all those factors that affect or are affected by the components of the system, but are not themselves components of the system. The external space contains the real-value control parameters that control the behaviour of the system, i.e., the connection weights, biases, thresholds, learning regime and, in networks whose structural properties are implemented as real-value parameters (Raijmakers et al. 1996a), the structure of the system. The internal structure together with the external structure constitutes the total structure of the system.

In dynamical systems, the fast internal dynamics are often accompanied by slow external dynamics. The external dynamics consist of the temporal paths in the external control space. In our case, the external dynamics consist of the network's learning dynamics (the learning rule, such as back-propagation, Hebb's rule etc.) and the dynamics that determine structural changes as the system learns, such as the rules for inserting nodes in cascade correlation and growing radial basis function networks.

When the network receives input, activation spreads from the input units to the rest of the network. Each pattern of activation values defines a vector, or a point, within the activational space of the system whose coordinates are the activation values of the pattern. The activation rules determine the state transitions that specify the internal dynamics of the system. In other words, the functions that determine how the system evolves in time by specifying how the state of the system at time $t \pm dt$ is a function of the state of the system at time t. Thus, the behaviour of such a system is depicted as a trajectory between points in the activational state space.

The activation rules, the number of units, the pattern of their connectivity, and the learning rate(s) of the network determine the architecture of the system when it starts its interaction with the environment. The aforementioned factors of a system are determined by its long-term history of experiences, since the class of networks discussed here may modify either their patterns of connectivity, as they learn, by adding nodes, deleting nodes, and sharpening their connections, or their biases and learning rates. The activation vectors and, hence, the behaviour of the system evolve as a result of the synergies among the architecture of the network, the input it receives, and the previous activity of the network,[3] under the control of the external dynamics, that is, the learning dynamics and the dynamics governing structural changes.

The behaviour of the system, therefore, is a collective effect which assumes, simultaneously, the form of cooperation and competition (Kelso 1995). In the case of cognitive systems, the competition is due to the effort of the system to retain its current state in the face of incoming information. If this information cannot be assimilated by the system in its existing form (in neural networks this means that the system does not yield the correct output), then the weights of a network change and the network may alter its structure to accommodate the new input.

The activation states which a network may settle into after it is provided with an input signal, are the attractors of the system. These are the regions in state-space toward which the system evolves in time. The points in state-space from which the system evolves toward a certain attractor lie within the basin of attraction of this particular attractor. Thus, the inputs that land within the basin of attraction of an attractor will be transformed by the connectivity patterns of the network so that they end up at this attractor where the system will settle.

Networks in which the outputs change over time until the pattern of activation of the system settles into one of several states, depending upon the input, are called attractor networks. The sets of possible states into which the system can settle are the attractors. If the network is used to model cognitive behaviour, then the attractors can be construed as realizing cognitive (or mental) states to which the system moves from other cognitive states that lie within the attractor's basin of attraction. The idea that mental states could be modelled by attractors of neural systems that are viewed as dynamical systems was first introduced by Thom (1983) and Zeeman (1965).

The process by which the input patterns are transformed into attractor patterns is the following: a given input moves the system into an initial state realized by an initial point. This input feeds the system with an activation that spreads throughout the network causing the units of the system to change their states. The processing may take several steps, as the signal is recycled through the recurrent connections in the network. Since any pattern of activity of the

---

[3] The latter factor concerns the current history of the system and is reflected in the transient recent changes in connection weights and in the recent information that the system has received through its inputs, as this information is represented by the system through the processing of the input signal by the hidden units during the activation cycles before the system settles into equilibrium.

units corresponds to a point in activation space, these changes correspond to a movement of the initial point in this state space. When the network settles, this point arrives at the attractor that lies at the bottom of the basin in which the initial point had landed; the inputs fed into the system are the initial conditions of the dynamic system. As a dynamical system settles into a mode depending on its initial conditions, so the neural network settles into the attractor state in whose basin of attraction the input falls.

For instance, in a semantic network, meanings of words are represented as patterns of activity over a large number of semantic features. However, only some of the combinations of semantic features are features of objects. The patterns that correspond to these combinations are the attractors of the network, which are points (or sets of points) in the state space corresponding to the semantic features of the prototype of the object signified by the word. These attractors are the meanings of words.

The concepts 'attractor' and 'basin of attraction' suggest a way of simulating the classical notion of symbol. The attractor basins that emerge as the network interacts with specific inputs might be construed as having symbolic-like properties, in that inputs with small variations that fall within the same attractor basin are pulled toward the same attractor (or cognitive state) of the system. Thus, various inputs (tokens) give rise to the same stable point of attraction, the attractor (type), which in this sense offers a dynamical analogue of the classical symbol.

For example, in Elman's (1995) network, tokens of the same lexical item filling different roles are distinguished by virtue of producing small differences in the activational state space. The basins of attraction that embody 'Tom' and 'Titikos', that is, two different cats, or two appearances of 'Tom' in differing circumstances, are different. At the same time, these tokens are identified as tokens of the same type on account of the fact that they are all located in a region of the state space which constitutes the basin of attraction of the lexical item (type) and which contains no other vectors except the tokens of this specific type. The universal term 'cat' is represented only in the sense that all tokens of tokens of cats are represented in nearby locations in the system's activational state space. Similarly, in Sirois et al.'s (2000) simulations of artificial grammar learning by infants, the networks trained learn to extract the type (prototype) from a restricted set of training tokens and then can generalize their knowledge to novel tokens, by treating them as instances of the same type.

The dynamical 'symbols', unlike the symbols of classical cognitivism, are dynamic and fluid rather than static and context independent. The dynamic properties result from the dynamical nature of the activations of associative patterns of units. As the network learns and develops, the connection strengths continuously change. The same happens when new units emerge and old units 'die' and the system reconfigures to maintain its knowledge and skills. All these cause changes in the original pattern in which an attractor/symbol was created in the first place, and as a result, subsequent activations differ. The same effects are caused by the different contexts in which the 'symbol' may be activated. This happens because connections from the differing contextual features bias the activation of the units of the original pattern in different ways emphasizing some feature of the pattern or other. Thus, the attractor/symbol is almost never instantiated with the same activation values of the units that realize it. As the network changes, attractors change and their activations covary with the context.

There is a price to be paid, of course, for the advantages of the dynamical attractor/symbols. This is that attractors do not have all the properties of classical context independent symbols. For instance, as a result of the context dependency, they do not hold their variable bindings through a series of deductive inferences. Current research on this issue attempts to empower attractors with these desirable binding properties. A first attempt by Pollack (1990) and Smolensky (1990) resulted in networks that achieve conjunctive static bindings. Shastri and Ajjanagadde (1993) and Hummel and Holyoak (1997) suggest ways to implement dynamic bindings in neural networks, but much remains to be done in order for dynamic neural networks to simulate adequately the binding properties of classical symbols.

The activational state-space of a network is a high-dimensional mathematical entity, a landscape. The state transitions in such a system are trajectories from one point on the landscape to another. As mentioned earlier, attractors correspond to cognitive states and the activation pattern that realizes each state is a vector, or a point (the tip of the vector), within the multidimensional activational space of the system, its landscape. Thus, each cognitive state is realized by a point on this landscape. Since the distributed encoding of a cognitive state does not usually involve all units of the system, there will be points on the activational landscape that will realize more than one cognitive state. This is so because the set of coordinates of a point may satisfy the partial coordinates given by several activational vectors of subsets of the system's units.

To get a better understanding of this landscape and of its role, think of a recurrent network that is given a certain input and goes through various processing cycles before it settles down into a certain attractor state, i.e. before it stabilizes at a certain output. During the phase of activation changes the system passes through various outputs. All these outputs can be viewed as lying on an energy surface. When the system passes through a certain output-state whose energy is not lower than the energies of the neighbouring states, it goes through another phase of activation-value changes in order to reduce the energy of the output state. When it reaches a point at which all the neighbouring states have higher energies, it settles.

These states of minimum local energy are the attractors and can be construed as valley bottoms on energy surfaces. Thus, attractors should be distinguished from the networks' outputs in general. Not all outputs are settling points. Attractors form a subset of the set of outputs of a network, in that they are those outputs at which the system can settle. Attractors can be also formed on the activations of the hidden units of a recurrent network. When the input of the system is such that the activation state of the system lies within the walls of the valley, the system will settle at the attractor that corresponds to its bottom. Hence, the valley is the basin of attraction that leads to the specific attractor-state of minimum energy. Since the network has many attractors, and therefore basins of attraction, the relative positions of a valley with respect to others will shape the relief of the activational landscape of the system, which determines the possible trajectories in the state space. A landscape is a multidimensional space of overlapping attractors and basins of attraction, whose contours of the valleys, that is, the topological distribution of the systems' attractors and basins of attraction (which constitute the dynamics of the system), direct the trajectories of state changes within the system/environment whole structure. Thus, the dynamics of the system determine the possible trajectories in the state space.

Modelling the dynamics of cognitive change

In this framework, cognitive change results from the moulding of the activational landscape, as a result of changes in the weights and the architecture of the network, as the network attempts to accommodate new input signals. The moulding may result either in the emergence of new, and/or disappearance of old, attractors, or in the reshaping of the basins of attraction. This process corresponds to a trajectory on the activational landscape. The idea that change is to be modelled by means of transitions in the state space of a dynamic system is at the heart of dynamical theories of cognition. Transitions in the state space of a dynamic system substitute for the algorithmic syntactically governed transitions of cognitivism.

The relief of the landscape determines the trajectories that are allowed, and thereby the possible transformations among cognitive states. Cognitive change, thus, depends on the activational landscape of the system that learns. When information enters it, the system tends to assimilate it within the existing framework of knowledge, which, in neural networks, is determined by the connection weights and the architecture of the network, which, in their turn, distribute the points that realize cognitive states on the network's landscape.

At this juncture, it would be useful to address the issue of change in real time versus change in developmental time. The behaviour of such systems is seen as a trajectory through the state space over time. This trajectory may be a movement from an existing attractor state to another existing attractor state, as when the initial conditions change in real time (that is, when different inputs are fed into the system) and these inputs fall within different basins of attraction leading, thus, the network to settle into different attractors. Thus, the system produces different activations of its output units due exclusively to the differences in the initial conditions, without any changes in its connection weights. This means that the system changes its behaviour in real time due to different initial conditions. This change, however, is not deemed to be a cognitive change. Cognitive change, as we have seen, presupposes the moulding of the activational landscape, and this can be the result of changes (either quantitative or qualitative) in the weight space of the system. When weights change, then the same input fed into the system leads to different attractor states.

Up to this point, it seems that the distinction between real-time change, or behaviour over time, of the system and conceptual change over time stands firm. But if we look more carefully at the dynamics of the system, a different picture emerges. Changes in the weight space result as the system attempts in real time to learn some task. More specifically, as the system is trained in the task, it reorganizes its weight space trying to acquire the desired output activations (in networks with a fixed structure). It is the differences between actual outputs and desired outputs that guide the changes in the weight space. Thus, since the production of outputs is the activity of the system in real time, the cause of conceptual change is the activity of the system in real time. In this sense, as Thelen and Smith (1994) also claim, real time and developmental time are unified. They become continuous in that the factors that cause behaviour in real time tasks are the same factors that cause developmental change.

We have posited certain types of cognitive change. How are these types realized at the middle level of mathematical formal description? Which factors are responsible for the types' differences in their cognitive functions? If change involves, for instance, repositioning of old content-realizing points on the system's landscape (that eventually result in changes in the bases of attraction of existing attractors), and/or appearance of new such points (appearance of new attractors and a moulding of the relief of the landscape due to the formation of new basins of attraction), then the aforementioned types must be realized by different ways of positioning content-realizing points and of transforming the landscape's relief. In what follows we will sketch the dynamic realization of our types of change.

Mappings
Bridging combination   This type of change involves the combination of structures in such a way that the existing content realizing points (including attractors) and the landscape's relief (their basins of attraction) of the system are not affected. The new structure is superimposed on the constituent structures.

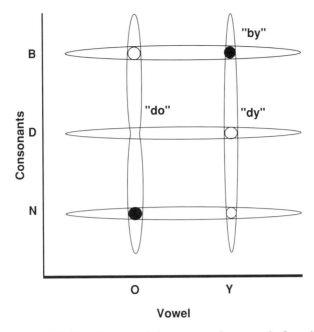

Figure 2.2. How the network learns to read non-words. Learning the pronunciation of words gives rise to the emergence of componential attractors, whose combination provides the pronunciation of the non-words. Only two componential attractors are depicted here. The basins of attraction for the word 'by' and the non-word 'dy' are the intersections of the sub-basins for pronunciation of 'b', 'd', and 'y', that is, the regions in the state space in which these sub-basins overlap. The solid circle is the attractor for the word 'by', and the open circle is the attractor for the non-word 'dy'. The reduced componentiality of the exception words is depicted as a deformation of the intersection of the salient attractors for the onset 'd' and the vowel 'o'. (Based on Plaut et al. 1996)

For example, let us consider the networks that simulate learning to pronounce words and non-words (Plaut and Shallice 1993; Plaut et al. 1996; Plaut 1999). These networks learn the pronunciation of both regular and irregular words, by building the appropriate attractors. The attractors of regular words consist of componential attractors, in which case the basin of attraction is the intersection of the sub-basins of attraction of the componential attractors. The exception words have their own attractors with a lesser degree of componentiality. In this case, combination explains the ability of the network to learn the pronunciation of both words and non-words, in that this knowledge is the result of the combination of the sub-knowledge encoded by the componential attractors, as is shown in Figure 2.2.

In this figure only two componential attractors are depicted, for onset and the vowel in the reduced two-dimensional state space (the activation space of the phonemic units of the network). The basins of attraction for the word 'by' and the non-word 'dy' are the intersections of the sub-basins for pronunciation of 'b', 'd', and 'y', that is, the regions in the state space in which these sub-basins overlap. The black circle is the attractor for the word 'by', and the striped circle is the attractor for the non-word 'dy'. The trained network learns to pronounce words by applying its knowledge regarding the pronunciation of the parts of the words (and of the role of context in pronunciation when it comes to exception words). The reduced componentiality of the exception words is depicted by means of a deformation of the intersection of the salient attractors for the onset 'd' and the vowel 'o'. The componential attractors and their basins of attraction remain unaltered, which means that the combined structures do not change.

Consider, further, the acquisition of the notion 'striped apple'. Suppose that a net has learned the concepts 'apple' and 'stripedness'. As a result of learning, the activation space of the hidden units consists of two basins of attraction with the corresponding attractors that stand for the prototypical 'apple' and 'striped-ness'. Suppose further that the net has never encountered a striped apple, it is fed that information and it has the capability to learn the concept 'striped apple'. The features that characterize any concept are encoded distributively as patterns of activity over a subset of the network's units. The features that character-ize apples and the features that characterize stripedness are non-overlapping, which means that the corresponding attractor basins are orthogonal to each other. This is depicted in Figure 2.3, in which the two basins of attraction are shown in the reduced two-dimensional activation space of the system's hidden units.

After the new concept is learned, the two basins change their relative posi-tions in the state so that they intersect. Their intersection (i.e. the pattern cor-responding to both sets of features) forms a new basin, which is the area in which the two basins overlap (Figure 2.4). The appearance of a new basin of attraction represents the learning of a new concept (Thelen and Smith 1994). The new basin of attraction is superimposed onto the two intersecting basins of attraction.

The basins of attraction (sub-basins) and the attractors of the concepts 'apple' and 'stripedness' do not change. Whatever input was falling within one of the two basins before learning still does so after the network has learned the new concept. What was categorized as an apple, before, is still categorized as such. The only change after learning is that some inputs fall within the new basin of attraction and are categorized as 'striped apples', while being at the same time both 'apples' and 'striped'; this is a result of the superimposition of the new basin of attraction onto the two sub-basins.

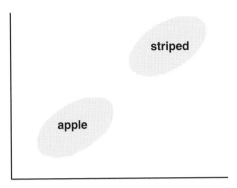

hidden unit 1

Figure 2.3. The two-dimensional depiction of the hidden unit's activation space of a network that has learned the concepts 'apple' and 'stripedness' and has never encountered a striped apple. The two attractor basins are orthogonal to each other, since the features that characterize apples and the features that characterize stripedness are non-overlapping.

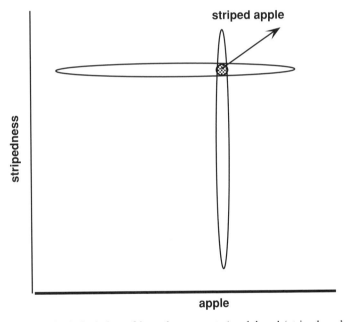

Figure 2.4. A depiction of how the concepts 'apple' and 'stripedness' are combined to produce the concept 'striped apple'. The two basins of attraction intersect, and as a result the new concept has all the characteristics of the two constituent concepts. The full circle represents the attractor for the concept striped apple.

We specified previously that any point on the activational landscape is the tip of the vector that has as dimensions the activation values of the units of the system that are activated when the system entertains the cognitive content that the point realizes. Hence, the new structure (striped apple) corresponds to the vector consisting of the activation of all units that distributively encode the new structure. Thus, the emerging structure has $n + m$ dimensions, where n and m are the numbers of units encoding the two constituent structures.

It may be, however, that when the sets of units that encode the combined structures are activated and give rise to the compound structure, some of the activation values of the units that distributively encode one of the structures are not the same as when the structure is activated alone. Since content is realized by the activation values of the units that encode the structure, when the activation values change the content of the emerging structure is, strictly speaking, different in some respect from the content of the structure when activated in other contexts. For instance, in the context of 'social lie', a lie ceases to express the liar's intention to harm the recipient in some way.

Interweaving   In interweaving the new structure establishes an attractor basin that affects the attractor basins of the constituent states in such a way that the latter are reduced, whereas the basin of attraction of the new structure is considerably wider than theirs. These events diminish the probability that activation patterns will fall within the basins of attraction of the constituent structures. At the same time the wider basin of attraction of the new structures has an increased probability to attract activation patterns within it.

Conflation   In conflation a persistent concurrence in experience leads to the formation of the belief that, for instance, more is up. Units that represent quantity get connected, or the pre-existing connections are strengthened, with units representing spatial information, in such a way that when an increase in quantity is encountered this is accompanied by the activation of the spatial concept 'up'. Although it is not clear whether the quantitative domain is shaped separately and subsequently gets connected with the spatial domain, or whether the quantitative domain is formed and structured by means of such connections with experiential domains, such as the spatial, one may argue with some plausibility that the content-realizing point corresponding to 'more' on the system's landscape is repositioned as a result of its connection with 'up'. This change in location on the landscape means that the activational pattern of 'more' is changed; thus, the concept acquires new content.

Restructuring   In *combination* the two structures that are combined are retained as they were before the combination, or undergo a minimal change in their conditions. When one of the existing structures is not compatible with the new structure ('light' in its Newtonian sense is not compatible with 'light wave'), then it has to be restructured for compatibility to be restored.

Restructuring, in its turn, is an instance of structure mapping, and it may involve quantitative and qualitative changes in the network, that is, the synaptic weights and the underlying structure, respectively, may change. The attractors and their basins change so that they may attract different patterns, since some activational patterns that were falling within the basin of attraction of the attractor may cease to do so and new patterns may now fall within the basin of attraction. For instance, what is categorized as light after the formation of the structure 'light wave' may be different from before, since other forms of radiation fall within the category of light.

In Figure 2.5 the restructuring of the concept 'light' and its transformation to 'light wave' is depicted. The old attractor for 'light' disappears, since the semantic features of light have changed, and a new attractor emerges as the system redeploys conceptual resources from the domain of wave mechanics (the source analogue) to the domain of the phenomena of light (the target analogue). The new attractor incorporates features from both the older attractors, since the new concept includes features of both.

Before the conceptual change took place (5a), the basins of attraction of 'light' and 'wave' were orthogonal (no overlapping of features). After the change has taken place (5b), the basin of attraction of light is reshaped and the new attractor basin intersects with the basin of attraction of 'wave', in so far as the two concepts share some features (recall that the dual nature of light as both a corpuscular and a wave entity precludes the inclusion of the basin of 'light' within the basin of 'wave'). Thus, a new basin of attraction is formed in the activational landscape. The overlap of basins is really a convergence zone that leads to the newly emerged superordinate attractor, which contains both component attractors within it.[4] Notice that this change is a strong one, in that it enhances the expressive capabilities of the system. The new content that emerges is not the sum of the constituent contents, as was the case in combination. Notice also that inputs that were classified as 'waves' will be reclassified after the change as instances of 'light' (X-rays that after the change are deemed to be different kinds of light) (5a, c).

The above picture depicts the moulding of the landscape when restructuring occurs. We do not claim of course that there are any neural models that could simulate restructuring in situations as complex as our example. This example is a clear case of conceptual redeployment from the domain of wave mechanics

---

[4] We wish to thank R. Lewis for this remark.

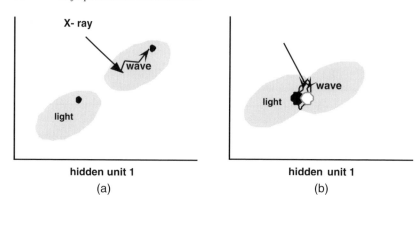

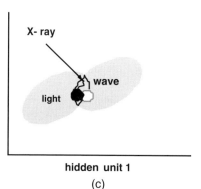

Figure 2.5. The restructuring of the concept 'light' and its transformation to 'light wave'. Before restructuring (a) the basins of attraction of 'light' and 'wave' were orthogonal (no overlapping of features). If an entity such as X-ray was deemed to be a wave, it could not be an instance of light. Hence, the corresponding input to the network would be attracted toward the attractor 'wave'. In the figure the input (X-ray) is represented by a straight arrow and the trajectory in phase space that corresponds to the gradual transformation of the input vector is represented by the curve. After restructuring (b) the new basin of attraction intersects with that of 'wave'. Thus, certain inputs fall within both basins and can be attracted toward both attractors, that is, they can be classified either as instances of light or of waves. Furthermore in (c), inputs (such as X-rays) that were classified as 'waves' will be reclassified after the change as instances of 'light'.

to the domain of light, or in other words, an example of the usage of analogical thought. To say that networks redeploy conceptual resources to a new domain is to say that the network can apply or transfer knowledge that it has acquired in one domain, that is, 'knowledge embedded in a connectionist model trained in one domain' (Dienes et al. 1999, 78) to quite a different domain.[5] Since the kinds of mappings discussed in this part are clear cut cases of analogical mappings, we will say now a few things about connectionist simulations of analogical thought.

Fusion   As mentioned above, structures within the neural net can be thought of as attractor states. Thus, the activation pattern of the structure attracts all other activation patterns that are similar enough to it (that is, all activation patterns that fall within the basin of attraction of the attractor). As a network learns, a new attractor state may emerge, which swallows the attractors that existed before. This is what happens in fusion. The two initial basins of attraction are also swallowed by the new one, so that all patterns that were falling within the one or the other now fall within the new basin of attraction. The system undergoes a phase transition that can be described as a reverse Hopf bifurcation (Figure 2.6), in which two stable states (bistability) are fused and disappear and a unique stable state emerges (unistability).

In Figure 2.7 one can see what happens when Galileo's notion of motion fused with the Aristotelian concepts of violent and natural motion. The basins of attraction of the initial concepts are fused into one, in such a way that the patterns previously captured by each of the initial attractor basins are now captured by the new basin. In other words, what was categorized as a natural or a violent motion before is categorized, after Galileo, as motion simpliciter. The new attractor abstracts some of the features of the previous attractors (such as the motion toward or away from the earth.

Figure 2.8 displays the phase transitions associated with the fusion of 'counting from one' and 'memory retrieval' strategies (used by four- to six-year-old

---

[5] 'Quite a different domain' means a domain with arbitrary different content, provided of course that there are the appropriate perceptual, as it were, mappings between the two domains that will guide the redeployment of knowledge by enabling the identification of the appropriate source domain for a given target (similarities in certain respects between the behaviour of sound and of light, for instance). In the case of Dienes et al. model, which learns the implicit artificial grammar in one perceptual domain (sequences of tones differing in pitch) and transfers the acquired knowledge to a new perceptual domain (sequences of letters) so that it learns the new domain's implicit grammar, there must exist a linear mapping between the front-end contents of the two domains for the transfer to be successful. The network of course does not have any kind of access to the 'common structure' that it transfers from one domain to the other, and it cannot report it; it simply does so. This means that in order for the mapping to be stored explicitly a second system that reads off the first is needed. This is of course the more general problem regarding the access of neural networks to their own contents.

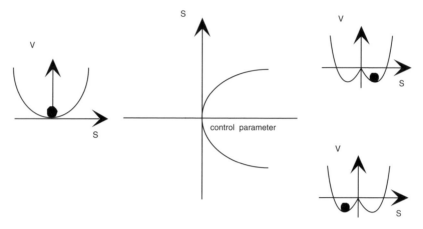

Figure 2.6. The inverted Hopf bifurcation where two stable states become unstable and one stable state emerges. Fusion can be seen as such a phase transition from bistability to unistability. The diagram is a plot of the time evolution of the landscape in state space. Attractors are represented as local energy minima.

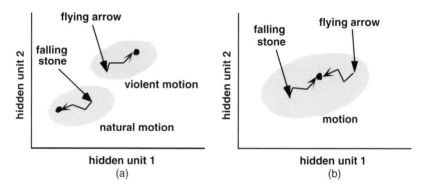

Figure 2.7. Fusion: the two distinct basins of attraction corresponding to the phenomena of violent and natural motion are fused and a single basin emerges that unifies all instances of motion.

children in simple arithmetic tasks) to the 'memory retrieval' strategy that becomes predominant between six and seven years of age.

The generative networks designed by Shultz et al. (1995) to model a series of cognitive tasks (balance scale, seriation, potency and resistance, distance, time and velocity concepts, and acquisition of pronouns) simulate the variability of the strategies available to children with respect to these tasks. Thus, they

counting   retrieval

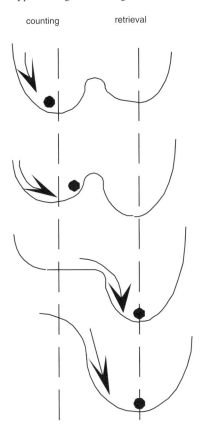

collective variable (age)

Figure 2.8. The phase transition in the fusion of counting and retrieval strategies. Originally both strategies are within the cognitive repertoire, as is shown
by the existence of two stable attractors. However, as age increases, the counting strategy becomes unstable, its basin of attraction becomes more shallow
and less curved and finally that attractor disappears and leaves the other attractor (the retrieval strategy) as the only available strategy.

report networks that at some stage of their training to learn to solve the balance-
beam tasks may 'employ' two different strategies to solve the same problem
and which, as training continues, progress to using reliably the more advanced
strategy. These networks may be said to implement 'fusion', by moving from
bistability to unistability.

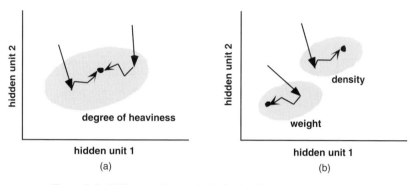

Figure 2.9. Differentiation: a single basin of attraction (a) is split into two new basins of attraction (b). As a result, some of the phenomena that children thought of as manifestations of the undifferentiated concept 'degree of heaviness' are now thought of as manifestations of 'density' and others are thought of as manifestations of 'weight'.

Tuning

Differentiation   In differentiation, the opposite phenomenon occurs. An existing attractor disappears and new attractors appear in its place (as in the differentiation of the concept 'degree of heaviness'). The initial basin of attraction is split, as it were, into two basins of attraction, so that the activational patterns that were falling within the original basin now fall within either one of the two. This is depicted in Figure 2.9, which shows the basins of attraction of the hidden units' activation space. Furthermore, it is possible that new patterns may fall within one of the two. Thus, some of the phenomena that children used to think of as manifestations of the undifferentiated concept 'degree of heaviness', after 'differentiation' occurs, are thought of as manifestations of 'density', and others are thought of as manifestations of 'weight'.

The networks that learn the grammar of a language differentiate a previously undifferentiated domain, by forming a new landscape. Words acquire grammatical roles, the language is structured, and rote memorization of sentences cedes its place to systematic construction of sentences. In Figure 2.10, one can see the result of a Principal Component Analysis (*PCA*) on the set of hidden units in the Visitation Set Gravitation (*VSG*) network of syntactic processing of Tabor and Tanenhaus (1999), which learns the syntactic structure of an artificial language. This network consists of two components, a simple recurrent network (Elman 1990) and a dynamical gravitation module that operates on the set of states of the hidden units visited by the recurrent network, as the signal cycles through it, and uses a gravitational mechanism to group these

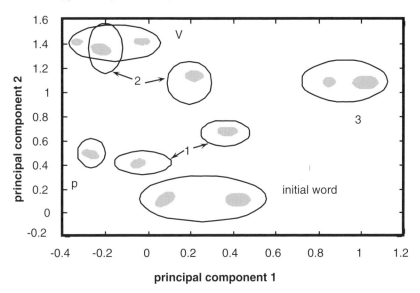

Figure 2.10. The result of a Principal Component Analysis (PCA) on the set of hidden units in the Visitation Set Gravitation (VSG) network of syntactic processing of Tabor and Tanenhaus (1999), which learns the syntactic structure of an artificial language. Six basins of attraction are formed, whereas previously the space was unstructured. Each basin corresponds to the major categories of the grammar, namely, initial word, verb word, word 1, word 2, word 3, and final word. The two attractors within each basin correspond to the two parse hypotheses. (Based on Tabor and Tanenhaus 1999)

states into distinct classes. After training, *PCA* yields the diagram shown in Figure 2.10. The state space has ten degrees of freedom but the figure depicts only a two-dimensional projection of the landscape.

As one can see, the landscape consists of six basins of attraction, each with two distinct attractors. Each basin corresponds to the major categories of the grammar, namely, initial word, verb word, word 1, word 2, word 3, and final word. The two attractors within each of five basins correspond to the two parse hypotheses, that is, that the verb is the main verb of the sentence, or, alternatively, that the verb is in a relative clause (McRae et al. 1998).

Refinement   The dynamical characterization of this type remains unrealized by connectionist models. It is not clear to us, yet, how neural networks could model this type of change. In this sense, it is a problem to be addressed by future research in the field.

Strong and weak cognitive change

In dynamical connectionism, learning and cognitive change consist of changes in connection weights, the structure and the learning rates of the network. More specifically, in connectionist networks an individual's state of knowledge is determined by the weights of the hidden units of the system. Cognitive representational change is regarded as the individual's actual path through the space of possible synaptic configurations, that is, as the transformations of the weight vector in an n-dimensional weight space, where n is the number of the weights in the neural network.

The appearance of novel cognitive states, and thus, the appearance of new attractors and the disappearance of old ones, implies a change of relief in the network's landscape (moulding). Since the relief depends largely on the structure of the network, that is, the number of nodes, their connectivity and the activation functions, its moulding is the result of changes in the structure of the network. Networks evolve as a result of the system's effort to adapt to a new environment, so that it responds properly to new input patterns, by superimposing new representations on those already existing. Thus, the system modifies the 'knowing assumptions' that do not fit the new environment, as it learns its features.

Modelling weak and strong conceptual change

The account of cognitive change at the mathematical level allows us to recast the discussion regarding strong and weak representational change in terms of dynamic systems theory. Whether a cognitive change is deemed to be weak or strong depends on whether the new structure increases the expressive (representational) resources of the system. Since in distributed neural networks, representations are patterns of activities of the hidden units, that is points in the state space of the system, the expressive contents of the system correspond to such points.

If, on the one hand, the relief of the landscape is such that the system cannot settle at a content realizing point, that is, if this point is not a possible attractor state, then the content that is realized by this point is not within the expressive capabilities of the system. When changes in the relief render this point a possible attractor, then this change is a radical one, since it results in an increase in the representational capacity of the system. That is, the system can now represent something that was beyond its expressive potential beforehand.

But the mere appearance of an attractor does not necessarily imply that a radical change has taken place, or that this is a novel attractor state. This is so if the content realizing point that appears as a new attractor was in fact expressible within the system; that is, if the system could have settled at that point, even if it had not done so, up to that time. Consider the first encounter of the system with a red apple. This input causes some perturbations, which the system attempts to absorb or dissipate. The system eventually does that, since its resources allow the assimilation of this input within its existing framework. It just adds, as it were, information regarding 'red' and information regarding 'apple' and gets the concept 'red apple'. In dynamic terms, the two basins of attraction are superimposed and form a new superordinate attractor.

More specifically, when the structures 'striped' and 'apple' are combined an attractor state 'appears', in the sense that the system acquires, at the cognitive level, the new notion of 'striped apple'. This 'new' attractor is a region in the state space, which realizes the content 'striped apple' and is superimposed on the attractors of 'apple' and 'striped'. But this is not a novel attractor, because this content was already within the expressive power of the system, since the relief of the landscape was such that the system could have settled, if fed with the appropriate input at this point. In other words, the 'new' attractor was situated at a local energy minimum in which the system could have settled if it had been fed with the appropriate input. That is, if the system had the experience of a striped apple, a simple repositioning of its basins of attraction, so that they intersect, could handle the new information. The new attractor appears without the landscape being moulded and this attractor is just the sum of information expressed by the other attractors, which remain intact. In this case, the ensuing change is weak.

When the input is not as accommodating, however, then the perturbation cannot be handled locally and the system gets far away from equilibrium. The only means to dissipate the tension is to reorganize itself by reorganizing its landscape, that is, by moulding the topographical distribution of its attractors. This change is qualitative 'in so far as it consists in a transformation of the over-all dynamic organization, not merely a quantitative adjustment in the existing structure' (Juarrero 1999, 160). Such qualitative changes, in which as the system reorganizes itself novel attractors (that is, behaviours or cognitive states) appear and old ones may disappear, are called phase changes. Phase changes alter the dynamics of the system and that is why the steps in the self-organized processes are new. New modes of behaviour or representational states become available to the system, which thus increases its representational capacity.

Consider the case of the formation of the concept 'light wave'. No mere intersection of existing basins of attraction, or any simple repositioning, could accommodate this salient input. Instead, a reshaping of attractor basins is required, as well as the disappearance of an older attractor and the emergence of a new one. These changes mould the landscape and allow the appearance of new local energy minima. Thus, it is the combination of changes with respect to both attractors and the shapes of the basins of attraction that renders a strong change.

In contrast, weak change refers to changes in the semantic content of representations, which broaden the field of application of these representations but do not increase the expressive capabilities of the system. In these cases, attractors are merely repositioned in the landscape, which means that the activation patterns that define them do change, but no new attractors are added in the system. Hence, repositioning of an attractor state is a weak change (Horgan and Tienson 1996), in so far as it concerns the change of position of an existing attractor, and not the appearance of a novel one. Reposition of any content realizing point is accompanied by changes in the activation values that constitute the point's activation pattern, and changes in its spatial relations with other content realizing points. Since semantic information in dynamic systems is captured, as we have seen, by means of the relative positions of content realizing points on the landscape, repositioning is accompanied by semantic changes. Repositioning by itself, however, does not impose a change in the relief of the system, and thus the change is a weak one.

When new information is learned with minimum change in the distribution of attractors and basins of attraction, and attractors are preserved (though the slope of the basins may change, with some becoming steeper, and thus more attractive, and others becoming less steep), the resulting change is weak, that is, the content-expressive power of the system does not change. Hence, merely updating the connection weights seems to be sufficient to cause this kind of change.

If the assimilation of new information is not possible within the existing landscape, and mere change in weights does not suffice to ensure learning, then the landscape is moulded by changes in the network's structure (Horgan and Tienson 1996). This may induce the appearance of new attractors; since the attractors are points on the landscape, the appearance of new cognitive states realizing points on this landscape, the disappearance of old ones and changes in the basins of attraction constitute strong changes and the content-expressive power of the system is altered.

It is now possible to address the issue of Chi's (1992) claim to the effect that no psychological operations bearing on existing concepts can lead to radical cognitive change. Chi's thesis emanates from her view that learning and change involve search within a defined representational space, as well as from a firm distinction between processing and the data that are processed. In fact, Chi reformulates Fodor's (1981) learning paradox, according to which the acquisition of new knowledge is impossible because no mechanisms operating upon existing knowledge-structures could add content that did not already exist in the structures that are being operated upon.

The discussion of change in dynamic neural networks offers an alternative to this picture of learning as a search within a defined problem space. According to this alternative picture, learning itself induces changes in the structures that are involved in the learning process. That is, the architecture of the network also changes as a function of learning. As Quartz and Sejnowski (1997, 585) remark: 'What is crucial to answer Fodor's challenge is the requirement that increases in representational power be a function of learning rather than that the increase in representational power not be a discrete change to the architecture (such as the addition of new units).' Generative networks with adaptive learning rates and insertion criteria exemplify such an approach.

The modification of structure as a function of learning allows the appearance of new attractor states, by positioning of new content-realizing points on the system's landscape. Thus, the system builds representations as it learns, and thus shapes the hypothesis space (as Baum 1989 showed, such networks can solve any learning problem in polynomial time). In other words, the structure of the training data and thereby the structure of the problem domain from which these data are drawn as well as the processing characteristics of the learner shape the hypothesis space to their constraints and requirements. This is due to the fact that learning depends crucially on the statistical regularities of the problem input, and the structural characteristics of the learner. Thus, psychological operations acting upon existing concepts can, with help from the environment and the processing characteristics of the learner, bring about radical change.

Hence, learning and the eventual change need not be inductive searches through a hypothesis space delineated by fixed representations that restricts search to solutions that can be expressed only by means of the pre-existing representations. Another implication of the above picture of learning is that the distinction between process and data breaks down, because processing in neural networks consists of employing the connection weights to activate the system's units when an input is provided, but the knowledge of the system is 'stored' in these weights. The result is that processing strategies and representations co-evolve (Clark 1993; Horgan and Tienson 1996). New attractors and basins of attraction appear, while results of processing reshape the landscape's relief, and thereby alter processing.

Mechanisms of change

At the cognitive level the main mechanisms driving conceptual changes are the Piagetian assimilation, accommodation and equilibration. The five types of change discussed above do not explain two important aspects of cognitive change. That is, first, they do not explain how the various concepts or operations used by any of them for the sake of the construction of a new mental unit are compared and evaluated for their relevance and usefulness in the construction process. Second, the five types of change also do not explain how the new mental units, once created, are tagged or marked so that they can be identified and stored for future use. To that end one needs some additional mechanisms: though in this chapter we have neither argued for nor attempted to simulate them, we have proposed elsewhere (Demetriou and Raftopoulos 1999) two general mechanisms, metarepresentation and symbolic individuation, that would be able to take up the aforementioned issues.

Metarepresentation is a process which looks for, codifies and typifies similarities between mental experiences. In logical terms, metarepresentation is analogical reasoning applied to mental experiences or operations, rather than to representations of environmental stimuli. For example, when a child realizes that the sequencing of the *if. . . then* connectives in language is associated with situations in which the event preceded by *if* always comes first and that it leads to the event introduced by *then*, this child is actually formulating an inference schema that leads to predictions and interpretations specific to this schema. The guiding system behind metarepresentation resides in the hypercognitive maps, which provide examples of past performance in situations similar to the present goal or the present task encounter. These examples can be recalled and tried as possible solutions to the present problem. Thus, metarepresentation, by monitoring and regulating these processes, abstracts patterns of operations, which are common between past similar problem-solving attempts and a current attempt. As the effects of this monitoring-regulation process are carried over across occasions, they are 'formalized' as new action schemes or criteria, which are more appropriate than the ones activated at the beginning for the present problem. Thus, they become available for future use, whenever a similar situation is encountered. Moreover, once in place, the new units avail themselves as origins for new constructions. Hence, metarepresentation is the active aspect of the hypercognitive system that integrates and interconnects the functioning of the various other mechanisms themselves, thereby creating general patterns of reasoning that transcend the particular domains.

Symbolic individuation pairs newly generated ideas with specific symbols. These symbols may be idiosyncratic, like mental images or personal scripts, or conventional, like language or scientific formalisms. Tagging a new mental construction with a symbol provides a distinct identity that enables or facilitates people to store, recall, and mentally manipulate this construction for the sake of problem solving and further development.

Thus, assuming these mechanisms offers a construct to the theory that would explain at one and the same time non-linear or strong conceptual changes together with concomitant changes in self-awareness and self-regulation. That is, when the products of any of the types of change discussed here are symbolically tagged and reflected upon, they themselves can become building blocks for new constructions in the future. In a sense, these two mechanisms together may be regarded as the equivalent of Piaget's (1975) reflective abstraction.

It is time now to consider the mechanisms driving change at the representational level. In each of the five types of change discussed previously, the processes that lead to the change are the same, always reducing to quantitative and qualitative changes in connection weights and the architectural structure of the network respectively. These processes cause the repositioning of existing attractors, the disappearance of old ones and the appearance of new ones, and also cause changes in the basins of attraction that shape the relief of the landscape. It could hardly be otherwise. In connectionism the computational mechanisms are domain general, statistical learning mechanisms, based on brain-style computation, that is, (a) on the spreading of the activation of each unit to other units, (b) on the modification of the connection weights, and (c) on the modification of the network structure.

McClelland (1995) argued that Piagetian 'assimilation' corresponds to the activation spread in a network when a signal is presented to the input units and propagates through the network causing the activation of its units. The alteration of the weights, as a result of the network's learning, models Piaget's 'accommodation', that is the change that the network undergoes trying to fit in new experiences.

Shultz and Schmidt (1991), Shultz, Schmidt, Buckingham, and Mareschal (1995) and others, on the other hand, have proposed networks that adapt their structure as they learn by increasing one by one their hidden units to accommodate the demands of the task they attempt to solve. These researchers offer a variation of McClelland's account, a variation that is suited better for networks that can modify their structure. According to this view, the quantitative phase of error reduction and weight change may correspond to Piaget's 'assimilation' of information in a pre-existing structure, whereas the qualitative change of unit and connection change may correspond to Piaget's 'accommodation' of the structure to handle unassimilated information. They claim that quantitative change renders possible knowledge acquisition within an existing representational framework, whereas qualitative change of structure allows an increase in representational capacities.

As we have said when discussing weak vs. strong conceptual change, the latter may require changes in neural architecture, whereas the former could be accomplished by means of gradual quantitative changes in connection weights. We are currently working on specifying the exact kind of processing mechanism, or combination thereof, involved in each of the types of change, by analysing the performances of the network simulations that could implement the five types of change. It seems, for instance, that *fusion* (exemplified by neural networks simulating the four-stage development observed in the balance-beam tasks) requires structure modification through the adoption of new hidden units. *Combination*, implemented by neural networks that simulate learning to pronounce words and non-words, seems to be amenable to weight modifications, in that simple recurrent networks can show this kind of change without any structure modification. We do not wish of course to claim that all kinds of combination could be accomplished by means of weight modifications, and it is highly plausible that more complex cases, especially non-linearly separable problems, would require more than that.

Besides the five types of changes that are produced by the processing mechanisms discussed above, our theory stipulates, as we have said, two additional mechanisms of change that belong to the hyper-cognitive level. What is lacking is an account of these mechanisms at the representational level; that is a discussion of dynamic neural networks that could implement them. This is a project for future work, although we must stress outright that these mechanisms should not be construed as kinds of homunculi-type hyper-cognitive devices that 'read' the activity of the mechanisms at the cognitive level. They are, instead, neural networks that receive input from other networks at a lower level in the cognitive hierarchy and process this signal. If, for example, dynamic binding is achieved through the synchronous activity of network nodes, then one of the tasks of these hypercognitive mechanisms will be the detection of coincidence among their inputs.

Researchers working with adaptive networks argue that only this class of networks can successfully meet Fodor's challenge, since it is only through the modification of the network's structure that the system can increase its representational capacities and learn 'new' concepts. Indeed, throughout this chapter, in our attempt to model change, we have focused on adaptive networks, that is networks that grow as they learn. Dynamical theory offers an alternative to this picture, in that it provides an explanation of how qualitatively new modes may emerge, not as a result of structural changes in the network, but because of the internal function of a self-organizing system (Raijmakers 1997). In this case, it seems that only a single mechanism of change needs to be posited, that of continuous and gradual small changes in the connection weights of a network (Elman et al. 1996).

Tabor and Tanenhaus's (1999) *Visitation SET Gravitation* model of a dynamic network is an example of a network that may be construed to implement differentiation and exhibit all the characteristics of a strong conceptual change, while during learning its structure is fixed and learning is accomplished by weight modifications only.

More specifically, the non-linear dynamics of a system can result in more expressively powerful structures by means of self-organization and of the non-linear dynamic governing the activation functions of their processing units (the Sigmoid activation function, for instance). Such transitions from a lower to a higher level of complexity, when the control parameters of a system transcend a threshold and critical mass effects occur, abound in dynamical theory, as in Kelso's (1995) studies of rhythmic finger motion, Thelen and Smith's (1994) study of treadmill stepping, Elman's (1995) study of language, the famous Belousov-Zhabotinsky chemical reaction (Kunnen and Bosma 2000) dynamic systems approach to development of meaning making. In these cases the values of control parameters change continuously and the changes may be arbitrarily small, and yet they lead to an increase in the expressive power (measured as computational complexity) of a system.

From these studies, a common thread emerges. The internal synergies of the coupled systems that interact and the underlying non-linear dynamics may result in phase transitions and in the emergence of qualitatively new, more complex, modes: 'Certain preferred collective states of the system are depicted as synergetic wholes that can be brought forth (but not programmed) by the action of some control parameter' (Clark 1997, 473). In fact, Rumelhart and McClelland (1986) and Hinton and Sejnowski (1986) prove that small, continuous, changes in the weight values of the hidden units of the system can occasionally produce abrupt and large changes in the partitions in the activation space. These changes are manifested by a discontinuous, stage-like, increase of the level of performance of the system, that is, by dramatic changes in the network's output (behaviour). These changes reveal a critical mass effect in which, when the training set reaches a critical size, the network exhibits a sudden transition between two modes of representation (Elman et al. 1996; Plunkett and Sinha 1992; van der Maas et al. this volume). These transitions correspond to the state transitions of dynamical systems.

Raijmakers et al. (1996b) have shown, however, that feed forward *PDP* networks cannot model phase transitions and show qualitatively different behaviour in dynamic regimes separated by a phase transition. For that recurrent connections are required. Such networks are Pollack's (1995) sequential cascade network (in which induction is seen as a phase transition) and Raijmakers' *Exact ART* (Raijmakers et al. 1996a), in which structural properties of the network are implemented as low-dimensional real-value parameters. In this network phase transitions occur as the values of the parameters vary continuously, without qualitative structural changes. Still, the phase transitions are not a function of learning, a result that limits the application of the network in modelling cognitive behaviour. If this can be done, that is, if the phase transitions could be modelled to be the result of learning itself, and it is entirely possible that it can, then, as Quartz and Sejnowski (1997, 585) remark: 'that would represent an alternative response to Fodor's challenge, one that stands besides other responses, such as the neural constructivism one'.

Conclusion

This article aims to sketch a theory of change recast in terms of dynamical connectionism. The discussion suggests some tentative answers to the three main questions that constitute the binding thread of this volume, namely, what develops, why it develops, and how does it develop?

Demetriou and Raftopoulos (1999) attempted to answer these questions at the cognitive level. This account assumes that the mind is organized in three main levels, to wit, the environment-oriented domain-specific systems, the self-oriented monitoring and representation processes, and the constraints of the processing potentials. Thus, the structures in these two first levels and the constraints are the subjects of *what* changes.

The theory also answers the other two questions. As to the *why* of change, the theory posits that, to develop, a system must regularly come under conditions that cause inefficient or erroneous operation with respect to its current goals. *How* the system changes is determined by means of (a) the standard Piagetian mechanisms of assimilation, accommodation and equilibration, and (b) the two hypercognitive mechanisms that complement the standard Piagetian mechanisms.

Returning to the representational level, the answers to the 'what, why, and how' are recast in terms of the dynamic connectionist networks. The constraints are among those things that change over development and training, the *what* question. The *speed of processing* is modelled as the propagation of signal through the units of the network. Though at a first glance, processing speed seems to evade modelling in feedforward networks, since activation is propagated in a single time step, Shultz (2003) argues that autoassociator networks can be used to implement latencies for responses generated by feedforward networks. The greater the error the greater the clean-up time of the network, which means that as the error decreases over training, so does the clean-up time, and thus, the network's responses.

Similarly, in recurrent networks things' response times, and hence, processing speed, have a natural expression by means of the cycles the network needs to settle on an attractor stable state. The better the network is tuned to the environment, the faster it stabilizes. Endogenous changes in processing speed that are related with maturational brain processes could be modelled by means of the learning rate, e, or the update rate in autoassociative networks.

Changes in memory, finally, can be modelled by means of the cascade correlation networks of Schultz, in which the number of context units increases as a function of time and experience.

The discussion regarding the mechanisms implementing change answers the *how* question. As we have argued, the quantitative phase of error reduction and weight change corresponds to Piaget's 'assimilation' of information in a pre-existing structure, whereas the qualitative change of unit and connection change may correspond to Piaget's 'accommodation' of the structure to handle unassimilated information. Quantitative change renders possible knowledge acquisition within an existing representational framework, whereas qualitative change of structure allows an increase in representational capacities.

Recall, moreover, that dynamical theory offers an alternative to this picture, in that it provides an explanation of how qualitatively new modes may emerge, not as a result of structural changes in the network, but because of the internal function of a self-organizing system. In this case, it seems that only a single mechanism of change needs to be posited, that of continuous and gradual small changes in the connection weights of a network. More specifically, the non-linear dynamics of a system can result in more expressively powerful structures by means of self-organization and of the non-linear dynamic governing the activation functions of their processing units (e.g. the Sigmoid activation function).

We saw that within dynamical connectionism, the behaviour of the system is a collective effect, which assumes, simultaneously, the form of cooperation and competition. In the case of cognitive systems, the competition is due to the effort of the system to retain its current state in the face of incoming information. If this information cannot be assimilated by the system in its existing form (in neural networks this means that the system does not yield the correct output), then the weights of a network change and the network may alter its structure to accommodate the new input. This constitutes the answer to the *why* question.

As has become obvious from the discussion in this chapter, there are many issues that have not been addressed and remain open. Further research is needed (a) to provide implementations of types of change such as refinement; (b) to elaborate on networks that could simulate complex cases of conceptual redeployment; (c) to come up with a realistic and ecologically valid solution to the problem of lifelong learning in neural networks; (d) to show how neural networks could address non-linearly solvable problems with increasingly abstract hidden structure; (e) to provide an account of the hypercognitive mechanisms, while avoiding the infinite regress lurking in the homunculus problem; and (f) to show how the system has access to the representational contents of its own mechanisms and their products, that is, how meaning infuses the system. It goes without saying that the above do not exhaust the list of all problems related to modelling cognitive change.

Moreover, the model of change advanced here will have to be evaluated and extended by further empirical and theoretical research. It is important that the different types of change which were described and modelled in this article are tested both in vitro and in vivo. In vitro testing may be effected through simulations that would actualize each of these mechanisms to see if they really produce new constructs out of existing ones. In vivo testing might include the study of actual learning in real classrooms and other environments where cognitive development occurs. Using microgenetic methods of recording change (Siegler 1996) we will have to locate and zoom in on examples of each of the mechanisms analysed here. Second, it requires learning experiments in which participants will systematically be led to construct new mental units by using existing ones according to the specifications of the construction process that characterizes each of the mechanisms. Under these conditions, the component units and the construction processes themselves will have to be systematically manipulated in a laboratory context.

Experiments of this kind are necessary to test if the construction of different types of mental units does require the different mechanisms. Experiments of this kind would provide a hard test to the theory because they would examine directly whether the enforcement of the different mechanisms on the developing person does lead to the expected change. Falsifying this expectation would of course suggest that the theory is not valid. It is only under these conditions that we can see if the mechanisms can really be implemented as causal agents of cognitive change.

REFERENCES

Baum, E. B. (1989). A proposal for more powerful learning algorithms. *Neural Computation, 1*, 201–7.
Carey, S. (1985). *Conceptual change in childhood*. Cambridge, MA: The MIT Press.
    (1992). The origin and evolution of everyday concepts. In R. Giere (ed.) *Cognitive models of science*. Minneapolis: Minnesota University Press.
Carey, S. and Spelke, E. (1994). Domain-specific knowledge and conceptual change. In L. A. Hirschfeld and S. A. Gelman (eds.) *Mapping the mind: domain specificity in cognition and culture*. Cambridge: Cambridge University Press.
Chi, M. T. H. (1992). Conceptual change within and across ontological categories. In R. Giere (ed.) *Cognitive models of science*. Minneapolis: Minnesota University Press, 129–86.
Chi, M. T. H., Glaser, R. and Rees, E. (1982). Expertise in problem solving. In R. J. Sternberg (ed.) *Advances in the psychology of human intelligence* (vol. 1). Hillsdale, NJ: Erlbaum.
Clark, A. (1993). *Associative engines*. Cambridge, MA: The MIT Press.
    (1997). The dynamical challenge. *Cognitive Science, 21*(4), 461–81.
Crutchfield, J. P. (1998). Dynamical embodiments of computation in cognitive processes. *Brain and Behavioral Sciences, 21*, 635.
Dawson, M. R. W. (1998). *Understanding cognitive science*. Cornwall: Blackwell.
Demetriou, A. (1998). Cognitive development. In A. Demetriou, W. Doise, K. F. M. van Lieshout (eds.) *Life-span developmental psychology* (pp. 179–269). London: Wiley.
Demetriou, A., Efklides, A. and Platsidou, M. (1993). The architecture and dynamics of developing mind: experiential structuralism as a frame for unifying cognitive developmental theories. *Monographs of the Society for Research in Child Development, 58* (5–6, Serial No. 234).
Demetriou, A. and Kazi, S. (2001). *Unity and modularity in the mind and the self: studies on the relationships between self-awareness, personality, and intellectual development from childhood to adolescence*. London: Routledge.
Demetriou, A. and Raftopoulos, A. (1999). Modelling the developing mind: from structure to change. *Developmental Review, 19*, 319–68.
Demetriou, A. and Valanides, N. (1998). A three level theory of the developing mind: basic principles and implications for instruction and assessment. In R. J. Sternberg and W. M. Williams (eds.) *Intelligence, instruction, and assessment* (pp. 149–99). Hillsdale, NJ: Lawrence Erlbaum.

Dienes, Z., Altmann, G. T. M., and Gao, Shi-Ji (1999). A neural network model of transfer of implicit knowledge. *Cognitive Science, 23*(1), 53–82.

Edelman, G. M. (1987). *Neural Darwinism.* New York: Basic Books.

(1992). *Bright air, brilliant fire. On the matter of mind.* New York: Basic Books.

Elman, J. L. (1990). Finding structure in time. *Cognitive Science, 14,* 179–211.

(1995). Language as a dynamic system. In R. F. Port and T. Van Gelder (eds.) *Mind as motion: exploration in the dynamics of cognition.* Cambridge, MA: The MIT Press.

Elman, J. L., Bates, E. A., Johnson, M. H., Karmiloff-Smith, A., Parisi, D. and Plunkett, K. (1996). *Rethinking innateness: a connectionist perspective on development.* Cambridge, MA: The MIT Press.

Fauconnier, G. (1997). *Mappings in thought and language.* Cambridge: Cambridge University Press.

Fodor, J. (1981). *Representations: philosophical essays on the foundations of cognitive science.* Cambridge, MA: The MIT Press.

Hinton, G. E., and Sejnowski, T. J. (1986). Learning and relearning in Boltzmann machines. In D. E. Rumelhart, J. L. McLelland, and the PDP Research Group (eds.) *Parallel distributed processing: explorations in the microstructure of cognition,* vol. 1: Foundations. Cambridge, MA: MIT Pres.

Hummel, J. E. and Holyoak, K. J. (1997). Distributed representations of structure: a theory of analogical access and mapping. *Psychological Review, 104*(3), 427–66.

Horgan, T. and Tienson, J. (1996). *Connectionism and the philosophy of psychology.* Cambridge, MA: The MIT Press.

Johnson, M. (1981). *The body in the mind: the bodily basis of meaning, imagination, and reason.* Chicago, IL: University of Chicago Press.

Juarrero, A. (1999). *Dynamics in action.* Cambridge, MA: The MIT University Press.

Kelso, S. (1995). *Dynamic patterns: the self organization of brain and behavior.* Cambridge, MA: The MIT Press.

Kunnen, S. E., and Bosma, H. A. (2000). Development of meaning making: a dynamic systems approach. *New Ideas in Psychology, 18,* 57–82.

Lakoff, G. (1987). *Women, fire, and dangerous things: what categories reveal about the mind.* Chicago, IL: University of Chicago Press.

McClelland, J. L. (1995). A connectionist perspective on knowledge and development. In T. J. Simon and G. S. Halford (eds.) *Developing cognitive competence: new approaches to process modeling* (pp. 157–204). Hillsdale, NJ: Lawrence Erlbaum.

McRae, K., Spivey-Knowlton, M. J., and Tanenhaus, M. K. (1998). Modelling the influence of thematic fit (and other constraints) in on-line sentence comprehension. *Journal of Memory and Language, 38,* 283–312.

Marr, D. (1982). *Vision: a computational investigation into human representation and processing of visual information.* San Francisco, CA: Freeman.

Newell, A. (1980). Physical symbol systems. *Cognitive Science, 4,* 135–83.

Newell, A. and Simon, H. A. (1972). *Human problem solving.* Englewood Cliffs, NJ: Prentice Hall.

Piaget, J. (1975). *The development of thought: equilibration of cognitive structures.* Oxford: Basil Blackwell.

Plaut, D. C. (1999). A connectionist approach to word reading and acquired dyslexia: extension to sequential processing. *Cognitive Science, 23* (4), 543–69.

Plaut, D. C. and Shallice, T. (1993). Deep dyslexia: a case study of connectionist neuropsychology. *Cognitive Neuropsychology, 10*, 377–500.

Plaut, D. C., McClelland, J. L., Seidenberg, M. S. and Patterson, K. (1996). Understanding normal and impaired word reading: computational principles in quasi-regular domains. *Psychological Review, 103*(1), 56–115.

Plunkett, K. and Sinha, C. (1992). Connectionism and developmental theory. *British Journal of Developmental Psychology, 10*, 209–54.

Pollack, J. B. (1990). Recursive distributed representations. In G. Hinton (ed.) *Connectionist symbol processing*. Cambridge, MA: The MIT Un. Press.

(1995). The induction of dynamic recognizers. In R. F. Port and T. Van Gelder (eds.) *Mind as motion: exploration in the dynamics of cognition*. Cambridge, MA: The MIT Press.

Pylyshyn, Z. (1984). *Computation and cognition: toward a foundation for cognitive science*. Cambridge, MA: The MIT Press.

Raftopoulos, A. (1997). Cognitive and perceptual limitations and learning: an excursion to connectionism. *Human Development, 40* (5), 293–319.

Quartz, S. R. and Sejnowski, T. J. (1997). The neural basis of cognitive development: a constructivist manifesto. *Behavioral and Brain Sciences, 20*, 537–56.

Raijmakers, M. E. J. (1997). Is the learning paradox resolved? *Behavioral and Brain Sciences, 20*, 537–96.

Raijmakers, M. E. J., van der Maas, H. L. J. and Molenaar, P. C. M. (1996a). Numerical bifurcation analysis of distance-dependent on-center off-surround shunting neural networks. *Biological Cybernetics, 75*, 495–507.

Raijmakers, M. E. J., van Koten, S. and Molenaar, P. C. M. (1996b). On the validity of simulating stagewise development by means of PDP networks: application of catastrophe analysis and an experimental test of rule-like network performance. *Cognitive Science, 20*, 101–36.

Rumelhart, D. E., McClelland, J. L. and the PDP Research Group (1986). *Parallel Distributed Processing: explorations in the microstructure of cognition*, vol. 1: Foundations. Cambridge, MA: MIT Press.

Sejnowski, T. and Rosenberg, C. (1986). NETtalk: a parallel network that learns to read aloud. The Johns Hopkins University, *Technical Report JHU/EEC-86/01*.

Shastri, L. and Ajjanagadde, V. (1993). From simple associations to systematic reasoning: a connectionist representation of rules, variables, and dynamic binding using temporal synchrony. *Behavioral and Brain Sciences, 16*, 417–94.

Shultz, T. R. (2003). *Computational developmental psychology*. Cambridge, MA: The MIT Press.

Shultz, T. R. and Schmidt, W. C. (1991). A cascade-correlation mode of balance scale phenomena. In *Proceedings of the Thirteenth Annual Conference of the Cognitive Science Society*. Hillsdale, NJ: Lawrence Erlbaum, 635–40.

Shultz, T. R, Schmidt, W. C., Buckingham, D. and Mareschal, D. (1995). Modelling cognitive development with a generative connectionist algorithm. In T. J. Simon and G. S. Halford (eds.) *Developing cognitive competence: new approaches to process modelling*. Hillsdale, NJ: Lawrence Erlbaum.

Siegler, R. S. (1981). Developmental sequences within and between concepts. *Monographs of the Society for Research in Child Development, 46* (2, Serial No. 189).
(1996). *Emerging minds.* Oxford: Oxford University Press.
Sirois, S., Buckingham, D. and Schultz, T. R. (2000). Artificial grammar learning by infants: an auto-associator perspective. *Developmental Science, 3*(4), 442–56.
Smith, C. S., Carey, S. and Wiser, M. (1985). On differentiation: a case study of the development of concepts of size, weight, and density. *Cognition, 21,* 177–237.
Smolensky. P. (1990). Tensor product variable binding and the representation of symbolic structures in connectionist systems. In G. E. Hinton (ed.) *Connectionist symbol processing.* Cambridge, MA: The MIT Press.
Tabor, W., and Tanenhaus, M. K. (1999). Dynamical models of sentence processing. *Cognitive Science, 23*(4), 491–517.
Thagard, P. (1992). *Conceptual revolutions.* Princeton, NJ: Princeton University Press.
Thelen, E., and Smith, L. (1994). *A dynamic system approach to the development of cognition and action.* Cambridge, MA: The MIT Press.
Thom, R. (1983). *Mathematical models of morphogenesis.* Ellis Horwood.
Wosilait, K., Heron, P. R. L., Shaffer, P. S. and McDermott, L. C. (1999). Addressing student difficulties in applying a wave model to the interference and diffraction of light. *Physics Education Research Supplement, American Journal of Physics 67*(7) S5–S15.
Zeeman, C. (1965). Topology of the brain. *Mathematics and computer science in biology and medicine.* Medical Research Council.

3   Developmental patterns in proportional reasoning

Han van der Maas, Brenda Jansen and Maartje Raijmakers

The editors of this book asked the contributors to answer three basic questions about cognitive development: what, how and why. We will attempt to answer these questions by a careful study of one famous case of cognitive development: Piaget's balance scale task for assessing proportional reasoning.

In the past, we have investigated this task in various ways and we will take the present opportunity to summarize and integrate our main findings. We approach the study of cognitive development from a methodological point of view. In each of the forthcoming sections, we apply a new technique in order to get a new perspective on the developmental process.

We first shortly discuss the background of research on the balance scale task. In the second section we attempt to resolve the criticism of Siegler's (1981) rule theory, the main theory for balance scale reasoning, by introducing categorical latent structure models for rule assessment. In the third section we attempt to validate and extend this rule theory with response time (RT) measures. Using RTs allows the test of the rule theory in great detail and leads to a number of specifications and improvements of the theory. Fourth, we summarize our study of the transitions between the rules. Knowledge of these transitions is an important step in understanding the mechanisms involved in the development of proportional reasoning. We focus on a particular transition, from Rule I to Rule II, to investigate whether this transition is a genuine phase transition. Based on our results, we present a restricted overlapping waves model of proportional reasoning, in which some transitions are sudden and others are more continuous. We will describe an ACT-R model that implements the model and thereby partly explains the what, how and why of cognitive development.

History of research on the balance scale task

In the balance scale task, children are asked to predict the movement of a balance scale. Equally heavy weights can be placed on the arms of the scale, at equally spaced distances. Figure 3.1 shows a graphical display of a balance scale problem. Blocks underneath the arms prevent the scale from tipping. The

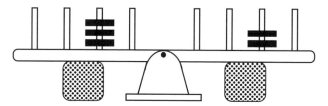

Figure 3.1. Example of a balance scale item.

task assesses proportional reasoning as it requires the understanding of the multiplicative relation between the dimensions.

Inhelder and Piaget (1958) formulated a developmental course of performance on the task, which is characterized by several qualitatively distinct, increasingly complex, stages. The stages range from considering the number of weights only to comparing the products of weight and distance of both sides of the scale (torque-rule). However, stages cannot be observed directly. Although responses to balance scale problems are probably related to the developmental stages, the relation is not perfect as both false positive errors (e.g. when children incidentally derive the correct response by guessing) and false negative errors (e.g. when children err) may occur.

Mainly in the context of another Piagetian task, conservation, researchers have asked what criteria need to be fulfilled to determine that a child possesses true knowledge (Braine and Shanks 1965; Brainerd 1973; Gruen 1966; Inhelder, Bovet, Sinclair and Smock 1966; Smedslund 1963, 1969; Smith 1992, 1993). Researchers have argued that a clearer picture of children's true knowledge is derived from children's explanations of their responses. Supporters of this 'Judgment and justification view' believe that the probability of a false positive error decreases when an explanation is asked for. Supporters of the 'Judgment-only view' reasoned that both types of error occur with a verbal method, as there is no one-to-one correspondence between logic and action nor between logic and language. A false positive error occurs if a child who does not understand the principle of torque is taught the correct justification for the balance scale task. However, when the child is presented with a slightly different problem, the child will not be able to give the correct justification. False negative errors may occur because children are not always able to express their mental operations verbally. Boden (1994) notes that knowledge must exist in action before it can be verbalized. Hence, a verbal justification may be a sufficient, but not a necessary, condition. Brainerd (1973) claims that asking for verbal justifications even increases the probability of false negative errors. According to Brainerd, asking for judgments alone does not necessarily cause an increased probability of false positive errors.

Research on the complex social interaction between experimenter and child during the verbal task (Bijstra, van Geert and Jackson 1989; Donaldson 1978; Elbers 1989; McGarrigle and Donaldson 1975; Rose and Blank 1974) and the linguistic aspects of the test situation (Schiff 1983; Moore and Frye 1986) showed that practical problems of the verbal method are evident as well. Siegal (1991) noted many reasons why a child may misinterpret the experimenter's intent. For instance, the child may start doubting because the experimenter asks the same question twice or may consider the task a game. Furthermore, the lack of consensus about which justifications of children demonstrate true knowledge (Brainerd 1973) constitutes an important problem of a verbal procedure.

Non-verbal versions of Piagetian tasks do not have these theoretical and practical disadvantages. Moreover, the advantages of a non-verbal test are innumerable: more items can be assessed in the same amount of time and other media, like computers and paper-and-pencil tests, are applicable. Training of experimenters and complex coding of tape-recorded justifications are not required. As will be shown below, the problem of false positive and negative errors can be ruled out to a large degree when an adequate methodology is used.

Siegler (1981) designed the Rule Assessment Methodology (RAM) to assess children's performance on the balance scale task in a non-verbal way. RAM involves a careful selection of item types that elicit specific response patterns. These patterns can be linked to rules, comparable to the original stages. Each rule, represented in Figure 3.2, is hypothesized to consist of consecutively executed steps. Each step is indicated with a parameter (in italics) that indicates the duration of executing the step. We hypothesize that the time involved with solving a balance scale item equals the sum of the duration of the steps that are completed. This hypothesis leads to a number of predictions, which are tested in a later section.

Complexity of rules increases with development as each rule consists of the steps of the preceding rule, extended with one or more extra steps. Rule I is the simplest rule as it involves only one step, which consists of comparing the numbers of weights (w). Participants who use Rule I decide that the scale will tip to the side with the largest number of weights when the numbers are unequal and that the scale will remain in balance when the numbers are equal. Participants who use Rule II also compare the numbers of weights on all items and decide that the scale will tip to the side with the larger number of weights when the numbers differ. However, when the numbers are equal, they also compare the distances at which the weights are placed (d). Rule III is more complex than Rule II because it contains two additional steps. Rule III-users derive the correct response on simple items by comparing the numbers of weights in the first step and comparing the distances at which the weights are placed in the second step. The first additional step is performed if both the weights and the distances are unequal and includes determining

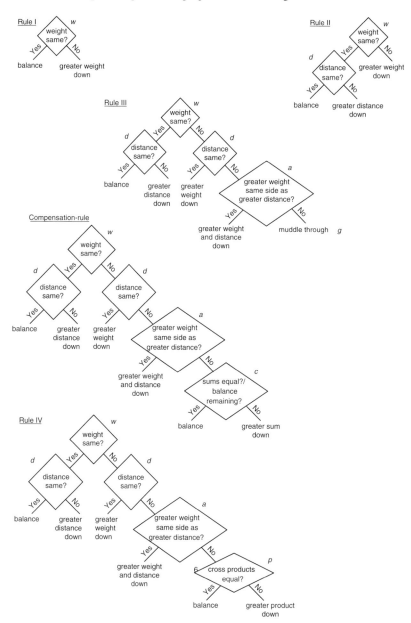

Figure 3.2. Rules defined by Siegler (1981). Also depicted is the compensation-rule. Lowercase italics w, d, a, c, g, and p indicate duration of a step. (Adapted from van der Maas & Jansen 2003)

whether the dimensions agree (*a*; i.e. whether the greater weight is on the same side as the greater distance). If the dimensions conflict, the second additional step is performed. It implies 'muddling through' or guessing (*g*). Although Rule IV contains the same number of steps as Rule III, Rule IV is more complex because of the complexity of the last step. It includes executing the torque-rule on items with conflicting dimensions (*p*).

To assess the use of these rules, Siegler designed (1976, 1981) six item types. On simple-balance items ('sb'), both arms of the scale hold the same number of weights, equidistant from the fulcrum. On simple-weight items ('sw'), the arms contain unequal numbers of weights, equidistant from the fulcrum. Simple-distance items ('sd') involve equal numbers of weights, placed at different distances from the fulcrum. On conflict items, one arm contains a greater number of weights, whereas the weights on the other arm are placed at a greater distance. The scale tips to the side with the larger number of weights on conflict-weight items ('cw'), tips to the side with the weights placed at the greater distance on conflict-distance items ('cd') and remains in balance on conflict-balance items ('cb'). Table 3.1 shows that each rule results in a specific response pattern on these item types. The indices in italics represent the duration of executing a rule, given item type.

RAM inspired many researchers to study children's behaviour on the balance scale task (Roth 1991). Ferretti and Butterfield (1989) focused on different populations whereas Halford, Andrews, Dalton, Boag and Zielinski (2002) and Richards and Siegler (1981) focused on younger children. Others designed alternative methods (Chletsos, De Lisi, Turner and McGillicuddy-De Lisi 1989; Kliman 1987; Marini and Case 1994; McFadden, Dufresne, and Kobasigawa 1987). Siegler and Chen (1998) performed a microgenetic study. Also the effects of training (Ferretti and Butterfield 1992; Phelps and Damon 1989; Warton and Bussey 1988) and the relationship between balance scale performance and other abilities or personality traits (Ferretti, Butterfield, Cah, and Kerkman 1985; Pauen and Wilkening 1997; Surber and Gzesh 1984) were studied. Finally, RAM motivated researchers to model children's behaviour by means of AI models and neural networks (McClelland and Jenkins 1991; Schmidt and Ling 1996; Shultz, Mareshal and Schmidt 1994; van Rijn, van Someren and van der Maas 2003).

Some studies resulted in the proposal of alternative rules (Wilkening and Anderson 1982). The addition-rule (Ferretti et al. 1985; Normandeau, Larivée, Roulin and Longeot, 1989; Jansen and van der Maas, 1997, 2002) is most frequently discussed. It results in the same response pattern as the buggy-rule (van Maanen, Been and Sijtsma 1989). On conflict items, the first three steps in these rules are similar to the steps in Rules III and IV: comparing both the values on the weight and the values on the distance dimension and deciding

Table 3.1. *Predicted proportion of correct items and RT for each rule, given item type.*

Item type	Example		Rule			
		Rule I	Rule II	Rule III	Compensation	Rule IV
simple-balance		1.00	1.00	1.00	1.00	1.00
simple-weight		w	$w + d$	$w + d$	$w + d$	$w + d$
		1.00	1.00	1.00	1.00	1.00
simple-distance		w	w	$w + d$	$w + d$	$w + d$
		.00[a]	1.00	1.00	1.00	1.00
conflict-balance		w	$w + d$	$w + d$	$w + d$	$w + d$
		.00[b]	.00[b]	.33[c]	—[d]	1.00
conflict-weight		w	w	$w + d + a + g$	$w + d + a + c$	$w + d + a + p$
		1.00	1.00	.33[c]	—[d]	1.00
conflict-distance		w	w	$w + d + a + g$	$w + d + a + c$	$w + d + a + p$
		.00[b]	.00[b]	.33[c]	—[d]	1.00

Note. [a] Answers that the scale will remain in balance. [b] Answers that the scale will tip to the side with more weights. [c] Guesses or muddles through. [d] Response depends on configuration of weights and distances. w, weight comparison; d, distance comparison; a, deciding whether the weight and distance dimension agree; g, guess or muddle through; c, compensation; p, compare products.

whether the dimensions conflict. At the fourth step, the addition-rule involves adding weight and distance on each side of the scale and comparing the sums, whereas the buggy-rule involves shifting the larger number of weights away from the fulcrum. One weight is removed for every shift, until the distances or the weights of both sides are equal. Halford et al. (2002) recognized the compensational character of both rules and we adopt their designation of these rules as 'compensation-rule'. Figure 3.2 contains the representation of the compensation-rule, whereas Table 3.1 shows that the rule results in the correct response to all simple items, and to some conflict items.

Statistical test of the rule assessment methodology

Although RAM proved to be a useful, non-verbal, method for studying children's knowledge, the method also met with criticism. Most importantly, the existence of rules was doubted. McClelland (1995) doubted whether humans use explicit rules, because studies by McClelland (1989) and McClelland and Jenkins (1991) showed that even connectionistic models, that do not contain explicit rules, do show rule-like behaviour. In these studies, data, generated with simple connectionistic models, were analysed with RAM. The results lead to the claim that the simple connectionistic models showed rule-governed behaviour and that they even acquired knowledge in a stage-wise process of rule acquisitions. Ferretti and Butterfield (1986) observed that the classifications in rules varied with the problem set used: children were classified as users of more complex rules if the items in a set contained larger product differences than when items with smaller product differences were used. In other words, the items of one type were not homogeneous and the rule classification depended on the items used.

To decide whether children truly use rules, we need empirical criteria for the concept 'rule'. Reese (1989) distinguished six criteria for rule inference, of which an important one is that observed behaviour is consistent with expected behaviour. Although RAM seems an elegant method to assess this criterion, there is a risk that the rules are an artifact of RAM (see Strauss and Levin 1981). First, RAM does not include any statistical fit measures to evaluate the fit of the rule classification to the empirical data. Second, the criterion of matching responses that is used to classify response patterns (e.g. 20 out of 24 responses correspond to a rule) is chosen arbitrarily and does not lend itself to statistical testing. As the criterion changes with the number of items, comparison of classifications based on different data sets, obtained with different tests, is difficult. Finally, with RAM, only the rules that are known a priori can be detected. A statistical approach to the classification of response patterns to rules is required to solve these problems.

The unobserved rule that a child uses can be regarded as a latent property that determines the child's responses to a set of balance scale items. The idea of a latent property corresponds to the concept of a latent variable, as postulated in latent structure models (Clogg 1995). Latent structure models are 'models that introduce latent variables to account for the observed pattern of association between the manifest variables' (Lazarsfeld and Henry 1967, in Heinen, 1996, p. 3). This means that the unobserved latent property (proportional reasoning) determines the behaviour of a person's manifest indicators (balance scale problems).

The latent class model is a latent structure model that deals with categorical latent and manifest variables. It is obvious that the manifest variables are measured on a categorical scale, as the responses to balance scale problems are 'left side down', 'right side down', and 'the two sides balance'. It is assumed that the latent variable, the ability to solve balance scale items, is also only measurable on a categorical scale, as a child's ability to solve balance scale problems is assumed to correspond to mastery of either Rule I, Rule II, Rule III or Rule IV. These rules cannot be viewed as points on a continuous scale as the procedures that are associated with the rules differ qualitatively from each other. The rules are increasingly complex but cannot easily be ordered. Consider for example the expected number of correct responses given Rule II and Rule III. Children who use Rule II answer more conflict-weight items correctly, whereas children who use Rule III answer more of the other conflict items correctly (see Table 3.1). However, the expected numbers of correct items are equal. Hence, it can be assumed that the measurement level of the latent ability of proportional reasoning is categorical and that each rule forms a category.

Collins and Wugalter (1992) and Rindskopf (1987) already demonstrated the usefulness of LCA for the analysis of developmental data. With LCA, the number of rules, and their response patterns, can be determined. In these response patterns, children's error processes can be modelled. A child's response may be inconsistent with the rule that the child is using because of carelessness, for instance (Rindskopf 1987). The deviation from the expected response pattern can be accommodated in a latent class model. Hence, the criterion used to classify children into classes (i.e. to rules) is based on a statistical criterion, rather than an arbitrary criterion. LCA also eases the comparison of classifications based on different data sets, collected with different tests. Another advantage is that LCA does not require information on the content of rules but detects clusters of response patterns in the data, which can later be interpreted as (alternative) rules. Most importantly, LCA can falsify the hypothesis concerning rule use, because a latent class model, associated with rule use, can be tested statistically.

Latent class analysis

LCA divides the population into a finite number of latent classes. Within each class, the manifest variables are assumed to be statistically independent. A latent class model consists of unconditional probabilities, representing the proportions of the classes, and conditional probabilities, representing the probabilities of giving the response 'left side down', 'right side down', or 'balance' on a particular balance scale item, within a given latent class.

We test whether two items are of the same difficulty, for subjects in a certain latent class, by restricting the conditional probabilities of these items, in the given class, to be equal to each other. In this way, Ferretti and Butterfield's (1986) claim, that rule classification depends on the product difference of the items in a specific set, can be tested. The claim is falsified when the conditional probabilities, associated with items of one type, can be restricted to be equal across items, within each latent class.

To select a model, we first determine the fit of a two-class model by considering the likelihood ratio, G^2, with respect to the number of degrees of freedom (df). In addition to the theoretical distribution of G^2, we use an empirical distribution, which is obtained by means of parametric bootstrapping (Langeheine, Pannekoek, and Van de Pol 1995). We increase the number of classes until a model is found with an insignificant G^2. Next, restrictions are applied to the unrestricted model and the tenability of the restrictions is judged by applying the likelihood-ratio difference test. Additionally, models with insignificant G^2 are compared by means of the Bayesian Information Criterion (BIC), which combines fit and parsimony. The model with the lowest value is selected. Subjects are assigned to the latent classes by means of posterior probabilities, based on the selected model.

We apply LCA to two empirical data sets, and to a data set that was derived with the PDP model for the balance scale task (McClelland 1989). This allows for testing the claim that the PDP model can simulate children's behaviour on the task, which was supported by the results of the RAM. Analyses are performed with PanMark (van de Pol, Langeheine, and de Jong 1996).

Application of LCA to responses to balance scale items

Data sets IA and IB

The first empirical data set (Data set IA), collected by van Maanen et al. (1989), consists of the responses of 484 children to a paper-and-pencil test of 25 balance scale items. Children were in grades seven and eight. The simulated data set (Data set IB) was generated with the same items and consists of the same number of response patterns. Both data sets consist of dichotomous responses (false/correct). Analyses were carried out for each item type individually to test

Table 3.2. *Fit-measures of latent class analyses of conflict-balance items, for data-sets IA and IB.*

Model	G^2	df	$p(G^2)$	$pb(G^2)$	ΔG^2	Δdf	BIC
			Data set IA (empirical data set)				
2	84.77	20	.00	.00	–	–	152.54
3	33.16	16	.01	.01	–	–	125.58
4	19.80	11	.05	.07	–	–	143.02
5	13.30	8	.00	.06	–	–	155.01
4e	34.19	24	.08	.09	14.39	13	77.32
			Data set IB (PDP data set)				
2	134.47	21	.00	.00	–	–	196.04
3	68.09	17	.00	.00	–	–	154.29
4	27.06	14	.00	.00	–	–	138.17
5	13.53	11	.13	.13	–	–	138.07

Note. Adapted from Jansen and van der Maas (1997). *pb*, bootstrapped p-value.

the hypothesis that children respond consistently to items of a single type. As Table 3.1 suggests, the probability of answering an item correctly depends only on the item type (and the rule that a child applies). Any other item characteristics (e.g. product difference) are not expected to affect response probabilities. Equality restrictions between items within each class are introduced to test consistency.

As an example, we present the results of the analyses of the cb-items. LCA of responses to this item type should result in three latent classes. One class is expected to consist of children who answer cb-items correctly because they use Rule IV or the compensation-rule. The compensation-rule does not necessarily result in a correct response to cb-items, but it does given the items in this test. A second class is expected to consist of children who use Rule III and who guess on cb-items. A third class is expected to consist of children using Rule I or Rule II, who will answer that the scale will tip to the side with the larger number of weights (see Table 3.1) and hence fail cb-items. Table 3.2 shows the fit measures of the latent class models of both data sets.

In case of the empirical data set, a four-class model is chosen, as this is the model with the smallest number of latent classes that fits the data. In model 4e, the conditional probabilities were restricted to be equal within each of the first three classes. When all five conditional probabilities of the fourth latent class were constrained to be equal, the model was rejected. Inspection of the item characteristics revealed that all cb-items could be solved by performing the buggy-rule. However, only one buggy was needed to solve the third and fourth item, whereas two buggies were needed to solve the remaining items. Hence, we restricted the conditional probabilities of the first, second, and fifth item to the same value and restricted the conditional probabilities of the third and the fourth item to the same value. The likelihood-difference test showed that the restrictions of model 4e were acceptable ($p > .05$). The BIC value of model 4e was also lower than that of the unrestricted four-class model.

The selected model is presented in Figure 3.3. The largest class ($\pi = 0.36$) showed low conditional probabilities of answering cb-items correctly, which matched the expected responses of children who use either Rule I or Rule II. The second class ($\pi = 0.26$) showed conditional probabilities that approximated a guessing level (Rule III). The third class ($\pi = 0.25$) showed high conditional probabilities of answering cb-items correctly, and was expected to comprise children who used Rule IV or the compensation-rule. The smallest class ($\pi = 0.13$) was unexpected. It was characterized by high probabilities of answering cb-items 3 and 4 correctly, but probabilities that suggested guessing on the remaining items. Apparently, children in this class used the buggy-rule but applied it poorly. They seemed to guess when the conflict item was not reduced to a simple item after making one buggy.

In case of the data set generated with the PDP model, it was more difficult to find a model that described the data adequately. The fit measures in Table 3.2 indicate that five latent classes were needed to describe the data, but the five-class model, represented in Figure 3.3, was highly sensitive to the choice of starting values. This instability suggests that the LCM is not suitable. Moreover, only a single class was compatible with Siegler's rules (showing a response pattern that was characterized by low conditional probabilities of answering cb-items correctly and hence matched Rule I and Rule II). This class accounted for 0.38 of the cases.

The analyses of the cb-items were representative of the analyses of the remaining item types. The latent classes in the models of the empirical data set matched Siegler's rules (Rule I, Rule II) or could be interpreted as stemming from plausible alternative rules (compensation-rule). The evidence for Rule IV was less convincing, but the children in data set IA were probably too young to display this rule. Rule III was detected in some, but not all, latent class models. Simulation studies showed that it is difficult to detect a guessing rule like Rule III with LCA. Some children, who used a buggy version of the compensation-rule, had difficulty applying this rule as they resorted to guessing when it took more than one buggy to reduce the conflict item to a simple item. Equality restrictions showed that children responded consistently to items of the same type. This result conflicts with the inconsistency Ferretti and Butterfield (1986) observed.

empirical data **NN data**

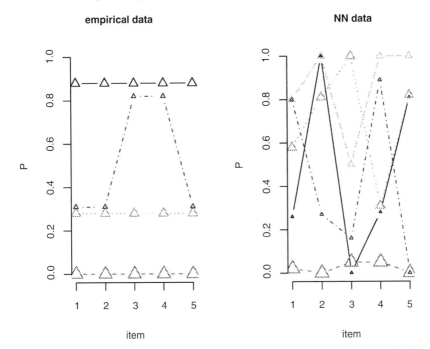

Figure 3.3. Latent class models of children's data and data generated with the PDP model (NN) of McClelland (1989). Sizes of the triangles indicate proportions of the classes. The items are five conflict-balance items. (Adapted from Jansen & van der Maas 1997)

Data set II

The second empirical data set (Data set II) features in Jansen and van der Maas (2002), and consists of the responses of 805 subjects to another test of 25 balance scale items. Subjects' ages ranged from five to nineteen years. Data set II consists of trichotomous responses (left/balance/right). Analyses of individual item types showed that responses to items of one type were homogeneous. It then can be concluded that an item is representative for other items of the type. We present a latent class model of responses to a combination of item types. Only with a combination of item types can all Siegler's rules be detected. We selected the responses to two sd-items, two cw-items and two cb-items. The items that were used to collect data set II were constructed in such a way that the use of the compensation-rule resulted in the incorrect response 'in balance' to cw-items, and in the correct response to the remaining conflict items. The expected response patterns for Siegler's rules and the compensation-rule differed importantly in this set of items (see Table 3.3). We expected a five-class model, with each class representing a rule.

Table 3.3. *Expected latent classes for latent class model of a combination of items.*

			conditional probabilities						
distance			conflict-weight			conflict-balance			
left	balance	right	left	balance	right	left	balance	right	interpretation
0.00	1.00	.00	*1.00*	.00	.00	.00	*0.00*	1.00	Rule I
1.00	.00	.00	*1.00*	.00	.00	.00	*.00*	1.00	Rule II
1.00	.00	.00	*.33*	.33	.33	.33	*.33*	.33	Rule III
1.00	.00	.00	*1.00*	.00	.00	.00	*1.00*	.00	Rule IV
1.00	.00	.00	*.00*	1.00	.00	.00	*1.00*	.00	compensation-rule

Note. The probabilities for the correct response are printed in italics. For the conflict-balance items, the right side has the larger number of weights. Adapted from Jansen and van der Maas (2002).

A seven-class model was selected as this was the first model that showed an adequate fit to the data (G^2 (671) = 174.70, $pb(G^2)$ >0.05) and because this model had a lower value of BIC than models with more classes. Table 3.4 shows the selected model. Table 3.4 only contains the conditional probabilities of one item of each type, to save space, and because the probabilities were quite similar.

Comparison of Tables 3.3 and 3.4 shows that the first five classes in the selected model matched the five expected latent classes. The children in the first additional class ($\pi = 0.02$) responded that the scale would tip to the side with the smallest distance on sd-items. On conflict items, these children also responded that the scale would tip to the side with the smallest distance (or the largest number of weights). These children perhaps thought that the scale always tipped to the side with the smallest distance (SDD-rule). The responses of the children in the second additional class ($\pi = 0.17$) to the sd-items and to the cw-items were similar to those of the children in the fifth class, but the responses to the cb-items differed. Possibly, these children used some mix of Rule III and the compensation-rule.

Conclusion

The results of LCA suggest that children actively employ rules in solving balance scale problems. The value of the application of LCA to the balance scale task has been confirmed by the latent class analyses of balance scale data reported by Boom, Hoijtink, and Kunnen (2001). They demonstrated that even

Table 3.4. *Latent class model of responses to a combination of items.*

		Conditional probabilities									
		distance 4			conflict-weight 4			conflict-balance 4			interpretation
t	$p(t)$	left	balance	right	left	balance	right	left	balance	right	
1	.27	.00	.96	.04	.96	.01	.02	.00	.00	1.00	Rule I
2	.15	.70	.21	.09	.87	.13	.00	.00	.00	1.00	Rule II
3	.09	.98	.02	.00	.44	.23	.34	.66	.07	.27	Rule III
4	.11	*1.00*	.00	.00	.82	.11	.07	.00	*1.00*	.00	Rule IV
5	.18	.97	.01	.02	.03	.95	.02	.10	.90	.00	compensation-rule
6	.02	.17	.17	.67	.92	.08	.00	.00	.08	.92	SDD
7	.17	.93	.07	.00	.24	.66	.10	.04	.39	.57	Rule III/comp

Note. t = latent class, $p(t)$ = proportion of latent class t. The probabilities for the correct response are printed in italics. For each type, item 4 is shown. For the conflict-balance items, the right side has the larger number of weights. Rule III/comp is a combination of Rule III and the compensation-rule. SDD is the Smallest Distance Down Rule. Adapted from Jansen and van der Maas (2002).

LCA of large data sets, with 20 items, is feasible. An additional advantage of the application of LCA is that we were able to detect alternative rules, like the compensation-rule. Contrary to the rule classifications of RAM, the latent classes reflect the structure in the observed data and arise independently from the rules postulated in a theory.

The difficulties of interpreting the LCA models for the PDP data set were striking. Although fitting latent class models was possible, the results were often unstable (i.e. dependent on starting values). Furthermore, the response patterns of the classes did not show consistency within item types, and hardly matched Siegler's rules or any plausible alternative rule. Probably, no rules underlie the response patterns of this connectionist model, in spite of the results that were obtained by applying RAM (McClelland 1989; McClelland and Jenkins 1991). These results are in accordance with the results of Raijmakers, van Koten, and Molenaar (1996). It seems that the RAM is too liberal and may falsely suggest the presence of rules. Strauss and Levin's (1981) criticism that rules are an artifact of the methodology seems correct. However, application of the statistical technique of LCA allows for the falsification of the rule theory. We conclude that it is possible to reveal the rules children use by combining RAM with LCA, even without asking children to clarify their responses.

The restrictions that were applied to items of the same type proved that items of one type are homogeneous. The influence of product difference on rule classification that Ferretti and Butterfield (1986) detected was not observed here. A reason for this may be that we did not increase the product differences between the two sides of the scale as Ferretti and Butterfield did. As claimed elsewhere (Jansen and van der Maas 1997, 327), this indicates that their conclusion is based only on the extreme values of the product differences used in their experiment. As the conditional probabilities associated with the items can be restricted to be equal for each item type, it is possible to analyse the sum scores of each item type with finite mixture analysis. As Turner and Thomas (2002) noted, this technique can deal with smaller samples and a larger number of variables. However, the analysis of cb-items showed that items of a type are not necessarily homogeneous for all rules.

Rules and response times

We have proposed a new and promising method of validation of the rules in van der Maas and Jansen (2003) by using RTs. In this section we discuss the main results of this study. Figure 3.2 and Table 3.1 represent the predictions concerning RTs that can be derived from Siegler's (1981) rule theory. The predictions concerning RTs are tested by fitting regression models to RT data. Next, we propose and test several new predictions.

Table 3.1 shows that the RTs on all item types are predicted to equal w for participants who use Rule I. The RTs for Rule II-users on items with different numbers of weights, i.e. sw- and conflict items, are predicted to equal w, whereas the RTs on items with equal numbers of weights, i.e. sb- and sd-items, are expected to be longer, i.e. $w + d$. The RTs of participants who use Rule III, Rule IV, or the compensation-rule are expected to equal $w + d$ on simple items. On conflict items, the RTs are predicted to equal $w + d + a + g$, $w + d + a + p$, or $w + d + a + c$ for users of Rule III, Rule IV, or the compensation-rule, respectively. Of course, the RTs for all rules also include a constant amount of time for common processes like the motor response. However, the duration of this constant cannot be estimated independently of w as both processes always occur together.

Testing the RT predictions of the basic model

The parameters w, d, a, g and c, derived from Siegler's (1981) basic model, can be used as independent variables in regression analysis in which RT is the dependent variable. To perform this type of regression analysis, we collected the responses (left, balance, right) and the RTs of 147 children (six to fifteen years of age) and forty-four undergraduate psychology students for seventy balance scale items, presented in a computer test. The item set consisted of ten sets of seven items (sb, sw, sd, cbB, cw, cd, cbA). Both cba and cbb items are conflict-balance-items, but cba items can be solved correctly with the compensation-rule whereas cbB items cannot.

Rule assignment was done with RAM and with iterative cluster analysis on the sum scores per item type and not with latent class analysis in view of the large number of items (70). The results of these methods agreed well (Cohen's Kappa of 0.85). The classification that resulted from the cluster analysis was used in the RT analyses.

RT data were analysed per subject and per item, allowing for the incorporation of subject characteristics (like age) and quantitative item characteristics (like product difference). Model A contained parameters w, d, g, c, and p, but not parameter a because of identification problems. Model A also contained parameters that modelled the 'law of practice' ($i_1 e^{-i_2 I}$; where I is the order of the item in the test). The law dictates that the speed of responding increases during administration of a test (see, e.g., Thorndike 1913). In model A, comparing weights (w) was estimated 2.75 s, whereas comparing distances (d) was estimated at -0.22 s. The duration of guessing, performing the production rule, and performing a compensation process were estimated at 2.28 s (g), 2.62 s (p), and 2.39 s (c), respectively. The law of practice was modelled as $1.83e^{-0.07I}$.

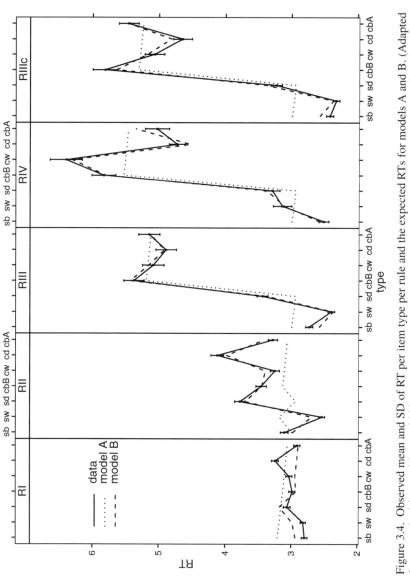

Figure 3.4. Observed mean and SD of RT per item type per rule and the expected RTs for models A and B. (Adapted from van der Maas and Jansen 2003)

Extending the basic model

Model A is extended with additional parameters, resulting in Model B. Different parameters were introduced and estimated for comparing equal and comparing unequal numbers of weights. Furthermore, the basic process of comparing equal weights (estimated at 2.02 s) was slowed with 0.18 s for each extra weight in each pile. Comparing unequal weights took 2.60 s, independent of the size of the difference between the numbers of weights.

From model B, it was concluded that Rule II-users compared distances at any item, whether the numbers of weights were equal or not. Although the response patterns showed that Rule II-users always answered that the scale would tip to the side with the larger number of weights, their RTs showed that they did consider the distance dimension when the numbers of weights differed.

Deciding that the distances were identical was easy when the piles were placed at the pegs next to the fulcrum or at the furthest pegs from the fulcrum. The decision took 0.66 s more when the piles were placed near the centre of each arm. Deciding that the piles of weight were placed at different distances was mediated by the difference between the distance on the left and the distance on the right side. An increase of distance difference of one slowed users of Rule II by 0.34 s.

Users of the complex rules, Rule III, the compensation-rule and Rule IV, were considered to compare weights and to compare distances at each balance scale item. The steps proceeded in the same way as for users of Rule I and Rule II. However, the process of comparing unequal distances turned out to be different for users of complex rules. An increase of distance difference of one *shortened* RT by 0.41 s. Probably, the difference between the distances was more easily noted when the difference was large. Parameter *a* was estimated at 1.29 s.

It was concluded that the RT of Rule III-users was 0.27 s longer when the sum of the difference between the values on the weight dimension and the difference between the values on the distance dimension increased by one. Possibly, these participants could not decide when both dimensions were salient. It seems likely that their decision is based on the careful consideration of the possibilities and does not imply pure guessing as the RTs were relatively long and comparable to those associated with the compensation-rule and Rule IV.

Although the response patterns for the addition-rule and the buggy-rule do not differ, the predictions concerning the RTs associated with the rules do differ. We conclude that participants used a buggy-rule and not an addition-rule because model B demonstrated that RT was affected only by parameters that were related to predictions that followed from the buggy-rule: RT increased by 1.13 s for each required buggy and increased by 0.23 s for each weight in the pile that needed to be shifted.

Model B showed that Rule IV-users consider whether a conflict item contains any symmetries: RT was 0.37 s shorter when the distance at which the weights were placed on one arm was equal to the number of weights on the other arm (see Figure 3.1 for an example). Moreover, RT was lengthened by 0.12 s when the sum of products of weight and distance increased by one, resulting in an increase of product difficulty.

An extra parameter was added to improve the description of the RTs of users of Rule IV. This parameter referred to the hesitation, lasting 0.74 s, to answer that the scale would tip to the side with the larger number of weights. Although the parameter did improve the fit of the model, we do not consider it a very reliable parameter.

The base speed rate of older children was faster than that of younger children. Finally, a positive relation was observed between rule inconsistency (deviance of the observed response pattern from the cluster pattern) and increase of RT.

Model B described the data significantly better than model A, which demonstrated that inclusion of quantitative item characteristics improves the prediction of RTs considerably.

Weight-distance items

The last six items of the balance scale test were so-called weight-distance items. Weight-distance items are items in which the larger number of weights is on the side of the larger distance. All subjects should solve these simple items easily. Users of Rule I and II are expected to take into consideration the weight dimension (w) only, whereas users of higher rules are expected to look at the distance dimension (d) too, and even check whether the larger weight is on the side with the larger distance (a). This results in the provoking prediction that older and more advanced subjects are expected to respond more slowly to these easy items. This prediction was confirmed by the data. Mean RT for Rule I and II was 2.63 s, whereas the mean RT for Rule III, the compensation-rule and Rule IV was 3.96 s. This large difference was significant ($t (52) = -5.02$, $p < .01$).

Conclusions

The analyses of the RTs validated Siegler's rule models to a large extent. Next, it was possible to refine the rule models greatly by using both subject (age and rule inconsistency) and item characteristics (e.g. number of buggies). It was concluded that the compensation-rule is actually a buggy-rule and not an additive rule and that Rule II-users always consider the distance dimension but that they nevertheless neglect it in their response. This result matches Siegler's (1981) observation that many children who demonstrated Rule II in their response patterns did indicate the use of the distance dimension in their explanation afterwards. Further study of this finding is required. Finally, the results showed that inconsistent rule use was associated with increased RT. A complete analysis of these data can be found in van der Maas and Jansen (2003).

Transition from Rule I to Rule II

Having established a clear idea of children's strategies for solving balance scale problems, it is time to study whether the transitions between the strategies proceed either continuously or discontinuously. Although the character of transitions between stages constitutes a central and recurrent issue in developmental psychology, criteria to distinguish the two types of development were lacking (Brainerd 1978). Recently, van der Maas and Molenaar (1992, 1996) proposed to use catastrophe theory to test for discontinuities. Catastrophe theory (Thom 1975) is a general mathematical theory of transitions, which are defined as large sudden jumps as functions of small continuous changes in independent variables. The most popular model of catastrophe theory is the so-called cusp model which has two independent variables. For instance, the freezing and melting of water and ice can be modelled with the cusp model. This transition is controlled by two independent variables, temperature and pressure.

Cusp-like processes are characterized by a number of phenomena, so-called catastrophe flags, among which are the sudden jump, bimodality, inaccessible region, critical slowing down, hysteresis and divergence (Gilmore 1981). The last two are convincing indicators of discontinuity. Hysteresis occurs when the sudden jump position depends on the direction of change in the normal variable. For instance, ice melts at $0°C$ but water freezes (in disturbance free conditions) at $-4°C$. Divergence means that the system is forced to choose between two alternative modes when the splitting variable increases. For instance, at low pressure, water at $-2°C$ can be in an in-between state. When pressure increases to 1 atmosphere, either the solid state or the fluid state is selected and the in-between state becomes unstable. Figure 3.5 depicts the cusp model, where α is the normal variable and β is the splitting variable, and the main catastrophe flags. The proposal of van der Maas and Molenaar (1992) is to use the flags as criteria for detecting developmental transitions.

A cusp model for the Rule I to Rule II transition

Bimodality is a necessary, although not sufficient, indicator of transitions. Bimodality is clearly shown in the distribution of sum scores of sets of distance items. The distribution shows a strong distinction between two modes

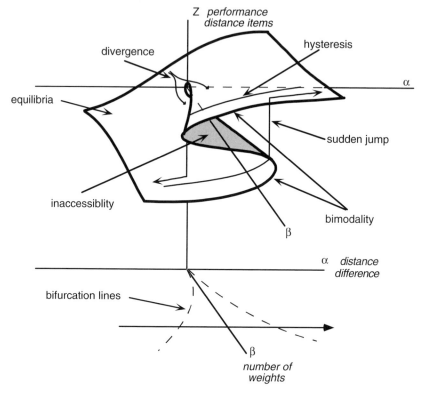

Figure 3.5. The cusp model of the Rule I to Rule II transition. (Adapted from Jansen and van der Maas 2001)

of responses: all incorrect (Rule I) or all correct (Rule II or a more complex rule) (Raijmakers, van Koten, and Molenaar 1996; Jansen and van der Maas 1997, 2001; see also Section 2). This inspired us to think about a cusp model of the Rule I to Rule II transition. A good choice of the dependent variable is the percentage correct (or some transformation of this percentage) on sets of distance items as Rules I and II differ only in the responses to these items. A selection of independent variables, i.e. the normal and the splitting variable, is more difficult. The normal variable gives rise to sudden jumps and hysteresis, the splitting variable to divergence.

According to Siegler and Chen (1998), the main difference between Rules I and II is the ability to encode distance. We emphasized the saliency of the distance dimension to increase the awareness of the distance dimension of Rule I-users. Increase of awareness may result in encoding the dimension and, eventually, in a switch to using Rule II. Saliency was emphasized by increasing the distance difference between the two sides of the scale in distance items. Hence, we chose the difference in distance between the weights on the left and the weights on the right side of the scale as the normal variable.

We chose the number of weights used in a distance item as the splitting variable. This choice is based on the premise that more weights increase the confidence of both Rule I- and Rule II-users. Since Rule I-users only take the number of weights into account, a more salient weight dimension should increase the probability that they answer according to this rule. On the other hand, increase of weights increases the product difference between left and right. Rule II-users may have more confidence in their answer because the momentum for the side with the larger distance increases. This polarization for items with equal distance differences and different amounts of weights is a divergence effect (see Figure 3.5).

With the choice of these two variables, the cusp model is complete, as depicted in Figure 3.5. The following main predictions can be derived from this model:

(1) Sudden jump: by increasing the distance difference, some (transitional) Rule I-users spontaneously jump to Rule II.
(2) Bimodality/inaccessibility: scores on a set of distance items are bimodally distributed, the intermediate scores have low probability.
(3) Divergence: When the number of weights increases, the distribution of the observed scores becomes increasingly bimodal.
(4) Hysteresis: the distance difference at which Rule I-users jump to Rule II when the distance difference is increased is larger than the distance difference at which Rule II-users switch to Rule I, when the distance difference is decreased.
(5) Critical slowing down: subjects are easily perturbed in the area where the transition is likely to occur (between the bifurcation lines; see Figure 3.5). A possible effect is an increase in RTs (van der Maas, Raijmakers, Hartelman, and Molenaar 1998).

Divergence and hysteresis

The main difference between catastrophe theory and other models for developmental transitions (Brainerd 1979; Eckstein 2000; Thomas and Lohaus 1993; van Geert 1998; Wilson 1989) is that catastrophe theory explains instead of assumes abruptness. In addition, the criteria divergence and hysteresis are unique to catastrophe theory. Hence, in our studies we have focused on these two catastrophe flags.

We used six distance items with a distance difference of two to test for divergence. Three of these items have five weights and three items have a single weight. The bimodality on the first three items should be more pronounced.

We used special series of items to test for hysteresis. In these series, we started with a distance item with a distance difference of one. Distance difference increased to five (the scale in the experiment had six pegs) in the next four items, and decreased again, in the next four items, to one. In a control series, which should not lead to jumps and hysteresis, the greyness of the weights was increased and decreased. The control and hysteresis series were counterbalanced. In a second experiment we also included a series in which distance difference was first decreased and then increased.

Given these hysteresis series of nine items, six possible types of patterns can occur, of which five are predicted by the cusp model. The first two patterns contain either correct responses only (Rule II) or incorrect responses only (Rule I). The 'delay' pattern refers to the hysteresis pattern: the jump to Rule II takes place at higher distance difference than the jump back to Rule I. In the 'enhanced contrast' pattern the jump to Rule II takes place earlier than the jump back from Rule II to Rule I. This pattern should not occur according to the cusp model. In the 'Maxwell' pattern, both jumps take place at the same distance difference. The 'sudden jump' pattern implies that subjects switch from Rule I to Rule II but never switch back, which can be interpreted as a strong delay pattern. Finally, residual irregular patterns may occur.

Experiments

In our first experimental study, we administered a paper-and-pencil test to 314 children (between six and ten years old). The test included practice items, a pre- and a post-test to determine the rule used, and the hysteresis, divergence and control series. The pretest analysis showed that about 50 per cent of the children responded according to Rule I, 40 per cent responded according to Rule II and about 10 per cent responded inconsistently. Most of the children who used Rule I and Rule II were stable rule-users and were not expected to be sensitive to our manipulations. This was the reason to test a large group of children.

The divergence manipulation proved to be unsuccessful. Both the distribution of scores for the items with one weight and the distribution of scores for the items with five weights were strongly bimodal. The distributions were very similar ($\chi^2(3, N = 314) = 1.97, p = 0.58$).

The hysteresis manipulation was more successful. We classified response patterns with both the RAM and LCA. For the later method, we formulated a confirmatory latent class model that included classes that corresponded to the five expected patterns (Rule I, Rule II, delay, Maxwell, sudden jump) and a residual group. Classes that contained response patterns associated with hysteresis (delay, Maxwell, sudden jump) were necessary to obtain a fitting model, whereas classes that contained response patterns associated with enhanced

Table 3.5. *Proportions of hysteresis patterns on hysteresis test and control test.*

	LCA		RAM	
	Hysteresis test	Control test	Hysteresis test	Control test
Rule I	.341	.395	.315	.357
Rule II	.350	.427	.325	.401
Delay	.029	.003	.022	.000
Maxwell	.035	.000	.035	.000
Jump upward	.096	.038	.083	.029
Residual	.092	.073	.162	.150
Missing values	.057	.064	.057	.064

$N = 314$. Adapted from Jansen and van der Maas (2001).

contrast worsened the model significantly. Table 3.5 shows the proportions of hysteresis patterns for the hysteresis and the control test, for the analysis with both RAM and LCA.

As expected, most subjects stuck to their rule. About 15 per cent of the subjects (control test: 4 per cent) showed delay, Maxwell, or sudden jump patterns. In a second experiment, we found similar results. At series in which distance difference first decreased (from 5 to 1) and then increased, the percentage of hysteresis patterns was a little lower but still statistically significant.

Model evaluation

The present results indicate that the transition from Rule I to Rule II shows important characteristics of a genuine phase transition. The evidence for bimodality and inaccessibility is convincing as the score distributions of sets of distance items are strongly bimodal. Although we did not find evidence for divergence, we do not think that the failure of the divergence test falsifies the whole idea of a cusp-like process. Either our choice of the control variable (number of weights) or our operationalization of this variable was not adequate. Moreover, the hypothesis of discontinuity is confirmed by the results supporting the other flags, especially hysteresis. We showed, in various ways, that the small number of subjects showing hysteresis in their responses could not be attributed to chance. In addition, in the analysis of the RTs (van der Maas and Jansen 2003; see Section 3), we found evidence for an increase in RTs when responses were inconsistent. This effect is particularly strong for Rule I-users. This phenomenon may be interpreted as an instance of another important catastrophe flag, i.e. 'critical slowing down'.

A developmental model for problem-solving behaviour on the balance scale task

Consistency of responding during the administration of a balance scale test was analysed to study whether children who use Rule II, Rule III, Rule IV, and the compensation-rule do so as consistently as children who use Rule I. For this analysis, we used empirical data set II (Section 2). For this data set, participants responded to five blocks of items. Responses to the second and third block of the test were analysed separately from the responses to the last two blocks of the test, with LCA. The results of the first two blocks were similar to those of the last two blocks, which were reported in Section 2. LCA of the data demonstrated evidence for the use of Rule I, Rule II, Rule III, Rule IV, the compensation-rule, a combination of Rule III and the compensation-rule, and the SDD-rule.

Children were assigned to the most probable latent class on both parts of the test by means of posterior probabilities. The results of the assignments are represented in Table 3.6. Use of latent Markov models is preferred to model rule consistency, but, as Turner and Thomas (2002) noted, using this method causes huge computational problems because of the large number of parameters.

The application of Rule I was found to be stable as almost 0.86 of the children who used this rule on the first part of the test continued to use it on the later part. This supports our claim that the transition from Rule I to Rule II happens discontinuously. By contrast, only 0.55 of the children who used Rule II on the first part continued to use this rule on the later part of the test. Many children switched to using either Rule III (0.20) or the mix of the compensation-rule and Rule III (0.14). The use of the compensation-rule, Rule III, and the combination of Rule III and the compensation-rule was also quite inconsistent. Children who were at this level of performance seemed to *muddle through* the rules in their repertory: sometimes they compared sums, sometimes they guessed, etc. However, there was a considerable proportion of children (0.62) who consistently applied the compensation-rule. Another interesting finding was that children who used Rule III, or the mix of the compensation-rule and Rule III, on the first part of the test switched to using Rule II on the second part of the test. The high proportion (0.91) of children who used Rule IV on both parts of the test suggested that, once children have learned the correct rule, they always apply it. No conclusions are drawn on the consistency of the use of the SDD-rule as only a few children were identified as users of this rule.

In summary, both the use of Rule I and Rule IV was quite consistent, but there seemed to be much switching between Rule II, Rule III, the compensation-rule, and the combination of Rule III and the compensation-rule. The progress of

Table 3.6. *Turnover table for rule use on first and last part of the test.*

		Last part						
		Rule I	Rule II	Rule III	compensation	Rule III/comp	Rule IV	SDD
	Rule I	.855	.120	.013	.004	.004	.000	.004
	Rule II	.016	.549	.197	.025	.139	.049	.025
	Rule III	.063	.188	.458	.042	.125	.104	.021
First part	compensation	.000	.005	.081	.621	.207	.086	.000
	Rule III/comp	.030	.212	.081	.192	.394	.091	.000
	Rule IV	.000	.030	.000	.015	.045	.910	.000
	SDD	.000	.091	.091	.182	.000	.000	.636

Note. Rule III/comp is a combination of Rule III and the compensation-rule. Adapted from Jansen and van der Maas (2002).

children who start by using Rule II to using Rule III or the compensation-rule can be explained by spontaneous learning. Children who use Rule II already know that the distance dimension can be important. Their RTs indicate that they consider it for any item (see Section 3), but their responses indicate that they only incorporate it in their strategy when the weights are equal. Merely presenting these children with balance scale items may sensitize them to the distance dimension and may convince them of the importance of the distance dimension. However, they do not know how to combine the two dimensions yet. This is consistent with the interpretation of Rule III. A different mechanism from learning must be responsible for regressing from Rule III or the compensation-rule to Rule II. Finally, many children switched between Rule III, the combination of Rule III and the compensation-rule, and the compensation-rule. This finding supports the hypothesis that children who use Rule III sample from an ensemble of strategies and that switching between these strategies is inherent to Rule III.

Switching between strategies seems to contrast with a so-called staircase model that underlies Siegler's hierarchy of rules. In a staircase model of development, children apply a rule for a long period and then suddenly shift to a next rule that is associated with a more advanced level of ability. The staircase model implies consistent rule use.

Siegler (1996) proposed the overlapping waves model to explain more gradual transitions between phases in development. In an overlapping waves model, each mode of behaviour (or developmental phase) is represented by a wave. As waves are overlapping, the change from one mode of behaviour to the next can be gradual and children may even display several modes of behaviour concurrently. The extent of overlapping can vary. With development, children's preference for a mode of behaviour develops.

We contend that a restricted form of the overlapping waves model (Siegler, 1996) can describe the development of problem solving on the balance scale task. The model contains greatly overlapping waves as well as hardly overlapping waves (similar to the stairs in a staircase model). This restricted overlapping waves model is depicted in Figure 3.6, together with a staircase model and an overlapping waves model. All models are idealizations and describe the development of a given individual. The ages on the x-axis are derived from a multigroup LCA of data set II, with age groups featuring as group indicator. The results of this multigroup LCA clearly demonstrated the rule hierarchy that Siegler (1976, 1981) proposed. Rule I, which was mainly used by children between five and seven years old, was succeeded by Rule II, which was observed with children from eight years. Use of Rule II decreased among older children. Rule III was used by children of almost all ages, but was most frequent among children of ten years old. The onset of Rule IV was quite sudden and was first observed with children of fourteen years old. The compensation-rule was one of the most frequently used rules in children from eleven years old. The mix of the compensation-rule and Rule III was noted among children between nine and sixteen years old. Hence, the two alternative rules followed Rule III in the rule hierarchy. Finally, the SDD-rule was used by only a few children, of various ages. It should be noted that the analysis showed that children in different age groups may demonstrate similar behaviour and that children of the same age may demonstrate different rules. Hence, the values on the x-axis were chosen somewhat arbitrarily.

Figure 3.6 represents our hypothesis that Rule I and Rule II are non-overlapping waves and that the development from Rule I to Rule II is mainly discontinuous. Rule II and Rule III are depicted as overlapping waves. As Rule II-users improve their perception of the distance dimension, they may increasingly integrate it in their strategies. Their behaviour gradually changes to the use of Rule III because they want to combine the two dimensions but do not know how. We propose that Rule III should be considered as an ensemble of strategies that each can be described as waves. Each strategy includes a combination of the distance and the weight dimension, except multiplication. The rules are used concurrently, but the preference for a certain rule changes with age. It is not clear why and how this preference changes. The transition to using Rule IV is supposed to be sudden. We contend that children shift to a higher level of formal operations (Inhelder and Piaget 1958), or that they learn the torque-rule through instruction at school, which results in its sudden application. This rationale of the restricted overlapping waves model was based on the

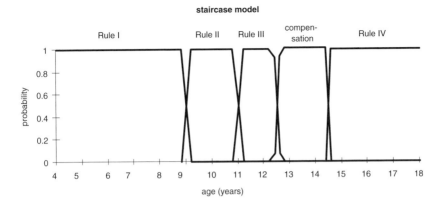

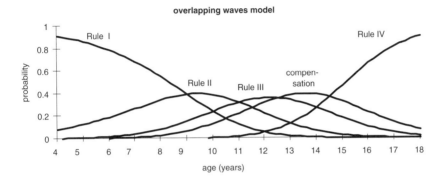

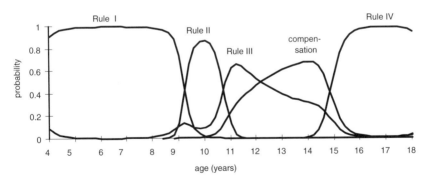

Figure 3.6. Staircase model, overlapping waves model, and restricted over-lapping waves model for development of reasoning on the balance scale task. The x-axis represents age in years. The y-axis represents the probability of the use of a rule. (Adapted from Jansen and van der Maas 2002)

analyses of cross-sectional data. Of course, a longitudinal study is necessary to test the hypotheses that follow from this model.

Computational model of proportional reasoning

Several computational models have been developed to capture the developmental phenomena associated with the balance scale task. These models, which originate in different computational traditions, attempt to explain phenomena of development in proportional reasoning. So far, none of these models has been able to explain all empirical data.

Recently, van Rijn et al. (2003) proposed a computational model that is implemented in ACT-R (Anderson and Lebiere 1998). This model can be viewed as an implementation of the restricted overlapping waves model. The validity of the model and alternative computational models was judged with regard to four empirical phenomena: (1) Stable phases and transitions: the behaviour of the model should obey the Rules and the model must be able to explain the transitions between Rules. (2) Rules: a complete model should include all known empirical rules and explain the order in which they occur. (3) Transition phenomena: the sudden jump and hysteresis patterns, as demonstrated in the hysteresis experiments, should be explained. From a computational point of view it would be difficult to simulate these patterns, without using feedback about the correct response, as all existing computational models work because of feedback. (4) Torque difference effects: a computational model should explain the within item type homogeneity for moderate torque differences (Jansen and van der Maas 1997) and within type heterogeneity for extreme torque differences (Ferretti and Butterfield 1986). Table 3.7 summarizes the extent to which each existing computation model satisfies these criteria.

ACT-R

ACT-R is a hybrid cognitive 'architecture'. It is a theory for simulating and understanding human cognition (Anderson and Lebiere 1998) in which the use of symbolic knowledge is mediated with quantitative parameters. It uses declarative memory with chunks that represent descriptive knowledge ('more weights left') and procedural memory containing production rules in the form of IF-THEN rules ('more weights left, then left side down'). The presence of goals (like 'solve the balance scale problem') constrains the activity of the memory. The activity of each chunk of production rules is determined by its past use and success, costs and random noise.

Development is possible since ACT-R models are able to expand their knowledge both by external input (perception) and internal modifications (declarative

Table 3.7. *Overview of empirical criteria per model.*

	Model Type				
	Production Rules		Decision Trees	Neural Networks	
Empirical criteria	KS'78	SL'87	SL'96	McC'95	S'95
EC1: Rule-like behaviour	–	√	√	–	–
EC2: Rule sets	√	+	+	–	+
EC3: Transition patterns without feedback	–	–	–	–	–
EC4: Torque difference effect	–	–	+	√	√

Note. √: Criterion fully satisfied, +: Criterion partly satisfied, –: Criterion not satisfied. KS'78: Klahr and Siegler (1978), SL'87: Sage and Langley (1983), SL'96: Schmidt and Ling (1996), McC'95: McClelland (1995), S'95: Shultz et al. (1995). Adapted from van Rijn et al. (2003).

chunks from production rules). Van Rijn et al. (2003) also apply a new ACT-R method, called production composition (Taatgen and Anderson 2002). Production composition creates new rules by joining production rules that occur in succession. This composition mechanism also applies to learning new behaviour from declarative descriptions of problem-solving actions. These declarative actions can be matched and executed by 'interpretative production rules'. Composed production rules have generally lower costs than the parent rules together and therefore the new production rules are favoured.

Set-up of model

In the construction of the model, van Rijn et al. (2003) distinguish three factors. The first factor concerns how the development proceeds, the second and third factors relate the order and timing of developmental events. Figure 3.7 displays the role of these factors in the set-up of the model.

The first factor underlying the behaviour of the model concerns mechanisms in ACT-R, explained above, and task-general knowledge. This task-general knowledge is implemented as declarative representations of actions associated with the general strategy 'answer a balance scale problem by searching for differences between the left and right side of the scale'.

The second factor relates to task-specific concepts. It specifies when task properties like weight, distance, addition and multiplication become available.

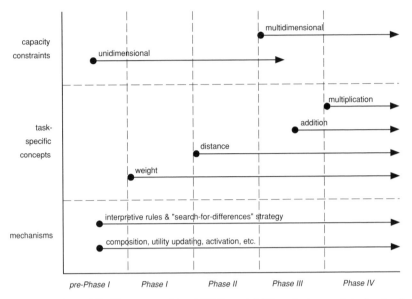

Figure 3.7. The set-up of the ACT-R model. Three factors explain the development of proportional reasoning: mechanisms, task-specific concepts and capacity constraints. (Adapted from van Rijn et al. 2003)

Two assumptions are made about these properties: weight precedes distance and multiplication precedes addition.

The third factor is capacity. As in most developmental theories (for instance the Neo-Piagetian theories), van Rijn et al. (2003) assume that a limited capacity initially constrains the generality of the 'search for difference' strategy. Initially only one difference can be detected, later in development more than one difference can be searched for.

Simulation

Exact description of the simulation of the model can be found in van Rijn et al. (2003). Roughly, the following development takes place. Initially, neither the weight nor the distance property is encoded because the associated activation levels are below threshold. Therefore, the model answers by guessing. After each guess, feedback is given about the correctness of the given answer. As the proportion of correct answers based on guessing is low, the production rules representing this strategy have a low utility. Therefore, as soon as the weight property becomes available, the model will start to incorporate this concept in the decision process, yielding Rule I behaviour. As this increases the proportion of correct answers, the production rules associated with Rule I are preferred over the pre-Rule I production rules. Since the proportion of successful answers is still relatively low, distance is incorporated shortly after it becomes available to the model. However, as the available capacity is insufficient to incorporate both properties in the decision process at the same time, the model switches its attention to distance, discarding the weight information. As determining the answers based solely on weights is less successful when the weights are equal than when the weights are unequal, the shift from weights to distances only occurs when the weights are equal. When the capacity has increased sufficiently to make it possible to use a strategy that incorporates both weights and distances, the model progresses to Rule III behaviour. In this phase, the weights and distances are examined regardless of whether the number of weights is equal or not. However, as knowledge about combining the weights and distances is as yet unavailable, the model can only guess the answer if the weights and distances are both unequal. Only when the concept of addition or multiplication becomes available is the model able to progress to the compensation-rule, and finally to Rule IV.

The model can also be tested on series of items used in the hysteresis experiment (see Section 4). No feedback is given in this simulation. The increased perceptual saliency of the distance cue allows the model to switch from Rule I to Rule II. Under certain activation conditions, hysteresis occurs. Also torque difference effects can be simulated in this way.

Evaluation of the model

This ACT-R model is based on the evaluation of success of applied knowledge, combined with a mechanism to construct new knowledge by searching for differences between the left- and right-hand sides of presented balance scale problems. This model accounts for the main empirical phenomena as well as for the recently reported empirical phenomena, such as learning without feedback and hysteresis.

The successful reproduction of the empirical phenomena by our model was partly realized with features that were also used in previous computational models. Like the symbolic models, behaviour in the ACT-R model is based on the application of production rules, which results in rule-like behaviour. As in the previous models, new production rules are learned by extending the already present knowledge. However, instead of containing a few complex production rules, our model consists of a larger number of smaller production rules. Each of these production rules executes only a small part of the complete answering process. Therefore, newly constructed production rules can simply replace older production rules instead of requiring a complex mechanism to modify existing production rules. As in the neural net models of balance scale behaviour, quantitative information plays an important role in the ACT-R model (i.e., utility and activation). The dynamics of these quantitative variables are important for the description of the empirical phenomena.

The combination of features from ACT-R and the symbolic and neural net type of models provides the basis for a number of achievements specific for this model: (1) The model produces the relatively abrupt transitions, which are problematic in the non-symbolic models. (2) It explains transitions without feedback and the related transition patterns, which cannot be explained from the learning methods used in the previous models. (3) The model demonstrates that, given a non-biased training set, Rule IV will not easily be learned because of the high success-rate of the Addition Rule. (4) The presented model is able to explain both phenomena related to long-term development and phenomena that are only observable during short time-spans. (5) The model makes explicit that the notion of 'search for differences' combined with a gradual increase in capacity and knowledge is sufficient to explain development on the balance scale task.

Discussion

This chapter summarizes and integrates a number of recent studies on development of proportional reasoning as assessed with the balance scale task. We applied latent structure models for rule assessment, RT analysis to further analyse the rules, catastrophe theory to investigate the transition from Rule I to Rule II, and finally ACT-R modelling to test our ideas about how development proceeds on this type of task by simulation. Due to space limitations, we provided only a brief description of the method and results. Yet, we hope that the readers have seen enough to grasp the potential of these methods and importance of the outcomes.

First, we showed that the criticism on the concept of rules, as well as the criticism on the RAM, can be overcome by the application of LCA. In a latent class model, rules are interpreted as categorical values of a latent variable. Since a priori expectations are not necessary, new rules can be detected, with the SDD-rule as a nice example. Next, the set of rules and each rule separately can be subjected to statistical testing. This takes away the arbitrariness of traditional rule assessment methods. Using LCA, we were able to falsify the claim that a specific connectionist model shows rule-like behaviour, similar to the behaviour of children. We also evidenced an important assumption underlying Siegler's rules, namely that behaviour is homogeneous within item types. Finally, we reached a number of conclusions about the actual rules used by children in solving balance scale problems.

Second, we further validated the rules with an analysis of RTs. To our own surprise it was possible to use these data to extend the rule theory with predictions relating to all kinds of quantitative characteristics of balance scale items. For instance, it was possible to show that the compensation-rule is in fact a so-called buggy-rule and not an addition-rule. We also found some unexpected results. The most important was that users of Rule II seem to invest time in perceiving the distance cue also when the number of weights on the left side differs from the number of weights on the right side. This unexpected phenomenon indicated that Rule II is very similar to Rule III. The difference is that users of Rule III guess when the two cues conflict, whereas users of Rule II apparently decide to ignore the distance cue in the choice of their response.

Third, we reported our study of the Rule I to Rule II transition. We developed a cusp model for this transition, derived unique predictions of this model and tested them in two studies. We found strong evidence for the presence of the catastrophe flags bimodality and inaccessibility and some evidence for hysteresis but we failed to find evidence for divergence. In the reaction time study, we found an indication of critical slowing down, another catastrophe flag. Although these findings require further study, it seems that this is the first time real evidence for a genuine phase transition in cognitive development is shown.

Fourth, we integrated these findings into a new general model of development of reasoning on the balance scale task. This model is a restricted version of Siegler's (1996) overlapping waves model in which some transitions are rather sudden and others are more gradual. By analysing transition matrices between latent class models of different parts of a balance scale test and by analysing the relation to age, we were able to specify this overlapping waves model quite precisely, as shown in Figure 3.6.

Finally, we formulated a computational model of balance scale learning. One spin-off of such an attempt is that one is forced to be very explicit about the mechanisms, constraints and assumptions underlying the model. Our present model consists of ACT-R mechanisms, general knowledge, assumptions about task-specific properties and the role of memory capacity constraints. We were able to explain the main empirical phenomena with this model. We think that the restricted overlapping waves model and the ACT-R model at least partly answer the 'why' and 'how' questions posed in the introduction. The LCA and RT analyses partly answer the 'what' question. Cognitive development in this and probably many other domains can be characterized as a progression through a series of increasingly complex and accurate task-specific rules or strategies.

This view of cognitive development is clearly consistent with other approaches to the study of development. The originality of our work lies more in the use of new advanced formal methods (statistical, mathematical and computational) than in the basic theory. Yet a few additional theoretical remarks should be made.

In the dynamical (e.g. Thelen and Smith 1994) and in the connectionist (Bates and Elman 1993; McClelland 1995) accounts, the concepts of rules and symbols are often explicitly rejected. We use dynamical concepts (catastrophe theory concerns non-linear dynamical systems) and connectionist ideas (the sub-symbolic level in ACT-R), yet we adopt the traditional view of rules in explaining higher mental processes (see also van der Maas 1995). We think the results of the latent class analyses and the response time analyses support our point of view.

Our approach is generally consistent with the Piagetian and neo-Piagetian theories (e.g. Demetriou, Christou, Spanoudis and Platsidou 2002) in that it tries to explain constructive development. A number of ideas, like the importance of cognitive capacity, perceptual cues (field dependency) and processing speed of mental procedures are adopted from these approaches. In the ACT-R model, for instance, one important factor is the continuous increase in cognitive capacity or memory span. Finally, we mention that it might be possible to interpret certain ACT-R mechanisms used here as implementation of Karmiloff-Smith's concept of representational redescription (Taatgen, van Rijn and Zondervan 2003).

Of course, many new questions arise and some are still unresolved. There are at least three major steps required to test our ideas. The first is to acquire individual data over time by using a microgenetic or longitudinal design. The restricted overlapping waves model is drawn from cross-sectional data and data from the hysteresis experiment. A valid test clearly requires longitudinal data. Second, it would be wise to validate our results with other proportional reasoning tasks, like the shadow task (Siegler 1981). Third, the present ACT-R model was not tested on the RT data. ACT-R models are known for their ability to predict RTs. The present model must be able to mimic our results to a large extent. We see this test as important validation since the model was not constructed for this type of data simulation.

REFERENCES

Anderson, J. R. and Lebiere, C. (1998). *The atomic components of thought.* Mahwah, NJ: Lawrence Erlbaum Associates, Inc.

Bates, E. A. and Elman, J. L. (1993). Connectionism and the study of change. In Mark H. Johnson (ed.) *Brain development and cognition.* Oxford: Blackwell.

Bijstra, J., van Geert, P. and Jackson, S. (1989). Conservation and the appearance–reality distinction: what do children really know and what do they answer? *British Journal of Developmental Psychology, 7*, 43–53.

Boden, M. A. (1994). *Piaget.* London: Fontana Press.

Boom, J., Hoijtink, H. and Kunnen, S. (2001). Rules in the balance: classes strategies, or rules for the balance scale task. *Cognitive Development, 16*, 717–35.

Braine, M. D. S. and Shanks, B. L. (1965). The development of conservation of size. *Journal of Verbal Learning and Verbal Behavior, 4*, 227–42.

Brainerd, C. J. (1973). Judgements and explanations as criteria for the presence of cognitive structures. *Psychological Bulletin, 79,* 172–9.

(1978). The stage question in cognitive-developmental theory. *The Behavioral and Brain Sciences, 2,* 173–213.

(1979). Markovian interpretations of conservation learning. *Psychological Review, 86,* 181–213.

Chletsos, P. N., De Lisi, R., Turner, G. and McGillicuddy-De Lisi, A. V. (1989). Cognitive assessment of proportional reasoning strategies. *Journal of Research and Development in Education, 23,* 18–27.

Clogg, C. C. (1995). Latent class models. In G. Arminger, C. C. Clogg and M. E. Sobel (eds.) *Handbook of statistical modeling for the social and behavioral sciences.* New York: Plenum Press.

Collins, L. M. and Wugalter, S. E. (1992). Latent class models for stage-sequential dynamic latent variables. *Multivariate Behavioral Research, 27,* 131–57.

Demetriou, A., Christou, C., Spanoudis, G. and Platsidou, M. (2002). The development of mental processing: efficiency, working memory, and thinking. *Monographs of the Society for Research in Child Development, 67*(1).

Donaldson, M. (1978). *Children's minds.* London: Fontana.

Eckstein, S. G. (2000). Growth of cognitive abilities: dynamic models and scaling. *Developmental Review, 20,* 1–28.

Elbers, E. (1989). Het conservatie-experiment en de verwachting van het kind over de interaktie met de proefleider. *Tijdschrift voor Ontwikkelings Psychologie, 16,* 42–8.

Ferretti, R. P. and Butterfield, E. C. (1986). Are children's rule-assessment classifications invariant across instances of problem types? *Child Development, 57,* 1419–28.

(1989). Intelligence as a correlate of children's problem solving. *American Journal on Mental Retardation, 93* (4), 424–33.

(1992). Intelligence-related differences in the learning, maintenance, and transfer of problem-solving strategies. *Intelligence, 16*(2), 207–23.

Ferretti, R. P., Butterfield, E. C., Cah, A. and Kerkman, D. (1985). The classification of children's knowledge: development on the balance-scale and inclined-plane tasks. *Journal of Experimental Child Psychology, 39*(1), 131–60.

Gilmore, R. (1981). *Catastrophe theory for scientists and engineers.* New York: Wiley.

Gruen, G. E. (1966). Note on conservation: methodological and definitional considerations. *Child Development, 37,* 977–83.

Halford, G. S., Andrews, G., Dalton, C., Boag, C. and Zielinski, T. (2002). Young children's performance on the balance scale: the influence of relational complexity. *Journal of Experimental Child Psychology, 81,* 417–45.

Heinen, T. (1996). *Latent class and discrete latent trait models: similarities and differences.* Thousand Oaks, CA: Sage Publications.

Inhelder, B. and Piaget, J. (1958). *The growth of logical thinking from childhood to adolescence.* New York: Basic Books.

Inhelder, B., Bovet, M., Sinclair, H. and Smock, C. D. (1966). On cognitive development. *American Psychologist, 21,* 160–4.

Jansen, B. R. J. and van der Maas, H. L. J. (1997). Statistical test of the rule assessment methodology by latent class analysis. *Developmental Review, 17,* 321–57.

(2001). Evidence for the phase transition from Rule I to Rule II on the balance scale task. *Developmental Review, 21*, 450–94.

(2002). Development of children's rule use on the balance scale task. *Journal of Experimental Child Psychology, 81*(4), 383–416.

Klahr, D. and Siegler, R. (1978). The representation of children's knowledge. In H. Reese and L. Lipsitt (eds.) *Advances in child development and behavior* (pp. 61–116). New York: Academic Press.

Kliman, M. (1987). Children's learning about the balance scale. *Instructional Science, 15*, 307–40.

Langeheine, R., Pannekoek, J. and van de Pol, F. (1995). *Bootstrapping goodness-of-fit measures in categorical data analysis.* CBS, Statistics Netherlands.

Marini, Z. and Case, R. (1994). The development of abstract reasoning about the physical and social world. *Child Development, 65*, 147–59.

McClelland, J. L. (1989). Parallel distributed processing: implications for cognition and development. In M. G. M. Morris (ed.) *Parallel distributed processing, implications for psychology and neurobiology* (pp. 8–45). Oxford: Clarendon Press.

(1995). A connectionist perspective on knowledge and development. In T. J. Simon and G. S. Halford (eds.) *Developing cognitive competence: new approaches to process modeling* (pp. 157–204). Lawrence Erlbaum Associates.

McClelland, J. L. and Jenkins, E. (1991). Nature, nurture, and connections: implications of connectionist models for cognitive development. In K. van Lehn (ed.) *Architectures for intelligence: the twenty-second Carnegie Mellon Symposium on cognition* (pp. 41–73). Pittsburgh, PA: Lawrence Erlbaum Associates.

McFadden, G. T., Dufresne, A. and Kobasigawa, A. (1987). Young children's knowledge of balance scale problems. *Journal of Genetic Psychology, 148*, 79–94.

McGarrigle, J. and Donaldson, M. (1975). Conservation accidents. *Cognition, International Journal of Cognitive Psychology, 3*, 341–9.

Moore, C. and Frye, D. (1986). Context, conservation and the meanings of more. *British Journal of Developmental Psychology, 4*, 169–78.

Normandeau, S., Larivée, S., Roulin, J. L. and Longeot, F. (1989). The balance-scale dilemma: either the subject or the experimenter muddles through. *Journal of Genetic Psychology, 150*, 237–50.

Pauen, S. and Wilkening, F. (1997). Children's analogical reasoning about natural phenomena. *Journal of Experimental Child Psychology, 67* (1), 90–113.

Phelps, E. and Damon, W. (1989). Problem solving with equals: peer collaboration as a context for learning mathematics and spatial contexts. *Journal of Educational Psychology, 81* (4), 639–46.

Raijmakers, M. E. J., Van Koten, S. and Molenaar, P. C. M. (1996). On the validity of simulating stagewise development by means of PDP networks: application of catastrophe analysis and an experimental test of rule-like network performance. *Cognitive Science, 20*(1), 101–36.

Reese, H. W. (1989). Rules and rule-governance: cognitive and behavioristic views. In S. C. Hayes (ed.) *Rule governed behavior: cognition, contingencies, and instructional control* (pp. 3–84). New York: Plenum Press.

Richards, D. D. and Siegler, R. S. (1981). Very young children's acquisition of systematic problem-solving strategies. *Child Development, 52*, 1318–21.

Rindskopf, D. (1987). Using latent class analysis to test developmental models. *Developmental Review, 7*, 66–85.

Rose, S. A. and Blank, M. (1974). The potency of context in children's cognition: an illustration through conservation. *Child Development, 45*, 499–502.

Roth, W. M. (1991). The development of reasoning on the balance beam. *Journal of Research in Science Teaching, 28*, 631–45.

Sage, S. and Langley, P. (1983). Modeling cognitive development on the balance scale task. In A. Bundy (ed.) *Proceedings of the eighth international joint conference on artificial intelligence* (vol. 1, pp. 94–6). Karlsruhe, Germany.

Schiff, W. (1983). Conservation of length redux: a perceptual–linguistic phenomenon. *Child Development, 54*, 1497–1506.

Schmidt, W. C. and Ling, C. X. (1996). A decision-tree model of balance scale development. *Machine Learning, 24*, 203–30.

Shultz, T. R., Schmidt, W. C., Buckingham, D. and Mareschal, D. (1995). Modeling cognitive development with a generative connectionist algorithm. In T. J. Simon and G. S. Halford (eds.) *Developing cognitive competence: new approaches to process modeling* (pp. 205–61). Hillsdale, NJ: Lawrence Erlbaum Associates.

Siegal, M. (1991). *Knowing children: experiments in conversation and cognition. essays in developmental psychology.* Hove, UK: Lawrence Erlbaum Associates.

Siegler, R. S. (1976). Three aspects of cognitive development. *Cognitive Psychology, 8*, 481–520.

  (1981). Developmental sequences within and between concepts. *Monographs of the Society for Research in Child Development, 46*(2), 1–74. (With commentary and reply from Sidney Strauss and Iris Levin.)

  (1996). *Emerging minds: the process of change in children's thinking.* New York: Oxford University Press.

Siegler, R. S. and Chen, Z. (1998). Developmental differences in rule learning: a microgenetic analysis. *Cognitive Psychology, 36*(3), 273–310.

Smedslund, J. (1963). Development of concrete transitivity of length in children. *Child Development, 34*, 389–405.

  (1969). Psychological diagnostics. *Psychological Bulletin, 71*, 234–48.

Smith, L. (1992). Judgements and justifications: criteria for the attribution of children's knowledge in Piagetian research. *British Journal of Developmental Psychology, 10*, 1–23.

  (1993). *Necessary knowledge: Piagetian perspectives on constructivism*, Essays in Developmental Psychology Series. Hove, UK: Lawrence Erlbaum Associates.

Strauss, S. and Levin, I. (1981). Commentary on Siegler's 'Developmental sequences within and between concepts'. *Monographs of the Society for Research in Child Development, 46* (2, serial no. 189), 75–81.

Surber, C. F. and Gzesh, S. M. (1984). Reversible operations in the balance scale task. *Journal of Experimental Child Psychology, 38*, 254–74.

Taatgen, N. A. and Anderson, J. R. (2002). Why do children learn to say 'broke'? A model of learning the past tense without feedback. *Cognition 86* (2), 123–55.

Taatgen, N. A., van Rijn, H. and Zondervan, K. (2003). Explaining developmental transitions through constrained generalization. In preparation.

Thelen, E. and Smith, L. B. (1994). *A dynamic systems approach to the development of cognition and action.* Cambridge, MA: MIT Press.

Thom, R. (1975). *Structural stability and morphogenesis: an outline of a general theory of models.* Reading, MA: Benjamin.

Thomas, H. and Lohaus, A. (1993). Modeling growth and individual differences in spatial tasks. *Monographs of the Society for Research in Child Development, 58*(9, serial no. 237).

Thorndike, E. L. (1913). *Educational psychology: the psychology of learning (vol. 2).* New York: Teachers College Press.

Turner, F. W. and Thomas, H. (2002). Bridging the gap between theory and model: a reflection on the balance scale task. *Journal of Experimental Child Psychology, 81(4),* 466–81.

van de Pol, F., Langeheine, R. and De Jong, W. (1996). *PANMARK 3. Panel analysis using Markov chains. A latent class analysis program* [User manual]. Voorburg, The Netherlands.

van der Maas, H. L. J. (1995). Beyond the metaphor? *Cognitive Development, 10,* 621–42.

van der Maas, H. L. J. and Jansen, B. R. J. (2003). What response times tell of children's behaviour on the balance scale task. *Journal of Experimental Child Psychology, 85,* 141–77

van der Maas, H. L. J. and Molenaar, P. C. M. (1992). Stagewise cognitive development: an application of catastrophe theory. *Psychological Review, 99,* 395–417.

    (1996). Catastrophe analysis of discontinuous development. In A. von Eye and C. C. Clogg (eds.) *Categorical variables in developmental research. Methods of analysis.* San Diego, CA: Academic Press.

van der Maas, H. L. J., M. E. J. Raijmakers, Hartelman, P. A. I. and Molenaar, P. C. M. (1998). Reaction time as recovery time after pertubation. In Savelsbergh, G., van der Maas, H. L. J. and van Geert, P. (1999). *Nonlinear analysis of developmental processes.* Amsterdam: KNAW.

van Geert, P. (1998). A dynamic systems model of basic developmental mechanisms: Piaget, Vygotsky, and beyond. *Psychological Review, 105(4),* 634–77.

van Maanen, L., Been, P. H. and Sijtsma, K. (1989). The linear logistic test model and heterogeneity of cognitive strategies. In E. E. Roskam (ed.) *Mathematical psychology in progress* (pp. 267–88). Berlin, Germany: Springer-Verlag.

van Rijn, H., van Someren, M. and van der Maas, H. L. J. (2003). Modeling developmental transitions on the balance scale task. *Cognitive Science, 27*(2), 227–57.

Warton, P. and Bussey, K. (1988). Assisted learning: levels of support. *British Journal of Developmental Psychology, 6* (2), 113–23.

Wilkening, F. and Anderson, N. H. (1982). Comparison of two rule-assessment methodologies for studying cognitive development and knowledge structure. *Psychological Bulletin, 92,* 215–37.

Wilson, M. (1989). Saltus: a psychometric model of discontinuity in cognitive development. *Psychological Bulletin, 105,* 276–89.

4   Building general knowledge and skill: cognition and microdevelopment in science learning

Marc Schwartz and Kurt W. Fischer

Consider what knowledge, skills or insights you might need to meet this challenge successfully: light a bulb with only *one* length of wire and a battery.[1] What do you need to know, and how do you integrate this knowledge? What role did development play in preparing you for this challenge? Science educators can identify the skills that are necessary to deal with this task. Cognitive scientists can outline the developmental progression of skills that learners build and organize to create possible solutions. In this chapter we put together cognitive development with task performance. We use a research-based practical definition for skills that allows educators and cognitive scientists to judge the complexity of activities and solutions, and to identify the processes and steps by which learners build richer understandings as they cope with challenges such as turning on the light bulb.

With these tools, we present a model of how by groping in context with a new task, people (a) construct novel skills and thus novel understanding and (b) generalize the new skills to related contexts (Fischer, Yan, and Stewart, 2003). This analysis is generally consistent with Piaget's (1952/1936; 1950/1947) emphasis on groping and adaptation as mechanisms for creation of new knowledge. It adds specific tools for describing how people use groping and adaptation to build new knowledge in specific contexts and to generalize that knowledge to other contexts. Other theories of ontogenesis have generally neglected this question and process, except in research on microdevelopment (Granott and Parziale 2002). They have typically either assumed that new knowledge can be readily created and generalized, or they have not considered the question specifically. Piaget himself did approach the question in a broad way, and the framework that we present explicates his explanation in terms of groping and adaptation (Fischer and Connell 2003).

The authors thank Thomas Bidell, Nira Granott, James Parziale and Phillip Sadler for their contributions to the concepts and research in this paper. Preparation of the paper was supported by grants from Mr and Mrs Frederick P. and Sandra P. Rose and the Harvard Graduate School of Education.
[1] Before continuing, you might want to spend a few minutes considering how you would proceed with this task.

Framework for analysing skills

The concept of skills shows up frequently in both cognitive development and education and is prominent in the literature on science education, science literacy, and national and state science standards. Skills are often characterized as generalized abilities such as completing electrical circuits, designing experiments, graphing data, or understanding motion and force (AAAS 1989; AAAS 2001; NRC 1996) – a framework based in the psychometric tradition and prominent in much of cognitive science (Carey 2000; Demetriou, Christou, Spanoudis and Platsidou 2002; Ferrari and Sternberg 1998; Horn and Hofer 1992). However, such a characterization has posed two specific problems for educators and cognitive scientists:

(1) The framing in terms of general abilities obfuscates the need and value of analysing these abilities in terms of their cognitive demands.[2]

(2) Generalized abilities have been notoriously difficult to teach (Case 1998; Detterman 1993; Fischer and Immordino-Yang 2002; Salomon and Perkins 1989).

Furthermore, such a conceptualization of skills makes certain questions hard to answer. How can educators determine with any confidence what has been learned? How can cognitive scientists evaluate student progress in learning general abilities such as designing experiments, graphing data, or wiring complete circuits? We will show that an analysis in terms of specific activities and skills obviates these problems and facilitates useful analysis of what students learn.

Analysis of components of skill-building

To achieve this analysis requires moving beyond a simple dichotomy of right versus wrong solutions and building instead a deeper analysis of the components or units that learners need and use in creating answers to specific tasks. Most frameworks analysing long-term changes in cognitive development (including many in this book) neglect the short-term building of components for specific tasks. A skill framework illuminates these components, highlighting the form in which students think as they try to meet the light bulb task and one other challenge – how to build a bridge (from toothpicks and marshmallows) that supports its own weight across an eleven-inch span. The framework provides tools for analysing the developmental processes in learning a task or solving a problem, a process that is called *microdevelopment* or *microgenesis* (Fischer 1980a; Granott and Parziale 2002; Schwartz and Sadler in preparation; Werner 1948; Yan and Fischer 2002).

---

[2] Cognitive demand: the degree of coordination of more basic ideas required by a learner to construct a more complex concept.

The first goal of the chapter is to use both tasks (light bulb and bridge) to characterize student achievements within a comprehensive cognitive framework that reveals the richness and complexity of understanding as well as the evolution of that understanding. This chapter uses both tasks to explore what it means to understand and how to compare development and variation in understanding over time. Analysis of student responses exposes the units of variation and characterizes the deeper understandings that learners achieve when coordinating these units into workable solutions. This framework helps identify what is missing in any partial or developing understanding. Also, in this chapter we try to support deeper understanding in you, the reader, by creating some of the experiences that students have as they work with a task and build skill and understanding.

Skill theory, a dynamic model of cognitive development and learning, provides a framework for recognizing and quantifying changes in understanding (Fischer 1980a; Fischer and Bidell 1998). This cognitive model of human development offers two powerful tools for research: a set of procedures for defining skills and an empirically established complexity scale for assessing levels of skill construction in both learning and long-term development. Concepts of skills and levels, which are related to Piaget's (1983) original global characterization, have been refined into a set of fine-grained tools for analysis. This hierarchical model provides a framework that identifies changes and variations in understanding and can support the conceptualization of educational interventions to help students build more sophisticated understandings. In this framework, skills are cognitive structures that learners use in specific contexts and that vary in complexity, while abilities such as graphing or building complete circuits (and other such capacities that are sometimes called 'skills') will be referred to as competencies, which are made up of many related skills in our sense.

The second goal of the chapter is to demonstrate how skill analysis can capture the specific trajectories that students move through in reaching more complete understanding, often by using more complex skill levels. This type of analysis sharpens the picture of what it means to understand by identifying the levels of skills that students use and the experiences that they have to make sense of when confronting new concepts and problems. This type of analysis also highlights how new understandings are dynamic because the skill levels that individuals display are intimately associated with and dependent upon changes in context and individual state. With skill analysis, any understanding can be characterized both for its uniqueness and for its general properties, combining specification of the specific skills used and their temporal quality with their level on the general scale of skill complexity (see also Case, Okamoto, with Griffin, McKeough, Bleiker, Henderson et al. 1996; Dawson 2002; Dawson and

Gabrielian 2003; Fischer and Bidell 1998; Schwartz and Sadler in preparation; (http://gseacademic.harvard.edu/~hcs/base/index.shtml).

Scale for developmental analysis

Skill theory describes the changes in cognitive structures that are observed in the long term as human beings mature and in the short term as they confront new tasks (Fischer 1980; Fischer and Bidell 1998). Despite the large amount of research on cognitive development, most developmental scales have been simply used with empirical validation of their scale properties. At best, stages in other frameworks have been tested primarily for their Guttman properties (Case 1991; Dawson 2001, 2002; Dawson and Gabrielian 2003; Fischer et al. 1993; Fischer and Silvern 1985). In skill theory each level is an increasingly complex coordination and differentiation of earlier levels. Each level forms a real point on a developmental scale, because it has been documented by evidence of discontinuities with emergence of each level and evidence of strong separation of levels in Rasch scaling analysis. Also, each level seems to have specific correlates in development of brain activity (Fischer and Rose 1996). So far, research indicates that there are thirteen hierarchical levels grouped into four tiers (or stages in the terminology of Case 1991, and Piaget 1983). Ten of these are most relevant for normal cognitive development and learning in children and adolescents and are used in the analyses in this chapter; there is strong empirical support showing clusters of discontinuities at specific ages for all ten (Fischer and Bidell 1998; Fischer and Rose 1996).[3]

This framework has allowed researchers to use the same scale to identify and describe similar changes in understanding in a variety of areas (for example, Bidell and Fischer 1994; Commons et al. 1998; Dawson 2002; Fischer and Bidell 1998; Fischer, Yan, and Stewart 2003; Granott 2002; Rose and Fischer 1998; Yan and Fischer 2002). Skill analyses can reveal the range of cognitive skills used by students confronting specific tasks through descriptions of the levels of understanding they use as they solve problems. In addition, educators can use this kind of analysis to identify where interventions have affected students' specific skills and where they have not had the intended effect. The analyses provide educators and cognitive scientists insights into the patterns of activity and understanding that students demonstrate as they try to build general competencies.

---

[3] In this chapter the levels are numbered as follows: the first level of the tier of sensorimotor actions is labelled Sm1 and the remaining levels in that tier are Sm2 and Sm3. The levels of the tier of representations are Rp1, Rp2, and Rp3. The levels of the tier of abstractions are Ab1, Ab2, Ab3, and Ab4, for a total of ten levels. (See Fischer and Bidell 1998 and Fischer, Yan and Stewart 2003 for more detailed explanation.)

The patterns of activity demonstrate pathways of skill development. Each pathway involves a range of skill levels within the hierarchy of skills and depicts the underlying structures of the activities and concepts that students create. In the pathways individual students show distinct trajectories that are the outcome of the dynamic interaction of the students' activities with particular contexts. The individual trajectories are not well-marked highways that all students follow to mastery, although different trajectories may share characteristics that mark common pathways. The same type of skill structure can support misunderstandings that are just as complex as a correct understanding. Analogously, buildings may look different from the outside, but the supportive inner skeleton is still recognizable to any engineer because all buildings must withstand the same forces of nature.

In summary, skill theory provides educators and cognitive scientists the same kind of perspective that structural engineering provides architects by revealing the inner structure of understanding. This perspective is useful in not one but two important time frames. Skill levels are useful in characterizing both long-term cognitive development from birth to early adulthood and short-term learning. The developmental levels in the skill framework for long-term development can also serve as a ruler to quantify observed changes in understanding that result from learning in the short term. The rationale of this approach is that learning is a form of short-term development – the organizing principle behind the skill analysis of microdevelopment (Fischer and Granott 1995; Granott and Parziale 2002; Yan and Fischer 2002).

Microdevelopment

Even though development through the levels observed from birth through adulthood is a process supported by maturation, people do not reach the same level of sophisticated skill and concept use in all domains – a finding that is evident throughout the literature in the widespread prevalence of unevenness or *décalage* across domains in cognitive development (Case 1991; Demetriou et al. 2002; Fischer 1980b; Flavell 1982). This phenomenon has been explored in research with children and adults confronting new problems (Bidell and Fischer 1994; Fischer and Granott 1995; Granott 2002; Parziale 2002; Yan and Fischer 2002). When learners begin the problem-solving process in a new situation, they first use primitive skills, not their most sophisticated ones. They start with less sophisticated skills in order to familiarize themselves with the problem and to start anew the process of coordinating skills into more complex, novel structures (Granott, Fischer and Parziale 2002). As they interact with the problem and gain understanding through the use of less sophisticated skills, they build a foundation specific to the problem they are working on – one that will support the construction of more sophisticated skills similar to those already developed over time in more familiar areas. Thus the process of short-term coordination mirrors the process of long-term coordination observed over years of development.

Microdevelopment is the process of recovering and reorganizing skills when confronting novel problems in order to construct new skills that are needed to meet the demands of the new problem. Microdevelopment is learning structured in the short term in ways similar to development over a lifetime (Wertsch and Stone 1978; Granott 2002).

The complexity of any problem a learner expects to solve cannot exceed the highest skill level s/he has achieved through the process of long-term development. This upper limit of performance in solving problems, called the *optimal level*, does not occur automatically in every situation a person faces, because skill performance is a function of support, context, emotional state, and practice in coordinating component skills (Fischer and Bidell 1998; Fischer, Bullock, Rotenberg and Raya 1993; Vygotsky 1978). Conditions especially conducive to eliciting optimal-level performance are high degrees of contextual support marked by priming of key task components, which offer learners conditions that facilitate new skill construction and organization.

Many researchers and educators have emphasized the role of support in the development of new skills (Lave 1993; Rogoff 1990; Vygotsky 1978), but it is often assumed that students can simply transfer ideas from one area to another. Research clearly shows that students rarely accomplish such transfer with school knowledge (Case 1998; Fischer and Immordino-Yang 2002; Griffin 1995; Nardi 1996; Pea 1993; Salomon and Perkins 1989). Support allows students to make use of familiar skills in new contexts and to function at higher developmental skills that they have not yet fully mastered. Support helps guide students toward the sophisticated understandings that science requires and that science activities without support seldom produce. A person that needs assistance to perform a skill today can gradually build toward an expert performance of that skill on her own tomorrow (Granott, Fischer, and Parziale 2002).

Development is thus a phenomenon that is observable not only as people mature but on smaller time scales of seconds to days. This short-term development, observed in learners facing new problems or familiar problems in new contexts, has been investigated in numerous studies (Granott and Parziale 2002). For example, Granott (2002) investigated the evolution of strategies that adults develop for understanding how Lego robots work. Yan and Fischer (2002) studied the learning process for adults learning to use computers to do statistical calculations. Parziale and Fischer mapped the pathways school-age students follow to learn how to build bridges with marshmallows and toothpicks (Parziale 2002; Parziale and Fischer 1998). Bidell and Fischer (1994) analysed how children deal with the tower of Hanoi problem. Schwartz (2000; Schwartz and Sadler in preparation) investigated how students learn to build magnets from a nail, a battery, and wire and how they understand whether objects will float or sink in water. Because skills vary along the same levels in long and short-term development, microdevelopmental analysis can capture changes in understanding in time frames that are normally encountered in classrooms and other learning environments.

Microdevelopment in action

We will explore in some detail the development of understanding in three different areas – building bridges, juggling and understanding circuits. The analysis of bridge building provides a general introduction to the skill levels that students encounter while trying to build a stronger bridge. Juggling illuminates the process of coordination of components in skills. Understanding circuits elucidates in further depth the nature of the levels that people use when confronting the bulb challenge.

Building bridges

James Parziale in his study of middle school students learning to build bridges employed skill analysis to evaluate changes as student dyads used marshmallows and toothpicks to build a bridge that could successfully span an eleven-inch gap (Parziale 2002; Parziale and Fischer 1998). Student dyads produced interactive dialogue that both revealed the skills that each student used and often supported or prompted use of more complex skills. Figure 4.1 illustrates the outcome of an interaction between two students, fifth-graders Josh and Will. Two kinds of changes were coded during 120 separate interactions between Josh and Will during one laboratory period: (1) the skill complexity evident in the dyad's activities and (2) the complexity of the bridge itself. The interactions included a variety of activities, such as testing the strength of a toothpick, connecting toothpicks and marshmallows, announcing a new observation, or posing a question.

From actions to representations

The dashed line in the graph represents the students' skill level at each recorded activity while working with the bridge components. At level Sm1: single actions, which is the simplest level in the present analysis, one student picked up a toothpick and focused on its properties ('It's warped.'). At all sensorimotor levels, the focus is on actions with the marshmallows and toothpicks, with understanding still limited to physical sensorimotor experience or action.[4] At

---

[4] Piaget claimed that such an understanding belongs to the sensorimotor stage. In skill theory this stage is referred to as the action tier.

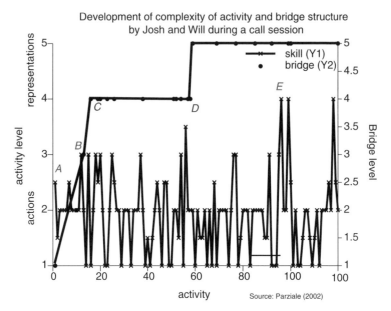

Development of complexity of activity and bridge structure by Josh and Will during a call session

C and D mark an increase in complexity of the bridge structure. A, B, and E mark changes to new levels and other significant events in construction activities. Note the correspondence between the patterns for the most complex activities and the progress in the complexity of the bridge.

Figure 4.1. Relation of counting speed to span. (Adapted from Case 1985, 361)

Level Sm1 Josh and Will do not yet attempt to link actions with toothpicks (or marshmallows) to meet the challenge of building a bridge.

The next two levels (levels Sm2 and Sm3) involve relating actions together, such as joining toothpicks in order to make a longer section. The earlier level, Sm2, called a sensorimotor mapping, appears early in Josh and Will's activities at the start of the graph, marked A; it involves a simple relation of two actions to create a new sensorimotor understanding. Josh and Will related bridge components (connecting marshmallows and toothpicks to form a chain), because they recognized that toothpicks had to be connected to span the gap. However, the students were not yet using any guiding principle beyond a simple chain to organize the toothpicks into a bridge. At activity 15 in Figure 4.1 at the point marked B, the students began to recognize that a simple chain of toothpicks would not span the gap, because the links collapsed under the bridge's weight. They then experimented with more complex connections of toothpicks and marshmallows, building skills at level Sm3, sensorimotor systems. Thus their activities with the task supported the emergence of more complex skills.

Toward the end of the session (from interactions 96 to 120, starting at point E) Josh's and Will's work together supported the emergence of a new representation. They coordinated actions involving marshmallows and toothpicks into a new level of complexity, demonstrating a qualitatively new form of understanding (level Rp1, single representations). They had previously carried out many systems of actions that revealed the properties of the toothpicks and marshmallows by uniting the materials in various ways, and here they brought those actions together in the recognition that only certain configurations led to a stronger bridge section. They focused on a representation of one set of configurations that are strong and stable – a triangular strut.

This new skill involves a transformation from understandings based on actions to a new form of understanding involving representations that are independent of specific actions, although based upon them.[5] Will and Josh discovered the triangular strut as a special configuration by coordinating various actions while working with the material. In future conversations the students used the word 'strut' to capture the essence of this stronger configuration. They no longer needed to see or build the strut to represent its properties. They could also use words other than 'strut' to encapsulate this new discovery, with any representation they used serving the same purpose – capturing the actual configuration of this stronger bridge section.

The new form of understanding that emerged at level Rp1 also coincides with an improvement in the bridge structure – the triangular struts are now included in the bridge to help distribute the weight of the bridge components. Using the same complexity scale, we can compare the changes in skill level at each activity to the complexity of the bridge that each dyad built during the same interval (the solid line). The graph illustrates how the skill structures that appear in the students' interactions can be related directly to changes in the bridge. The activities only involved building parts of the bridge, and so they typically remained less complex than the bridge itself; but the most complex activities match advances in building a more effective bridge (points C and D in Figure 4.1), which reflects an increased complexity in design not observed earlier.

The association between skill development and bridge complexity provides a start for understanding the relation between student ideas and the scientific concepts behind bridge building. This relation does not proceed far without contextual support, however, because achieving higher-order skills in science is not easy to do alone or even in peer groups (Bredderman 1983; Schwartz 2000). Student ideas in science are often not only different from a scientist's understanding, but resistant to influence from teachers and curricula (Driver,

---

[5] Piaget first identified this kind of understanding as belonging to the early pre-operational stage. In skill theory this level begins the representational tier.

Guesne and Tiberghien 1985; Driver, Squires, Rushworth and Wood-Robinson 1994; Shamos 1995).

Developmental range

Student concepts and activities involve variable, not permanent structures, demonstrating a range of skill complexity that varies with support and other factors. This flexibility in performance occurs within the learner's *developmental range*, which describes an array of skills at various complexity levels, as reflected in the ups and downs of activities in Figure 4.1. At the lower end of the range, learners are typically solving problems alone or in low-support environments and are thus operating at or below what we call a *functional level*, the best that they can do without support. When learners act in highly supported or scaffolded contexts, they can perform at their optimal level, the highest level that they are capable of. For Josh and Will their optimal levels were level Rp3 representational systems or level Ab1 single abstractions, depending on the domain. In the bridge-building activities in Figure 4.1, they never reached their *optimal level*.

An individual's developmental range – the interval between their functional and optimal levels, between the best that they can do without and with contextual support – changes with development. Using the skill hierarchy, researchers and educators can describe the specific range of variations that a person shows in learning a skill and the pattern through which they grow their skill. Different individuals in different tasks will produce diverse growth patterns, and also two skills of the same complexity can have diverse content.

Cycle of levels in tiers

Understanding within the action tier for the task of building a bridge begins with individual actions using toothpicks and marshmallows. For example, learners explored the materials (e.g. Do toothpicks bend easily? In which direction do they best withstand compression?). They next discovered ways in which action understandings about toothpicks might or might not extend to the marshmallows. Success in coordinating multiple actions ultimately supported the emergence of a new tier of understanding, a new kind of skill called a representation.

The same general strategy of coordination repeats in parallel fashion in the representational tier through the integration of earlier levels into later levels. The four levels of representations are single representations,[6] mappings of representations, systems of representations and coordinations of systems into single abstractions. Each tier shares the same general pattern of coordination, as

[6] Note that in the bridge example, single representations were identified only as a level Rp1 skill or understanding.

shown by the names of the levels – for the action tier, single actions, mappings of actions, systems of actions, and coordinations of systems into single representations (Fischer 1980b; Fischer and Rose 1996). This pattern also appears in the final developmental tier of abstractions: single abstractions, mappings of abstractions, systems of abstractions, and coordinations of systems into principles.

To illuminate the nature of coordination that unfolds in any tier we use a juggling heuristic. Learners are coordinating skills within their developmental range in the same fashion that jugglers learn to keep more and more balls coordinated. The juggling heuristic highlights the strategy of skill development as learners coordinate skills at earlier levels into more complex skills at later levels.

Juggling skills – a heuristic

In learning how to juggle, training books recommend that learners begin with one ball and learn how to pass this ball back and forth skilfully from one hand to the other (Ashman 2000). This technique allows the learner to focus on the ball, the movements their arm makes, and the trajectory of the ball as it leaves the hand. This accomplishment may not look like juggling, but it serves as a foundation for juggling. At the next level, the juggler adds an additional ball to the task. The juggler will now pass the ball from each hand to the other hand. This activity still does not look like juggling, but this new level of coordination is necessary before a third ball can be successfully added. This technique of building towards increasing levels of coordination is analogous to the coordination of single representations into first mappings, and then mappings into systems of representations.

The nature of building new skills can thus be seen as two operations. The first operation is strategic in that increased competency is demonstrated by keeping more balls or representations coordinated. The second operation is tactical in that the juggler must choose different items to juggle: balls, knives or torches present different challenges. The difference in objects is analogous to the difference in ideas and activities found in various disciplines that are coordinated into more complex understandings. This strategy of increased coordination is what we will explore in more detail as learners respond to another task, lighting an electric bulb, by discovering ways of coordinating representations into increasingly more complex solutions.

The juggling heuristic offers three other insights about skills and skill development besides the strategic/tactical distinction. First, juggling has a temporal quality that suggests that new or developing skills can only be observed once the balls (knives or torches) have been set in motion. The immediacy of juggling nicely illustrates the learner's dynamic enterprise of building more complex activities. Support and practice play vital roles in the stability and variability of any new activity. New skills exist as a fragile temporal-spatial relation of components like the juggler coordinating and keeping in motion additional balls. New understandings show the same lack of stability that jugglers face when attempting to coordinate an additional ball in a routine that they have already learned to handle.

The second insight is how juggling is context-dependent. A juggler may be able to juggle three balls, but that does not mean that s/he can juggle three knives. Being able to juggle three balls also does not mean that the juggler can juggle three balls while balancing on one foot at the top of a stepladder. A skill is not just the description of a behaviour. A skill is the display of a specific behaviour in a particular context. Skill levels change as contexts change. Knowledge varies powerfully across contexts – even contexts in which the 'same' skill could be used.

Third, the nature of juggling changes as learners develop more stable higher order skills. In juggling balls, the initial assumption was that each ball was a stable structure symbolizing a single representation. When a juggler is dealing with moving one ball in his hand, mapping two balls in motion together is enormously challenging. As the juggler develops a skill of mapping two balls to each other, the mapping itself can become a stable structure. To coordinate a mapping, the learner unites the two balls into a larger, more complex structure that becomes a single, stable unit of its own. At this level of competence the learner begins passing the mapping from hand to hand before other mappings and/or single representations are added to the juggling act to meet the demands of more complex tasks, where the necessary or required understanding is a more complex structure (such as a system of representations)

Learning to juggle skills is not an easy task, yet nature endows people with the ability to juggle from birth. As the nature and number of items being juggled changes, new skills and skill levels emerge. The same juggling operation helps learners reach greater complexity in each tier.[7] Each new tier offers learners a qualitatively new way of understanding their world that encapsulates earlier understandings, and the coordination of more complex skills in the new tier proceeds in the same way.

In the next section we elaborate both the transition between tiers and the emergence of new skills, exploring the differences in skill level and their implications for learners working towards an effective solution. The observation that

---

[7] There are four documented tiers: reflex, action, representation and abstraction. More information about the reflex tier can be found in Fischer (1980b) and Fischer and Hogan (1989). The reflex tier is not introduced in this chapter because it is observed only in infants during their first months of life. Reflexes are ultimately coordinated into single actions, which is the first time infants control a movement relatively independently of postural constraints (such as reaching for a ball or following a ball with their eyes).

there are alternative pathways that can lead to an ideal solution reinforces the idea that there is not one linear series of steps that all learners take to achieve an expert understanding. Student understandings can reflect different uses of the same skills, which lead them to different conclusions about the natural world.

Building electrical circuits

The prevalence of diverse solutions to tasks such as the light bulb problem was first illustrated in the documentary *Minds of our own* (1997). The film highlights the variety of beliefs new graduates and scholars at a leading American university hold about electricity and circuits, many of them wrong in a strict technical sense. For the purposes of this chapter, the solutions suggested by those interviewed in *Minds of our own* as well as many other responses from student interviews show a range of understandings that when unpacked provide a richly textured view of the nature of understanding, the relation between alternative solutions, and the microdevelopmental progression of creating a novel understanding.

Each solution or strategy that a student uses represents different choices about how to coordinate beliefs about the world with specific content encountered in and out of school. Science educators have often focused on the *misconceptions* implied by unworkable strategies, claiming that they impede understanding. Evidence of misconceptions or naive conceptions is well documented in science education (Driver et al. 1985, 1994; Novak 1987), but we argue that these misunderstandings are better understood as alternative pathways of understanding, often based in a schema or metaphor that frames a range of skills and can lead to better understanding. (Schemas are to be distinguished from what Piaget (1983) calls 'schemes', which are the general structures for acting and knowing that each person uses.) Students grope with tasks by means of these schemas, and through the groping they can create an understanding that is novel for them. The diverse pathways provide important information for scientists and educators to develop insight into how learners coordinate skills to form more powerful understandings.

The initial solutions offered by three adults attempting the light bulb task provide a way to explore how skills evolve in complexity (Figure 4.2). The three drawings may also summarize or highlight achievements you have made in understanding circuits. For example, you should have little difficulty recognizing the wire in each solution.

If you recognized the wire, you might ask yourself, 'How did I do that?' The wire's appearance is different in each case. To recognize the wire in each drawing requires a more fundamental understanding embedded in an earlier form of understanding – sensorimotor or action understanding. You know from prior experiences that wire is easy to bend, that it can maintain different shapes,

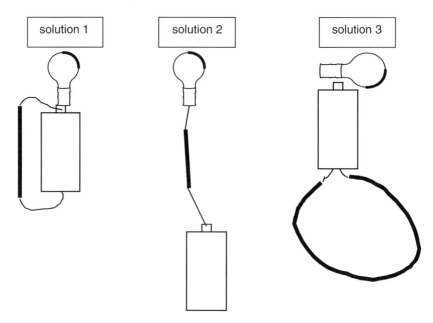

Figure 4.2. Three attempted solutions to lighting a bulb with one piece of wire and a battery.

that there is often a covering on the wire that can be brightly coloured or not, and that under the cover is a shiny metallic core. All of these observations and experiences with wire are key levels of action understanding embedded and already coordinated in the first tier of skill development. However, as adults we have lost touch with the work involved in creating symbolic understandings from our actions, and as a result we no longer recognize or appreciate the importance of this transition.

Transitioning from actions to representations

The transition from action understanding to representational understanding is a powerful experience. Before considering further the representations unique to circuits, we want to explore the nature of the transition from level Sm3, the last level of the action tier, to level Rp1, the first level of the representational tier. This transition is just as powerful as the transition from representations to abstractions or from abstractions to principles, but it can be harder to illustrate. To experience the impact of the transition from actions to representations and the new world that unfolds as we coordinate these representations into ever

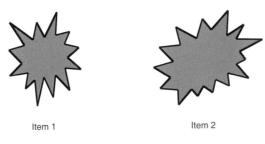

Figure 4.3. Blurbs.

more complex structures, we will examine a representation that you do not yet recognize (Figure 4.3).

Item 1 in Figure 4.3 is a 'blurb'. You don't know what blurbs are yet, but after looking at the first blurb, you will probably suspect that Item 2 in Figure 4.3 is also a 'blurb'. Why? This ability to recognize similar objects and to recognize these objects by name is a conspicuous skill in toddlers because single representational skills mark the leading edge of what they are learning to accomplish on their own (Corrigan 1983; Fischer and Corrigan 1981). Toddlers name objects without knowing what they are or the purpose they serve. You are experiencing the same effect with blurbs. However, for you in contrast to a toddler, the time spent at this first level of the representational tier will be relatively short-lived. Pay attention to your experience as we add the following information about 'blurbs': the blurbs in Figure 4.3 have been magnified 100 times, and blurbs are always found at the end of sentences.

At this point you may recognize that the authors are talking about 'periods'. The moment that blurbs become periods, literate individuals can quickly coordinate other related representations with this single representation. For example, writers do not use blurbs (periods) after questions, and probably do not use them after bullets in lists. Three periods in a row means something different from one period at the end of a sentence. Readers expect only one period after a sentence like this one. Being able to distinguish blurbs in a world full of non-blurbs is a level of understanding characterized by the first level of the representational tier. Recognizing the relations of blurbs to other entities is an indication of the coordination entailed when operating at later levels in the tier.

An important point about single representations is their ability to persist as characteristics specific to objects that vary along some dimensions. For example, size, shape and shading are characteristics of blurbs. If you encounter a blurb-like object that is twice as big as Item 1 or 2, or has only two or three points, or has the outline of a blurb but is white inside, is this new object still a blurb? There is a range along which each characteristic can be amplified or dampened without inadvertently creating a new object or new representation. It is difficult to say where the limits are for each person, but they frame the boundaries that allow people to recognize objects that belong to the same group. When the acceptable range for blurbs has been exceeded, then people are no longer sure whether the new object is a blurb or not.

Single representations act as foundational skills that serve as the platform for building more complex representations. Each successive level for understanding the light bulb task is organized and coordinated into increasingly more complex cognitive structures. The levels of understanding that students and adults reach with the light bulb task reside mostly in the representational tier. The levels of understanding within this tier are typically sufficient for handling many of the problems we encounter in life, with no need for abstractions (Fischer, Yan and Stewart 2003; Yan and Fischer 2002).

Level Rp1: single representations in circuits

A second question about the three solutions in Figure 4.2 will help introduce another single representation necessary to understand circuits. Which object is the battery? Recognizing batteries, like the wire, requires a rich tactile and visual range of coordinated actions. Batteries are hard; the ends are shiny. One end has a little bump. The other end often has a dimple. There are a number of continua along which batteries might change that can eventually disrupt the pattern of actions necessary to separate batteries from non-batteries.

Young children easily demonstrate the limits of this skill as they are learning to master single representations. In one pilot study of seven three-year-olds, the children easily identified AAA, A, and D batteries as all batteries even though they differed in size. Varying the size of the batteries in this way did not change the representation for these children, but the range of the size dimension can be exceeded. When these children, all becoming proficient at many skills at level Rp1 (single representations), were shown a lithium watch battery, the battery[8] representation broke down. Most asked, 'What is it?' Some claimed it might be money or even the tip of a bigger battery. When the interviewer (Marc Schwartz) asked whether the object could be a battery, most of the children said that it was too small to be a battery, or they asked, 'Where does it go?' – where does it fit on a battery?

Experience easily expands the range of a dimension. One boy, Jimmy, was not confused by the watch battery; his father was the maintenance man at the preschool where the pilot study was conducted. He looked at the AAA battery

---

[8] You might take a few moments to consider why you are not confused. What skills have you coordinated that allow you to include lithium watch batteries in the group of objects called batteries?

and did not hesitate, 'That's a "Duracell".' When shown the watch battery, he immediately explained, 'That's a button battery, and it has acid inside. Acid makes the battery work.'

The difference in performance between Jimmy and his playmates can be reproduced in adults by altering the context in which they have become accustomed to seeing a battery. If you saw the drawing of the battery (as drawn in Figure 4.2) on a yellow diamond road sign, would you recognize the battery, or would you see something else? In this context, your challenge is to create a single representation, which most likely begins with the question, 'What am I looking at?'

Even though young children and adults are developmentally prepared to handle single representations, the skill is not a fixed structure guaranteed to surface when needed. Changing the context or changing one or more characteristics beyond an acceptable range can degrade or interfere with the single representational skill so that understanding requires that the individual move to a lower level skill to become reacquainted with the object through sensorimotor actions.

Level Rp2: Mappings of representations in circuits

With the juggling heuristic, the comfort in handling single representations is like the ability of handling one ball skilfully in the hand. What would it mean to handle or juggle two balls? An understanding at the second level of the representational tier requires that individuals coordinate an additional dimension to relate two different characteristics that vary along relevant dimensions. Individuals discover the relation of both characteristics to the initial representation, which leads to a meaningful new understanding about the representation. At level Rp1, learners could vary the size of the battery considerably without being confused about whether it was still a battery. For example, when asked why some batteries were bigger than others, Juliette (from the toddler pilot study) pointed to the D battery and explained, 'That's a Papa battery' and continued, pointing to the AAA battery, 'That's a baby battery.' Most of her classmates responded to this question in a similar fashion by repeating back salient characteristics about its size – the bigger battery is taller or the smaller battery is skinnier.

However, these same children had difficulty coordinating related information about batteries. When I asked Juliette what batteries are for, she told me a story about how her doll needs batteries to talk. She knows that batteries are necessary to make the doll talk, but this knowledge acts as a separate uncoordinated single representation about dolls. Talking dolls need batteries. Or as Jimmy will say with confidence, the battery has acid in it, and flashlights need them. But neither child can yet create a mapping of representations about batteries, such as explaining why batteries come in different sizes or what is changing in batteries as they get bigger or smaller.

Around 3.5 to 4.5 years children begin to create a new kind of skill across many contexts, coordinating an additional dimension to form level Rp2 mapping of representations. The additional dimension about batteries that most children, adolescents, and adults in well-developed countries recognize is that they are a source of electricity[9] for toys and tools. Thus a new dimension in which batteries can vary is the amount of electricity they provide. One possible way to vary the amount of electricity the battery provides is to vary the size of the battery. Coordinating variations along both the dimensions of size and amount of electricity in the battery changes the understanding about the representation in consideration. A big battery provides lots of electricity. A small battery provides less electricity. Juliette knows for example that her talking doll needs batteries to work, but at age three she did not yet coordinate battery size with amount of electricity. Being able to coordinate both variables would be an indication of the emergence of level Rp2.

When children coordinate both dimensions, they can seek to improve the function of an electrical device by asking for a bigger battery (Schwartz 1998). They may claim that a bigger battery is more powerful. Even if the size to power relation is not technically correct, this view is coherent with one popular hypothesis, schema, or metaphor about the world: bigger is better (Lakoff and Johnson 1980). The metaphor 'bigger is better' is a powerful reminder of one of the mapping relations that people observe in many situations in life.

Schemas, metaphors or central conceptual structures provide general frameworks or shells that conveniently capture relations or dimensions about the world and form frameworks for many skills (Case 1991; Fischer and Immordino-Yang 2002; Granott et al. 2002; Lakoff 1987; Perkins 1997). Many schemas help people organize understanding at the mapping and higher levels. For example, the number line serves as a general structure that grounds many different activities involving the use of number (Case et al. 1996). These structures organize causal relations that people have discovered in the world and thus are useful in shaping the predictions people make about how the world works.

A schema that shapes understanding electricity is the source metaphor, which specifies three components: a source, a delivery mechanism, and a user at the other end. Students typically rely on their experience with plumbing to organize all three components: a reservoir serves as the source, the pipes become the delivery mechanism, and the consumer waits at the faucet. Ten- and eleven-year-olds will explain that electricity flows through the wire to the bulb like water flowing through a pipe (Shipstone 1985; Schwartz 1998).

---

[9] Children and adults also use alternatively the following terms: energy, stuff or power.

The source metaphor seems to lead to a way of coordinating knowledge about the battery and the wire – battery as providing power and wire as serving as a path. From the perspective of juggling, the source metaphor helps establish and stabilize relations between these ideas, resulting in a richer understanding of circuits. With the metaphor students can consolidate several dimensions, and instead of juggling two separate balls, they can handle both balls as one larger, more complex structure bonding the balls together. The first ball symbolizes the battery and one salient characteristic – the electricity it provides. The second ball symbolizes the wire and its special property as a path. There are a number of different types of paths that are possible (e.g. one-way, two-way, narrow, etc.), but the plumbing metaphor draws the learner's attention to the one-way path required by the source metaphor. The learner as juggler is thus focusing on one variation in each representation. In the resulting mapping, the source of energy and the path are coordinated into an understanding about circuits (that the battery is a source and the wire is a one-way path).

Children and adults using solution 2 in Figure 4.2 demonstrate this form of mapping. They explain that the wire acts as a pipe to get electricity from the battery to the bulb. Relevant dimensions highlighted by the source metaphor are 'source versus non-source' and 'one-way path versus alternative paths'. Each single representation within a mapping can hypothetically embody a variety of characteristics that vary along independent dimensions, but in an active skill at the mapping level, only one dimension is under consideration for each representation.

In general, proposed solutions at the mapping level do not suffice to actually light the bulb. Building additional mappings will not create a solution either, but they can lay the groundwork for a solution constructed at the next skill level. For example, some learners point out that batteries are a source of energy and that all batteries have two sides that are different. Although this mapping alone is not useful as a solution to the light bulb task, it will play a role in more complex solutions. New mappings and dimensions of the representations need to be coordinated to create a successful solution. This increased level of coordination is embodied in solution 1 in Figure 4.2 and in the descriptions learners used to justify that solution.

Level Rp3: a system of representations

Solution 1 is a less common alternative, and although incorrect, it nevertheless illustrates a more complex, sophisticated skill. Student explanations for this solution reveal a new coordination of two mappings. This new skill level generates a novel view about batteries. Some students explain that the battery must be activated or charged before it will work, and so they use the wire to connect both ends of the battery. Charged batteries are on (empowering the battery to deliver energy) and uncharged batteries are off (and thus the battery cannot deliver energy). The second mapping used in this new skill level is an outgrowth of the plumbing idea from the source metaphor: the wire is used to turn the battery on by making electricity flow. Students using this skill place the bulb on top of the battery, explaining that they don't really need the wire to connect the bulb to the battery. Essentially the shortest path from the source to the bulb is to simply lay the bulb on the battery – which will not light the bulb, in fact.

This new skill, which coordinates two mappings at the same time, illustrates the third level of representational thinking – level Rp3, a representational system. A new mapping concerning batteries is being coordinated with the earlier source metaphor/mapping. In terms of juggling, the student has put in play together two mapping skills: a new representational mapping for batteries coordinated with a mapping for simplified circuits captured by the plumbing metaphor.

Students who use this particular system, as embodied in their explanation of solution 1, quickly discover that the bulb does not light. Thus they quickly see that this representational system is not reliable. For the student there are a number of possible problems: one of the dimensions within the system of mappings is not relevant, or another more promising dimension in one of the mappings has not been considered, or the two mappings chosen for coordination are not appropriate. When a student makes any of the changes implied by these problems, s/he has to coordinate new mappings to create a new system skill.

When students fail to light the bulb, they are forced to examine the reliability of the system they are attempting to coordinate. The potential problem with this system creates an opportunity to challenge both the importance of the mappings and their dimensions as well as to consider investigating new dimensions in one or both mappings. One student explained that she felt certain that there needed to be a source that delivers electricity to the bulb. Thus the source metaphor or mapping remained intact, which allowed the student to shift her attention to the 'charged battery' mapping, and to think about the 'charged versus not charged dimension' that she was holding (and attempting to juggle) concerning batteries. Even though she explained that she had never seen such an arrangement with batteries and wires, she still needed to see if the battery needed to be 'charged' before abandoning this mapping – trying out the arrangement in action. Note the important role that understanding at the action tier plays in supporting skill development (such as seeing that the light does not turn on). After this student made this observation, she felt free to discard the incorrect mapping.

A new and relevant dimension about batteries surfaces when students attend to the fact that there are two sides of the battery, and that each side is different. Students who discover that solution 1 does not work become more sensitive to the two sides of batteries (which is not to say that students have to pass through solution 1 in order to appreciate that both ends of the battery are different). Some students claim that any solution requires that both ends of the battery be used (although they may not be sure why). Some may point out that one side is positive and the other is negative without being able to explain what makes one side positive or negative. The new mapping provides an altered focus, which is powerful enough to change the way students attempt to light the bulb.

With this new focus, some students for the first time talked about whether the circuit was complete or not. The dimension of complete vs. incomplete circuits is a new and important concept, which begins to take shape in a strategy such as 'solution 3'. Note that in solution 3 the wire forms a circle to illustrate 'completeness' by joining both ends of the wire at one of the ends of battery. However, a complete circuit must coordinate several dimensions about the battery – both making the wire close the circuit and including both sides of the battery. Even though students were still not sure how to coordinate these dimensions with the materials at hand, they quickly abandoned solution 3 not only because the strategy failed to light the bulb, but also because the solution failed to use both ends of the battery even though the circuit looked complete. The key to lighting the bulb is to coordinate the correct two dimensions in the circuit mapping.

Students working with the materials began talking about the bulb in terms of two contact points instead of one. They examined the bulb more closely, sometimes questioning whether there are two sides of a bulb, and if the position of the bulb on the battery matters. Students sometimes experimented with this new dimension as a variation of solution 2 in Figure 4.2. Instead of putting the wire to the end of the bulb, they attached the wire to the side of the bulb. When asked to predict what would happen, students often admitted that they did not think this strategy would work, but they felt strongly that they needed to test the dimension before they could move beyond it.

You may have noted that this testing phenomenon is the second example of students building a design that they did not believe would work. Why would anyone do this? One explanation comes from the microdevelopmental perspective. Students need to build representations based on their own sensorimotor understandings. The advantage of testing the design is that the sensorimotor outcome provides direct information, not information coming from an outside authority (such as a teacher or book). Once students have created their own sensorimotor understanding, they are usually ready to accept the resulting representations as their own. This is an important point for educators who believe that representational knowledge can be transferred to students by simply telling it to them – a process that forces them to 'borrow' representations instead of 'building' their own (Schwartz and Fischer 2003).

Exploring whether the side of the bulb is different from the end of the bulb is sometimes productive because some students experiment with one contact point versus two contact points. At this point students used either the side or the end of the bulb as one of the contact points for the battery, which leaves the other side of the battery and the unused contact point on the bulb as the contact points to be connected by the wire. With this new configuration, the bulb for the first time will light. (If you have not worked with circuits, you may have to make an effort to juggle the representations together to understand this solution.)

The skill for this working solution is at the same skill level as the earlier incorrect solution (number 1 in Figure 4.2) because only two mappings need to be coordinated in order to light the bulb: bulbs and batteries have two active sites (or contact points), and the path has to connect all the sites. The one-site versus two-site dimension can also be framed as 'incomplete versus complete circuits', and the dimension of 'one-way path versus some alternative path' can be framed as 'flow versus non-flow'. This new coordination is initially tenuous in most students. Its fragility is evident, for example, when a teacher asks a student whether it matters which side of the battery is connected to the bulb. In practice, this new question can be resolved quickly by reversing the battery to find out that the side doesn't matter, but students usually grope and stumble to construct that understanding.

Being able to coordinate two mappings at the same time is the template for a representational system. In Figure 4.2, solutions 1 and 3 reflect different mappings coordinated into a level Rp3 representational system. This fact may not be intuitively obvious, but the skill analysis of each student's explanation indicates the similarity in these apparently different solutions. For students to make the transition to the next level, single abstractions, they need to coordinate several such representational systems to create the new kind of skill.

Level Ab1: systems of systems of representations, which are single abstractions

Although the dimension of two poles versus one pole (negative versus positive sides of batteries) was not needed to solve the original problem, polarity becomes one more necessary dimension about batteries that students must coordinate to move to the next level of understanding – systems of systems of representations, which are single abstractions. As learners coordinate multiple representational systems, a new and qualitatively new form of understanding emerges – abstract thinking. The number of representational systems that need to be coordinated to develop an abstract understanding about circuits is not fixed. In the simplest case, two coordinated representational systems (including the dimension of polarity) may be sufficient for an emerging abstraction. The coordination of multiple systems leads to a richer abstract concept of circuit.

Table 4.1. *Dimensions along which representations about the bulb task may vary.*

Objects Represented	Bulb	Wire	Battery
Dimensions	– State of the bulb: on vs. off. – Contact points: one versus two. – Incomplete vs. complete circuit: Both contact points must be part of the circuit.	– Path vs. non-path: The path must establish a route for electricity. A string could not provide this function. – Incomplete for complete circuit.	– Source vs. non-source – Charged vs. not charged – Two sides of the battery: Each side must be part of the path. – Batteries have two poles.

An abstraction about circuits coordinates the multiple dimensions of the initial three single representations (batteries, wires, bulb) into an intangible, generalized concept of circuit. The essential feature of abstractions in the new tier is that circuits are understood through concepts that go beyond the concrete particulars, so that representations no longer need to be the immediate focus. Ultimately abstractions about circuits need to coordinate a number of dimensions about batteries, wires and bulbs. Table 4.1 summarizes the several dimensions that abstractions can coordinate to form a broad concept of circuit.

Educational implications

Even though cognitive development, practice and scaffolding support increasingly more sophisticated skills as students gain experience and maturity, there is no guarantee that they will recognize and effectively coordinate the representations that are afforded by the worlds of school and the rest of life. Learning is a process where people make use of their developmental history to build the skills necessary to face new problems in a manner that is similar to the development of skills from infancy to adolescence. Learning is a constructive process in which a person must juggle and coordinate several events or characteristics concurrently to create a new skill. Students have the potential to address new problems by using their maturing cognitive capacities to build new skills, and this process is always fundamentally affected by context. Support and scaffolding play important roles in facilitating microdevelopment (learning) as students have opportunities to perform at their optimal levels, and thus to take advantage of their most sophisticated skills.

A powerful and compelling tool that students use to organize skills is schemas, metaphors or central conceptual structures. Schemas are an important platform for students in that they support the organization of actions and concepts in particular forms. The languages and cultural practices embody schemas, metaphors and central conceptual structures, and consequently children live in the presence of many structures that can support their learning and understanding (Case 1991; Fischer and Immordino-Yang 2002; Granott et al. 2002; Lakoff 1987; Perkins 1997). Schemas serve as first approximations about how nature works by focusing attention on a limited number of dimensions. While schemas thus offer insight, they also constrain more widely coordinated views about the world. When students have the opportunity to use their schemas to address tasks or problems such as the bulb and bridge-building tasks, they are challenging their view of the world.

Teachers and class activities must address the schemas and metaphors (and 'misconceptions') students use by inviting them first to recognize the structures they are using, and then to challenge these structures in new contexts. For example, students who use plumbing as a source metaphor explain that the electricity flows through the wire, but when a teacher points out that the wire is solid, students have the opportunity to reconsider the limits of the metaphor.

Identifying the cognitive structures students use in addressing key tasks is an important platform for educators. Recognizing these structures helps educators understand the range of understandings used in a population of students, and also highlights the skills that need to be supported to help students reach new levels of competence in science (Demetriou et al. 2002; Fischer and Immordino-Yang 2002; Griffin and Case 1997).

Conclusion: creating new understandings

In this chapter we aimed to show how people construct new understandings by tracing the cognitive structures that students use when trying to solve two kinds of science problems. We used skill theory, a neo-Piagetian framework, to trace the trajectory of understanding from sensorimotor through representational and on to abstract skills that students coordinated in order to understand the solutions they created to solve the bridge and light-bulb tasks.

Students used sensorimotor actions to build up single representations about batteries, wires and bulbs (or marshmallows, toothpicks and bridges), but in terms of the task of lighting a bulb, the representations alone did not empower students to do anything more than recognize a few similar features in the objects. By acting on the objects and exploring them, students built on their representations and uncovered a number of dimensions that added depth to the representations; and some of the dimensions turn out to be relevant to solving the task. In single representations, students handle one dimension at a time, focusing on one variable aspect of the object or representation, which has important similarities to juggling one ball. Coordinating two representations that each vary along one dimension in a representational mapping is similar to juggling two balls.

Schemas or metaphors such as the source metaphor can help stabilize this mapping coordination and direct thinking and learning (leading to both misconceptions and conceptual advance). Schemas and metaphors capture some aspect of the world that people have experienced in multiple contexts, and they are typically embodied in language and cultural practice.

Students coordinate mappings to create representational systems, like juggling four or more balls. A representational system is necessary to solve and explain the light-bulb task, but representational systems can also generate incorrect answers. To intervene effectively to facilitate student learning, educators need to know the dimensions that students must attend to in order to learn, as well as the other dimensions that students typically use, especially those that they favour. However, solutions that do not work are not simply incorrect. They provide clues into how students are thinking and how curricula might challenge their alternative solutions – information to help students build microdevelopmental pathways to better knowledge. Skill theory provides the cognitive framework to analyse the microdevelopmental processes through which students use skill structures to construct new understandings and generalize them to solve problems, both in school and in their daily lives.

REFERENCES

AAAS (1989). *Project 2061: Science for all Americans*. Washington DC: American Association for the Advancement of Science.
  (1993). *Benchmarks for science literacy*. Washington DC: American Association for the Advancement of Science and National Science Teachers Association.
AAAS and NSTA (2001). *Atlas of science literacy*. Washington DC: American Association for the Advancement of Science and National Science Teachers Association.
Ashman, S. (2000). *Juggling – all you need to know to develop amazing juggling skills*. Bath, UK: Paragon.
Bidell, T. R. and Fischer, K. W. (1994). Developmental transitions in children's early online planning. In M. M. Haith, J. B. Benson, R. J. R. Jr., and B. F. Pennington (eds.) *The development of future-oriented processes* (pp. 141–76). Chicago: University of Chicago Press.
Bredderman, T. (1983). Effects of activity-based elementary science on student outcomes. *Review of Educational Research*, *53*, 499–518.
Carey, S. (2000). Science education as conceptual change. *Journal of Applied Developmental Psychology*, *21*, 13–19.
Case, R. (1992). *The mind's staircase: exploring the conceptual underpinnings of children's thought and knowledge*. Hillsdale: Erlbaum.

(1998). The development of conceptual structures. In D. Kuhn and R. S. Siegler (eds.) and W. Damon (series ed.) *Handbook of child psychology: vol. 2. Cognition, perception, and language*. New York: Wiley.

Case, R., Okamoto, Y., with Griffin, S., McKeough, A., Bleiker, C., Henderson, B. and Stephenson, K. M. (1996). *The role of central conceptual structures in the development of children's thought. Monographs of the Society for Research in Child Development, 61* (5–6, serial no. 246).

Commons, M. L., Trudeau, E. J., Stein, S. A., Richards, F. A. and Krause, S. R. (1998). Hierarchical complexity of tasks shows the existence of developmental stages. *Developmental Review, 18*, 237–78.

Corrigan, R. (1983). The development of representational skills. In K. W. Fischer (ed.) *Levels and transitions in children's development. New directions for child development, 21*, 51–64. San Francisco: Jossey-Bass.

Dawson, T. L. (2001). A comparison of three developmental stage scoring systems. *Journal of Applied Measurement, 3*, 146–89.

(2002). New tools, new insights: Kohlberg's moral reasoning stages revisited. *International Journal of Behavior Development, 26*, 154–66.

Dawson, T. L. and Gabrielian, S. (2003). Developing conceptions of authority and contract across the lifespan: two perspectives. *Developmental Review, 23*, 162–218.

Demetriou, A., Christou, C., Spanoudis, G. and Platsidou, M. (2002). *The development of mental processing: efficiency, working memory, and thinking. Monographs of the Society for Research in Child Development, 67* (1, serial no. 173).

DESIGNS (1994). *Proposal to the National Science Foundation*. Cambridge, MA: Harvard-Smithsonian Center for Astrophysics.

Detterman, D. K. (1993). The case for the prosecution: transfer as an epiphenomenon. In D. K. Detterman and R. J. Sternberg (eds.) *Transfer on trial: intelligence, cognition, and instruction* (pp. 1–24). Norwood, NJ: Ablex.

Driver, R., Guesne, E. and Tiberghien, A. (1985). Some features of children's ideas and their implications for teaching. In R. Driver, E. Guesne and A. Tiberghien (eds.) *Children's ideas in science* (pp. 193–201). Milton Keynes: Open University Press.

Driver, R., Squires, A., Rushworth, P. and Wood-Robinson, V. (1994). *Making sense of secondary science: research into children's ideas*. London: Routledge.

Ferrari, M. and Sternberg, R. J. (1998). The development of mental abilities and styles. In D. Kuhn and R. S. Siegler (eds.) and W. Damon (series ed.), *Handbook of child psychology: vol. 2. Cognition, perception, and language* (5th edn, pp. 899–946). New York: Wiley.

Fischer, K. W. (1980a). Learning and problem solving as the development of organized behaviour. *Journal of Structural Learning, 6*, 253–67.

(1980b). A theory of cognitive development: the control and construction of hierarchies of skills. *Psychological Review, 87*, 477–531.

Fischer, K. W. and Bidell, T. R. (1998). Dynamic development of psychological structures in action and thought. In R. M. Lerner (ed.) and W. Damon (series ed.) *Handbook of child psychology: vol. 1. Theoretical models of human development* (5th edn, pp. 467–561). New York: Wiley.

Fischer, K. W., Bullock, D., Rotenberg, E. J. and Raya, P. (1993). The dynamics of competence: how context contributes directly to skill. In R. Wozniak and K. W.

Fischer (eds.) *Development in context: acting and thinking in specific environments* (pp. 93–117). Hillsdale, NJ: Erlbaum.

Fischer, K. W. and Connell, M. W. (2003). Two motivational systems that shape development: epistemic and self-organizing. *British Journal of Educational Psychology: Monograph Series II, 2,* 103–23.

Fischer, K. W. and Corrigan, R. (1981). A skill approach to language development. In R. Stark (ed.) *Language behavior in infancy and early childhood* (pp. 245–73). Amsterdam: Elsevier.

Fischer, K. W. and Granott, N. (1995). Beyond one-dimensional change: parallel, concurrent, socially distributed process in learning and development. *Human Development, 38,* 302–14.

Fischer, K. W. and Hogan, A. E. (1989). The big picture for infant development: levels and variations. In J. J. Lockman and N. L. Hazen (eds.) *Action in social context: perspectives on early development* (pp. 275–305). New York: Plenum Press.

Fischer, K. W., and Immordino-Yang, M. H. (2002). Cognitive development and education: from dynamic general structure to specific learning and teaching. In E. Lagemann (ed.) *Traditions of scholarship in education.* Chicago: Spencer Foundation.

Fischer, K. W. and Pipp, S. L. (1984). Process of cognitive development: optimal level and skill acquisition. In R. J. Sternberg (ed.) *Mechanisms of cognitive development* (pp. 450–80). New York: Freeman.

Fischer, K. W. and Rose, S. P. (1996). Dynamic growth cycles of brain and cognitive development. In R. Thatcher, G. R. Lyon, J. Rumsey, and N. Krasnegor (eds.) *Developmental neuroimaging: mapping the development of brain and behavior* (pp. 263–79). New York: Academic Press.

Fischer, K. W. and Silvern, L. (1985). Stages and individual differences in cognitive development. *Annual Review of Psychology, 36,* 613–48.

Fischer, K. W., Yan, Z. and Stewart, J. (2003). Adult cognitive development: dynamics in the developmental web. In J. Valsiner and K. Connolly (eds.) *Handbook of developmental psychology* (pp. 491–516). Thousand Oaks, CA: Sage.

Flavell, J. (1982). On cognitive development. *Child Development, 53,* 1–10.

Granott, N. (2002). How microdevelopment creates macrodevelopment: reiterated sequences, backward transitions, and the zone of current development. In N. Granott and J. Parziale (eds.) *Microdevelopment: transition processes in development and learning.* Cambridge: Cambridge University Press.

Granott, N., Fischer, K. W. and Parziale, J. (2002). Bridging to the unknown: a transition mechanism in learning and problem-solving. In N. Granott and J. Parziale (eds.) *Microdevelopment: transition processes in development and learning* (pp. 131–56). Cambridge: Cambridge University Press.

Granott, N., and Parziale, J. (eds.) (2002). Microdevelopment: transition processes in development and learning. Cambridge: Cambridge University Press.

Griffin, M. M. (1995). You can't get there from here: situated learning, transfer, and map skills. *Contemporary Educational Psychology, 20,* 65–87.

Griffin, S. and Case, R. (1997). Rethinking the primary school math curriculum. *Issues in Education: Contributions from Educational Psychology, 3*(1), 1–49.

Harvard-Smithsonian Center for Astrophysics (1997). *Minds of our own.* Science Education Department, Science Media Group. Cambridge, MA.

Horn, J. L. and Hofer, S. M. (1992). Major abilities and development in the adult period. In R. J. Sternberg and C. A. Berg (eds.) *Intellectual development* (pp. 44–99). Cambridge: Cambridge University Press.

Jacobs, Kawanaka and Stigler (1999). Integrating qualitative and quantitative approaches to the analysis of video data on classroom teaching. *International Journal of Education Research, 31,* 717–24.

Lakoff, G. (1987). *Women, fire, and dangerous things: what categories reveal about the mind.* Chicago: University of Chicago Press.

Lakoff, G. and Johnson, M. (1980). *Metaphors we live by.* Chicago: University of Chicago Press.

Lave, J. (1993). Word problems: a microcosm of theories of learning. In P. Light and G. Butterworth (eds.) *Context and cognition: ways of learning and knowing* (pp. 74–92). Hillsdale, NJ: Lawrence Erlbaum Associates.

Martin, M. O., Mullis, I. V. S., Gonzalez, E. J., Smith, T. A. and Kelly, D. L. (1999). *School contexts for learning and instruction: IEAS third international mathematics and science study (TIMSS).* Chestnut Hill, MA: Boston College.

Nardi, B. (1996). Studying context: a comparison of activity theory, situated action models, and distributed cognition. In B. Nardi (ed.) *Context and consciousness: activity theory and human–computer interaction* (pp. 69–102). Cambridge, MA: MIT Press.

National Research Council (1996). *National Science Education Standards.* Washington DC: National Academy Press.

(1999). *How people learn: bridging research and practice.* M. Donovan, J. Bransford, and J. Pellegrino (eds.) Washington DC: National Academy of Science.

(2001). *Knowing what students know: the science and design of educational assessment.* Washington DC: National Academy Press.

Novak, J. D. (1987). *Proceedings of the second international seminar: misconceptions and educational strategies in science and mathematics July 26–29, 1987,* vol II. Ithaca, NY: Department of Education, Cornell University.

Novak, J. D. and Gowin, D. B. (1984). *Learning how to learn.* New York: Cambridge University Press.

Parziale, J. (2002). Observing the dynamics of construction: children building bridges and new ideas. In N. Granott and J. Parziale (eds.) *Microdevelopment: transition processes in development and learning* (pp. 131–56). Cambridge: Cambridge University Press.

Parziale, J. and Fischer, K. W. (1998). The practical use of skill theory in classrooms. In R. J. Sternberg and W. M. Williams (eds.) *Intelligence, instruction and assessment* (pp. 96–110). Hillsdale, NJ: Lawrence Erlbaum Associates.

Pea, R. D. (1993). Practices of distributed intelligence and designs for education. In G. Salomon (ed.) *Distributed cognitions: psychological and educational considerations* (pp. 47–87). Cambridge: Cambridge University Press.

Perkins, D. N. (1997). *Knowledge as design.* Mahwah, NJ: Erlbaum.

Piaget, J. (1950). *The psychology of intelligence* (M. P. D. E. Berlyne, trans.). New York: Harcourt Brace. (Originally published 1947.)

(1952). *The origins of intelligence in children* (M. Cook, trans.). New York: International Universities Press. (Originally published, 1936.)

(1983). Piaget's theory. In P. M. Mussen (ed.) *Handbook of child psychology* (vol. 1, pp. 103–28). New York: Wiley.

Rogoff, B. (1990). *Apprenticeship in thinking*. New York: Oxford University Press.

Rose, S. P. and Fischer, K. W. (1998). Models and rulers in dynamical development. *British Journal of Developmental Psychology, 16* (pt 1), 123–31.

Sadler, P., Coyle, H. and Schwartz, M. (2000). Engineering competitions in the middle school classroom: key elements in developing effective design challenges. *Journal of the Learning Sciences, 9*, 299–327.

Salomon, G. and Perkins, D. N. (1989). Rocky roads to transfer: rethinking mechanisms of a neglected phenomenon. *Educational Psychologist, 24*, 113–42.

Schwartz, M. (1998). The role of standard designs in goal setting in a science activity. Unpublished Qualifying Paper, Harvard University. Cambridge, MA.

　(2000). Design challenges: a new path to understanding science concepts and skills. Unpublished doctoral dissertation. Harvard Graduate School of Education. Cambridge, MA.

Schwartz, M. and Fischer, K. W. (2003). Building vs. borrowing: the challenge of actively constructing ideas. *Liberal Education* (Summer), 22–9.

Schwartz, M. and Sadler, P. (2001). *Goals and technology education: the example of design challenges*. Proceedings of the Second AAAS Research in Technology Education Conference. AAAS: Washington, DC.

　(submitted) Empowerment in science curriculum development: a microdevelopmental approach. *International Journal of Science Education*.

Shamos, M. H. (1995). *The myth of scientific literacy*. New Brunswick: Rutgers University Press.

Shipstone, D. (1985). Electricity in simple circuits. In R. Driver, E. Guesne and A. Tiberghien (eds.) *Children's ideas in science* (pp. 33–51). Milton Keynes: Open University Press.

Vygotsky, L. (1978). *Mind in society: the development of higher psychological processes* (Cole, M., John-Steiner V., Scribner, S., Souberman, E, trans.). Cambridge, MA: Harvard University Press.

Werner, H. (1948). *Comparative psychology of mental development*. New York: Science Editions.

Wertsch, J. V. and Stone, C. A. (1978). Microgenesis as a tool for developmental analysis. *Quarterly Newsletter of the Laboratory of Comparative Human Cognition, 1*(1), 8–10.

Yan, Z. and Fischer, K. W. (2002). Always under construction: dynamic variations in adult cognitive development. *Human Development, 45*, 141–60.

5   Cognitive change as strategy change

Joke Torbeyns, Laurence Arnaud, Patrick Lemaire and Lieven Verschaffel

The goal of this chapter is to epitomize the contribution of the information-processing perspective to cognitive development. A key feature of this perspective is its focus on (changes in) mental structures and processes that help us understand (changes in) cognitive performance. In the first section of the chapter we examine several theoretical and methodological issues that the information-processing perspective of cognitive development has made important to address. We begin with a brief discussion of the conceptual framework of Siegler and collaborators as a prototypical example of this perspective. The overlapping waves theory (Siegler 1996, 2000), the model of strategy change (Lemaire and Siegler 1995) and the strategy choice and discovery simulation (Shrager and Siegler 1998) are presented. In the second part of the first section we discuss two research methods and tools that are typical for the information-processing perspective on human learning and development, namely the microgenetic method (Siegler and Crowley 1991), and the choice/no-choice method (Siegler and Lemaire 1997). In the second section the above-mentioned theoretical and methodological approaches are exemplified by means of two recent studies. The first study (Chen and Siegler 2000) illustrates how the microgenetic method can be applied successfully to study changes in toddlers' strategy use in the domain of problem solving. The second study (Lemaire and Lecacheur 2002a) deals with changes in children's and adults' strategy characteristics in the domain of computational estimation, using the choice/no-choice method. Strengths and weaknesses of the information-processing approach – in comparison to some other current theoretical and methodological approaches to cognitive development – and some indications for its further development and integration with other approaches are discussed in the final section.

The information-processing perspective: theoretical and methodological issues

Theoretical issues

Since the cognitive revolution in psychology at the end of the 1950s, the information-processing perspective heavily influenced theoretical and empirical studies of human learning and development (De Corte, Greer and Verschaffel 1996; Demetriou, Christou, Spanoudis and Platsidou 2002; Greeno, Collins and Resnick 1996; Greer and Verschaffel 1990; Kail 1996; Klahr and MacWhinney, 1998). One of the main features of this perspective is its attempt to describe, at a very high degree of precision, the cognitive structures and processes that underlie cognitive performance. Cognitive phenomena are described and explained in analogy with computer operations: observable stimuli (input) activate internal knowledge structures; these knowledge structures are manipulated by mental procedures, which leads to a specific reaction (output).

Information-processing models of cognition typically consist of internal representations of information and mental processes that operate on these representations; (changes in) observed reactions to specific stimuli are explained in terms of (changes in) internal representations and mental procedures that use, edit and create these representations.

Information-processing psychologists further argue that a profound understanding of the cognitive structures and processes that underlie cognitive performance necessarily requires a detailed understanding of the task of interest. In line with this argumentation, they tend to develop detailed models of cognition for specific task domains (e.g. solving simple addition problems, understanding the working of the balance beam . . .). Syntheses of scrutinized analyses of these domain-specific models are assumed to highlight common cognitive structures and processes as well as general developmental mechanisms and functions (Kail 1996).

A third characteristic of the information-processing perspective is that models of cognition are preferably formalized as computer simulations (Greer and Verschaffel 1990). Computer simulations do not only ensure greater rigour in the construction and specification of cognitive models, but also allow researchers to test the sufficiency and necessity of the assumptions within any specified model. Such enterprise can lead to revising proposed models.

All these features of the information-processing perspective have been embedded in several influential research programs. Siegler and collaborators' research program is a good example. We start with a discussion of Siegler and Lemaire's theoretical framework on cognitive change, as expressed in the 'overlapping waves theory' (Siegler 1996, 2000) and the 'model of strategy change' (Lemaire and Siegler 1995), and continue with a detailed description of the underlying change mechanisms, as specified in the 'Strategy Choice And Discovery Simulation' (SCADS; Shrager and Siegler 1998). SCADS serves as a good illustration of the information-processing perspective on cognitive development.

Strategy change

In line with the information-processing perspective, Siegler and Lemaire focus on changes in the strategic aspects of cognitive performance to better understand cognitive changes that occur with age and/or experience (Lemaire and Siegler 1995; Siegler 1996, 2000).[1] A strategy is defined as 'a procedure or set of procedures for achieving a higher level goal or task' (Lemaire and Reder 1999, 365). Stated otherwise, a strategy is a series of procedures that an individual uses to accomplish a cognitive task. Siegler and Jenkins (1989) distinguish two major types of strategies: 'back-up' strategies and 'retrieval'. Back-up strategies are defined as rather time-consuming, procedural strategies (like, for instance, the so-called sum strategy, which involves first representing each addend by counting it out, starting from 1, and next counting out both addends, starting from 1, to get the sum; e.g., '3 + 8 = 1, 2, 3 . . . 1, 2, 3, 4, 5, 6, 7, 8 . . . 1, 2, 3, 4, 5, 6, 7, 8, 9, 10, 11'). Retrieval refers to the (quasi-) automatic activation of the answer to the problem from long-term memory (e.g. '3 + 8 = 11, I know this by heart').

According to Siegler (1996, 2000), the development of cognitive strategies has traditionally been portrayed in terms of the staircase metaphor. This metaphor depicts cognitive change as a series of 1:1 equations between ages and ways of thinking. Children of a given age use a particular strategy to solve a cognitive task; cognitive change involves a relatively brief period of transition, during which multiple strategies conflict with each other, leading to the substitution of the previously used strategy for a qualitatively better one. Taking into account the results of recent studies on strategy use and strategy change, Siegler (1996, 2000) criticizes these traditional depictions of cognitive change, and proposes the overlapping waves theory as an alternative theory for describing and understanding cognitive development.

The overlapping waves theory is based on three assumptions (Siegler 1996, 2000). The first assumption is that people use multiple strategies, rather than just one single strategy, to solve cognitive tasks. This variability in strategy use has been documented in a diversity of domains, including simple arithmetic, scientific reasoning, reading, spelling, memory tasks, etc. Moreover, strategy variability can be observed at all ages, between individuals (i.e. different subjects use different strategies to solve the same task or the same problem) as well as within individuals (i.e. one subject uses different strategies to solve a particular task on two occasions close in time or even within a single trial). The second assumption is that the different strategies coexist and compete with each other over prolonged periods of time, rather than just during brief transition

---

[1] The discussion of the theoretical framework on cognitive development offered by – especially – Siegler, is based on his 1996 and 2000 publications. These publications provide a good overview of Siegler's earlier work (Siegler 1986, 1987, 1991, 1998).

periods. The third assumption states that increasing experience with a cognitive task leads to changes in the relative frequency with which the different strategies are used, as well as the development of new strategies for solving the task. These new strategies are added to the repertoire of already-acquired strategies, rather than simply replacing it, and applied with gradually changing frequencies. In other words, the overlapping waves theory depicts cognitive development as characterized by a continuously changing repertoire of coexisting strategies which are applied with continuously changing frequencies and proficiencies.

In the perspective of the overlapping waves theory, Lemaire and Siegler (1995) distinguished four dimensions along which learning and cognitive development occur. The first dimension, strategy repertoire, involves the variety of strategies that are used to solve a task (i.e. which strategies are used?). The second dimension, strategy distribution, refers to the relative frequency with which each of these strategies is used. The third dimension, strategy efficiency, concerns the accuracy and the speed of strategy execution. The fourth dimension, strategy selection, refers to the mechanisms by which individual strategies are chosen on each trial. These trial-by-trial choices enable subjects to be adaptive in their strategy choices, in the sense of increasing the accuracy and speed of their task performance. Changes in strategy use can thus occur in at least four different ways: the acquisition of new strategies and the abandonment of old ones (dimension 1), changes in the relative frequency with which each of the available strategies is used (dimension 2), changes in the accuracy and the speed of strategy execution (dimension 3), and changes in the individual strategy choices (dimension 4). According to this model, at the beginning of the learning process, the learner frequently, if not exclusively, chooses rather primitive back-up strategies (like, for instance, the sum strategy), which he or she executes rather inefficiently (i.e. inaccurately and slowly). Moreover, the learner is not able to choose among the different strategies in the most economical way. With experience, the learner uses more efficient back-up strategies (such as, for instance, the min strategy, which consists in counting up from the larger addend the number of times indicated by the smaller addend; e.g., '3 + 8 = (8), 9, 10, 11') and retrieval, which he or she executes ever more frequently, more efficiently, and also more adaptively.

These changes along the four dimensions of Lemaire and Siegler's model of strategy change are assumed to emerge from a competitive negotiation between associative and metacognitive knowledge systems. As discussed in detail by Crowley, Shrager and Siegler (1997), the human mind consists of both associative and metacognitive knowledge systems. The associative knowledge systems consist of implicit, non-verbalizable, domain-specific knowledge that might be best expressed as a set of learned associations among tasks, actions, and outcomes. The metacognitive knowledge systems involve explicit, potentially verbalizable knowledge of production rules, plans and heuristics that can be used to solve tasks in a given domain. Whenever the human mind is confronted with a task from a given domain, both the domain-specific associative and metacognitive knowledge systems encode the task, match their representation of the task to their respective knowledge bases, and select an appropriate strategy to solve the task. The outcome of these independent but competing encoding and selection processes is in large part determined by the amount of the experience the human mind has with the task. In case of novel tasks, the associative system often lacks sufficient knowledge to select an appropriate strategy, while the more broadly applicable metacognitive system can make a more confident decision about which strategy to use best. If, in contrast, the human mind is presented with a familiar task, the fast associative system almost automatically produces an appropriate strategy, before the slower metacognitive system is able to make its selection. The outcome of the encoding and selection processes is also determined by the goals of the metacognitive system. In novel contexts, the metacognitive system just aims to solve the task. To reach this goal, the metacognitive system monitors the correct application of the strategy chosen by giving commands to the associative system that executes this strategy. In familiar contexts, however, the associative system almost automatically produces a strategy, which enables the metacognitive system to focus on aspects other than supervising the execution process, like, for instance, checking the partial results of the problem solving process. In such situations, the metacognitive system might notice interesting aspects of prior solutions or strategies that are not directly related to the (traditional) goal of solving the task, and adopt the (new) goal of solving the task in a particular way. To reach the latter goal, the metacognitive system tries to increase its control of the selection and execution processes, and tries to direct the associative system to solve the task in the suggested way.

Shrager and Siegler (1998) formalized the idea of a competitive negotiation between associative and metacognitive knowledge systems in a computer simulation, namely the Strategy Choice And Discovery Simulation (SCADS). The next section describes the structure and functioning of SCADS, and discusses how it generates gradual changes in the repertoire, distribution, efficiency and selection of strategies.

*The Strategy Choice And Discovery Simulation (Shrager and
    Siegler 1998)*

SCADS (Shrager and Siegler 1998; see also Siegler 2001) is a computer simulation that models the cognitive structures and processes that allow people to

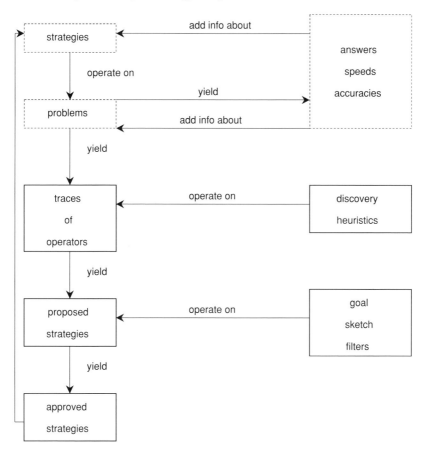

Figure 5.1. Structures and processes as specified in the Strategy Choice And Discovery Simulation. (From Shrager and Siegler 1998, 408)

make adaptive strategy choices and discover new strategies in the domain of simple addition.[2] Figure 5.1 describes SCADS's organization.

---

[2] SCADS's predecessors, the 'distributions of associations model' (Siegler and Shrager 1984) and the 'Adaptive Strategy Choice Model' (ASCM; Siegler and Shipley 1995), both simulate the development of people's strategy choices in the domain of simple addition from the age of four onward. The distributions of associations model and ASCM are tested and validated by comparing performance of computer models with strategy choices of elementary-school children while solving single digit additions. SCADS maintains all of the strategy choice mechanisms of its predecessors (associative learning mechanisms), and extends them by adding strategy discovery mechanisms (interplay between associative and metacognitive mechanisms).

Strategy choices   The dotted boxes in Figure 5.1 identify the associative knowledge system of the model. The database of the model, with information about problems (answers) and strategies (speeds, accuracies), plays a key role in the strategy choice process. The first type of information, information about problems, consists of problem–answer associations, i.e. associations between individual problems and potential, correct as well as incorrect, answers to these problems (e.g. 2 + 3 could be associated with 1, 4, 5, and 6). The associations between individual problems and potential answers differ in strength; the associative strength is expressed in a value ranging from 0 (no association) to 1 (strong association). The second type of information, information about strategies, includes (a) global data, i.e. data about each strategy's efficiency aggregated over all problems (e.g. the speed and accuracy of the sum strategy on single digit additions, like 2 + 3, 4 + 1, or 6 + 7); (b) featural data, i.e. information about the efficiency of each strategy on problems with a particular feature (e.g. the speed and accuracy of the sum strategy on single digit additions with both addends smaller than 5, like 2 + 3 and 4 + 1); (c) problem-specific data, i.e. data about each strategy's efficiency on particular problems (e.g. the speed and accuracy of the sum strategy on 2 + 3); and (d) novelty data, i.e. information about the newness of each strategy (e.g. how often has the sum strategy already been used to solve single digit additions?).

Whenever SCADS is presented with a problem, it activates the global, featural and problem-specific data about the speed and accuracy of each of the available strategies.[3] The model weights these data in function of (a) the amount of information they reflect (the less frequently a strategy has been used on the problem, the more global and featural data are weighted; the more frequently a strategy has been used on the problem, the heavier problem-specific data are weighted); and (b) how recently they were generated (the more recently the data were generated, the more they are weighted). Weighted efficiency and novelty data[4] for each strategy provide the input for stepwise regression analyses, which compute the projected strength, i.e. the projected speed and accuracy of the different strategies on the problem. The strategy with the highest projected strength relative to that of all strategies has the highest probability of being chosen.

Strategy execution   SCADS attempts to execute the selected strategy on a given trial. The model forms a working-memory trace of all operations and partial results produced during the problem-solving process (traces of operators;

---

[3] For a more technical description of the operation of SCADS and its predecessors, we refer the interested reader to Shrager and Siegler (1998); Siegler (1996); Siegler and Shipley (1995); and Siegler and Shrager (1984).

[4] SCADS assigns additional novelty points to newly discovered strategies, which allows them to be chosen, even if the information about their efficiency is limited.

Figure 5.1). If the retrieval strategy is chosen, the model sets two parameters. The first parameter is the 'confidence criterion', which specifies the minimum strength of the problem–answer association that must be reached before it will be retrieved by the model (e.g. the strength of the problem–answer association is at least 0.3). The second parameter is the 'search length criterion'. This parameter determines the maximum number of attempts that the model will make to retrieve the answer to the problem (e.g. maximum three retrieval attempts). Once these parameters are set, the model activates potential problem–answer associations relative to their strength. If the strength of the activated association exceeds the value of the confidence criterion, the answer is stated. If the strength of the activated association does not exceed the value of the confidence criterion, the model activates another problem–answer association. The sequential activation of potential problem–answer associations is repeated until the value of the confidence criterion or the value of the search length criterion is reached. In the latter case, another strategy is chosen.

The execution of a back-up strategy is represented as a modular sequence of operators. For instance, the execution of the sum strategy is represented as follows: all fingers down, choose hand, choose addend, say addend, clear echoic buffer, count out fingers to represent addend, switch hands, switch addends, say addend, clear echoic buffer, count out fingers to represent addend, clear echoic buffer, count all fingers, end (Shrager and Siegler 1998). The model executes the sequence of operators in the specified order, and states the result. The first time SCADS executes a particular back-up strategy, like for instance the sum strategy, the model devotes its attentional resources (which are not included in Figure 5.1 but are critical to the model's functioning) to ensuring the correct execution of the strategy. The model's decision on whether attentional resources need to be devoted to the supervision of the strategy execution process is based on the strength of the association between the successive operators in the strategy relative to a threshold that varies randomly from trial to trial. To the degree that SCADS has little experience with the execution of a strategy, the strength of the association between the successive operators in it is weak, and attentional resources are required to ensure its appropriate application. Each time SCADS executes the strategy, the strength of the association between the operators in it becomes stronger, which allows the model to devote less attentional resources to the execution process.

The execution of the strategy chosen promotes gradual changes along each of the higher described dimensions of strategy change. First, the strategy execution process yields information about the answer to the problem as well as the speed and accuracy of the strategy on the problem. This information modifies SCADS's database, which, in turn, influences future strategy choices. The execution of the strategy chosen thus results in gradual changes in strategy selection, and, consequently, gradual changes in strategy distribution. Second, the execution of a strategy brings an increase in its speed and accuracy, and a decrease in the attentional resources that are needed to ensure its appropriate execution. Frequent practice with a strategy leads to an increasingly fast, accurate and effortless execution, which allows the model to devote its attentional resources to, for example, the discovery of new strategies (see below). In other words, the strategy execution process promotes gradual changes in the efficiency and repertoire of strategies too.

Strategy discovery   The solid boxes in Figure 5.1 describe the structures and processes that are involved in the strategy discovery process. The metacognitive system of the model plays a central role in the generation of new strategies. The metacognitive system consists of three components, namely (a) the higher-mentioned attentional resources, (b) discovery heuristics, and (c) goal sketch filters.

As mentioned before, SCADS attempts to execute each strategy chosen. The more frequently the model executes a strategy, the more strongly the operators in the strategy become associated, and the less attentional resources SCADS needs to monitor this strategy's execution. SCADS allocates these freed attentional resources to the discovery heuristics.

SCADS includes two discovery heuristics: (a) when a redundant sequence of behaviours is detected, delete one of the sets of operators that caused the redundancy; and (b) if the data base indicates that a strategy is faster or more accurate when it is executed in a particular order, then create a specialized version of the strategy that always uses that order (Shrager and Siegler 1998). These discovery heuristics analyse the working-memory trace of the most recent strategy execution. When doing so, the discovery heuristics sometimes propose new strategies, some valid, others flawed (proposed strategies).

SCADS evaluates the strategies proposed by the discovery heuristics for consistency with the goal sketch filters. The goal sketch filters indicate the criteria that legitimate strategies in the domain of simple addition must meet (e.g. both addends have to be represented in the proposed strategy). If the proposed strategy violates the conceptual constraints specified by the goal sketch filters, it is abandoned. If the proposed strategy is in accord with the conceptual constraints (approved strategies), SCADS adds it to its strategy repertoire. The newly discovered strategy thus modifies the model's database and, consequently, influences future strategy choices.

A final remark concerns the value of the computer simulation. SCADS's performance in simple additions (single digit additions and additions with one addend above 20) is highly consistent with the strategy choice and discovery phenomena that can be observed in four- and five-year-old children (Shrager and Siegler 1998). Just like four- and five-year-olds, SCADS uses multiple strategies to solve simple additions. With increasing experience, the model applies the retrieval strategy ever more frequently, executes the available strategies ever more efficiently, and makes ever more adaptive strategy choices. As practice with simple additions grows, SCADS also discovers new strategies. SCADS never executes illegal new strategies. The discovery of new strategies takes place following correct as well as incorrect trials; the generalization of the newly discovered strategies proceeds gradually. All these phenomena closely resemble empirical data from preschoolers' simple arithmetic; this supports the validity of the structures and processes described in SCADS.

Methodological issues

Siegler and collaborators (e.g., Siegler 1996, 2000; Siegler and Lemaire 1997) propose the use of two different methods to study cognitive (i.e. strategy) change. The first method, the microgenetic method, offers the researcher three fundamental guidelines that allow the study of change processes while they are occurring. The second method, the 'choice/no-choice' method, is a necessary tool to gather unbiased data about (changes in) strategy efficiency and adaptiveness.

The microgenetic method
Siegler and Crowley (1991) define the microgenetic method in terms of three key characteristics. The first characteristic refers to the period of data collection: data are collected during the entire period of change in the competence of interest, i.e. from the beginning of the change until the time at which the changing competence reaches a relatively stable state. The second – and most important – characteristic involves the frequency or density of data collection: the researcher gathers data about the changing competence on as much measurement times as possible; a high density of observations during the period of change relative to the rate of change benefits the quality of the data. The third characteristic refers to the data analyses: the data are examined on an intensive trial-by-trial basis, rather than aggregated over all subjects and/or over all items.

The high density of observations during the period of change provides the researcher the kind of fine-grained information needed to capture and examine change while it is occurring. As discussed in detail by Siegler and Crowley (1991) and Miller and Coyle (1999), cross-sectional and longitudinal approaches yield valuable data about individual children's competencies at different measurement times or different ages. The neat comparison of children's performances at the different measurement times allows the researcher to describe in detail *what* exactly changes in their competencies over time. However, the time between the observations is usually too great to understand the specifics of the process that gave rise to the observed changes. In contrast, by densely sampling individual children's competencies during periods of rapid change, the microgenetic method yields a detailed portrayal of the conceptual and/or behavioural changes that occur over time in and between testing sessions. This fine-grained information not only allows researchers to give a detailed depiction of *what* changes in each individual's behaviour over time. It also allows them to formulate plausible hypotheses about the path, rate, breadth, variability and sources of the change. In other words, it also allows researchers to identify what goes on during the period of change, i.e. *how* change occurs.

The microgenetic method proved useful for studying changes in a wide range of content domains and age groups (Kuhn 1995). The microgenetic method has been used to examine change processes in diverse domains, including number conservation (Siegler 1995), simple addition (Siegler and Jenkins 1989; Siegler and Stern 1998), problem solving (Chen and Siegler 2000; Siegler and Chen 1998), scientific reasoning (Kuhn, Amsel and O'Loughlin 1988; Kuhn, Garcia-Mila, Zohar and Andersen 1995; Kuhn, Schauble, and Garcia-Mila 1992), and map drawing (Karmiloff-Smith 1992). Moreover, it has been applied to deepen our understanding of toddlers' (Chen and Siegler 2000), preschoolers' (Siegler and Jenkins 1989), school-age children's (Siegler and Stern 1998), adolescents' and adults' (Kuhn et al. 1995) cognitive development.

The choice/no-choice method

To obtain unbiased information about the efficiency of strategy use and the adaptiveness of individual strategy choices, Siegler and Lemaire (1997) propose the use of the choice/no-choice method. The choice/no-choice method requires testing each subject under two types of conditions. In the choice condition, subjects can freely choose which strategy they use to solve each problem. In the no-choice condition, subjects must use one particular strategy to solve all problems. The number of no-choice conditions equals the number of strategies available in the choice condition. For instance, if there are two strategies available in the choice condition, there will be two no-choice conditions: one no-choice condition in which subjects are experimentally forced (i.e. instructed) to use one strategy on all problems, and one no-choice condition in which they have to use the other strategy on all problems.

The obligatory use of one particular strategy on all problems in the no-choice condition by each participant allows the researcher to obtain unbiased estimates of the speed and accuracy of the strategy. As discussed in detail by Siegler and Lemaire (1997), the data about the speed and the accuracy of strategies obtained in the choice condition can be biased by selection effects: a strategy that is used mainly to solve easy problems, or primarily applied by the most able subjects, will seem more efficient than a strategy that is almost exclusively used to solve the most difficult problems, or employed most frequently by the least skilled subjects. Requiring all subjects to solve all problems with one particular strategy makes such selective assignments of strategies to problems and/or subjects impossible in the no-choice condition, and thus yields unbiased data about the strategy's efficiency. Moreover, comparison of the data about the accuracy and the speed of the different strategies as gathered in the no-choice conditions, with the strategy choices made in the choice condition, allows the researcher to assess the adaptiveness of individual strategy choices in the choice condition accurately: does the subject (in the choice condition) solve each problem by means of the strategy that yields the best performance on this problem, as evidenced by the information obtained in the no-choice conditions?

Siegler and Lemaire (1997; Lemaire and Lecacheur 2001a) studied the adaptive nature of adults' strategy choices in multiplication and currency conversion tasks successfully using the choice/no-choice method. Furthermore, Lemaire and Lecacheur (2001b, 2002b) applied this method to describe developmental differences in nine- and eleven-year-olds' strategy use in the domains of computational estimation and spelling. Likewise, Luwel, Verschaffel, Onghena and De Corte (2003) demonstrated the usefulness of the choice/no-choice method in studying young adults' strategy characteristics in the domain of numerosity judgement. Finally, Torbeyns, Verschaffel, and Ghesquière (2002, 2004a) examined the strategies that six- to twelve-year-old children of different mathematical ability use to solve simple additions and subtractions by means of this method.

Two illustrative studies

This section illustrates the above-mentioned theoretical and methodological approaches by means of two recent studies. The first study (Chen and Siegler 2000) addresses changes in toddlers' problem-solving strategies in terms of Lemaire and Siegler's model of strategy change as well as Shrager and Siegler's SCADS, using the microgenetic method. The second study (Lemaire and Lecacheur 2002a) investigates the characteristics of the strategies that children and adults use to solve computational estimation tasks, starting from the model of strategy change, using the choice/no-choice method.

Strategy development in toddlers' problem-solving

Chen and Siegler (2000) studied developmental changes in toddlers' problem-solving competencies by means of the microgenetic method. In line with Lemaire and Siegler's model of strategy change, they examined (changes in) the repertoire, frequency, efficiency and adaptiveness of the strategies that toddlers use to solve problems. Special attention was given to the acquisition and further development of one specific problem-solving strategy, namely the tool strategy (see below).

Method   Eighty-six toddlers (aged 18 to 35 months) participated in the study. The toddlers were divided into two groups on the basis of their age. One group consisted of 42 toddlers aged between 18 and 26 months (= younger toddlers). The other group included 44 toddlers between 27 and 35 months of age (= older toddlers).

All toddlers individually solved a toy-retrieval task. An attractive toy was put in the middle of a table, too far away for the toddler to reach. On the table, between the toddler and the toy, were six tools that might be used to retrieve the toy. Only one tool, the target tool, had both a long enough shaft and the right kind of head to pull the toy to the child. The other tools were too short, had no head, or had an ineffective head to obtain the toy.

All toddlers solved three parallel problems of the toy-retrieval task in one of three learning conditions, namely the modelling condition, the hint condition, or the control condition. Each problem consisted of five trials, i.e. five one-minute-periods during which toddlers had the opportunity to try to reach the toy. On the first three trials of each problem, toddlers were encouraged to obtain the toy; they were also told that they could use the tools to do so. After the third trial of each problem, the experimenter demonstrated to the toddlers in the modelling condition how to use the target tool to obtain the toy, and encouraged them to do the same. Toddlers in the hint condition saw, after the third trial of each problem, the experimenter pointing to the target tool, while asking them: 'Can you use this to get (the toy)?' Toddlers in the control condition did not receive any instruction after the third trial of the problems. Following this, toddlers in all three conditions were presented two more trials on the same problem. All toddlers solved the three problems during one testing session; a two- to three-minutes-break was offered between the subsequent problems.

Chen and Siegler registered for each toddler and for each trial the toddler's problem-solving activities (direct observation of problem-solving behaviour), his or her success in obtaining the toy, and the time the toddler needed to reach the toy.

Results   Using Lemaire and Siegler's framework of strategy change as the guiding principle for the data analysis, Chen and Siegler examined changes in the repertoire and distribution of the strategies that toddlers used to solve toy-retrieval problems throughout the experiment. Moreover, they analysed in detail the processes that generated change in the use of the tool strategy over the three problems, over successive trials within a single problem, and within a given trial.

Strategy repertoire   Trial-by-trial analyses of toddlers' problem-solving behaviour revealed that toddlers used multiple strategies to solve the toy-retrieval task. This variability in strategy use was found over the three problems, over the trials within a single problem, and even within a given trial. Chen and Siegler observed four different strategies: (a) the tool strategy, i.e. toddlers use a tool to reach the toy; (b) the forward strategy, i.e. toddlers lean forward and reach for the toy; (c) the indirect strategy, i.e. toddlers ask their parent for help; and (d) no strategy, i.e. toddlers just face the toy and hope that someone will give it to them. Seventy-four per cent of the toddlers used either three or four strategies to solve the problems; only three of the 86 toddlers (i.e. 3 per cent) relied on a single strategy during the entire experiment. The mean number of strategies used by each toddler was 3.04.

The variability in strategy use continued after the toddlers discovered the tool strategy, although the degree of variability differed between the three learning conditions and between the younger and older toddlers in each condition. Once the older toddlers in the modelling and hint conditions had discovered the tool strategy, they applied the other types of strategies on only 4 per cent of the trials. The younger toddlers in the modelling and hint conditions used strategies other than the tool strategy on respectively 23 per cent and 20 per cent of the trials after the discovery of the tool strategy. The older toddlers in the control condition continued to use strategies other than the tool strategy on 48 per cent of the trials after the first time they applied the tool strategy; the younger toddlers in the control condition did so on 84 per cent of such trials.

Strategy distribution   The frequency with which toddlers applied the four strategies clearly changed throughout the experiment. On the first trial of the first problem, most toddlers (i.e., about 80 per cent of the toddlers) used either no strategy or the forward strategy; the indirect strategy and the tool strategy were applied by a minority of them. Throughout the experiment, the frequency of the forward strategy first increased but gradually decreased afterwards. The frequency of no strategy decreased considerably. The tool strategy was used ever more frequently, and became the most frequent strategy at the end of the experiment. The indirect strategy was used only occasionally throughout the entire experiment, with almost no changes in the frequency of its application.

The changes in strategy frequency throughout the experiment differed greatly between the three learning conditions, between younger and older toddlers in each learning condition, and even between individual toddlers within a given age group and learning condition. The frequency of the forward strategy decreased considerably among older toddlers in the modelling and hint condi-tion, but remained high both among younger toddlers in the modelling and hint conditions and among older and younger toddlers in the control condition. Next, the older and younger toddlers in the modelling and hint condition decreased the number of trials on which they used no strategy to reach the toy, but the frequency of no strategy did not change among older and younger toddlers in the control condition. Finally, the older and younger toddlers in the modelling and hint condition applied the tool strategy increasingly frequently throughout the experiment; in contrast, the frequency of the tool strategy remained low among the older and younger toddlers in the control condition.

Development of the tool strategy   Fine-grained analyses of individual toddlers' use of the tool strategy on the three problems, on the subsequent trials within a problem, as well as within a given trial, provided highly valuable information about the path, rate, breadth, variability, and sources of change in this strategy, or, stated otherwise, about the specifics of the change process itself (how does change occur?).

Most toddlers discovered the tool strategy, i.e. applied the tool strategy on at least one trial. The discovery of the tool strategy differed between the three learning conditions: the number of toddlers who discovered the tool strategy was greater in the modelling condition (100 per cent) than in the hint condition (86 per cent), which was, in its turn, greater than in the control condition (56 per cent).

Toddlers who discovered the tool strategy applied it increasingly frequently and consistently on subsequent trials within a problem and on subsequent problems. The accessibility of the tool strategy increased too: toddlers used this strategy ever more frequently as their first strategy on a trial, rather than as a later strategy. With experience, toddlers also refined their strategy choices. They did not only choose the tool strategy more often. When they chose to use the tool strategy, they also used the target tool (rather than an inefficient tool) more frequently. Finally, the toddlers improved their execution of the tool strategy. They became more skilful in using the target tool to reach the toy, which led to an increased success in obtaining the toy, and to a decreased time to reach the toy.

The rapidity with which these changes in the use of the tool strategy occurred varied greatly with toddlers' age and learning condition. Older toddlers in both the modelling and hint conditions learned rather quickly, while the application of the tool strategy changed more gradually among younger toddlers in the latter two conditions. Older and younger toddlers in the control condition showed a more meandering path of change, with less systematic changes in strategy use throughout the experiment.

Conclusions   Chen and Siegler's results provide strong empirical evidence for the validity of Lemaire and Siegler's conceptual framework in the domain of problem-solving. In line with the overlapping waves theory, toddlers used multiple strategies to solve the toy-retrieval task, and applied these strategies with changing frequencies throughout the experiment. Moreover, they added a new strategy, namely the tool strategy, to their strategy repertoire. As toddlers' experience with the tool strategy grew, the frequency, efficiency and adaptiveness with which they applied this new strategy increased too, which is in line with the developmental changes proposed by Lemaire and Siegler's view of strategy change. Each of the just-mentioned changes in the use of the tool strategy can be explained in terms of the change mechanisms described in SCADS. As documented by Chen and Siegler (2000), from the start of the experiment toddlers possessed some conceptual understanding of the task and the types of strategies that might be successful in reaching the toy (= goal sketch filters). The tool strategy, taught by the experimenter to all toddlers in the modelling and hint condition and discovered by about half of the toddlers in the control condition, allowed toddlers to make contact with the desired toy and pull the toy to them. Stated otherwise, the tool strategy met the criteria that potential strategies for solving the toy-retrieval task must meet, as specified by the goal sketch filters, and was thus added to the toddlers' strategy repertoire. The goal sketch filters probably facilitated the transfer of this newly-acquired strategy to subsequent trials within a problem and to subsequent, superficially different, problems. The successful application of the tool strategy on subsequent trials within a problem and on subsequent problems presumably changed its strength relative to the strengths of the other available strategies, which, in its turn, influenced future strategy choice and strategy execution processes.

The study of Chen and Siegler also documents the value of the microgenetic method to study developmental changes in young children's strategy use. The frequent trial-by-trial observations of individual toddlers' problem-solving behaviour, success in reaching the toy, and time needed to obtain the toy, and the fine-grained analyses of these data, made it possible to describe in detail the quantitative and qualitative changes in the use of the tool strategy. Moreover, it allowed Chen and Siegler to analyse the influence of distal variables like toddlers' age, instruction received, and toddlers' growing experience with the task, on the change processes. Finally, it enabled them to deepen our understanding of the underlying change mechanisms.

Strategy development in children's and adults' computational estimation

The second illustrative study that exemplifies the characteristics and strengths of the choice/no-choice method in detail concerns computational estimation skills. Computational estimation is one type of estimation that involves imprecise calculation. More formally, it can be defined as finding an approximate answer to arithmetic problems without (or before) actually computing the exact answer (e.g. $146 + 69 + 48 = 260$; $7 \times 53 = 3500$). Compared to other arithmetic skills, this is a fairly under-investigated area. It is surprising because investigating cognitive processes involved in computational estimation skill provides information about children's general understanding of mathematical concepts, relationships and strategies (e.g. Bestgen, Reys, Rybolt and Wyatt 1980; Carpenter, Coburn, Reys and Wislon 1976; Dehaene, Spelke, Pinel, Stanescu, and Tsivkin 1999; Lemaire, Lecacheur and Farioli 2000; Sowder 1988, 1992; Sowder and Wheeler 1989). Not only is computational estimation an important component of mathematical cognition, but it is also often used in everyday situations in which a rough answer provides a contextually appropriate degree of precision. Examples of such situations involve (a) determining how much a dinner that costs 150 French francs (or 22.5 euros) would cost in US dollars, (b) converting the height of a 3000-metre mountain to feet, or (c) converting a temperature presented in degrees Fahrenheit to the corresponding temperature in degrees Centigrade (e.g., Carpenter et al. 1976; Rubenstein 1985; Trafton 1978). Lemaire and Lecacheur (2002a) ran a study that was aimed at furthering our understanding of age-related changes in strategic aspects of computational estimation skills. In particular, their data document age-related changes in strategy frequency, efficiency and adaptiveness. Strategy repertoire was held constant, so that all age-related differences on any other dimension of the model of strategy change could not be attributed to base-line differences in strategy repertoire.

Method   Two hundred and sixteen participants were asked to provide estimates of 72 three- by three-digit addition problems (e.g. 249 + 743). There were 72 young adults ($M = 21.5$ years, 27 males and 45 females), 72 fourth-grade children ($M = 9.7$ years, 38 boys and 34 girls), and 72 sixth-grade children ($M = 11.9$ years, 42 boys and 30 girls). Two particular strategies were investigated in this project: round-down strategy (i.e. rounding both operands down to the closest smaller decades like doing 230 + 780 to find an estimate for 236 + 789) and round-up strategy (i.e. rounding both operands up to the closest larger decades like doing 240 + 790 for 236 + 789). These two strategies have been shown to be of crucial importance in previous research on computational estimation (e.g., LeFevre, Greenham and Waheed 1993; Lemaire et al. 2000).

The choice/no-choice method was used, so that strategy frequency could be investigated in the choice condition, strategy efficiency could be studied in the no-choice conditions, and strategy adaptiveness could be looked at with measures from both choice and no-choice conditions. Each participant solved the 72 computational estimation problems under one condition only: in each age group, a third of participants was tested in the choice condition, a third was tested under the no-choice/round-down condition, and a third under the no-choice/round-up condition. In the choice condition, participants were informed that they could use either the round-down or the round-up strategy on each problem. In each of the round-down and round-up/no-choice conditions, all 72 problems had to be solved by round-down and round-up strategy respectively. In the choice condition, participants were asked to say which of the two available strategies they had used after solving each problem.

All participants were tested individually and were asked to provide their estimates as fast and as accurately as possible. After an initial set of ten practice trials no participant had any problems with understanding the task or with executing rounding strategies. Each problem was presented centred on a computer screen, after a 1000-ms warning signal. Timing started when problems appeared on the computer screen and ended after participants' response.

Results Data were analysed so as to address the set of issues pertaining to the strategic dimensions pointed out by Lemaire and Siegler (1995). Concerning strategy frequency, Lemaire and Lecacheur wanted to know which of the two computational estimation strategies was used most often and whether strategy preferences changed with age. Regarding strategy efficiency, we asked if both strategies are equally fast and yield as accurate estimates, as well as how relative speed and accuracy of strategies change with age. For strategy adaptivity, data analyses enabled Lemaire and Lecacheur to determine how adaptive computational strategy choices are and how adaptivity of computational estimation changes with age.

Strategy distribution Several findings were of interest for our understanding of age-related differences in computational estimation strategy use. First, all participants used round-down strategy more often than round-up strategy ($M = 61$ per cent vs. $M = 39$ per cent). The former strategy was used on 63 per cent, 62 per cent, and 59 per cent of trials by adults, fourth-, and sixth-graders respectively. Second, the round-down strategy was used more often ($M = 68$ per cent) on small-unit problems (i.e. problems with sum of unit digit smaller than 10) than on large-unit problems ($M = 54$ per cent). Finally, the round-down strategy was used more often with small-unit problems than with large-unit problems in adults ($M = 72$ per cent vs. $M = 53$ per cent) and in sixth-grade children ($M = 70$ per cent vs. $M = 54$ per cent), but not in fourth-grade children ($M = 61$ per cent vs. $M = 56$ per cent).

Strategy efficiency Analyses of strategy efficiency enabled understanding of how fast and how accurately each strategy was executed in each age group and for each type of small- and large-unit problem. Mean solution latencies and per cent deviations were therefore analysed as a function of age group, strategies and problem type. Per cent deviations are differences between estimates and correct sums divided by correct sums. To illustrate, if a participant responded

570 for 132 + 453 he or she would be 2.56 per cent away from the correct sum ([(570 − 585)/585] * 100).

Results showed that round-down strategy yielded shorter solution times and better estimates than round-up strategy in choice and no-choice conditions. In addition, in both choice and no-choice conditions, adults were significantly faster (choice: $M = 6.6$ s, no-choice: $M = 5.6$ s) than sixth-graders (choice: $M = 12.8$ s, no-choice: $M = 10.1$ s) who were significantly faster than fourth-graders (choice: $M = 17.5$ s, no-choice: $M = 16.4$ s). These latencies were not compromised by speed-accuracy trade-offs as corresponding analyses on mean per cent deviations showed that adults (choice: $M = 1.52$ per cent, no-choice: $M = 1.59$ per cent) and sixth-grade children (choice: $M = 1.54$ per cent, no-choice: $M = 1.70$ per cent) provided estimates that were closer to correct sums than fourth-graders (choice: $M = 2.06$ per cent, no-choice: $M = 1.97$ per cent). Thus, as in other math activities, computational estimation performance increased with age, and this is not (only) the result of older participants' using more efficient strategies more often.

Strategy selection   Analyses of strategy selection enabled understanding of the determiners of strategy use overall and in each age group separately. It was of interest to know whether strategy choice processes were influenced by the same variable, and if so to the same extent, in each age group. It was also of interest to know whether strategy choices are adaptive in each age group, whether the determiners of strategy choices were the same or different across age groups. To answer these questions, Lemaire and Lecacheur (2002a) ran a series of correlation and regression analyses with the goal of predicting mean per cent use of round-down in the choice condition as a function of two types of predictors, namely problem and strategy features. Problem characteristics involve stimulus attributes such as (a) problem size (as assessed by correct sums); (b) whether the operand includes specific numbers, like 0, 1, 5, or 10; or (c) size of the larger operand. Strategy characteristics refer to relative strategy performance with a given strategy in the no-choice conditions. (d) Relative speed was measured as the mean latencies for round-up strategy under no-choice/round-up – mean latencies for round-down strategy under no-choice/round-down. (e) Relative precision was measured as the mean per cent deviations for round-up strategy under no-choice/round-up – mean per cent deviations for round-down strategy under no-choice/round-down. These two types of problem and strategy features proved crucial in past outcomes of research on arithmetic strategies (see Ashcraft 1995, for a review).

Correlation analyses suggested that adults and sixth-graders chose strategies on individual problems based on distances between unit digits and their closest decades, as well as on relative precision. In contrast, fourth-graders made strategy choices mostly on the basis of size of hundred and decade digits and to a much lower extent on the basis of size of unit digits. Size of hundred and decade digits captures calculation difficulty, suggesting that fourth-graders used round-down more often on problems involving large numbers in order to decrease calculation difficulty. These results were confirmed by regression analyses that showed a unique significant predictor in all age groups. This best predictor of strategy use was the sum of unit digit in adults ($R^2 = .60$) and in sixth-graders ($R^2 = .41$). Fourth-graders' strategy use was best predicted by sum of hundred and decade digits ($R^2 = .13$). Differences in R^2 magnitudes suggest that children were much less systematic than adult participants.

Conclusions   The study of Lemaire and Lecacheur (2002a) documents the value of the choice/no-choice method to examine age-related changes in strategic aspects of children's computational estimation performance. First, the no-choice condition results showed that estimates of relative strategy performance may be biased by strategy choices when they are not controlled for. Such bias, when not controlled, undermines any conclusions regarding age-related changes in strategy execution. Second, the pure estimates of strategy performance in the no-choice condition enabled unbiased assessments of the role of relative strategy performance on strategy choices, as well as effects of problem features above and beyond effects of strategies.

What also makes the choice/no-choice method nice is that, when combined with detailed conceptual task analyses, participants' performance is easily understood. For example, in Lemaire and Lecacheur's study, it is easy to understand how the round-down strategy yielded better performance than the round-up strategy, and consequently was used more frequently by participants. Figure 5.2 shows a diagrammatic representation of cognitive processes involved within each round-down and round-up strategy. Although both strategies involve approximately the same cognitive processes (except for round-up which involves an extra process, incrementing decade digits), these processes make different cognitive resource demands. Encoding could be easier when executed within round-down than within round-up because round-down could be executed accurately without encoding unit digits. Moreover, rounding processes were probably easier to execute within round-down than within round-up for two reasons: (a) round-down did not require calculating differences between unit digits and the closest larger decades, (b) round-up processes had to be executed with decade digits stored in working memory whereas working memory was much less involved in executing rounding processes within round-down, as the manipulated decade digits were displayed on the computer screen while trying to find estimates.

Of course, the Lemaire and Lecacheur study involves a number of limits (see Lemaire and Lecacheur 2002a, for a detailed discussion of these limits), such as the two types of strategies that were investigated, the types of problems

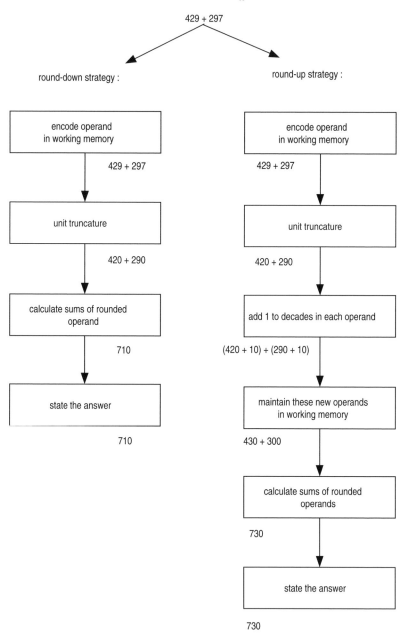

Figure 5.2. Conceptual task analysis of cognitive processes involved within each computational estimation strategy in Lemaire and Lecacheur's (2002a) study.

that were tested or the between-subject nature of the choice/no-choice variable. However, generalization of Lemaire and Lecacheur's findings with more than two strategies or two other strategies, with all types of problems and with each participant being tested under both choice and no-choice conditions, is easy to test. Similarly, individual differences other than age and expertise (environmental constraints such as different levels of speed and/or accuracy pressure) may be easily tested to run fine-grained analyses of the main determiners of children's computational estimation performance, as well as age-related changes in these performances.

Conclusion and discussion

One of the main goals of cognitive developmental psychologists is to understand children's cognition; another one is to understand cognitive development. Understanding children's cognition entails knowing how children accomplish cognitive tasks in a variety of domains. Understanding cognitive development requires being able to describe and explain (in terms of mechanisms) age-related cognitive changes. Major theories of cognitive development – Piagetian, neo-Piagetian, Vygotskian, contextualist and neo-nativistic (see Flavell, Miller and Miller 1993 for a review) – have made several claims regarding both general features of children's cognition and cognitive development. Information-processing approaches to cognitive development made important unique contributions. These contributions have a number of implications for further understanding and investigating cognitive development. We discuss these theoretical and methodological implications in this final section. At the same time we will mention some limitations of this approach, and point to some ways for its further development and integration with other work.

Changing our view of cognitive development

As shown in the two above-mentioned illustrative empirical studies in the domains of problem solving and computational estimation, respectively, and in many other cognitive domains, it can no longer be held that, to accomplish a cognitive task, children of one age use one given strategy and older children use a different strategy. At all ages, children use several strategies. As developmental psychologists who want to know how cognitive changes occur and how children approach cognitive tasks, it is important to acknowledge that this cognitive variability is an important feature of human cognition at all points throughout life. Otherwise, our understanding of children's thinking is biased and does not correspond to reality (Siegler 1996, 2000).

Acknowledging cognitive variability leads us to investigate different issues in children's cognition, in particular issues involving strategic aspects of children's cognitive performance. These issues concern strategy repertoire, distribution, efficiency and selection. It also leads us to investigate how changes occur in all these strategy dimensions. First, it is important to understand strategy repertoire. That is, for any given cognitive task or domain, we want to know what are the strategies that children use or could use to correctly accomplish the task. This can be done both theoretically (via conceptual task analyses of the type portrayed in Figure 5.2) or empirically (e.g. through video-recordings or via verbal protocols). For some cognitive domains, the same strategy repertoire is used by children of varying ages. For other domains, different strategies may be used. In any case, it is important to know strategy repertoire if we want to understand children's cognition.

The second strategy dimension that contributes to cognitive development is strategy distribution. Information-processing approaches suggest viewing cognitive development as changes not necessarily in the type of strategies that are used but in the strategy mix. One strategy that is most frequent at a given age may be no longer the most frequently used a few months or years later. The overlapping waves model proposed by Siegler is a very picturesque and yet adequate way of characterizing children's thinking; it makes crucial the goal of describing cognitive development as a succession of distributions of modes of thinking.

The two other strategy changes that characterize cognitive development and that become more important to understand if we want to provide better descriptions and explanations of cognitive growth in children are strategy efficiency and selection. As data in different domains suggest, execution of each strategy improves with age. That is, strategies become triggered and executed much more quickly and more accurately as children grow older and become more expert at cognitive tasks. This occurs, among other things, through automatization (e.g. Lemaire, Barrett, Fayol and Abdi 1994).

Acknowledging cognitive variability finally leads us to investigate how children of different ages choose among strategies (or mental representations) to accomplish cognitive tasks. Information-processing approaches have led to the discovery that children do not choose a given strategy for all trials before accomplishing the task; they choose each strategy on each trial. This suggested that researchers had to run some studies looking at what determines children's strategy choices. These choices appear to be dependent upon at least four types of factors, namely problem features (e.g. small vs. large arithmetic problems), strategy characteristics (speed or accuracy), situational constraints (e.g. speed/accuracy requirements), and individual differences (e.g. skills in a given domain). Previous works in the information-processing tradition abundantly documented the roles of problem and strategy features and skills (e.g. Geary 1996; Geary and Brown 1991; Lemaire and Lecacheur 2002a, b; Lemaire and Siegler 1995; Lemaire et al. 1994), and less abundantly the role of situational constraints (e.g. Bisanz and LeFevre 1990; Bjorklund and Rosenblum 2001). Future research will help understand the respective roles of these factors throughout cognitive development so as to know whether some factors are more important than others during some periods of cognitive development than during other periods.

In sum, information-processing approaches to cognitive development changed our view of what cognitive development is all about. It is no longer a succession of modes of thinking. Rather, it involves several modes of thinking co-existing and competing throughout development. Cognitive development proceeds gradually, with continuous changes in the repertoire, frequency, efficiency and adaptiveness of the co-existing strategies. It should be noted, however, that the overlapping waves model might not apply to all kinds of strategy developments. It can be argued that the well-documented smoothness of overlap that is evidenced by the gist of the above-mentioned studies is due to the fact that most of this research focuses on specific (sets of) problems whose solution becomes possible within a limited age range, such as, for instance, addition problems. However, if one focuses on strategies concerned with broader sets of (qualitatively different) problems, like, for instance, addition and algebra problems, the language for describing and interpreting strategy changes provided by the overlapping waves model may be less appropriate (Demetriou, Efklides and Platsidou 1993; Granott 1998; van Geert 1998). Further research is needed to reveal which (types of) strategy changes fit nicely with the overlapping waves model and for which this model does not yield the most appropriate theoretical account.

The information-processing approach did not only change our view of what changes during cognitive development, but also deepened our understanding of both general and specific mechanisms accounting for how and why these changes occur. As evidenced by Siegler and his associates, changes in cognitive performance are not merely the result of either increased automatization of associative knowledge or improvements in metacognitive understanding. Increased cognitive performance reflects changes in both associative and metacognitive knowledge systems, as well as their dialectic interaction. As formalized in SCADS, associative and metacognitive structures and processes dynamically interact and continuously change on the basis of experience, leading to gradual improvements along the higher-described dimensions of strategy competence. The change mechanisms specified in SCADS do not only apply to the domain of simple addition. As illustrated in the first empirical study (Chen and Siegler 2000), these change mechanisms do also play a key role in other cognitive domains, such as, for instance the domain of problem solving.

Although the metacognitive knowledge system plays a significant role in Siegler's theory of cognitive development, and although such a system makes part of computer simulation models like the SCADS model, it should be acknowledged that this theory and these computer models do not give us a very clear and convincing response as to what is exactly the role of these metacognitive processes, how they are activated, and how they work and develop themselves. Therefore, another valuable line of future research is to investigate the role of metacognition more intensively, both theoretically and empirically. For an example of a theory of cognitive development that has tried to integrate metacognition more explicitly and more systematically, we refer to the chapter by Demetriou and associates in this volume. Moreover, although Siegler's theory on cognitive development initially did not deal directly and analytically with the influence of other general factors besides metacognition on the process of change, like, for instance, processing efficiency and working memory, recent studies by Lemaire and collaborators (De Rammelaere, Duverne, Lemaire and Vandierendonck 2003; Imbo, Duverne and Lemaire 2003) revealed how working memory influences strategy choice and execution processes in the domain of mathematical cognition. These insights can help us to refine, elaborate, and integrate the models presented in this chapter with other models in which processing efficiency factors occupy a central role (e.g. Case, Okamoto, Griffin, McKeough, Bleiker, Henderson and Stephenson 1996; Demetriou et al. 2002; Halford, Wilson and Phillips 1998).

Changing our research methods to investigate cognitive development

New issues, or old issues revisited, brought to the forefront of the research agenda by cognitive developmental psychologists inspired by information-processing approaches, forced researchers to devise and use new research methods to better understand children's cognition and cognitive development. As discussed in the introduction, research methods such as formal, computational models of cognitive development and the microgenetic or the choice/no-choice methods proved to be well suited to addressing these issues.

Formal models of cognitive development, such as SCADS, developed by Siegler and collaborators, greatly advanced the field of cognitive development. Not only are these models characterized by rigorous, transparent, and empirically justifiable or testable assumptions, they also generate deeper understanding of old and new issues. For example, one pressing issue in cognitive development is age-related changes in strategy distribution. Models such as SCADS make it clear that one potential mechanism for age-related changes in strategy distribution or strategy choices involves changes in associative strengths among different problem components (strategies, operands, correct and incorrect answers). Such clear, rigorous and testable assumptions dissipate the mysterious nature of transition between modes of cognitive functionings at different points in the course of development.

By building more computational models and further testing their predictions, the field of cognitive development is sure to make important progress. It is also a sure way to explore issues for which they are mute. For example, how children of different ages modulate their strategy choices as a function of situational or contextual constraints (e.g. speed/accuracy pressures; solving problems with peers) is not yet understood within these models. Even though it is possible to assume mechanisms of modulation of associative strengths, whether such modulation requires conscious awareness and is part of metacognitive processes will have to be determined in future research.

Together with formal computational models of children's cognitive development, the information-processing perspective has devised new empirical methods. Two of these have been discussed in this chapter, namely microgenetic methods and the choice/no-choice method. Microgenetic methods are the type of methods that developmental psychologists needed to go deeper into investigating cognitive changes, above and beyond simply looking at age-related changes in average performance. Although microgenetic methods are resource demanding and time consuming, they are very useful tools to obtain precise and detailed measures of the determiners of changes (hence the mechanisms by which changes occur) and a more complete picture of individual differences in cognitive growth (for a more detailed discussion, see Miller and Coyle 1999).

The choice/no-choice method is the direct result of looking at children's cognition as inherently variable. As several empirical studies have now demonstrated, such methods not only control for potential artefacts present in previous investigations, thereby enabling firmer and clearer conclusions than before, but also open up new issues. To take one example, without collecting separate measures of strategy execution under choice and no-choice conditions, it was impossible to understand why we use several strategies, how we choose among them on each trial, and how one strategy becomes more frequent at some point. Thanks to the choice/no-choice method, it was possible to observe that having multiple strategies yields better performance than having just one (because some strategies are more efficient on some problems, and other strategies work best with other strategies); it was possible to document the crucial roles of problem and strategy characteristics on children's strategy choices at different periods in their life. What is nice about methods such as the choice/no-choice method is that they are not limited to the domain of mathematics in which they have been devised. Recent investigations documented their fruitfulness in other domains, such as spelling (Lemaire and Lecacheur 2002b; Rittle-Johnson and Siegler 1999). However, the choice/no-choice method has its limits too (Torbeyns et al. 2004b). First of all, within the choice/no-choice paradigm, the number of no-choice conditions must equal the number of strategies available in the choice condition. Taking into account the rich diversity of strategies that people use to accomplish cognitive tasks, most studies will have to replace the choice condition by a restricted-choice condition, in which the number of available strategies is limited by the experimenter. Otherwise, with more no-choice conditions different factors (e.g. fatigue, attention, motivation) may distort participants' optimal execution of strategies. Second, the choice/no-choice method requires that the experimenter has control over the strategies that subjects apply in both the choice and no-choice conditions. Since people (can) use – from an early age onwards – a variety of cognitive strategies that are not accompanied by observable problem-solving behaviours (like, for instance, counting silently or retrieving the answer to single digit additions), experimental control of the strategies used in the choice and no-choice conditions is necessary (by asking subjects to point to observable objects while counting to control the use of counting strategies, as far as counting is concerned, or by including a strict time limit to ensure the use of retrieval, in the case of retrieval). Consequently, strategy execution might become a (highly) artificial process within the choice/no-choice paradigm. Moreover, even with these experimental manipulations, one can question whether it is possible to really know which (other) unobservable cognitive strategies subjects applied during problem-solving.

In conclusion, conceptual and methodological contributions of information-processing approaches to cognitive development enabled us to better understand children's cognition and cognitive development. These approaches provided detailed descriptions and accounts of how children of different ages perform tasks in a variety of cognitive domains as well as new tools to investigate crucial issues in cognitive developmental psychology. Such a success has no reason to stop. Combined with other theoretical approaches, information-processing perspectives should make our field even more vibrant, active and productive than it has ever been.

REFERENCES

Ashcraft, M. H. (1995). Cognitive psychology and simple arithmetic: a review and summary of new directions. *Mathematical Cognition, 1*, 3–34.

Bestgen, B. J., Reys, R. E., Rybolt, J. F. and Wyatt, J. W. (1980). Effectiveness of systematic instruction on attitudes and computational skills of preservice elementary teachers. *Journal for Research in Mathematics Education, 2*, 124–35.

Bisanz, J. and LeFevre, J. A. (1990). Strategic and nonstrategic processing in the development of mathematical cognition. In D. F. Bjorklund (ed.) *Children's strategies: contemporary views of cognitive development*. Hillsdale, NJ: Lawrence Erlbaum Associates.

Bjorklund, D. F. and Rosenblum, K. E. (2001). Children's use of multiple and variable addition strategies in a game context. *Developmental Science, 4*, 184–94.

Carpenter, T. P., Coburn, T. G., Reys, R. E. and Wislon, J. W. (1976). Notes on national assessment: estimation. *Arithmetic Teacher, 23*, 296–301.

Case, R., Okamoto, Y., Griffin, S., McKeough, A., Bleiker, C., Henderson, B. and Stephenson, K. M. (1996). The role of central conceptual structures in the development of children's thought. *Monographs of the Society for Research in Child Development, 61* (1–2, serial no. 246).

Chen, Z. and Siegler, R. S. (2000). Across the great divide: bridging the gap between understanding of toddlers' and older children's thinking. *Monographs of the Society for Research in Child Development, 65* (2, serial no 261).

Crowley, K., Shrager, J. and Siegler, R. S. (1997). Strategy discovery as a competitive negotiation between metacognitive and associative mechanisms. *Developmental Review, 17,* 462–89.

De Corte, E., Greer, B. and Verschaffel, L. (1996). Mathematics teaching and learning. In D. C. Berliner and R. C. Calfee (eds.) *Handbook of educational psychology* (pp. 491–549). New York: Macmillan.

Dehaene, S., Spelke, E., Pinel, P., Stanescu, R. and Tsivkin, S. (1999). Sources of mathematical thinking: behavioural and brain-imaging evidence. *Science, 284,* 970–3.

Demetriou, A., Christou, C., Spanoudis, G. and Platsidou, G. (2002). The development of mental processing: efficiency, working memory, and thinking. *Monographs of the Society for Research in Child Development, 67* (serial no. 268).

Demetriou, A., Efklides, A. and Platsidou, M. (1993). The architecture and dynamics of developing mind: experiential structuralism as a frame for unifying cognitive developmental theories. *Monographs of the Society for Research in Child Development, 58* (5–6, serial no. 234).

De Rammelaere, S., Duverne, S., Lemaire, P. and Vandierendonck, A. (2003). The role of working-memory in simple and complex arithmetic verification problems. Manuscript submitted for publication.

Flavell, J. H., Miller, P. H. and Miller, S. A. (1993). *Cognitive development (3rd edn).* Upper Saddle River, NJ: Prentice-Hall, Inc.

Geary, D. C. (1996). The problem-size effect in mental addition: developmental and cross-national trends. *Mathematical Cognition, 2,* 63–93.

Geary, D. C. and Brown, S. C. (1991). Cognitive addition: strategy choice and speed-of-processing differences in gifted, normal and mathematically disabled children. *Developmental Psychology, 27,* 398–406.

Granott, N. (1998). A paradigm shift in the study of development: essay review of *Emerging minds* by R. S. Siegler. *Human Development, 41,* 360–5.

Greeno, J. G., Collins, A. M. and Resnick, L. (1996). Cognition and learning. In D. C. Berliner and R. C. Calfee (eds.) *Handbook of educational psychology* (pp. 15–46). New York: Macmillan.

Greer, B. and Verschaffel, L. (1990). Introduction to the special issue on mathematics education as a proving-ground for information-processing theories. *International Journal of Educational Research, 14,* 3–12.

Halford, G. S., Wilson, W. H. and Phillips, S. (1998). Processing capacity defined by relational complexity: implications for comparative, developmental, and cognitive psychology. *Behavioral and Brain Sciences, 21,* 803–64.

Imbo, I., Duverne, S. and Lemaire, P. (2003). Effects of working memory on strategic aspects of cognitive performance: insights from arithmetic computational estimation. Manuscript submitted for publication.

Kail, R. (1996). Information-processing theories of human development. In E. De Corte and F. E. Weinert (eds.) *International encyclopedia of developmental and instructional psychology* (pp. 92–7). Oxford, England: Pergamon Press.

Karmiloff-Smith, A. (1992). *Beyond modularity: a developmental perspective on cognitive science*. Cambridge, MA: MIT Press.

Klahr, D. and MacWhinney, B. (1998). Information processing. In D. Kuhn and R. S. Siegler (eds.) W. Damon (series ed.), *Handbook of child psychology: volume 2. Cognition, perception, and language* (5th edn, pp. 631–78). New York: Wiley.

Kuhn, D. (1995). Microgenetic study of change: what has it told us? *Psychological Science*, 6, 133–9.

Kuhn, D., Amsel, E. and O'Loughlin, M. (1988). *The development of scientific thinking skills*. San Diego: Academic Press.

Kuhn, D., Garcia-Mila, M., Zohar, A. and Andersen, C. (1995). Strategies of knowledge acquisition. *Monographs of the Society for Research in Child Development*, 60 (serial no. 245).

Kuhn, D., Schauble, L. and Garcia-Mila, M. (1992). Cross-domain development of scientific reasoning. *Cognition and Instruction*, 9, 285–327.

LeFevre, J. A., Greenham, S. L. and Waheed, N. (1993). The development of procedural and conceptual knowledge in computational estimation. *Cognition and Instruction*, 11, 95–132.

Lemaire, P., Barrett, S. E., Fayol, M. and Abdi, H. (1994). Automatic activation of addition and multiplication facts in elementary school children. *Journal of Experimental Child Psychology*, 57, 224–58.

Lemaire, P. and Lecacheur, M. (2001a). Older and younger adults' strategy use and execution in currency conversion tasks: insights from French franc to euro and euro to French franc conversions. *Journal of Experimental Psychology: Applied*, 7, 195–206.

(2001b, August). *Strategic change in children's computational estimation*. Paper presented in a symposium on 'Strategy changes and strategy choices in children's and adults' mathematical thinking: theoretical and methodological contributions' at the 9th Conference of the European Association for Research on Learning and Instruction, Fribourg, Switzerland.

(2002a). Children's strategies in computational estimation. *Journal of Experimental Child Psychology*, 82, 281–304.

(2002b). Applying the choice/no-choice methodology: the case of children's strategy use in spelling. *Developmental Science*, 5, 42–7.

Lemaire, P., Lecacheur, M. and Farioli, F. (2000). Children's strategies in computational estimation. *Canadian Journal of Experimental Psychology*, 54, 141–8.

Lemaire, P. and Reder, L. (1999). What affects strategy selection in arithmetic? The example of parity and five effects on product verification. *Memory and Cognition*, 27, 364–82.

Lemaire, P. and Siegler, R. S. (1995). Four aspects of strategic change: contributions to children's learning of multiplication. *Journal of Experimental Psychology: General*, 124, 83–97.

Luwel, K., Verschaffel, L., Onghena, P. and De Corte, E. (2003). Analyzing the adaptiveness of strategy choices using the choice/no-choice method: the case of numerosity judgement. *European Journal of Cognitive Psychology*, 15, 511–37.

Miller, P. H. and Coyle, T. R. (1999). Developmental change: lessons from microgenesis. In E. K. Scholnick, K. Nelson, S. A. Gelman and P. H. Miller (eds.) *Conceptual development: Piaget's legacy* (pp. 209–39). Mahwah, NJ: Erlbaum.

Rittle-Johnson, B. and Siegler, R. S. (1999). Learning to spell: variability, choice, and change in children's strategy use. *Child Development, 70,* 332–48.

Rubenstein, R. N. (1985). Computational estimation and related mathematical skills. *Journal for Research in Mathematics Education, 16,* 106–19.

Shrager, J. and Siegler, R. S. (1998). SCADS: a model of children's strategy choices and strategy discoveries. *Psychological Sciences, 9,* 405–10.

Siegler, R. S. (1986). Unities across domains in children's strategy choices. In M. Perlmutter (ed.) *Perspectives on intellectual development: the Minnesota symposia on child psychology* (vol. 19, pp. 1–48). Hillsdale, NJ: Erlbaum.

(1987). Some general conclusions about children's strategy choice procedures. *International Journal of Psychology, 22,* 729–49.

(1991). Strategy choice and strategy discovery. *Learning and Instruction, 1,* 89–102.

(1995). How does change occur: a microgenetic study of number conservation. *Cognitive Psychology, 25,* 225–73.

(1996). *Emerging minds.* New York: Oxford University Press.

(1998). *Children's thinking.* New Jersey: Prentice Hall.

(2000). The rebirth of children's learning. *Child Development, 71,* 26–35.

(2001). Children's discoveries and brain-damaged patients' rediscoveries. In J. L. McClelland and R. S. Siegler (eds.) *Mechanisms of cognitive development. Behavioral and neural perspectives* (pp. 33–63). Mahwah, NJ: Erlbaum.

Siegler, R. S. and Chen, Z. (1998). Developmental differences in rule-learning: a microgenetic analysis. *Cognitive Psychology, 36,* 273–310.

Siegler, R. S. and Crowley, K. (1991). The microgenetic method: a direct means for studying cognitive development. *American Psychologist, 46,* 606–20.

Siegler, R. S. and Jenkins, E. A. (1989). *How children discover new strategies.* Hillsdale, NJ: Erlbaum.

Siegler, R. S. and Lemaire, P. (1997). Older and younger adults' strategy choices in multiplication: testing predictions of ASCM using the choice/no-choice method. *Journal of Experimental Psychology: General, 126,* 71–92.

Siegler, R. S. and Shipley, C. (1995). Variation, selection and cognitive change. In T. Simon and G. Halford (eds.) *Developing cognitive competence: new approaches to process modelling* (pp. 31–76). Hillsdale, NJ: Erlbaum.

Siegler, R. S. and Shrager, J. (1984). Strategy choices in addition and subtraction: how do children know what to do? In C. Sophian (ed.) *Origins of cognitive skills.* Hillsdale, NJ: Erlbaum.

Siegler, R. S. and Stern, E. (1998). Conscious and unconscious strategy discoveries: a microgenetic analysis. *Journal of Experimental Psychology: General, 127,* 377–97.

Sowder, J. T. (1988). Mental computation and number comparison: their roles in the development of number sense and computational estimation. In J. Hebert and M. Behr (eds.) *Number concepts and operations in the middle grades* (pp. 182–97). Hillsdale, NJ: Lawrence Erlbaum.

(1992). Estimation and related topics. In D. A. Grouws (ed.) *Handbook of research on teaching and learning.* New York: Macmillan.

Sowder, J. T. and Wheeler, M. M. (1989). The development of concepts and strategies used in computational estimation. *Journal for Research in Mathematics Education, 20*, 130–46.

Torbeyns, J., Verschaffel, L. and Ghesquière, P. (2002). Strategic competence: applying Siegler's theoretical and methodological framework to the domain of simple addition. *European Journal of Psychology of Education, 17*, 275–91.

(2004a). Strategic aspects of simple addition and subtraction: the influence of mathematical ability. *Learning and Instruction, 14*, 177–95.

(2004b). Strategy development in children with mathematical disabilities: insights from the choice/no-choice method and the chronological-age/ ability-level-match design. *Journal of Learning Disabilities, 37*, 119–31.

Trafton, P. R. (1978). Estimation and mental arithmetic: important components of computation. In M. N. Suydam and R. E. Reys (eds.) *Developing computational skills.* Reston, VA: National Council of Teachers of Mathematics.

van Geert, P. (1998). A dynamic systems model of basic developmental mechanisms: Piaget, Vygotsky, and beyond. *Psychological Review, 105*, 634–77.

6   The emergence of mind in the emotional brain

Marc D. Lewis

Over the past ten years or so, the language of dynamic systems has become increasingly important for understanding cognitive and neural processes, both in the moment and over development (e.g. Kelso 1995; Port and van Gelder 1995; Skarda and Freeman 1987; Thatcher 1998; Thelen and Smith 1994; Varela, Thompson and Rosch 1991). According to the dynamic systems (DS) approach, cognition builds on itself, biasing its own outcomes and growing in coherence and complexity. This process is often called self-organization, defined as the emergence of novel structures or levels of organization resulting from the spontaneous synchronization of lower-order elements. At the psychological level of description, self-organizing cognitive wholes emerge from the synchronization of lower-order components, such as associations, expectancies, propositions, percepts, schemas and memories. At the biological level, these abstract entities are translated into populations of neurones and neural assemblies that become rapidly synchronized through electrochemical activities.

There is growing evidence that coherent mental events correspond with neural self-organization, both emerging from and constraining the synchronization of cellular events in the physical system of the brain (Engel, Fries and Singer 2001; Thompson and Varela 2001). This is a momentous discovery that promises to resolve the mind–body problem in a way never before possible. On this view, it appears that mind grows out of matter – specifically, brain matter – in a dynamic process that organizes the very matter from which it arises. The question I wish to address in this chapter is: how does emotion contribute to this process?

The aim of this book is to examine the development of cognition over the months and years of life. But in order to do so, it is important to try to understand how cognition emerges and coheres in the first place – that is, in the moment (or what is termed 'real time'). What develops in cognitive development must come together within occasions, perhaps many occasions, first. And indeed, both the momentary and developmental time scales can be modelled as self-organizing processes. Therefore, my first objective in this chapter is to look at the self-organization of cognition in real time, with particular attention to how emotion drives cognitive coherence. The medium I choose for this exploration is the brain, where I examine the tendency for rapid synchronization across the various levels of the neural axis, from primitive structures that control stereotypic behaviours to the executive systems of the cerebral cortex. Next, I examine the implications of this perspective for development, looking both at normative developmental acquisitions and at the development of individual cognitive differences.

Dynamic systems approaches – unanswered questions

According to dynamic systems (DS) accounts, variability in behaviour over development should not be considered 'noise', partly because it is the source of possibilities from which new forms arise (Thelen and Ulrich 1991; Thelen and Smith 1994). Moreover, this variability changes in systematic ways at the time of identifiable shifts in cognitive and motor development (Rose and Fischer 1998; van der Maas 1998; van Geert 1998). In cognitive development, for example, variability increases and then decreases at about three years, when new syntactic forms cohere and stabilize (Ruhland and van Geert 1998). The same profile of fluctuation, referred to as a *phase transition*, appears to hold for habits of attentional engagement in frustrating situations at 18–20 months (Lewis, Zimmerman, Hollenstein and Lamey 2004), the time of a hypothesized stage shift in cognitive development (Case et al. 1992b). The rise in variability at transitions evidently reflects the onset of new patterns of activity or thought, competing with each other and with previously established patterns. The subsequent reduction in variability reflects the increasing resilience of one form at the expense of others (e.g. scripts, schemas, strategies). However, it remains difficult to explain how and why *particular* forms develop. Given a broad range of possible outcomes, why do some cognitive forms emerge instead of others? What stabilizes them amid the flux of organismic and environmental changes? Why do they recur and strengthen over development while other forms disappear?

One approach to these questions is to look more closely at the real-time processes that underlie developmental change. Developmentalists who take a dynamic systems view have a unique window on microdevelopmental processes that complements more traditional findings from longitudinal research (Lee and Karmiloff-Smith 2002). In real time, as in development, cognitive outcomes arise out of background variability, achieving coherence and stability on a scale of seconds rather than months or years (Kelso 1995; Thelen and Ulrich 1991). These rapidly self-assembling forms include walking, crawling and reaching (Thelen and Ulrich 1991), semantic categorization (Smith 1995), emotion-related appraisals (Lewis 2000; Scherer 2000) and social behaviour (Vallacher and Nowak 1997). Many theorists assume that cognitive self-organization at this scale reflects the synchronization of activity across brain regions, and both neuroscientific research and computer simulations suggest the rapid convergence of neural oscillations (e.g. firing rates) when actions or mental states cohere (Skarda and Freeman 1987; Thatcher 1998; Thelen et al. 2001; Thompson and Varela 2001; Varela et al. 2001). But even if developmental emergence relies on momentary coherences, we are no closer to explaining which cognitive forms emerge. Why these and not others? What propels them within situations, and what causes them to recur across situations? These concerns reflect the three questions highlighted by this volume: What forms cohere in development? How do they cohere and recur? Why (according to what causal agency) do these processes take place?

DS developmentalists do not worry very much about the nature of the cognitive acquisitions that arise through self-organizing processes – the 'what' of cognitive development. DS approaches in the Piagetian tradition (e.g. Case et al. 1996; Demetriou et al. 2002; van der Maas and Molenaar 1992; van Geert 1994) measure generic change processes, exemplified by a variety of problem-solving and linguistic tasks, and they model systems that can exhibit those processes without regard to content. These modelling ventures are more concerned with the 'how' than the 'what' of development, and they frame the mechanisms of development with elegant equations that symbolize feedback processes leading to stabilization. DS approaches based on synergetics (e.g. Smith 1995; Thelen and Smith 1994) also examine a large variety of developing forms, suggesting that all emerge in more or less the same way – through the coordination of their components via action. Thelen and Smith supply at least one axiom for defining the 'what' of development. For them, coordination reflects function: cognitive, motor and perceptual coherences arise because they interface with the environment in a way that 'works'. These coherences are then selected in development. They recur and strengthen, becoming attractors in a developing landscape of skills and actions. In this way, the 'what' of cognitive development is defined abstractly as coherences that work, and the 'how' of development involves mechanisms of co-activation and selection.

Thus, for DS theorists, the 'what' of development remains highly abstract, and the 'how' of development is identified by general mechanisms such as feedback, coordination and selection. Perhaps as a result, the 'why' of development remains abstract as well. DS developmentalists cite general tendencies for complex systems to self-organize, according to principles such as 'negative entropy' and coupling due to energy flow. These tendencies are often explained by reference to physical, thermodynamic, chemical and biological systems, but there is not as much thinking about the causal force that propels human ontogenesis per se. Of course, it is a good idea to retain enough generality in one's model to make it relevant to a diverse set of tasks, domains and acquisitions. But it may be possible to model development in relation to general *human* forces and processes without losing this edge. Ideally, the functionality of enduring forms might be specified according to how we humans tune into what is functional; the feedback and coordination processes that give rise to such forms might be specified in terms of actual bodily mechanisms of synchronization; and the causal thrust that propels development might be specified in terms of human strivings and even human survival.

In the remainder of this chapter, I try to show that the 'what', 'how' and 'why' of cognitive development can be addressed by viewing emotion as the signpost of functionality, the fuel that drives feedback and synchronization in the brain, and the embodiment of goals that propel thought and action. First, if Thelen and Smith are correct, and functionality determines what develops, then it would probably be advantageous to apprehend functionality directly. Emotions are all about function. Phylogenetically, they mark the requirements for attending to and acting on situations of survival relevance and adaptive significance faced repeatedly by our ancestors. Ontogenetically, they index events that have acquired significance within the particular environments of family, community, culture and niche. The emotional system is ready-made to guide attention, action, and thought according to what is proficient and useful in these environments. So the 'what' of cognitive development – the forms that end up being functional – may be identified by what is emotionally effective. Second, the feedback and coordination that give rise to novel structures can be analysed in terms of brain systems that have evolved precisely for the purpose of coordinating perception and action through reciprocal information flow. At many levels of scale, from neurones to whole brain regions, these systems interact through multiple and reciprocal pathways. They settle into cooperative states of synchronization because of their intrinsic network dynamics and because of the chemical agents that constrain their activity. Most important, they settle into these states only when motivation is present (Damasio 1994), thus identifying the 'how' of development as neural synchronization driven by emotion. Finally, the causal force that propels human development – the 'why' of development – is more than an intrinsic property of complex systems. Perhaps it is an *intentionality* that focuses the mind on situations that are potentially beneficial or potentially harmful, where cognitive complexity can grow in the service of survival through the mediation of emotion. This kind of causation is a unique property of higher mammals, though it extends from more general principles of self-organizing systems in nature. According to this view, not only does mind grow out of matter, but mind grows out of matter through the mediation of emotions, and these emotions tap motives for gain, improvement, affiliation, and safety. Thus, all mental abilities, processes and skills may be shaped by their motivational origins.

Cognition and emotion – the view from psychology

In this section I briefly show how emotion guides converging cognitive patterns in real time, as well as over development, through reciprocal and recursive cognition–emotion interactions. The modelling presented here has been developed in several theoretical papers (e.g. Lewis 1995, 1996, 1997, 2000). Evidence for emotional effects on cognition comes from studies of emotional constraints on attention, reasoning, memory and planning, primarily conducted by emotion theorists. Evidence for emotional effects on development has been compiled by emotion theorists interested in trait-like continuities and developmentalists who study the role of emotion in personality formation.

Perhaps the main function of emotions is to direct attention to relevant aspects of the environment in the service of action tendencies for altering that environment (e.g. Ekman 1994; Frijda 1986; Izard 1993). From this perspective, attention is always 'motivated' (Derryberry and Tucker 1994), and cognition is generally constrained by the type of emotional state (e.g. sadness, anger, happiness, fear). This assumption corresponds well with our common sense. We know that an angry mood leads to thoughts of triumph and retaliation, anxiety leads to thoughts of danger and safety, and emotions such as interest or curiosity sustain our attention to detail and novelty. Supporting these intuitions, a good deal of research demonstrates the effects of emotional states on attention and other cognitive processes (e.g. Bower 1992). Sad versus happy emotions differentially affect attentional style and content, with sadness narrowing attention and focusing it on social contingencies (e.g. Isen 1990). Anxiety also biases and narrows attention, perhaps through its effects on filtering or inhibition (Wood, Mathews, and Dalgleish 2001). Emotion has also been found to bias perception (Mathews and MacLeod 1985; Niedenthal, Setterland and Jones 1994), memory retrieval (Eich and Metcalfe 1989; Isen 1985) and social judgment (Forgas and Bower 1988; Keltner et al. 1993), most often by enhancing the selection of emotion-relevant content (see review by Mathews and MacLeod 1994). Finally, emotion is theorized to select and configure cognitive organization whenever competing goals require resolution (Oatley and Johnson-Laird 1987).

From a DS perspective, the effects of emotion on cognition are one stream in a bidirectional exchange or feedback loop between the emotional and cognitive systems. In my own modelling, I have suggested that this reciprocal interaction gives rise to the coupling of cognitive, perceptual, and emotional elements to form self-organizing cognitive gestalts or appraisals that cohere and stabilize rapidly along with emerging motivational/emotional states (e.g. anger, interest, anxiety, relief). Thus, a cognitive appraisal or strategy converges in real time from the coordination of (lower-order) elements such as concepts, associations and perceptions, but it does so only in interaction with a consolidating emotional state (even a mild one, such as the mild enthusiasm you are hopefully feeling as you read these words). According to this model, a consolidating appraisal or strategy both generates and constrains emotional activation. At the same time emotional activation both generates and constrains attentional processes at work in the appraisal (Lewis 1995, 1997; Lewis and Granic 1999). This idea parallels notions of reciprocal causation discussed by other theorists (e.g. Izard, Ackerman, Schoff and Fine 2000; Malatesta and Wilson 1988; Teasdale and Barnard 1993).

Emotional constraints on cognition have been studied at the developmental scale as well. These constraints include enduring trait-like forms such as biases, associations, and emotional habits (e.g. Bradley, Mogg and Millar 2000; Mathews and MacLeod 1994). The effects of emotions on attention are often described in terms of such trait-specific biases, as when anxious subjects attend selectively to anxiety-related words (Mathews and MacLeod 1985, 1986) or faces (Fox, Russo and Dutton 2002), and depressive subjects attend to negative words (Wenzlaff et al. 2001) and recall negative experiences (Clark and Teasdale 1982). These clinical examples may be extreme variants of a normal tendency for cognitive forms to recur in particular situations because of recurring emotional states. Along these lines, Izard and Malatesta (e.g. 1987) have argued that enduring affective-cognitive 'structures' are the units of analysis of stable individual differences. This idea is extended in a recent book by Magai and Haviland-Jones (2002), where adult personality styles are shown to emerge from the recurrent coupling of emotions and appraisals over the years of child development. Examples of the development of cognitive-emotional biases can be seen in the acquisition of a hostile attributional bias in children with harsh or abusive parenting (e.g. Weiss, Dodge, Bates and Pettit 1992). Other lines of research examine core thematic memories with strong emotional components as the building blocks of personality (Thorne and Klohnen 1993).

In DS terminology, patterns laid down in development can be represented as attractors on a state space of 'possible' psychological states. Perceptual categories (Thelen and Smith 1994), linguistic categories (Smith 1995), motor coordinations (Hopkins and Butterworth 1997), cognitive skills (van Geert 1994), memories (F. D. Abraham 1995), belief systems (Goertzel 1995) and communicative frames (Fogel 1993) have all been proposed as attractors on a psychological state space. The presence of several attractors, representing several viable cognitive organizations, indicates a range of states to which interpretations can converge for the same individual. In the present model, some self-organizing cognition–emotion gestalts converge with increasing likelihood across occasions, such that they become characteristic responses to particular kinds of situations. These emerging attractors can be viewed as stabilizing individual differences in thought, feeling and behaviour, but they can also be studied as stage-specific constellations that characterize a particular period of development and then dissipate (Lewis 2001). Thus, an individual's cognitive repertoire at any stage of development can be depicted as a cluster of probable cognitive-emotional states, indeterminate and variable in real time but stable or continuous over some period of development.

This discussion suggests a DS reinterpretation of the effects of emotion on cognition in real time and development. Self-organizing cognition–emotion gestalts within occasions may lay down patterns of response across occasions, producing an emerging developmental profile. This profile describes characteristic cognitive appraisals and strategies catalysed by emotional processes on each occasion. This proposition goes beyond other DS models by defining 'what' develops as cognitive forms that feed back with emotions. Whatever constellations are redundant, ineffective, irrelevant, or arbitrary have no chance of developing because they have no purchase on the emotional world. In cognitive development, emotionally relevant constellations may best be viewed as insights, interpretations, or strategies that solve new kinds of problems, or old problems in new ways (in ways that 'work' – Thelen and Smith 1994) and hence correspond with interest, excitement and feelings of mastery. In personality development, these forms are better viewed as appraisals and strategies that attempt to solve difficult interpersonal problems, often with only partial success, and hence correspond with more negative emotions such as anxiety, anger and jealousy (cf. Thorne and Klohnen 1993).

However, the discussion so far leaves us little closer to the 'how' and 'why' of development, and even the 'what' of development as I have presented it up to this point is highly abstract and should be further reduced to specific categories of emotionally relevant operations. In the next section, we move from the psychological to the neural level of analysis, in order to better identify the forms, mechanisms and causal forces at work in cognitive and personality development.

The role of emotion in self-organizing neural processes

The brain is the ultimate self-organizing system. In the cerebral cortex alone, approximately twenty billion cells, with thousands of connections each, provide a massive population of interacting units in a state of continuous flux. Despite its potential for immense noise, chaos or disorder, this system converges rapidly to highly ordered, synchronous states (e.g. Thompson and Varela 2001). Each of those states taps enormous cooperativity across the elements in this system, even at relatively great distances. And this convergence, or synchronization, occurs whenever we pick up a tooth brush, tell the time or recall a poem. Corresponding with neural self-organization, but at a different level of description, the components of cognition and attention can be said to converge and form into coherent thoughts and plans. The various sensory and executive systems become linked, working memory becomes engaged, actions are selected and refined, and so forth. Some scientists have studied the parallels between neural coherences and cognitive coherence (e.g. Engel, Fries and Singer, 2001; Skarda and Freeman 1987; Thompson and Varela 2001). This research paradigm is still at a relatively early stage, but it seems likely that neural coherence at some level is necessary for cognitive coherence, and that the convergence of cognition depends on – and possibly contributes to – the synchronization of neural elements. (Yet, it should be noted that neural 'coherence' has not been clearly defined with respect to scale – and that 'synchronization' may only apply to a subset of neural components, a particular frequency band, or a limited time frame, for any given operation.)

In order to think about neural synchronization at the broadest scale, and to establish a possible role for emotion, it is necessary to consider not only cortical processes but processes at every level of the neuraxis. In fact, a more complete analysis would include bodily processes as well, though these go beyond the scope of the present chapter. We can roughly divide the brain into four levels, each more advanced and appearing later in evolution than the previous one. Figure 6.1 provides a rough sketch of some of the systems housed at each of these levels.

The brain stem

The shaft of nerve tissue at the core of the brain (divided into pons, medulla, and midbrain) contains sets of nuclei for programmed responses to internal and external events. These nuclei control relatively primitive, packaged response patterns (e.g. defensive and attack behaviour, vigilance, feeding, freezing, sexual behaviour, facial expressions), each highly independent and stimulus-bound, and many of which go back to our reptilian ancestors. In higher animals, the actions of many of these systems are regulated by or synchronized with activity in the hypothalamus, which sits just above them. Brainstem systems orchestrate emotional behaviour even in the absence of higher brain systems. For example, animals without a forebrain display 'sham rage', which has the behavioural appearance of rage. These systems have thus been referred to as basic emotion circuits (Panksepp 1998). According to Panksepp, partially

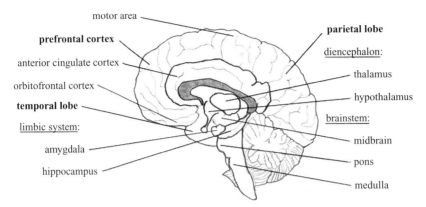

Figure 6.1. A sketch of the main systems of the brain. Particular attention is given to systems that mediate cognitive and emotional processes.

independent brainstem circuits can be identified for anger, fear/anxiety, anticipatory excitement, love/attachment, sadness, joy, and sexual desire. Critically, the brain stem also produces a great variety of neurochemicals that arouse the cortex and modulate processing in virtually all brain systems. These chemicals include the well-known neuromodulators dopamine, norepinephrine, serotonin, and acetylcholine, and they are manufactured and released to both specific and general targets in the brain whenever the organism is emotionally aroused. Many of these chemicals also affect bodily systems, such that bodily responses are prepared to correspond with brain changes.

The diencephalon

The thalamus and hypothalamus sit one above the other, at the top of the brain stem, and they coordinate functioning at a higher and more integrated level. The thalamus controls sensorimotor processes by mediating between sense organs and brain systems and by participating in motor feedback loops that orchestrate behavioural sequences. The hypothalamus controls the internal milieu, including the organs and vascular systems, partly through its output to the autonomic nervous system and partly through direct axonal pathways. It also receives information from these systems in return, thus functioning as a central regulator of bodily responses to relevant environmental events. The hypothalamus is densely connected with brainstem nuclei and it synchronizes with their activities in coherent modes of functioning. It also releases neurochemicals (i.e. neuropeptides) that set body and brain systems into coherent goal-directed

226   *Marc D. Lewis*

states, such as territorial aggression, scavenging for food, courting and mating, and so forth. These states are organized at a higher level than the more elementary modes of the brainstem, and their neurochemical outputs organize more comprehensive action orientations than the diffuse arousal modes elicited by brainstem neuromodulators (Panksepp 1998).

The limbic system

This is a rough semicircle of structures that grew out of the diencephalon and evolved profoundly in mammals. These structures are capable of learning and memory, whereas lower structures control perception and action according to fixed 'programs' that required no learning. The processing of sensory input and motor output is slowed down in the limbic system, so that responses can be fitted more precisely to the learned aspects of situations (Tucker, Derryberry and Luu 2000). According to Tucker and colleagues, this slowdown was necessarily accompanied by the evolutionary advent of emotions, whose motivational force works by maintaining the focus of attention and action rather than by triggering some 'fixed action pattern'. Indeed, the limbic system mediates emotional states that orient attention and action to whatever is presently meaningful. For example, the amygdala, a key limbic structure, tags neutral stimuli with emotional content (LeDoux 1995; Rolls 1999), thereby creating chains of associations based on emotional experiences. Connections from the amygdala to lower (hypothalamic and brainstem) structures activate motivational response systems given current stimulus events, and connections from the amygdala up to the cortex entrain perception, attention and planned action to these events. The amygdala requires the participation of lower structures to produce emotional states, while the converse is not true (Panksepp 1998). Other limbic structures, including the septal and hippocampal structures, also support emotional behaviours (e.g. play, sex, nurturance) and organize episodic memory and attention (e.g. MacLean 1993).

The cerebral cortex

The layers of the cortex surround the limbic system, and the recently evolved cells that inhabit these layers are the locus of what we normally call cognition, perception, and attention. In the cortex, the time between stimulus and response appears to be greatly stretched out (Tucker et al. 2000). Inputs from the world and potential actions connect with each other through a matrix of associations, comparisons, synthesis across modalities, planning, reflection and above all conscious control. These operations take time, and emotions maintain a coherent orientation to the world during that period of time. For example, deliberate action is guided by thought (in the form of plans), and thought (e.g. attention allocation to these plans) is constrained by emotion. Thus, cortically mediated actions are functional, not only at the level of some phylogenetically ancient blueprint, but also at the level of a continuously refined model of the world, accessed by motivated memories. The cortex is also a key system for the cognitive control of emotional responses, or emotion regulation. In particular, the prefrontal regions execute higher perceptual and cognitive activities (including attention, monitoring, decision-making, planning and working memory) which are recruited by (and which regulate) the emotional responses mediated by brainstem and limbic structures (Davidson and Irwin 1999; Barbas 1995; Bechara, Damasio and Damasio 2000). The orbitofrontal cortex and the anterior cingulate cortex are two prefrontal regions that are phylogenetically older and closer to the limbic system, and they are important for maintaining attention while modulating emotionally relevant action plans (Barbas 2000; Rolls 1999).

This hierarchy of brain levels is often construed in terms of domination or control of lower levels by higher levels. Indeed, each new level of the neuraxis does subordinate the more primitive functions of previous levels. However, as emphasized by Tucker, there are two important caveats. First, more primitive brain systems continue to evolve, so that their functions can provide support to the higher levels of control. For example, the brain stem has evolved to become a factory of neuromodulators that fuel the cortex, allowing the cortex to grow and strengthen synapses as the basis of learning. Synaptic changes have long been viewed as the vehicle of memory consolidation, but only recently have neurochemicals released by the brain stem been shown to be critical for synaptic shaping. Without the arousal caused by emotion, new synapses could not be formed. Thus, cortical plasticity depends on the cooperation of the most primitive neural regions. Second, the downward flow of control and modulation – e.g. from cortex to limbic system to brain stem – is reciprocated by an upward flow of motivational arousal and recruitment. The brain stem and diencephalon fuel the limbic system with information and arousal, locking in behavioural activation and inhibition systems, and they also fuel the cortex with chemicals that recruit its activities to ancient mammalian and even reptilian goals. Primitive agendas and requirements thus flow up the neuraxis from its most primitive roots at the same time as executive attention, planning, and knowledge subordinate each lower level by the activities of the cortex. If not for the bottom-up flow, the brain would have no energy and no direction for its activities. If not for the top-down flow, recently evolved mechanisms for perception, action and integration would have no control over bodily states and behaviour. It is the reciprocity of these upward and downward flows that links cognition with motivation, giving evolution a gameplan for continued improvements, and eventually producing a mind, albeit a motivated mind (see Figure 6.2).

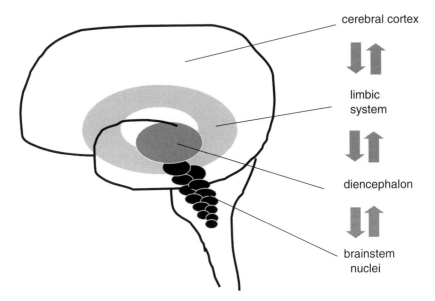

Figure 6.2. Vertical integration. Influence flows in both directions, upward and downward, between each level of the neuraxis.

The reciprocation of motivational and executive flows, up and down the neuraxis, appears to be responsible for the rapid synchronization of the entire brain through a process of 'vertical integration' (Tucker et al. 2000). This process of synchronization is hypothesized to occur whenever a significant change in internal or external events triggers an emotion, and thus demands the initiation of a cognitive or motor response. Vertical integration is considered necessary to coordinate perception, attention, and action planning with primitive action tendencies, so that the animal can behave flexibly, skilfully and intelligently when motivated (Tucker et al. 2000; cf. Buck 1999). But what are its implications for real-time cognitive processes? As mentioned earlier, cognitive operations (e.g. attentional focusing) require the synchronization of the cortex, the self-organization of a vast network of elements into a coherent, highly-ordered state. But the principle of vertical integration implies that cortical coherence is just the tip of the iceberg. It is suggested that cortical coherence relies on synchronization across *all* brain systems, especially those responsible for motivation and emotion. According to this view, the cortex does not act in isolation. It is part of a two-way stream of electrochemical traffic that binds motivation with control in every cognitive act. In other words, 'mind' cannot cohere through cortical self-organization unless supported by motivational agendas arising through the more primitive levels of the neuraxis. Mind not only needs matter, it needs motivated matter; and to the extent that motivation is expressed by feeling states that have evolved over millions of years, it needs emotion.

Feedback and synchronization between the cognitive and emotional systems was described earlier as the foundation for self-organizing mental gestalts. With some understanding of the neural underpinnings of cognition and emotion, this process can now be mapped out with more precision. Any event with the capacity to recruit neural activity turns on brainstem arousal systems, which in turn activate diverse regions of the diencephalon, limbic system and cerebral cortex. These systems in turn augment brainstem activity by magnifying and articulating the perception of the significant event. This initial process of spreading activation can be described as a positive feedback cycle, in which activity builds on itself and the process of change is self-augmenting. As more and more neural components become recruited to an emerging constellation, activation processes settle into an ongoing stable pattern, characterized by negative feedback. Now, deviations or fluctuations are damped, because many different systems reinforce each other's ongoing activity. The emergence of coherence and stabilization is a property of many interactive networks, including cellular automata (Nowak et al. 2000), constraint satisfaction networks (Thagard and Verbeurgt 1998) and neural networks in general (Rumelhart et al. 1986). In the human brain, coherence and stabilization settle across multilevel subsystems very rapidly. Synchronizing activity across these levels is what drives the brain into vertical integration, coupling cognitive and motivational functions, while the cortex itself settles into a coherent cognitive-perceptual constellation. In other words, a macroscopic pattern of activation settles across all levels of the neuraxis, linking emotion, attention, perception and action tendencies, through the spontaneous coordination of the many cellular systems that have been designed by evolution to work together. The functionality of cognition is thus supported, because cognition is generally *about* something important – at least important to the individual at the time. In Damasio's (1994) view, cognition is rooted in emotional states and is necessarily 'about' what is emotionally relevant.

If each momentary cognitive state relies on emotion, our next question should be: what are the implications for development? Once again, cognitive states imply neural coherence – the emergence of order in a complex, nonlinear system of interacting neurones. This is an ideal system for appreciating novelty. A self-organizing system can cohere in a multitude of ways depending on all sorts of parameters: in the case of human cognition, we often look to the environmental context as supplying those parameters. However, an *adaptive* self-organizing system also tunes itself, shaping its own tendencies in relation to previous patterns of cooperativity. A neural system shapes its own connection strengths through experience, and of course this provides a very useful model for cognitive development (Elman et al. 1996). As emphasized by Tucker, the incredible extent of human neoteny (i.e. developmental immaturity) provides the time span over which this self-organizing system becomes increasingly structured and organized. Neonates show vast cortical plasticity, and this plasticity serves as the foundation for massive learning as the cortex develops. Specifically, functional synapses are strengthened, and non-functional or redundant synapses are pruned, all under the pressure of real-time experience. According to the present model, however, no experience can have an impact on neural structure unless the brain converges to a coherent, global state of synchronization in the first place. And this process necessarily involves emotion. Given this criterion – the 'how' of development in the present model – experience can lay down structure by means of synaptic shaping in the limbic system and cortex. To summarize, if motivation and emotion constrain cortical self-organization in the moment, then they can also shape the outcomes of that self-organization, the laying down of structure in synaptic networks, over the years of childhood and adolescence. This means that emotion not only shapes cognition, it shapes cognitive development as well.

The emotional roots of cognitive development: three examples

In the remainder of this chapter, I wish to elaborate on the emotional origins of cognitive development with three related examples. The first is the emergence of effortful self-control at about the age of three to four in normally developing children. The second is a more molar look at correspondences between emotion-dependent changes and transitional nodes or stage shifts in cognitive development. The third is the emergence of individual attentional and cognitive biases, an important constituent of personality formation, driven by each child's focus on motivationally relevant events.

Effortful control

Effortful (or 'inhibitory') control is an acquisition emphasized by Posner, Rothbart, and Derryberry in particular, though it is also a favourite topic of cognitive developmentalists interested in executive function (e.g. Zelazo, Carter, Reznick and Frye 1997). Posner and Rothbart (1998, 2000) emphasize a major onset of inhibitory control at $3\frac{1}{2}$ to 4. At this age, children become capable of inhibiting actions on demand, restraining their approach to rewards, and directing their attention deliberately despite prominent 'misleading' cues. For example, they become capable of resisting the temptation to open a present while an adult is out of the room. The brain region held responsible for this cognitive acquisition is the anterior cingulate cortex (although orbitofrontal regions may also participate in some of these functions). This midline region of the frontal cortex is an attentional system that is considered very important for self-monitoring, selective attention, and error correction, functions that may be critical for the kinds of 'decentration' necessary for Piagetian tasks. Yet, despite its 'cognitive' function, the anterior cingulate is an extension of the limbic system. The cingulate layers grew out of the hippocampus in evolution, and they remain closely connected with it anatomically. However, the cingulate also receives massive input from the amygdala and other structures implicated in emotional response. In keeping with its limbic character, the anterior cingulate attaches emotional significance to pain. It has also been associated with various emotional activities, including the effects of nurturance, care, play, and sexual attraction. Most important, and befitting its role at the border between the limbic system and cortex, the anterior cingulate entrains cortical evaluation and monitoring to emotional needs and impulses (Lane et al. 1998). This function appears to be a direct expression of its participation in vertical integration.

Posner and Rothbart (1998) postulate that the role of the anterior cingulate in attention regulation grows out of its connection with emotion systems. In particular, infants are confronted with intense distress quite often, whereas school-aged children rarely cry. At some point between these ages, some part of the brain must become highly adept at regulating negative emotions, and in so doing, according to these authors, regulating competing choices more generally. In this case, the 'what' of cognitive development may be viewed as a broad skill that is highly functional, as Thelen and Smith (1994) might argue, but also one whose functionality is indexed by its power to change emotional states. Posner and Rothbart believe that self-regulation begins with emotion regulation – consistent with the 'how' of development in the present account. From an early age, children control emotions by shifting attention to non-distressing targets (Rothbart, Ziaie and O'Boyle 1992). The capacity to shift attention may become increasingly discrete, volitional and sophisticated because it is driven by the motivation to reduce distress. In turn, this capability may permit children to shift behaviour away from impulsive actions for the sake of non-immediate rewards, as four-year-old children have been observed to begin doing (Thompson, Barresi and Moore 1997). A capacity to monitor one's own behaviour in order to avoid distress before it occurs may simply be an extension of this switching mechanism. Finally, the cognitive processing benefits of effortful attention may become an end in themselves once children have learned to master distress regulation. All in all, a key cognitive-developmental milestone may be considered an epiphenomenon of the development of emotion regulation.

Developmental stages

The example of effortful control may be a case in point, and the influence of motivational shaping on cognitive development may extend to many or all normative acquisitions. In other words, each normative cognitive advance may be driven, not only by maturational timetables and social expectations, but also by emotional forces that contribute to brain synchronization, with new and more sophisticated patterns of coherence converging at each subsequent stage. Piagetian and neo-Piagetian theorists have investigated correspondences between cyles of cortical coherence and the timing of stage and substage transitions (Case 1992; Fischer and Rose 1996; Thatcher 1998). A number of corrrespondences have been persuasively demonstrated, especially in the earlier years. Moreover, both Case (e.g. Case, Hayward, Lewis and Hurst 1988) and Fischer (e.g. Fischer, Shaver and Carnochan 1990) have modelled the role of emotion in the organization of cognitive development, and Thatcher (1998) has used an explicit dynamic systems analysis as the basis of his model of cortical cycles. It would seem that these and other neo-Piagetian theorists would not be surprised if new patterns of cortical coherence were driven by emotional processes that serve as mediators of cognitive development.

Indeed, the plasticity of the brain and its openness to emotion-mediated change may shift in correspondence with developmental stages. We know that new cognitive-developmental acquisitions begin with a period of fluctuation and then achieve stability after some period of time (Case et al. 1996; Ruhland and van Geert 1998). The period of fluctuation demarcating each change may be marked by higher levels of emotional intensity, and the changes themselves may be coupled with emotional dynamics. Thus, for example, Lewis et al. (2004) found a rise in negative emotion related to frustration and a high degree of fluctuation in the attentional habits of toddlers at 18–20 months, the hypothesized age of the transition between the sensorimotor and interrelational stages in Case's (1985) model. It is often assumed that fluctuations in developmental profiles index phase transitions, as old skills give way and new skills take their place (Thelen and Smith 1994), but they may also reflect the emotional turmoil children experience as they attempt to fashion coherent interpretations and strategies out of several competing possibilities. According to this view, vertical integration driven by emotion may be a key mechanism of change when multiple cognitive strategies are competing for dominance at transitional nodes. This would explain the 'how' of cognitive development in terms of an emotional push at times of high variability. The 'what' of development – the actual patterns that cohere – could then be viewed as those cognitive organizations that 'work' to minimize anxiety and other negative emotions and to maximize pride, relief and satisfaction. Thus, the criterion of 'what works', supplied by Thelen and her colleagues, would be indexed directly by 'what feels good', and the 'why' of development would reflect the intentionality of the organism to pursue its goals as effectively as it can. According to this view, cognitive developmental stages would map onto a sequence of phases of stabilization and destabilization, with the impact of emotion greatest whenever new phases of stabilization begin to cohere.

Individual differences

The third example of the emotional shaping of development concerns the development of individual differences in the contents of cognition, that is, the individual's accumulating repertoire of appraisals, interpretations, and strategies, and the expectancies and biases that facilitate their reemergence over multiple occasions. The emotional origins of individual differences in cognitive development have been addressed by several theorists (e.g. Case et al. 1988; Fischer, Shaver and Carnochan 1990), and I have addressed similar issues in previous work. However, from the perspective of the brain, it is important to identify a second corticolimbic system as the locus for learning and maintaining habitual appraisals of the social world. The orbitofrontal cortex, on the bottom surface of the frontal lobes, encodes and holds attention to context-specific, motivationally relevant contingencies, both learned and unlearned (Rolls 1999). Like the anterior cingulate, the orbitofrontal system sits at the border region between the limbic system and cortex. It receives signals from the amygdala, alerting it to the emotional content of events, and reciprocates by regulating the amygdala (and other subcortical systems) in turn. Meanwhile, the amygdala's connections to more primitive diencephalic and brainstem structures ensure an unbroken chain between the most basic motivational responses and the monitoring of contingencies by the orbitofrontal cortex, again reflecting their co-participation in vertical integration.

According to Schore (1994), the orbitofrontal cortex is where rapid appraisals of emotionally relevant events take place, from earliest infancy onward. For example, early attachment experiences, in which the infant processes the mother's facial cues, vocal tone and touch, are encoded in the orbitofrontal cortex, building up a repertoire of expectancies and learned contingencies. For this learning to take place, the orbitofrontal cortex would be expected to participate in vertical integration through which it becomes entrained to present motivational agendas. Through this process it would maintain its focus on relevant events and sustain a state of activation – part of an overall cortical coherence – as fuelled by the upward flow of neurochemicals.

Attachment experiences, because of their high emotional tone, constitute the ideal occasions for a great deal of social learning. The 'how' of development may be demonstrated by the sensitivity of the cognitive system to this emotion-guided learning. Moreover, goals for achieving safety and interpersonal closeness are highly compelling, and the 'why' of development can be clearly envisioned as these goals propel the individual to make sense of the world in a way that feels tolerable. The 'what' of development may then be whatever works best to achieve and maintain tolerable emotional states. It does not take long for infants to develop appraisals and expectancies about the nature of interpersonal interactions, concerning, for example, their mother's likelihood of providing pleasure, disappointment or frustration. But what gets learned in the attachment – what Bowlby called internal working models – goes well beyond these early evaluations, to serve as individually unique templates for forming and monitoring interpersonal relationships throughout the lifespan. These working models represent the 'what' of social-cognitive development in the long term, because they set the course for the continual accretion of social learning. Returning to the neural perspective, as the orbitofrontal cortex becomes organized through repeated activation of a unique configuration of synapses, it also continues to process new interpersonal events in its own way, thus continuing to elaborate a store of expectancies about how people behave.

Conclusions

In this chapter I have examined the role of emotion in cognitive self-organization by looking at the coupling of brain systems in vertical integration. The spontaneous synchronization of brain regions, up and down the neuraxis from primitive to highly advanced structures, provides a mechanism by which emotion may help to shape emerging cognitive configurations in real time. In developmental time, these converging patterns were argued to shape neural circuits that become increasingly entrenched, and increasingly sophisticated, with repeated activation over occasions. In this way, I suggested, emotional contributions to cognitive coherence translate to emotional effects on cognitive development. In the final section, examples were provided to demonstrate that particular cognitive capacities, general patterns of normative development, and individual differences in the contents of cognitive development could all be explained by the participation of emotion in the real-time emergence of coherent neural assemblies.

The ideas presented here derive from research findings in several diverse fields and subfields: cognition–emotion relations, cognitive and emotional development, dynamic systems applications to brain and behavioural research, and the neurobiology of emotion and development. However, these ideas remain highly speculative. They constitute broad integrations that are difficult to test and require multi-disciplinary research strategies that are only now being developed. In our own research, my colleagues and I (e.g. Lewis and Stieben 2004) are setting out some of these research directions under the general banner of brain–behaviour relations in development. We are using dense-array electroencephalogram (EEG) techniques in order to measure the cortical activity of children of different ages when they are confronted with emotionally compelling events. Frontal patterns of brain activity, representing the cognitive control of emotional states, do change with age. They also change with treatment, in the case of clinical populations who learn to modulate their attention to emotionally distressing events more effectively. Beside the measurement of these changes, cortical EEG patterns can also be evaluated for synchronization and coherence, using a number of currently available techniques. We hope to show that synchronization parameters specific to certain kinds of cognitive operations change systematically with development, or with treatment, and that such changes correspond with behavioural acquisitions that come on-line concurrently. If it turns out that both sets of changes are mediated by the emotional contents of experimental tasks, we will have achieved a first step toward validating the framework outlined in this chapter.

REFERENCES

Abraham, F. D. (1995). Dynamics, bifurcation, self-organization, chaos, mind, conflict, insensitivity to initial conditions, time, unification, diversity, free will, and social responsibility. In R. Robertson and A. Combs (eds.) *Chaos theory in psychology and the life sciences* (pp. 155–74). Mahwah, NJ: Erlbaum.

Barbas, H. (1995). Anatomic basis of cognitive-emotional interactions in the primate prefrontal cortex. *Neuroscience and Biobehavioural Reviews. 19*, 449–510.

(2000). Connections underlying the synthesis of cognition, memory, and emotion in primate prefrontal cortices. *Brain Research Bulletin, 52*, 319–30.

Bechara, A., Damasio, H. and Damasio, A. R. (2000). Emotion, decision making and the orbitofrontal cortex. *Cerebral Cortex, 10*, 295–307.

Bower, G. H. (1992). How might emotions affect learning? In S.-Å. Christianson (ed.) *The handbook of emotion and memory: research and theory* (pp. 3–31). Hillsdale, NJ: Erlbaum.

Bradley, B. P., Mogg, K. and Millar, N. H. (2000). Covert and overt orienting of attention to emotional faces in anxiety. *Cognition and Emotion, 14*, 789–808.

Buck, R. (1999). The biological affects: a typology. *Psychological Review, 106*, 301–36.

Case, R. (1985). *Intellectual development: birth to adulthood*. New York: Academic Press.

(1992). The role of the frontal lobes in the regulation of cognitive development. *Brain and Cognition, 20*, 51–73.

Case, R., Hayward, S., Lewis, M. D., and Hurst, P. (1988). Toward a neo-Piagetian theory of cognitive and emotional development. *Developmental Review, 8*, 1–51

Case, R., Okamoto, Y., Griffin, S., McKeough, A., Bleiker, C., Henderson, B. and Stephenson, K. M. (1996). The role of central conceptual structures in the development of children's thought. *Monographs of the Society for Research in Child Development, 61* (serial no. 246).

Clark, D. M. and Teasdale, J. D. (1982). Diurnal variation in clinical depression and accessibility of memories of positive and negative experiences. *Journal of Abnormal Psychology, 91*, 87–95.

Damasio, A. R. (1994). *Descartes' error: emotion, reason and the human brain*. New York: Avon Books.

236   *Marc D. Lewis*

Davidson, R. J. and Irwin, W. (1999). The functional neuroanatomy of emotion and affective style. *Trends in Cognitive Sciences, 3*, 11–21.

Demetriou, A., Christou, C., Spanoudis, G. and Platsidou, M. (2002). The development of mental processing: efficiency, working memory, and thinking. *Monographs of the Society for Research in Child Development, 67* (1, serial no. 268).

Derryberry, D. and Tucker, D. M. (1994). Motivating the focus of attention. In P. M. Niedenthal and S. Kitayama (eds.) *The heart's eye: emotional influences in perception and attention* (pp. 167–96). San Diego, CA: Academic Press.

Eich, E. and Metcalfe, J. (1989). Mood dependent memory for internal versus external events. *Journal of Experimental Psychology: Learning, Memory, and Cognition, 15*, 443–56.

Ekman, P. (1994). All emotions are basic. In P. Ekman and R. Davidson (eds.) *The nature of emotion: fundamental questions* (pp. 15–19). New York: Oxford University Press.

Elman, J. L., Bates, E. A., Johnson, M. H., Karmiloff-Smith, A., Parisi, D. and Plunkett, K. (1996). *Rethinking innateness: a connectionist perspective on development.* Cambridge, MA: MIT Press.

Engel, A. K., Fries, P. and Singer, W. (2001). Dynamic predictions: oscillations and synchrony in top-down processing. *Nature Reviews Neuroscience, 2*, 704–16.

Fischer, K. W. and Rose, S. P. (1996). Dynamic growth cycles of brain and cognitive development. In R. W. Thatcher, G. R. Lyon, J. Rumsey and N. Krasnegor (eds.) *Developmental neuroimaging: mapping the development of brain and behaviour* (pp. 263–79). San Diego, CA: Academic Press.

Fischer, K. W., Shaver, P. R. and Carnochan, P. (1990). How emotions develop and how they organise development. *Cognition and Emotion, 4*, 81–127.

Fogel, A. (1993). *Developing through relationships: origins of communication, self, and culture.* Chicago: University of Chicago Press.

Forgas, J. P. and Bower, G. H. (1988). Affect in social and personal judgments. In K. Fiedler and J. Forgas (eds.) *Affect, cognition and social behaviour: new evidence and integrative attempts.* Lewiston, NY: Hogrefe.

Fox, E., Russo, R. and Dutton, K. (2002). Attentional bias for threat: evidence for delayed disengagement from emotional faces. *Cognition and Emotion, 16*, 355–79.

Frijda, N. H. (1986). *The emotions.* Cambridge: Cambridge University Press.

Goertzel, B. (1995). Belief systems as attractors. In R. Robertson and A. Combs (eds.) *Chaos theory in psychology and the life sciences* (pp. 123–34). Mahwah, NJ: Erlbaum.

Hopkins, B., and Butterworth, G. (1997). Dynamical systems approaches to the development of action. In G. Bremner, A. Slater and G. Butterworth (eds.) *Infant development: recent advances.* East Sussex, UK: Psychology Press.

Isen, A. M. (1985). The asymmetry of happiness and sadness in effects on memory in normal college students. *Journal of Experimental Psychology: General, 114*, 388–91.

 (1990). The influence of positive and negative affect on cognitive organization: some implications for development. In N. Stein, B. Leventhal and T. Trabasso (eds.) *Psychological and biological processes in the development of emotion.* Hillsdale, NJ: Erlbaum.

Izard, C. E. (1993). Four systems for emotion activation: cognitive and noncognitive processes. *Psychological Review, 100*, 68–90.

Izard, C. E., Ackerman, B., Schoff, K. and Fine, S. (2000). Self-organization of discrete emotions, emotion patterns, and emotion-cognition relations. In M. D. Lewis and I. Granic (eds.) *Emotion, development, and self-organization: dynamic systems approaches to emotional development* (pp. 15–36). New York: Cambridge University Press.

Izard, C. E. and Malatesta, C. (1987). Perspectives on emotional development I: differential emotions theory of early emotional development. In J. D. Osofsky (ed.) *Handbook of infant development* (pp. 434–454). New York: Wiley.

Kelso, J. A. S. (1995). *Dynamic patterns: the self-organization of brain and behaviour.* Cambridge, MA: Bradford/MIT Press.

Keltner, D., Ellsworth, P. C. and Edwards, K. (1993). Beyond simple pessimism: effects of sadness and anger on social perception. *Journal of Personality and Social Psychology, 64*, 740–52.

Lane, R. D., Reiman, E. M., Axelrod, B., Yun, L., Holmes, A. and Schwartz, G. E. (1998). Neural correlates of levels of emotional awareness: evidence of an interaction between emotion and attention in the anterior cingulate cortex. *Journal of Cognitive Neuroscience, 10*, 525–35.

LeDoux, J. E. (1995). Emotion: clues from the brain. *Annual Review of Psychology, 46*, 209–35.

Lee, K. and Karmiloff-Smith, A. (2002). Macro- and microdevelopmental research: assumptions, research strategies, constraints, and utilities. In N. Granott and J. Parziale (eds.) *Microdevelopment* (pp. 243–65). Cambridge: Cambridge University Press.

Lewis, M. D. (1995). Cognition-emotion feedback and the self-organization of developmental paths. *Human Development, 38*, 71–102.

(1996). Self-organising cognitive appraisals. *Cognition and Emotion, 10*, 1–25.

(1997). Personality self-organization: cascading constraints on cognition-emotion interaction. In A. Fogel, M. C. Lyra and J. Valsiner (eds.) *Dynamics and indeterminism in developmental and social processes* (pp. 193–216). Mahwah, NJ: Erlbaum.

(2000). The promise of dynamic systems approaches for an integrated account of human development. *Child Development, 71*, 36–43.

(2001). Personal pathways in the development of appraisal: a complex systems/stage theory perspective. In K. R. Scherer, A. Schorr and T. Johnstone (eds.) *Appraisal processes in emotion.* Oxford: Oxford University Press.

Lewis, M. D. and Granic, I. (1999). Self-organization of cognition-emotion interactions. In T. Dalgleish and M. Power (eds.) *Handbook of cognition and emotion* (pp. 683–701). Chichester: Wiley.

Lewis, M. D. and Stieben, J. (2004). Emotion regulation in the brain: conceptual issues and directions for developmental research. *Child Development, 75*, 371–6.

Lewis, M. D., Zimmerman, S., Hollenstein, T. and Lamey, A. V. (2004). Reorganization of coping behaviour at $1\frac{1}{2}$ years: dynamic systems and normative change. *Developmental Science, 7*, 56–73.

MacLean, P. D. (1993). Perspectives on cingulate cortex in the limbic system. In B. A. Vogt and M. Gabriel (eds.) *Neurobiology of cingulate cortex and limbic thalamus: a comprehensive handbook* (pp. 1–15). Boston: Brikhauser.

Magai, C. and Haviland-Jones, J. (2002). *The hidden genius of emotion: lifespan trans-formations of personality.* Cambridge: Cambridge University Press.

Malatesta, C. Z. and Wilson, A. (1988). Emotion/cognition interaction in personality development: a discrete emotions, functionalist analysis. *British Journal of Social Psychology, 27,* 91–112.

Mathews, A. M. and MacLeod, C. (1985). Selective processing of threat cues in anxiety states. *Behaviour Research and Therapy, 23,* 563–9.

  (1986). Discrimination of threat cues without awareness in anxiety states. *Journal of Abnormal Psychology, 95,* 131–8.

  (1994). Cognitive approaches to emotion and emotional disorders. *Annual Review of Psychology, 45,* 25–50.

Niedenthal, P. M., Setterlund, M. B. and Jones, D. E. (1994). Emotional organization of perceptual memory. In P. M. Niedenthal and S. Kitayama (eds.) *The heart's eye: emotional influences in perception and attention* (pp. 87–113). San Diego, CA: Academic Press.

Nowak, A., Vallacher, R. R., Tesser, A. and Borkowski, W. (2000). Society of self: the emergence of collective properties in self-structure. *Psychological Review, 107,* 39–61.

Oatley, K. and Johnson-Laird, P. N. (1987). Towards a cognitive theory of emotions. *Cognition and Emotion, 1,* 29–50.

Panksepp, J. (1998). *Affective neuroscience: the foundations of human and animal emotions.* New York: Oxford University Press.

Port, R. F. and van Gelder, T. (eds.) (1995). *Explorations in the dynamics of cognition: mind as motion.* Cambridge, MA: MIT Press.

Posner, M. I. and Rothbart, M. K. (1998). Attention, self-regulation, and consciousness. *Philosophical Transactions of the Royal Society of London, B, 353,* 1915–27.

  (2000). Developing mechanisms of self-regulation. *Development and Psychopathol-ogy, 12,* 427–41.

Rolls, E. T. (1999). *The brain and emotion.* Oxford: Oxford University Press.

Rose, S. P. and Fischer, K. W. (1998). Models and rulers in dynamical development. *British Journal of Developmental Psychology, 16,* 123–31.

Rothbart, M. K., Ziaie, H. and O'Boyle, C. G. (1992). Self-regulation and emotion in infancy. In N. Eisenberg and R. A. Fabes (eds.) *New Directions for Child Development, 55,* 7–23. San Francisco: Jossey-Bass.

Ruhland, R. and van Geert, P. (1998). Jumping into syntax: transitions in the development of closed class words. *British Journal of Developmental Psychology, 16,* 65–95.

Rumelhart, D. E., Hinton, G. E. and McClelland, J. L. (1986). A general framework for parallel distributed processing. In J. L. McClelland, D. E. Rumelhart and the PDP Research Group (eds.) *Parallel distributed processing: explorations in the microstructure of cognition* (pp. 45–76). Cambridge, MA: MIT Press.

Scherer, K. R. (2000). Emotions as episodes of subsystem synchronization driven by nonlinear appraisal processes. In M. D. Lewis and I. Granic (eds.) *Emotion, development, and self-organization: dynamic systems approaches to emotional development* (pp. 70–99). New York: Cambridge University Press.

Schore, A. N. (1994). *Affect regulation and the origin of the self: the neurobiology of emotional development.* Hillsdale, NJ: Erlbaum.

Skarda, C. A. and Freeman, W. J. (1987). How brains make chaos in order to make sense of the world. *Behavioural and Brain Sciences, 10*, 161–95.

Smith, L. B. (1995). Self-organizing processes in learning to learn words: development is not induction. In C. A. Nelson (ed.) *New perspectives on learning and development: Minnesota symposia on child psychology: vol. 28* (pp. 1–32). New York: Academic Press.

Teasdale, J. D. and Barnard, P. J. (1993). *Affect, cognition, and change: re-modelling depressive thought.* Hillsdale, NJ: Erlbaum.

Thagard, P. and Verbeurgt, K. (1998). Coherence as constraint satisfaction. *Cognitive Science, 22*, 1–24.

Thatcher, R. W. (1998). A predator–prey model of human cerebral development. In K. M. Newell and P. C. M. Molenaar (eds.) *Applications of nonlinear dynamics to developmental process modelling* (pp. 87–128). Mahwah, NJ: Erlbaum.

Thelen, E. and Smith, L. B. (1994). *A dynamic systems approach to the development of cognition and action.* Cambridge, MA: MIT Press/Bradford.

Thelen, E. and Ulrich, B. D. (1991). Hidden skills: a dynamic systems analysis of treadmill stepping during the first year. *Monographs of the Society for Research in Child Development, 56* (serial no. 223).

Thelen, E., Schoner, G., Scheier, C. and Smith, L. B. (2001). The dynamics of embodiment: a field theory of infant perseverative reaching. *Behavioural and Brain Sciences, 24*, 1–86.

Thompson, C., Barresi, J. and Moore, C. (1997). The development of future-oriented prudence and altruism in preschoolers. *Cognitive Development, 12*, 199–212.

Thompson, E. and Varela, F. J. (2001). Radical embodiment: neural dynamics and consciousness. *Trends in Cognitive Sciences, 5*, 418–25.

Thorne, A. and Klohnen, E. (1993). Interpersonal memories as maps for personality consistency. In D. C. Funder, R. D. Parke, C. Tomlinson-Keasey and K. Widaman (eds.) *Studying lives through time: personality and development* (pp. 223–53). Washington, DC: American Psychological Association.

Tucker, D. M., Derryberry, D. and Luu, P. (2000). Anatomy and physiology of human emotion: vertical integration of brainstem, limbic, and cortical systems. In J. C. Borod (ed.) *The neuropsychology of emotion.* London: Oxford University Press.

Vallacher, R. R. and Nowak, A. (1997). The emergence of dynamical social psychology. *Psychological Inquiry, 8*, 73–99.

van der Maas, H. L. J. (1998). The dynamic and statistical properties of cognitive strategies: relations between strategies, attractors, and latent classes. In K. M. Newell and P. C. M. Molenaar (eds.) *Applications of nonlinear dynamics to developmental process modelling* (pp. 179–98). Mahwah, NJ: Erlbaum.

van der Maas, H. L. J. and Molenaar, P. C. M. (1992). Stagewise cognitive development: an application of catastrophe theory. *Psychological Review, 99*, 395–417.

van Geert, P. (1994). *Dynamic systems of development: change between complexity and chaos.* New York: Prentice Hall/Harvester Wheatsheaf.

(1998). We almost had a great future behind us: the contribution of non-linear dynamics to developmental-science-in-the-making. *Developmental Science, 1*, 143–59.

Varela, F. J., Thompson, E., and Rosch, E. (1991). *The embodied mind: cognitive science and human experience.* Cambridge, MA: MIT Press.

Varela, F. J., Lachaux, J-P., Rodriguez, E. and Martinerie, J. (2001). The brainweb: phase synchronization and large-scale integration. *Nature Reviews Neuroscience, 2*, 229–39.

Weiss, B., Dodge, K. A., Bates, J. E. and Pettit, G. S. (1992). Some consequences of early harsh discipline: child aggression and a maladaptive social information processing style. *Child Development, 63*, 1321–35.

Wenzlaff, R. M., Rude, S. S., Taylor, C. J., Stultz, C. H. and Sweatt, R. A. (2001). Beneath the veil of thought suppression: attentional bias and depression risk. *Cognition and Emotion, 15*, 435–52.

Wood, J., Mathews, A. and Dalgleish, T. (2001). Anxiety and cognitive inhibition. *Emotion, 1*, 166–81.

Zelazo, P. D., Carter, A., Reznick, J. S. and Frye, D. (1997). Early development of executive function: a problem-solving framework. *Review of General Psychology, 1*, 198–226.

7 Practices of quantification from a socio-cultural perspective

Geoffrey B. Saxe

Children are engaged with mathematics in their everyday activities. Look around you – notice the children chanting numbers as they jump rope or haggling over their scores in handball. Children in urban centres in Brazil buy and sell goods (Carraher, Carraher and Schliemann 1985; Saxe 1991); toddlers in working and middle-class homes in the US play number games and sing number songs with their mothers (Saxe, Guberman and Gearhart 1987); inner-city teenage boys keep track of their statistics in league basketball play (Nasir 2002). Mathematics is interwoven in children's everyday collective activities, and yet the cognitive-developmental study of children's mathematics has often overlooked such activities as sites for analysis. The result is that treatments of development often do not capture adequately the role of children's participation in collective activities, nor the way that children themselves contribute to the mathematical norms, values and conventions that take form in collective life.

The purpose of the chapter is to present a conceptual framework for analysing the interplay between individual and collective activity in cognitive development, using mathematical cognition as an illustrative case. The framework is rooted in an assumption common to psychogenetic treatments, whether structural-developmental (Piaget 1970) or activity-theoretic (e.g. Leontiev 1981): new cognitive developments emerge as individuals create and accomplish goals in daily activities. In this chapter I present an exposition of the framework with particular attention to the 'what?', 'how?' and 'why?' of development.

Throughout the chapter, I limit my discussion of cognitive development to practices of quantification. Of course, quantification practices are not the only 'what?' of development, but I view quantification as a valuable arena for

I am grateful to The Spencer Foundation for support during the preparation of this chapter (no. 200100026). The data presented, the statements made and the views expressed are solely the responsibility of the author. Various individuals contributed to this paper. Maryl Gearhart provided extensive comments and recommendations for revision. Participating members of the Fractions Research Group at UC Berkeley also contributed to the framing of the chapter. They include Britte Cheng, Rachel Coben, Jenny Garcia de Osuna, Julie McNamara, Orit Parnafes, Behnaz Shahidi and Edd Taylor. Author's email address saxe@socrates.berkeley.edu exposition of my approach. I begin by considering practices associated with activities outside of school to highlight the cultural roots of quantification. I then go on to explain a genetic approach to exploring the 'how?' of development, illustrating with practices in school. I end with some consideration of the 'why?' of development, focusing on supports for developmental change.

The 'what?' of development: quantification practices

By quantification practices, I mean socially patterned ways in which individuals draw upon cultural forms (like number words, rulers, charts and geometrical shapes) to construct and accomplish mathematical goals in everyday activities. Children are engaged with a wide range of quantification practices both in school and out.

Consider the collective activity of Brazilian child candy sellers that I documented as sellers plied their trade (Saxe 1991). At the time of my observations, the Brazilian economy was in a period of rapid inflation. The price of a wholesale box of candy of 30, 50, or 100 units ranged between 6,000 and 20,000 cruzeiros, and these prices surged at irregular intervals at each of more than 30 downtown wholesale stores. In the streets, it was common to find boys[1] selling candy to individuals at bus stops, outdoor cafes and on pavements. The candies that they sold were of various sorts (hard candy, chocolate bars, wafers) and for various prices, but always constructed as a retail price ratio of a specific number of candies for either 1000 cruzeiros (e.g. 5 for 1000) or 500 cruzeiros (e.g. 2 for 500).

The values that candy sellers computed were large, and yet many sellers were unschooled, so how did they establish their retail prices? Many of the sellers could not read the numerals on the cruzeiro notes (they knew the notes by the pictures), and they had no knowledge of school algorithms for computation. One common quantification practice was to empty the contents of a just-purchased 30, 50 or 100-unit wholesale box onto the ground, and then return candies to the box in groups of 2, 3 or 4 that corresponded to several possible price ratios, such as '2 for 500' or '3 for 1000'. Children repeated the groupings until all candy was returned (see Figure 7.1). Thus, for a box of thirty candies, if a seller returned three at a time adding 1,000 cruzeiros for each return, the sum after ten returns would total 10,000 cruzeiros. If the total turned out to be about double the value that he had paid for the box, he would decide to use the price-ratio he had just used to reconstitute the box. If not, he would re-empty the box, make an adjustment in the price ratio and repeat the process. In this way, many sellers created a retail price that afforded them an

---

[1] Virtually all sellers were male.

Figure 7.1. A child computes what the gross price a wholesale box would yield if he sold units to customers in the street at 4 for 1000 cruzeiros.

adequate profit as well as likely sales. Widely used in the selling community, this double procedure was a convention termed 'meio-pelo-meio'.

Some features of quantification practices

The candy sellers' activities illustrate some general features common to quantification practices. These features are often neglected in theoretical and empirical treatments of the 'what?' of cognitive development.

Cultural forms in quantification practices

To price candy for sales, sellers utilize a wide array of cultural forms like candies, candy boxes, currency values and number words. When sellers return candies to the box in groups, they count candy groups using words to signify currency values (i.e. 'one thousand cruzeiros', 'two thousand cruzeiros', 'three thousand cruzeiros', . . .). The box is a form that serves as a convenient repository that represents the wholesale purchase and thus the completion of the calculation of the street price. These are just examples. The notion that individuals make use of cultural forms to accomplish problems is key to understanding quantification practices. These forms are both constitutive of problems and instrumental in the accomplishment of problems, and in an important sense, they are constitutive of sellers' quantifications. To date, developmental analyses of the way forms are appropriated and organized in the daily activities of children are limited (notable exceptions include Vygotsky's seminal works (Vygotsky 1978, 1987) and more recent cultural-developmental accounts (Cole 1996 and Wertsch 1985)).

Mathematical means and goals in quantification practices
Though cultural forms themselves are constitutive of quantification practices, in themselves, forms contain no intrinsic mathematical meaning. Rather, the meaning of a form emerges relative to the goals of individuals (and forms afford particular kinds of goals). For example, a seller has the goal of selling his candy to customers; to accomplish the exchange he uses a particular price ratio as a means of regulating the number of candies exchanged for a value of currency. In contrast, later the seller may use the price ratio as it is used in the mark-up activity as a means of accomplishing goals that involve computation of appropriate retail price. For example, after purchasing a box of fifty units and emptying the box on the ground, a seller may replace the candies in groups of five, in accord with a price ratio like '5 for Cr$1000', adding 1000 cruzeiros for each replacement until all fifty units are exhausted. In this process, he coordinates his groupings, placements and successive additions, turning the selling ratio into a mathematical means to accomplish the goal of mark-up. Thus, in activity, individuals turn forms into means to accomplish emerging goals and in the process the same form may take on different mathematical properties.

Presuppositions in quantification practices
In the context of an everyday mathematical activity like selling candy, interlocutors tend to assume that they are doing mathematics in the same way, and they do not bother to explain each action or utterance. Yet presuppositions about the meanings of forms may not be shared; the 'same' actions and utterances may serve different functions for different individuals. For example, a younger seller may interpret an older seller's vocal count of 'one, two, three' as simply a count of groups of candies, when the older seller is in fact counting cruzeiros in an accumulation of potential sales (as in 'one thousand', 'two thousand', etc.). The older seller uses simple number words to track a progressive summation of the money gained by each sale. His counting is efficient, and his abbreviations pose no problem to himself. But what does the younger seller make of the older's quantification? The younger seller uses different presuppositions about the activity of the older and normative ways of using number words. Asymmetry in presuppositions can become a source of problems in communication if interlocutors interpret the same forms as serving different functions.

Relations between practices of quantification and social history
Quantification practices are socially and historically situated in a number of ways. First, activities like candy selling with which particular practices are associated themselves emerge and shift over historical periods. It was not always the case that selling candy was an occupation of urban street children in Brazil's Northeast; nor was it the case that there was always an urban environment. Indeed, the social organization of candy selling took form during a particular period in history and itself was situated in relation to a web of changing economic and political conditions. Further, cultural forms like number words, cruzeiro notes and even the size of a whole box take form in varied activities unrelated to candy selling and the socially recognized functions to which they were linked are each linked to historical periods. Moreover, in the hands of individuals participating in socially organized activities like candy selling the normative functions that these forms serve shift as well. For example, the meio-pelo-meio convention was reported to have had historical roots in rural life; it was viewed by many as an idiom for a particular way of conceptualizing work and profit. It has taken on a new function in the hands of sellers.

In sum, quantification practices are at the crux of the doing of mathematics in everyday collective life. They are rooted in the understandings that individuals bring to activities, and take on mathematical properties as individuals construct goals and make efforts to accomplish them. Though practices are constructed in activity, they are not the independent inventions of individuals. Rather, practices are socially and historically situated, constituted as individuals draw upon cultural forms (and the functions they afford) that themselves have complex social histories.

The 'how?' of development

How do quantification practices develop? In this section, I offer a method of analysis to explore the question. To support the exposition, I contrast my analytic approach with some features of Piaget's well-known structural-developmental investigations. Of particular concern are (1) the broad questions that frame inquiry across the two approaches and (2) the genetic methods and empirical techniques used to address core framing questions.

Piaget's structural-developmental approach

Piaget's accounts of cognitive development and his treatment of mathematical cognition hardly need introduction. His seminal analyses of cognitive structures and qualitative changes in structures over age have had a lasting influence on cognitive and developmental studies. Here, our concern is merely to note that, in his focus on cognitive structures, Piaget sidesteps an account of practices of quantification. The reason for this is not one of simple neglect. Rather, it is deeper than this, rooted in the orienting questions and units of analysis that are foundational to his analytic approach.

Piaget's starting point for inquiry is a set of questions about mathematics that are epistemological in character – what are the structural properties of mathematical knowledge (like operations and their inverses), and what is the relation between mathematics and logic (Piaget 1970)? For Piaget, the child is an 'epistemic subject', and psychological investigations are a means of empirical inquiry into cognitive structures that are posited as universal in their origins, their developmental trajectories and their timeless logical properties.

Piaget's method of inquiry into mathematical cognition is well represented in *The child's conception of number* (Piaget 1965). Piaget begins the volume by identifying his targets of analysis – mathematical relations and concepts, including numerical one-to-one correspondences (cardinal correspondences, ordinal correspondences), quantitative invariants (conservation of discrete quantity, continuous quantities) and arithmetical operations (additive compositions). Though his framing questions are epistemological, his techniques for investigation are empirical. Through clinical interviews with children, he seeks to reveal the psychogenesis of these fundamental mathematical ideas. A core theoretical argument for which he seeks to produce support is that fundamental mathematical ideas are rooted in the development of operations and their inverses linked to a logic of classes (negations) and a logic of relations (reciprocities).

Piaget's empirical techniques involve the presentation of a wide range of carefully designed number tasks to children, exploring properties of their understandings and their logical basis through clinical interviews. For example, in one version of his well-known conservation tasks, Piaget presented children with a number of counters, asking them to produce the same number from an available set. Younger children produced solutions in which the configuration of their copy showed similarities to the model set – for example, some children aligned the endpoints of the two sets. Slightly older children established equality based upon one-to-one correspondences; however, if one set was then spread apart, they would revert back to an analysis based upon endpoints or be unsure about equality, sometimes noting co-variations in spatial extents and element separations. Still older children argued that the sets necessarily had the same number after the spatial transformation, often arguing that the greater spatial extent was compensated for by the greater spatial separation, an equation of differences.

Piaget used his findings on such tasks to argue that the development of conservation understandings shifted qualitatively over age, and that such changes were related to the development of logical operations of class and order. Piaget argued that children come to equate the changes in the length of a set and element separations through a coordination of order relations (ordering spatial lengths and spatial separations) and classification (classifying the difference in length and element separations as equivalent). Through such arguments, Piaget sought to support claims about the epistemological roots of number. Thus, Piaget's argumentation borders epistemology and developmental psychology.

Piaget's focus was on universal structures of mathematical knowledge and their roots in ontogenesis. Issues of the historical and social conditions of development were hence far in the background. Indeed, Piaget argued that cognitive structures develop independently of local social and historical circumstances (Piaget 1970). Cultural issues were generally equated with factors that may affect the rate of structural development, but not much more (Piaget 1972). From this orientation, quantification practices become stripped of their social and historical properties – the forms and functions that they serve in activity.

A cultural-developmental perspective

A cultural approach begins with a different set of orienting concerns related to relations between the child and social history. The child is not only an 'epistemic subject' engaged in particular kinds of conceptual coordinations, but also an 'historical subject'. Children engage in practices of quantification in particular communities with particular social histories; they participate in collective life in particular moments of historical time. The roots of this view lie in Vygotsky's seminal writings (Vygotsky 1978, 1987), and the perspective is elaborated in current treatments (see, for example, Cole 1996; Wertsch 1991).

This analytic approach is founded on the assumption that there is a reciprocal relation between the genesis of collective activity and the genesis of individual activity.[2] On the one hand, collective activities have their genesis in the concerted work of individuals. In candy selling, the interconnected actions of sellers, clerks, customers, all working with cultural forms like currency, candy and written representations of prices, create and re-create a pattern of social organization that endures. Indeed, the collectively patterned activity of candy selling is sustained over many years, even though the particular actors change. But on the other hand, individuals within these activities are each actors, with their own beliefs, understandings and motives. Each seller constructs and accomplishes mathematical goals as he plies his trade and his goals are his own constructions.

Working within a cultural-developmental approach, I find it useful to conceptualize the 'genetic method' as requiring three different but related strands of analysis. (1) Microgenesis: how do individuals make use of forms like currency, or candy, or number words in moment-to-moment activity? On a given occasion, how do these forms come to serve particular functions as goals emerge and are accomplished? (2) Ontogenesis: how do the forms that are used and

---

[2] The perspective is consistent with Vygotsky's early discussion of units of analysis in the study of relations between speaking and thinking, as well as activity theoretic perspectives on activity as a nexus of relations between individual and collective activity (Leontiev 1981).

the functions that they serve shift with age and increased participation in collective activities? (3) Sociogenesis: how do new forms and functions emerge, spread and come to be valued in the quantification practices of individuals and groups? Let's consider how these three genetic concerns might frame an analysis of sellers' mark-up practices.

Microgenesis

I noted earlier that forms do not have fixed functions. Candies can be treated as food to eat, objects to count, or commodities with monetary value. None of these functions is an inherent feature of candy; rather, the functions of candy take form in activity. A *microgenetic* analysis frames questions about the process whereby individuals turn cultural forms like currency, number words and price ratios into mathematical means for accomplishing emerging goals in activities.[3] Let's consider further the way that a seller uses the price ratio form (from selling) to mark up wholesale prices.

The price ratio's original function is to mediate customer-seller exchanges. In a microgenetic analysis of the mark-up practice, we find that sellers uproot the form from its original context and use it in new ways – the price ratio becomes a mathematical means that aids the seller in planning how to sell.

In this activity, the child makes use of the price ratio to create many-to-one correspondences between multiple candies and units of 1000 cruzeiro notes, modelling repeated sales transactions. As argued earlier, though the price ratio form and its use to mediate customer-seller transactions afford the use of the ratio in mark-up practices, the generative properties of these correspondences are not contained in the ratio form or in the act of selling. Rather their generative power emerges from the child's construction of a logic of many-to-one correspondences in their moment-by-moment activity – as candies and currency values are conceptualized in relation to one another. We find evidence of the logical properties of these correspondences in sellers' sometimes repeated adjustments during mark-up. If a calculated gross price is too low after back-to-box placements (based upon the 'meio-pelo-meio' convention), a seller anticipates how to raise the value by decreasing the number of candies in his to-be-sold groups, and then repeats the back-to-box placements. If too

---

[3] Some researchers have made use of 'microgenesis' to refer to a methodological approach involving the intensive study of shifts in children's strategies and/or cognitive structures over short periods (see, for example, Siegler and Crowley 1991). My use of the term is more consistent with earlier treatments of the construct (Vygotsky 1986; Werner and Kaplan 1963) in which the very process of schematization of a phenomenon, perceptually or conceptually, is understood as a short-term developmental process. As conceptualized in the present discussion, microgenesis is neither a methodological approach nor a small-scale version of ontogenetic change. Rather it is a process in which forms with the cognitive functions they afford are transformed into means for accomplishing emerging goals.

high, he compensates through a logical calculation by adding a candy to his to-be-sold groupings. In these ways, the ratio becomes a mathematical means for mark-up as it is incorporated into a system of mathematical relations generated by the seller but embedded in the activity of selling candy.

An analysis of microgenesis seeks to understand the transformation of forms and functions into means and goals in activity. However, it does not address questions of the origins of these forms and functions in ontogeny. I turn next to this issue.

Ontogenesis

An *ontogenetic* analysis frames questions about shifting relations between the acquisition and use of cultural forms and mathematical functions that these forms are used to serve over age and experience. To illustrate, let's compare, for example, the practices of younger and older candy sellers. Analyses of these cohorts' use of the price ratio form reveals three patterns of shifting relations. First, as sellers enter into the selling practice at any age, the price ratio is appropriated to serve an important function – a means of mediating exchanges of candy for currency with customers.

Second, with increasing age, sellers use the price ratio to serve the function of mark-up. Younger sellers do not mark-up their wholesale boxes. Rather, they either ask or are told the ratio to use by others (parents, sibs, peers, store clerks). It is only the older sellers that use the price ratio to serve in the computation of an appropriate retail price.

Third, among the older sellers who use the ratio in mark-up, we find a progressive abbreviation of the ratio form with age and experience. As sellers begin to engage in mark-up computations, they often directly model sales. For example, one approach is to pretend to sell their candy in order to compute mark-up, removing candy by groups at a particular ratio sale price to compute a street price for the box. In contrast, an older seller is more likely to produce a quick and abbreviated computation in which only a trace of the price ratio is visible. For example, a seller may count the candy in a 30-unit box with single numbers in two groups of three at a time as depicted in Figure 7.2, not even removing the candy from the box. Through this procedure, the seller concludes that the box would sell for '10,000 cruzeiros', making explicit that 'ten' means '10,000 cruzeiros'.

Such form-function shifts over ontogenesis are related to individuals' emerging capabilities at coordinating mathematical relations of many-to-one correspondences. For younger sellers, many-to-one correspondences are simple counts – one Cr$1000 note and a number of candies. For older sellers, many-to-one correspondences have multiplicative properties (e.g. five sales of three for Cr$1000 is equivalent to a sale of fifteen for Cr$5000). The gradual

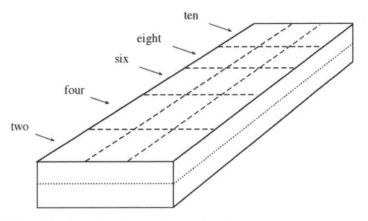

Figure 7.2. A seller's abbreviated use of the price ratio

shift from additive to multiplicative coordinations of relations over ontogenesis may well both give rise to and arise from mark-up activities. As sellers begin to engage in mark-up, they may explore the consequences of shifting the number of candies per note and exploring the effects of such alterations on the gross of potential sales.

Thus, over ontogenesis, we find a shifting relation between the forms used and the functions that they serve in quantification practices. Forms initially that may be used for a more elementary mathematical function, like the price ratio in seller–customer transactions, may gradually be used to serve new more complex mathematical functions in activities such as planning for sales in complex mark-up computations.

Sociogenesis

A sociogenetic analysis frames questions about the social origins and travel of cultural forms and their mathematical functions. Consider sociogenetic processes that occurred in approaches to mark-up with the price ratio. During the period of my study, inflationary surges led sellers to decrease the number of units sold for 1000 cruzeiros. These adjustments were often influenced by the pricing of others, leading to more general shifts for the price of candies in the streets. Similarly, during earlier periods, lower currency denominations were the valued root of the ratio – like the 500-cruzeiro note or the 100-cruzeiro note. Again, changes in the root bill value were probably initiated by some sellers, travelling through the community as new norms for selling; in turn, such shifts, perhaps initiated in the mark-up by some, led to shifts in selling practices as well as in the organization of mark-up computations by others.

In sum, my analytic tack is a departure from structural developmental analysis. In the Piagetian treatment, quantification practices are either analytically removed from an analysis of logical structures or bypassed by a focus on the results of clinical tasks that are often constructed without much concern for revealing the properties of cognition relative to collective life. In contrast, the focus here is on a dynamic cultural ecology of mathematics in which quantification practices are a key nexus in which we find a dynamic interplay between processes of micro-, onto-, and sociogenesis of cognitive activities.

The what?, how? and why? of development: a focus on practices valued in school

To explore the utility of the culturally oriented approach to developmental analysis, I turn to the practice of 'fair sharing' – dividing a quantity into equal fractional portions. I make use of the constructs sketched to provide a perspective on the what? how? and why? of development with regard to issues related to rational numbers.

Fair sharing is a common pragmatic strategy outside of school and it is also a typical instructional strategy for introducing children to fractions in elementary school. As in the case of candy sellers' mark-up computations, children's mathematical concern in fair sharing out of school is practical – to resolve claims to a limited resource, say a candy bar or a brownie. Children divide the resource with concern for an equitable portion. The motive is to obtain what is fair (if not an advantage!) over other stakeholders. Children are not necessarily concerned with quantifying the portions as fractional amounts, and they may not employ fractions and fraction words at all.

However, in school, teachers treat fair sharing in new ways. Curriculum designers and teachers have appropriated the out-of-school activity to support children's developing understanding of fractions. The instructional form of the activity typically engages children in using geometrical shapes (representing a commodity like brownies, cookies or pizza) and fraction words and numeric notation to refer to parts of those shapes. The register of fraction words, written notation and geometrical shapes are the forms used in practices of quantification in elementary school, and these are the targets of our developmental analyses.

A teacher's effort to draw upon out-of-school fair sharing activities to support a lesson on equivalent fractions

Consider an episode drawn from a fourth-grade class in which a teacher makes use of a fair sharing narrative to introduce fractions. We will see that some children interpret a 'fair share' as they would out of school, and differences between the presuppositions of the teacher and the students lead to problematic

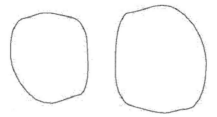

Figure 7.3. Ms Gates' drawing of the two 'huge cookies'

communications and repairs of various forms used in the activity (fraction words, geometrical shapes) and the mathematical functions that they are used to serve relative to fair sharing.The teacher's eventual recognition of the discrepancies leads to a pedagogical opportunity.

The teacher, Ms Gates, sits on a chair near the blackboard, and she tells her class about her recent trip to San Francisco. She describes her purchase of two huge cookies, and offers to share them among four students in the class.

1. TEACHER . . . I get these huge cookies [beginning to draw the first cookie on the blackboard – see Figure 7.3]. Two of them [drawing the second cookie]. And I say I am now going to choose four people. Derek, and Carrie, and Zed, and Ben [pointing to four children in her class]. And I am going to give – I'm going to share these cookies between these four people.
2. CHILD Equally?
3. TEACHER Equally! Of course. Are we democratic? Are we fair? Of course, equally!
4. CHILDREN [Background talk]
5. TEACHER Who can tell me [over the voices], wait a minute . . . [waiting for the noise to subside] how much cookie or cookies would each of those people get? [T calls on a child with his hand up] Lenny.
6. LENNY They'd each get two fourths.
7. TEACHER They'd each get two-fourths. [T now moves back to the board with chalk in hand.] So, what Lenny has done is he's said [T begins to partition the first drawn cookie with perpendicular lines through the first circle so that the drawn cookie is partitioned into quadrants. She's only partially finished when another child calls out]
8. CHILD FROM CLASS [Gary?] or one half
9. TEACHER Ok. It's going to help; it's going to really help if people don't call out.
10. ANOTHER CHILD [[Gary?] two fourths or one half
11. MORE CHILDREN [muffled task-related talk]
12. TEACHER [continues partitioning of the first circle into quadrants] I think this is why – tell me Lenny now am I wrong? You were saying that we'll get one cookie and we'll divide it between four people. So, each of them will get one of the quarters. And we divide the second cookie among the four people, so if it was Joey getting them, he'd get a piece from each.
13. CHILDREN [lots of task-related talk]
14. TEACHER And so Lenny said they'd get two quarters.

1 5. BACKGROUND CHILD TALK [lots more talk]
1 6. TEACHER [continues]. . . right, ok . . . [Teacher pauses] Lenny told me that it
would be 'two-fourths'. He also then added something to that – what did you tell
me Lenny?
1 7. LENNY [getting up and going to the board] The reason why I did two fourths was
because one cookie is bigger than the other [pointing to each cookie].
1 8. TEACHER Oh. . . . So . . . [looking momentarily confused] they'd get an equal
quarter from each one. But you know what they'd get an equal quarter from each
one. I'd have to make sure. So, do you hear what Lenny's saying? I just didn't
divide them into halves like this, because you know the people getting half from
here wouldn't get as much as those getting half from here. So I've given them
$\frac{1}{4}$ of this one and a fourth of this one, and together they'd have a whole cookie.
And Glen's point was you didn't need to do them that way. You could just divide
them into half. But you'd have to make absolutely sure the cookies were the same
size . . .

In this short episode, the teacher poses to her class a fair share problem
with some similarities to many children's everyday activities – if two cookies
were shared among four people, how much would each person receive? But in
the instructional context, the teacher's and the children's interpretations clash,
and communications are repaired. Let me now discuss how the cultural–genetic
framework frames the analysis of developmental processes in the quantification
practices captured in this episode.

Microgenesis and the fair sharing episode

During the whole class discussion, Ms Gates and Lenny are drawing upon
the same cultural forms – particular fraction words and the drawn circles –
but they are using them in different ways. For each of the participants, these
forms become representations of quantities; the fraction word 'two fourths'
refers to particular mathematical relations between parts and wholes. However,
Ms Gates' 'two fourths' and Lenny's 'two fourths' carry different meanings.

In her representation of the fair share, 'two fourths', Ms Gates is engaging in
what is a normative practice in schools, one in which graphical representations
are treated as idealized quantities. She assumes that two crudely drawn circles
will be taken as two circular cookies of equivalent size. This idealization appears
to be grounded in her intent to teach a lesson on equivalent fractions through
the example that 'two fourths' (as supported by the partitioning of circles in
Figure 7.4a) is equal to 'one half' (as supported by the partitioning of circles
in Figure 7.4b).

The microgenetic origins of Lenny's construction emerge from different
presuppositions. Lenny assumes that the cookies are different sizes (line 17),
an interpretation that is faithful to the blackboard drawing (Figure 7.4c). Thus,
for Lenny, the appropriate solution is one-fourth from each cookie, not one-
half from either. He interprets the goal of the task in terms of the pragmatic

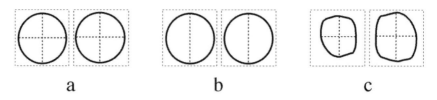

a   b   c

Figure 7.4. Three partitionings of Ms Gates' cookies.

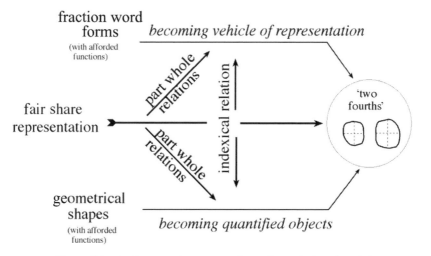

Figure 7.5. A microgenetic representation of Lenny's 'two-fourths'.

concerns of out-of-school sharing practices – he wants to be certain that the fair shares are equal.

The microgenetic processes in Lenny's and Ms Gates' activity reveal some formal similarities, even though the genetic origins of their microgenetic trajectories differ. In each case, we find a process that entails related strands of activity as depicted in Figure 7.5: treating fraction word forms as representations of quantities; partitioning shapes such that they become representations of quantities; and creating a relationship between word forms and shapes such that one serves to index the other.[4] Let's focus just on the microgenesis of Lenny's representation.

As depicted in the lower line, geometrical shapes become quantified objects as they are partitioned as fair shares of a whole. Lenny takes the two shapes as different sizes, each a different set of part–whole relations. As depicted in the

---

[4] This account shares some similarities with that which Werner and Kaplan (1984) present in their volume, *Symbol formation*.

higher strand, fraction words become treated as word forms that can carry the meanings of part–whole relations. For Lenny, the 'two' in 'two "fourths"' represents a cardinal value – the number of non-equivalent fourths. The meaning of 'fourths' is based on his interpretation of the value of each cookie as drawn. The dynamics of these processes are interrelated as depicted in the middle strand. The functions of word forms and shapes are constructed in relation to one another, such that the vehicle – in this case a cardinal word and fraction word – comes to index the object, in this case, a part of each cookie.

In Ms Gates' construction, there is a similar creation of quantified objects, representational vehicles and indexical correspondences. However, the process is rooted in different presuppositions regarding units, representations and the meaning of partitioning operations.

Sociogenesis and the fair sharing episode

Sociogenetic analyses focus on the emergence and spread of quantification practices. The use of geometric shapes for teaching fair share distributions is not an instructional innovation of Ms Gates' own design. The approach is common in curriculum units, and Ms Gates borrows and adapts it. Lenny brings his version of the fair sharing practice to the lesson. In her efforts to repair the communicative problem, Ms Gates tries to explain that there are two ways of taking the shapes as mathematical objects – idealized representations of quantities and their actual sizes. As this curriculum unit unfolds over the next few weeks, students will incorporate these two perspectives as they make sense of fair share solutions.

In sum, though practices are the construction of individuals, they certainly are not independent inventions. In the dynamics of collective activities, individuals are drawing upon forms with social histories and upon others' uses of such forms in the course of activity. It is in the context of use that innovations may emerge and spread as individuals interact with one another, making use of one another's constructions.

Ontogenesis and the fair sharing episode

The students in Ms Gates' classroom come to the fair share activity with prior experience with number and fraction words, geometrical shapes and activities of partitioning. Indeed, their interpretations of fair sharing have roots in much earlier periods of cognitive development when they used word forms, geometrical shapes and actions like splitting to serve functions that had little to do with the representations of fractions. In ontogenetic analyses, the concern is to understand these roots and trajectories of developmental change, with particular regard for the shifting relations between forms and functions in quantification practices. Let's consider some early activities that are arguably the ontogenetic roots of the quantification practices that Ms Gates is supporting in her classroom.

In early childhood, children engage in a wide variety of number activities. They use cardinal and ordinal number word forms in activities that include recognizing numerals on playing cards with parents, singing counting songs, telling their age, and racing with their friends (Saxe, Guberman and Gearhart 1987). Children also learn to name and differentiate geometrical shapes, including triangles, circles, squares and ovals, from picture books, educational activities involving plastic shapes and educational software. Finally, children engage in activities in which they split objects, as in out-of-school fair sharing activities. These varied forms are all ingredients of the practices that Ms Gates wants to support in her classroom, but in early development these forms serve very different functions than the representation of fractions.

To support an analysis of the ontogenesis of children's representational practices involving fractions, I am currently investigating how children come to use fraction words and geometric shapes to represent fractional quantities. My graduate students and I are interviewing third, fourth and fifth graders. We are finding that some children use whole number forms to represent their emerging understandings of part–whole relations (depicted in a drawing), while other children use fraction words to represent whole number conceptions. Consider how younger children responded to Figure 7.6a. Some children represented the fractional part as 'one out of four' (instead of the canonical form, 'one fourth'); other children said 'one third', using the canonical word form to represent a whole number count of the shaded pieces. Older students tended to use the canonical form in response to all items, and they were typically correct on item 6a. However, many students did not well differentiate the function of fraction words to represent discrete and continuous quantities, referring to 6b as 'one fifth', suggesting that while they used a canonical form to serve the function of representing a relation between parts and whole, they were not differentiating area, a continuous quantity, from a discrete quantity.

'Whys?': sources of change

Children construct new quantification practices through participation in collective activities like fair sharing and candy selling. Is it possible to identify the properties of such activities that support developmental processes of the sort that Ms Gates values in her classroom? I end the exposition by sketching a program of research that pursued this question.

The research focused on relationships between instructional practices and children's developing understandings of fractions. We tracked upper elementary children in twenty-one classrooms over the course of their instructional

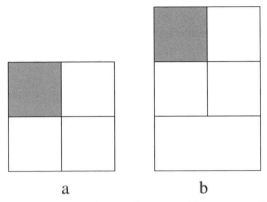

Figure 7.6. Greyed parts of areas used in a cross-sectional study with 3rd, 4th, and 5th graders 'Whys?': sources of change.

units (over 300 students participated). In each classroom, we followed two types of students from pre- to post-test – students who began instruction either with or without incipient understandings of fractions based on pre-test performance (Saxe, Gearhart and Seltzer 1999). We also rated the quality of fractions instruction based on observations of key lessons. With the rating system, we did not simply focus on the teachers' instructional moves. Rather, the concern was to capture the classroom as a collective, one in which student participation as much as teacher participation contributed to judgments about the quality of students' opportunities to learn. Gearhart, Saxe, Seltzer, Schlackman, Ching, Nasir, Fall, Bennett, Rhine and Sloan (1999) contains a complete description of this rating system as well as findings that bear on its validity as a measure of opportunities to learn in classrooms.

We expected that the two types of students would tend to generate different kinds of mathematical goals in their instructional activities, leading to differences in changes from pre-test to post-test performances depending on the quality of instruction. Children without incipient understandings would tend to interpret instructional tasks in terms of whole numbers, not part–whole and multiplicative relations, unless instructional practices guided them to re-conceptualize quantitative relations. In contrast, children with an incipient understanding of part–whole coordinations on elementary fractions tasks would be much more likely to progress during the unit even if instructional practices provided less support.

The findings are reported in Saxe, Gearhart and Seltzer (1999), and I sketch one strand of analysis here. Figure 7.7 is a plot of mean post-test performances[5]

[5] Post-test scores are adjusted by pre-test scores and language background of students in the classrooms.

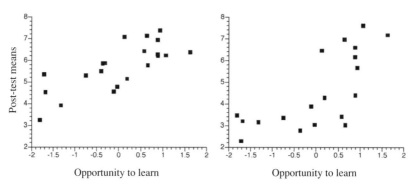

Figure 7.7. Adjusted post-test means for children with and without incipient knowledge in 21 classrooms as a function of opportunity to learn.

for each of the twenty-one classrooms as a function of the opportunity to learn ratings. The findings are consistent with our conjectures about the interaction of students' incipient knowledge and opportunity to learn. For the students with incipient understandings, the relationship between performance on post-test and opportunity to learn was linear; the greater their opportunity to learn fractions in the classroom, the more students progressed. For the students without incipient understandings, the relationship between performance on post-test and opportunity to learn was not linear. There was little gain for students whose classrooms were rated as providing limited opportunity to learn. However, there was a precipitous increase in student gain in classrooms rated more highly. Thus, when instruction is geared toward building upon what children understand, it is more likely that students – even with limited initial understandings – will make marked gains.

To deepen our understanding of these results, graduate students and I are analysing videotapes of fair share lessons collected in two contrasting classrooms to understand the interplay between micro-, onto-, and socio-genetic processes. One videotape was collected in a classroom that ranked highest on our scale of opportunity to learn; in this classroom there was no post-test gap between students who began instruction with and without incipient understandings, and the post-test means for both groups were high. The other is from a classroom that was ranked just below the median level on the opportunity to learn scale; in this classroom, the post-test scores of the group without incipient understandings were much lower than those of the incipient group.

The differences in classroom practices rated with different opportunities to learn revealed marked differences in the way students' efforts to structure and accomplish goals involving fractions were supported. In the classroom rated with greater opportunities to learn, the teacher built her instructional approach to the fair share problem on students' mathematical thinking, supporting their emerging mathematical goals as they worked to conceptualize and accomplish problems. For example, in this class, the teacher would pose a challenging problem that built on prior problems, and asked the students to solve it, encouraging them to enlist the help of a partner if needed. As she roved through the classroom, she observed students, sometimes asking them to explain their reasoning. As she queried and engaged a student in a brief conversation, she encouraged other students to comment and extend the dialogue. Students often listened and sometimes appropriated what they saw or heard into their own solutions. In the final discussion, the teacher asked students to share their strategies, and engaged the whole class in commentary on it. Her questions and comments generally followed students' line of reasoning, encouraging students to formalize their thinking and their representations. For example, she asked students to represent their work using both drawings and numeric notation, and to explain the relationships between the two.

In the classroom ranked below the median, the teacher tended to model how to partition fair shares, and she did not adopt a systematic approach to either graphic or numeric notation. In her opening lesson and in her interventions with individual students, her drawings tended to be unpredictable in size and shape, and her references to shapes and their parts were often a mix of canonical expressions (like 'one fourth') and whole number expressions, like 'a piece' or 'one piece', without well framing her intended meanings. Sometimes fractional parts were labelled with whole numbers and sometimes they were identified as fractions, but the relations between these different kinds of reference would be confusing to a child who does not readily conceptualize parts of areas in terms of fractions. When this teacher roved and when she led the final whole class discussion, she tended to correct students. She was not often engaged in understanding the students' approaches to the problem, or building the discourse on student understanding.

Concluding remarks

I end this sketch of a cultural developmental framework by briefly situating it in relation to some of the neo-Piagetian approaches to cognitive development.

I noted earlier that Piaget's major emphasis in his empirical and analytic work was to offer arguments about the origins and properties of universal cognitive structures and their developmental transformations. Piaget did not pursue analyses of individual differences nor processes whereby social factors might alter structural-developmental processes. These were largely concerns for psychology, and his occasional claims about such matters were peripheral to his seminal contributions to a genetic epistemology. In this regard, Piaget regarded the individual as an epistemic, not a psychological subject (Piaget 1970).

Neo-Piagetian frameworks have shifted methods and analytic techniques, treating the individual not only as a vehicle for epistemological inquiry, but also as a psychological subject. Methods are varied. They include cross-sectional and short-term longitudinal studies on batteries of cognitive tasks including variants of tasks used by Piaget like seriations and conservations (e.g. Case 1985; Pascual-Leone 1970). They also include training studies in which efforts are made to support children's improvements with particular regard for how learning may emerge in concert on subsets of assessment tasks (e.g. Case, Okamoto, Henderson and McKeough 1993; Demetriou, Christou, Spanoudis and Platsidou 2002). In addition, they include cross-national studies that make an effort to understand what are universal and specific developments in sets of cognitive abilities (e.g. Case, Okamoto, Griffin, McKeough, Bleiker, Henderson and Stephenson 1996; Demetriou et al. 2002). The psychological models that have given rise to and flowed from such studies have sought to explain consistencies and inconsistencies in cross-task performances over age in terms of domain-specific knowledge, like number or space, and domain-general constraints that regulate domain-specific constructions, such as constructs like working memory (e.g. Case 1985; Pascual-Leone 1970), processing efficiency (Demetriou, Christou, Spanoudis and Platsidou 2002) and webs of semantic connections within and across domains of knowledge (Case, Okamoto, Henderson and McKeough 1993).

The neo-Piagetian arguments for domain-specific cognitive structures are in accord with some current modularist positions (Butterworth 1999; Dehaene 1997) that attribute domain-specific processing mechanisms for particular kinds of knowledge (e.g. number). However, unlike these modularist accounts that tend to assume hard-wired numerical knowledge, at least some neo-Piagetian accounts posit and find support for a key role of individuals' constructive activity in the structural transformations of domain-specific knowledge over development (e.g. Karmiloff-Smith 1995).

In some respects, the framework sketched in this chapter travels on some similar ground with neo-Piagetian models. In focusing on emerging mathematical goals in everyday activities, I am concerned with domain-specific construction of logico-mathematical structures and their developmental transformation. Thus, in this chapter I delineated some of the features of structural-developmental progressions in sellers' coordination of many-to-one correspondences in their mark-up activities and in children's coordination of part–whole relations in fair sharing. Further, like Piagetian and neo-Piagetian formulations, the model I am proposing of (ontogenetic) development coordinated logico-mathematical operations is epigenetic. New structural coordinations are born from prior ones. Some supportive evidence for this thesis came from sellers' appropriation of their use of many-to-one correspondences in sales to their use of these correspondences in mark-up and the gradual working out of new mark-up strategies that involved more complex coordinations of correspondence relations. Finally, the studies on fractions as a function of different classroom practices are consistent with neo-Piagetian models that posit limits that enable and constrain children's construction of new mathematical understandings under educational interventions.

However, the present framework departs substantially from neo-Piagetian psychological models in important ways. From the perspective that I have elaborated, individuals are not only psychological subjects, as the neo-Piagetian models have emphasized, but also historical subjects. Indeed, whether we are discussing candy sellers in the streets of north-east Brazil or children participating in classroom communities, these children are actors enmeshed in webs of social organizations that sustain valued forms of collective representations with socially recognized functions. Such social organizations are themselves collective constructions that have been elaborated over the varied social histories of communities. Further, individuals play a constitutive role in both reproducing and producing alterations in these historical constructions through their participatory activities (Modell 1996; Saxe 1999; Saxe and Esmonde in press). In an autocatalytic process, the production, reproduction, and alteration of these forms create emerging environments that themselves become interwoven with the properties of individuals' own developmental trajectories in non-trivial ways. Thus an analysis of the individual must entail an analysis of social life, and vice versa. It is not that the psychologically oriented models do not attend to social factors. Indeed, in some impressive studies, authors like Case et al. (1996) and Demetriou, Kui, Spanoudis, Christou, Kyriakides and Platsidou (2003) have pointed to social and cultural variables that predict differences in the rate of particular developments of cognitive structures or structural-like processes. The problem is that, from a historical perspective, in these models and methods of study, the constructive activities of individuals as they emerge in social life remain all but invisible.

Taking the individual as an historical subject complicates but also enriches epistemological and psychological analyses of cognitive development. It requires the elaboration of new analytic units to support empirical inquiry, ones that open up opportunities for analysing the interplay between historical and developmental processes in the micro-, socio- and ontogenetic construction of knowledge. My sketch of the work on quantification practices is one emerging effort to re-situate the analysis of cognition in a perspective that coordinates not only epistemic and psychological concerns, but also the role of the individual as an actor, participating in, drawing from and contributing to continuities and discontinuities in forms and functions of knowledge not only in their own developments but in the social histories of communities.

262   *Geoffrey B. Saxe*

REFERENCES

Butterworth, B. (1999). *What counts: how every brain is hardwired for math.* New York: The Free Press.

Carraher, T. N., Carraher, D. W. and Schliemann, A. D. (1985). Mathematics in the streets and in schools. *British Journal of Developmental Psychology 3,* 21–9.

Case, R. (1985). *Intellectual development: birth to adulthood.* New York: Academic Press.

(1992). *The mind's staircase: exploring the conceptual underpinnings of children's thought and knowledge.* Hillsdale, NJ: Erlbaum.

Case, R., Okamoto, Y., Henderson, B. and McKeough, A. (1993). Analyzing diversity in developmental pathways: Methods and concepts. In R. Case and W. Edelstein (eds.) *The new structuralism in cognitive development: theory and research on individual pathways* (pp. 71–100). Contributions to Human Development, vol. 23. Basel: Karger.

Case, R., Okamoto, Y., Griffin, S., McKeough, A., Bleiker, C., Henderson, B. and Stephenson, K. M. (1996). The role of central conceptual structures in the development of children's thought. *Monographs of the Society for Research in Child Development, 61* (1–2), serial no. 246.

Cole, M. (1996). *Cultural psychology: a once and future discipline.* Cambridge, MA: Harvard University Press.

Dasen, P. R. and de Ribaupierre, A. (1988). Neo-Piagetian theories: cross-cultural and differential perspectives. In A. Demetriou (ed.) *The neo-Piagetian theories of cognitive development: toward an integration.* North Holland: Elsevier.

Dehaene, S. (1997). *The number sense: how the mind creates mathematics.* New York: Oxford.

Demetriou, A., Christou, C., Spanoudis, G. and Platsidou, M. (2002). The development of mental processing: efficiency, working memory, and thinking. *Monographs of the Society for Research in Child Development, 67*(1), serial no. 263.

Demetriou, A., Kui, Z. X., Spanoudis, G., Christou, C., Kyriakides, L. and Platsidou, M. (2003). The architecture and development of mental processing: Greek, Chinese, or universal? Unpublished manuscript. University of Cyprus.

Gearhart, M., Saxe, G. B., Seltzer, M., Schlackman, J., Ching, C., Nasir, N., Fall, R., Bennett, T., Rhine, S. and Sloan, T. F. (1999). Opportunities to learn fractions in elementary mathematics classrooms. *Journal for Research in Mathematics Education 30*(3): 286–315.

Karmiloff-Smith, A. (1995). *Beyond modularity: a developmental perspective on cognitive science.* Cambridge, MA: MIT Press.

Leontiev, A. N. (1981). The problem of activity in psychology. In J. V. Wertsch (ed.) *The concept of activity in Soviet psychology* (pp. 37–71). New York: Sharpe.

Modell, J. (1996). The uneasy engagement of ethnography and human development. In R. Jessor, A. Colby and R. A. Shweder (eds.) *Ethnography and human development: context and meaning in social inquiry* (pp. 479–504). Chicago: University of Chicago Press.

Nasir, N. S. (2002). Identity, goals, and learning: mathematics in cultural practice. *Mathematical Thinking and Learning, 4*(2 and 3), 213–47.

Pascual-Leone, J. (1970). A mathematical model for the transition rule in Piaget's developmental stages. *Acta Psychologica, 32,* 301–45.

(1988). Organismic processes for neo-Piagetian theories: a dialectical causal account of cognitive development. In A. Demetriou (ed.) *The neo-Piagetian theories of cognitive development: towards an integration* (pp. 25–64). Amsterdam: North-Holland.

Piaget, J. (1965). *The child's conception of number*. New York, Norton.

(1970). Piaget's theory. In P. H. Mussen (ed.) *Carmichael's manual of child psychology* (pp. 703–31). New York: Wiley.

(1972). Intellectual evolution from adolescence to adulthood. *Human Development, 15*(1), 1–12

Saxe, G. B. (1991). *Culture and cognitive development: studies in mathematical understanding*. Hillsdale, NJ: Lawrence Erlbaum Associates.

(1999). Cognition, development, and cultural practices. In E. Turiel (ed.) *Culture and development: new directions in child psychology* (pp. 19–35). San Francisco: Jossey-Bass.

Saxe, G. B., Guberman, S. R. and Gearhart, M. (1987). Social processes in early number development. *Monographs of the Society for Research in Child Development, 52*(2), serial no. 216.

Saxe, G. B. and Esmonde, I. (in press). Making change in Oksapmin tradestores: studies in shifting practices of quantification under conditions of rapid social change. *South Pacific Journal of Psychology*.

Saxe, G. B., Gearhart, M. and Seltzer, M. (1999). Relations between classroom practices and student learning in the domain of fractions. *Cognition and Instruction, 17*(1), 1–24.

Saxe, G. B. and Guberman, S. R. (1998). Studying mathematics learning in collective activity. *Learning and Instruction, 8*(6), 489–501.

Siegler, R. S. and Crowley, K. (1991). The microgenetic method: a direct means for studying cognitive development. *American Psychologist, 46*, 606–20.

Vygotsky, L. S. (1978). *Mind in society*. Cambridge, MA: Harvard University Press.

(1986). *Thought and language*. Cambridge, MA: MIT Press.

(1987). *Thinking and speech*. New York: Plenum.

Werner, H. and Kaplan, B. (1963). *Symbol formation: an organismic-developmental approach to language and the expression of thought*. New York: Wiley.

(1984). *Symbol formation: an organismic-developmental approach to the psychology of language*. Hillsdale, NJ: Lawrence Erlbaum Associates.

Wertsch, J. V. (1985). *Vygotsky and the social formation of mind*. Cambridge, MA: Harvard University Press.

(1991). *Voices of the mind*. Cambridge, MA: Harvard University Press.

8   Contributions of central conceptual structure theory to education

Sharon Griffin

Cognitive change lies at the very heart of the educational enterprise. It is what schooling is intended to produce. It underlies the changes in performance that are expected in school, in a variety of subject areas, as students progress through the grades and it underlies the competencies that are routinely measured in year-end assessments. Evidence of cognitive change is the single biggest factor that can earn a school a commendation, and the lack of such evidence the single biggest factor that can put a school out of business. Given the importance of this construct to education, it is disappointing that research in the field of cognitive change has not been made more available or accessible to educators – so that it can inform practice – and conversely, that current dilemmas in the field of education have not been made more salient to cognitive psychologists – so that insights gained in efforts to map the mind can be used to offer potential solutions to educational problems. A primary goal of the present chapter is to bridge this gap.

The three questions posed in the present volume – What is it that changes in cognitive development? How does change occur? Why does change occur? – provide an excellent starting point for this endeavour. By highlighting central aspects of cognitive change – aspects that any particular theory must address – they provide an opportunity for each author to describe (1) core postulates of a recent theory and (2), in the present chapter at least (see also Fischer, this volume; Adey, this volume), the educational implications that can be derived from each postulate. The theory that is described in the present chapter, *central conceptual structure theory*, is also an excellent candidate for this dual focus. It was conceived, developed and tested in schools of education and its form and character were shaped by this environment, not only by recent findings in the relatively new field of applied cognitive science, but also by broader educational concerns that permeated the very air we breathed. Finally, it was the fondest hope of the principal architect of this theory, Robbie Case, to whom the present volume is dedicated, that his work make a difference in real classrooms, for real children. Before his premature death, he had hoped to move his own scholarship in this direction and to articulate a theory of instruction that he believed was implicit in *central conceptual structure theory*. By describing the theory in such a way that it is accessible to educators and by drawing out some of its instructional implications, I hope to move his work in this direction.

I start by providing a brief description of Piaget's theory, with particular emphasis on (1) the answers this theory provides for the three questions that have been posed for the present volume (listed in the preceding paragraph) and (2) the educational implications that have been drawn from each answer. Because this theory provides a foundation for *central conceptual structure theory* and because it has had a larger and longer impact on education than any other cognitive developmental theory that has been advanced in the past century, it provides a useful context for the present discussion. I move next to a description of *central conceptual structure theory*, paying particular attention to the ways it differs from Piaget's theory and the additional contributions to education that these differences make possible. In the final section, I describe some educational applications that have been developed on the basis of the theory, the cognitive changes these applications support, and ways this applied research has, itself, prompted further refinements in the theory.

Piaget's theory

What is it that changes in cognitive development?

In contrast to most theorists who preceded him and most who followed him, Piaget attempted to describe cognitive change from birth to adulthood in terms of one set of intellectual structures, called operational structures or *structures d'ensembles* (structures of the whole), which become progressively complex as development proceeds and which can be used to explain an individual's performance across all domains of human functioning. To accomplish this broad mission, the structures Piaget proposed were modelled in very abstract terms and were called 'operational structures' or 'logical structures' so that they could explain performance across a broad range of content domains. In Piaget's theory the question 'What is it that changes in cognitive development? (i.e. 'What are the most important sequences of interest?') can thus be answered very simply. An individual's operational structures change.

In his theoretical formulations, Piaget described three major changes in operational structures that typically occur around the ages of two, six and eleven years of age, with each change ushering in a qualitatively different (i.e. more complex) form of thought. Development was thus described in terms of four major stages, proceeding from sensori-motor thought (birth to two years) to pre-operational thought (two to six years), to concrete operational thought (six to eleven years), to formal operational thought (eleven to eighteen years). Less major changes within each stage, in which the current form of thought is progressively differentiated, were also modelled in logical terms (e.g. as a change in an ability to handle an operation of the form $x = (f) \, y$, to an ability to handle an operation of the form $x = (f) \, y + z$, to an ability to handle an operation of the form $x = (f) \, y \times z$.

Not surprisingly, teachers, who are responsible for teaching subject matter knowledge (i.e. content knowledge), have had a hard time making use of descriptions of children's thought that are couched, almost exclusively, in structural terms (i.e. that are content free) and, of all the contributions Piaget has made to our understanding of cognitive change, his descriptions of what it is that changes in cognitive development have had the least impact on education. Several Piagetian scholars (notably Wadsworth 1996) have attempted to bring Piaget's stage characterizations (i.e. his operational structures) to life for teachers by providing a wealth of concrete, content-rich examples drawn from Piaget's own research. In the experience of the present author, these succeed in giving teachers a flavour of children's thought in particular stages; an appreciation of children's understanding of particular concepts (e.g. rules) at particular ages; and a vague sense that children's thought does indeed change across major stage transitions. However, like Piaget's own descriptions, these accounts fail to give teachers an understanding of the nature of the cognitive changes that Piaget has proposed and the manner in which one form of thought builds systematically upon another.

In an effort to capture these aspects of Piaget's theory for prospective teachers, the present author prepared a chart which lists, for each of Piaget's four major stages: (1) the information a child can represent and (2) the sorts of knowledge a child can construct, with the schemata/operational structures that are available in that stage (see Table 8.1). Although the categories selected for this effort – information represented and knowledge constructed – remain abstract, they are categories that are familiar to teachers. By moving Piaget's theory onto familiar ground and by addressing some of its implications for the content of children's thought, I hoped to make its relevance to education more apparent. Similarly, the at-a-glance chart, while it oversimplifies Piaget's theoretical formulations, has the advantage of highlighting (1) the systematic increase in structural complexity and (2) the attendant increase in the sophistication of children's knowledge structures that are central features of the cognitive changes Piaget proposed. I believe this chart has been useful in giving teachers a better intuitive understanding of the cognitive changes Piaget proposed but, in terms of shaping educational practice, its value has been limited.

How does change occur?

The mechanism that Piaget proposed to account for the emergence of new operational structures from previous ones can be illuminated by describing three constructs. The first, equilibration, rests on the assumption that individuals are

Table 8.1. *Piaget's stages.*

Stage[*]	Represents (has schemata for)	Knowledge constructed
sensorimotor: (0–2)	*current, available s-m experiences* e.g. represents smell, taste, touch, sound of sensory and motor acts	*physical knowledge* e.g. suckables, lookables e.g. animate–inanimate distinction
pre-operations (2–6)	*concrete objects and events* e.g. represents names and attributes of objects and events	*perceptual knowledge* e.g. big–little; heavy–light; red–blue e.g. self–other distinction
concrete operations (6–11)	*relationships btw. objects and events* e.g. represents transformations; how objects and events are organized in series, classes, dimensions	*logical (concrete) knowledge* e.g. dimensions of number, time, space, e.g. conservation; class inclusion e.g. inner–outer worlds distinction
formal operations (11–18)	*relationships btw. concepts* e.g. represents variables, dimensions; how concepts, classes of events are organized	*logical (abstract) knowledge* e.g. categories, systems e.g. analogies e.g. control of variables e.g. personality types distinction

[*] At each new level, previous levels are incorporated and integrated.

motivated to make sense of their world. When cognitive conflict occurs (i.e. when an individual encounters a situation that can't be interpreted satisfactorily with available operational structures), the individual will be motivated to change their existing structures to accommodate the new situation, either by expanding their existing structures to assimilate the new information or by changing the existing structures in more radical ways (e.g. by integrating two structures that were previously independent) to create a more powerful sense-making structure that provides a better fit for the present situation. When this mechanism is at work, schemata and operational structures become progressively differentiated and elaborated and, at certain points in development, hierarchically integrated, creating a new, higher-order structure that is qualitatively distinct from the previous structures from which it was built. Equilibration, differentiation and hierarchic integration thus play a central role in promoting change in this framework.

With these postulates, which are closely related to those described for the next question (why does change occur?), Piaget ushered in a radical change in the way knowledge and the knowledge construction process was construed. Knowledge construction was now seen as being squarely in the hands of the epistemic subject and dependent, to a large extent, on his own mental activity. This provides a sharp contrast to previously held beliefs that knowledge was 'imparted' to a largely passive subject by more knowledgeable experts or that knowledge was 'shaped' by reinforcement contingencies that were largely under environmental control (see Phillips and Soltis 1998, for a review of these theories).

Why does change occur?

Piaget proposed four factors to account for these changes. The first, maturation, is largely outside of the control of educators. The remaining three, however, have significant implications for education. These are: active experience (e.g. physical and mental exploration; problem-solving), social interaction (e.g. classroom communication), and disequilibrium. All three support the mechanism for change that Piaget proposed (described in the preceding paragraph) and all three can easily be influenced by the education process. The extent to which these factors and the ones described in the preceding paragraph have influenced education can be assessed, at least superficially, by the frequency with which the term 'constructivism' is found in the educational arena. Although derived directly from Piaget's work, this term has now transcended its author. It is used, today, to describe a set of principles that, to a greater or lesser extent, continue to shape a wide variety of educational initiatives. To provide a summary of Piaget's theory, four major constructivist principles and the educational implications that can be drawn from each are listed below. This is followed by a brief discussion of the extent to which each implication has been realized in US schools to date.

Constructivist principles
(1) All knowledge is constructed by the individual, through exploration and active participation in the physical and social world.
(2) Individuals use their current forms of thought to make sense of and to interpret self and the world.
(3) Development proceeds in an invariant sequence, by a process of differentiation and hierarchic integration in which new forms of thought build on and incorporate previous forms of thought.
(4) New forms of thought (adaptation) occur when there is an internal need (i.e. disequilibrium) and when the current form of thought doesn't work.

Implications for education

(1) Provide ample opportunity for students to explore actively the concepts you want them to learn and to discuss these ideas in a social context.

(2) For each discipline you want to teach, make sure you understand your students' current level of thinking and use this as a base to build on when you introduce new ideas.

(3) For each discipline that you want to teach, make sure you understand the levels of thinking that follow your students' current understanding so you can provide a carefully graded sequence of activities that will allow students to use their current understandings to construct new understandings at the next level up.

(4) Introduce cognitive conflict (e.g. by revealing shortcomings in students' current ways of thinking) and provide opportunities for students to construct more powerful understandings.

When one reviews the implications for education that can be logically derived from each of the four constructivist principles listed above, it becomes quickly apparent that only one of these implications (i.e. provide opportunities for active exploration) has had a notable impact on schooling in the US during the past half century. This implication has been realized in the many hands-on, discovery-based learning programs that were developed and implemented in the 1960s, 1970s and 1980s (with mixed results in terms of measurable gains in student learning and achievement) and it is evident today, in a more sophisticated form, in the problem-solving approaches to learning that characterize many mathematics and science curriculums that have recently been developed (see Griffin and Case 1997; Hiebert 1997, for a review of these approaches).

Although the second and third implications have been accepted by educators as good things to do, in principle, the lack of a framework and/or tools that teachers can use to assess children's current level of understanding in any domain (implication 2) or to identify the ways that knowledge in these domains is systematically constructed (implication 3) ensures that these implications are virtually invisible in the broader educational arena, rising to the level of consciousness only in isolated instances. Evidence that this is the case is available in a recent volume (Bransford et al. 1999) that was published by the National Research Council for the explicit purpose of informing educators of the importance of implications 2 and 3, among others, in the educational enterprise. Evidence that teachers are willing to implement these principles but lack the means to do so is available in the subsequent widespread demand for a follow-up volume that would provide concrete tools and examples to help teachers accomplish these goals. Thus, although Piaget pointed teachers in the right direction half a century ago, the general, abstract nature of his theoretical formulations provided insufficient guidance to educators to permit realization of the major implications of his theory.

The fourth implication (i.e. introduce cognitive conflict by revealing short-comings in students' current ways of thinking) has also not achieved broad currency in the educational arena (see Minstrell 1989, for a notable exception). For this failure, we can't blame Piaget for any lack of clarity in the manner in which this cognitive change mechanism has been presented, but rather we can consider the reluctance of US teachers to provide consequences for students' performance that are anything other than positive. This effectively eliminates any pedagogical efforts to pay serious attention to students' mistakes and to use these mistakes as sites for learning. Although this, too, is changing in the current educational climate (see Hiebert 1997), it is largely thanks to current, post-Piagetian theories of cognitive change, which provide a framework in which all the implications described above can more easily be realized. It is to one such theory that I now turn.

Central conceptual structure theory

Central conceptual structure theory was developed by Robbie Case and his colleagues and students over a twenty-year period. Although the theory evolved across this time period and went through several transformations (see Case and Okamoto 1996, for a review of this history), the goals of this effort remained constant; namely, to create a model of cognitive change that preserved the strengths of Piaget's theory and that overcame its weaknesses. In this section, I draw upon the current form of the theory to answer the three questions that have been posed in the present volume and to describe aspects of the theory that have direct implications for education. More detailed descriptions of the theory can be found in Case and Griffin 1990; Case 1992; Case and Okamoto 1996; Griffin and Case 1997.

What is it that changes in cognitive development?

In contrast to Piaget's more unitary theory of cognitive development, central conceptual structure theory can perhaps best be thought of as a two-part theory, with one part describing the form of children's thought and the other part, the content of children's thought. Because form and content can't exist independently, this distinction is somewhat artificial. However, it provides a useful rhetorical device to illuminate components of the theory that can be directly attributed to Piaget (i.e. the form of children's thought) and components of the theory that go beyond Piaget, and that address a major limitation in Piaget's theory (i.e. the content of children's thought). Each of these aspects of central conceptual structure theory is described, in turn, below.

The form of children's thought

In central conceptual structure theory, the form of children's thought (i.e. the organization of schemata) is seen to change systematically with development, to become increasingly complex, and to progress through four major stages and several minor substages, between birth and adulthood. As illustrated in Figure 8.1, the structural progression that is proposed is so similar to the one Piaget proposed that a description of the ways the two theories differ with respect to this progression will be sufficient to illuminate this aspect of central conceptual structure theory. The major differences are as follows.

First, in central conceptual structure theory a new mechanism – growth in working-memory capacity (Pascual-Leone 1970) – is used to explain the common form that children's thought is believed to assume across content domains. Because working-memory capacity has been found to grow systematically with development and to impose system-wide constraints on mental processing (Pascual-Leone and Goodman 1979), it provides a useful framework to reconcile the notions that children's thought may differ in content across content domains (discussed below) and still assume a common form across different domains of mental functioning.

Second, the substage transitions that are proposed in central conceptual structure theory are much more systematic within stages and consistent across stages than the ones Piaget proposed. These aspects of central conceptual structure theory have also been informed by research on working memory, which has suggested patterns not only in the rate at which cognitive change occurs but also in the form these changes assume at different developmental periods (Pascual-Leone 1969; Pascual-Leone 1970; Pascual-Leone and Goodman 1979). The stage and substage transitions that are illustrated in Figure 8.1 have been informed by this research. They can be summarized as follows: (1) Each major stage transition involves the hierarchic integration of two units of thought (e.g. two schemas) that were available only independently before; (2) Each substage transition involves a progressive elaboration of the new unit of thought from a single structure (e.g. a unidimensional structure in the first substage of the dimensional stage) to a double structure (e.g. a bidimensional structure in the second substage of the same stage) to a more fully integrated double structure (e.g. an integrated-bidimensional structure in the third and final substage of this major stage). Note that these postulates parallel the ones Piaget provided for substage transitions and described in more logical terms.

The remaining two differences between the present formulation and the one proposed by Piaget are relatively minor and can be summed up quickly. Third, in central conceptual structure theory, the names of three stages that succeed the sensori-motor stage have been changed to better reflect the type of information that is represented and the level of structural complexity that is achieved when

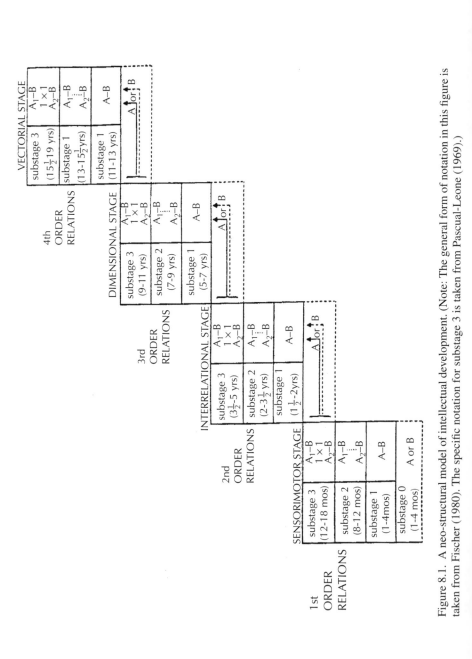

Figure 8.1. A neo-structural model of intellectual development. (Note: The general form of notation in this figure is taken from Fischer (1980). The specific notation for substage 3 is taken from Pascual-Leone (1969).)

each new unit of thought is created. For example, the label 'dimensional', applied to the third stage of development, is designed to capture the notion that the hierarchic integration of two fully developed 'interrelational' schemas from the previous stage makes it possible for a child to represent dimensions (e.g. of time, space, number) for the first time. Fourth and finally, the age at which the second major stage transition is believed to occur has been changed from six years to five years on the basis of a wealth of research evidence that has accumulated over several years, within the paradigms of both theories.

The content of children's thought

From the perspective of the thinker, as opposed to the observer of children's thought, there is no form of thought that is content-free. Spurred by this realization, Case and his colleagues devoted a considerable amount of attention to an exploration of the content of children's thought, across the middle childhood years, in domains of experience that are relevant to schooling (e.g. logical-mathematical understanding, narrative understanding, spatial-artistic understanding). Using the theoretical formulations described in the previous section, it was hypothesized that the content of children's thought in specific domains would change systematically in a manner that is consistent with the stage and substage transition postulates (i.e. the systematic increase in structural complexity) that had already been identified for this age range. The present theory represents the fruits of this initiative. By searching for content that conformed to the general form of children's thought, as identified and refined in half a century of research, we were able to identify a limited number of domain-specific central conceptual structures that we believed provided a more powerful and compelling description of cognitive change than any other we had encountered to date. Central conceptual structures became the cognitive sequences of interest to us in our subsequent research efforts and the current name of the theory reflects this focus.

What is a central conceptual structure? A central conceptual structure is a powerful organizing schema, consisting of a network of core concepts and relations that underpin most tasks in a particular domain, at a particular level of competence, and that serve as a foundation for the development of further competencies at higher levels. Several central conceptual structures have been identified to date and the three that are most fully articulated – the central numerical structure, the central spatial structure and the central narrative structure – are described here in some detail to illustrate this aspect of the theory. It is worth noting here that, although the term 'central conceptual structure' is typically used as a singular noun, to highlight the domain-specific content that each such structure embodies, it is also used to refer to a set of structures within a particular domain that describe the manner in which a particular central conceptual structure is created from precursor structures, and is progressively elaborated across substage transitions. In the latter case, the plural form of the term is sometimes used.

The cognitive sequences that have been identified for three content domains and for the age range of four to ten years are described below. Note that the age assigned to each sub-stage in these progressions represents the midpoint of a two-year interval in which most children in developed societies (e.g. those with adequate access to the opportunities the society presents) are able to demonstrate the particular form of knowledge described.

The central numerical structure

At four years of age, children have two knowledge structures available – a schema for making global quantity comparisons (e.g. saying which of two quantities is a lot or a little) and a schema for counting small sets of objects (e.g. saying the counting words as you touch each object in turn) – which are not yet linked. At this age, therefore, they are able to apply one *or* the other of these structures at any one time. For example, when presented with two stacks of weights on a balance beam, they can tell which is heavier and lighter and which side of the beam will go down if the difference between the stacks is perceptually salient. If it is not salient, the stacks will be judged to be equivalent, without any attempt at counting to verify the prediction (Siegler 1976). Alternatively, if counting is what is required in a task, children can rote count from one to five (or one to ten) with ease and, when shown a mixed array of seven yellow and eight red chips, can count just the red chips and tell how many there are.

At six years, the two 'precursor' structures from the previous stage have become integrated into a single super-ordinate structure – *the central numerical structure (also called the mental number line structure)* – in which numbers, conceptualized as an ordered series of number words, are intimately linked to quantities and are used to determine which of two quantities is a little or a lot. At this age, therefore, children know that small numbers indicate a little, that big numbers indicate a lot, and that each counting word they say up in the sequence means that a set has been increased by one. With this structure, children realize that numbers themselves have magnitude (e.g. that 9 is bigger than 7) and that a question about addition and subtraction (e.g. If you have four and you get three more, how many will you have?) can be answered simply by counting forward or backward along the counting string.

At eight years, the single integrated structure from the previous stage is differentiated into two such structures, allowing children to use numbers to make quantity determinations along two quantitative variables (e.g. tens and ones in the number system; hours and minutes in the time system; dollars and cents in the money system). With this more complex structure (called a *double mental number line structure*), they are able, for example, to understand place value; to solve mentally double-digit addition problems (e.g. 12 + 54); and to tell which of two double-digit numbers (e.g. 69 or 71) is bigger or smaller.

At ten years, the two components of the differentiated structure from the previous stage are more fully integrated, allowing children to make compensations along one quantitative variable to allow for changes along the other. With this new structure (called an *integrated double mental number line structure*), they are able, for example, to perform mental computations with double-digit numbers that involve borrowing and carrying (e.g. 13 + 39); to translate from one time dimension (e.g. hours) to another (e.g. minutes) to determine which of two times (e.g. two hours or 90 minutes) is longer; and to solve Balance Beam problems in which number of weights and distance from the fulcrum both vary and some compensation between these variables is required to determine which side of the beam will go down.

The major tool that was developed to identify this progression – the Number Knowledge test – is presented here in its entirety for the age range under consideration (see Table 8.2). For researchers, it provides operational definitions of the knowledge structures that have been proposed for each substage in this sequence. For teachers, it provides a tool that can be used: (1) to assess students' current level of understanding in this domain, and (2) to identify central conceptual understandings that can and should be taught at the next level up. More detailed descriptions of the central numerical structure and of the research base that supports the present formulation can be found in Case and Griffin 1990; Griffin et al. 1994; Griffin and Case 1997; Griffin 2002.

Before turning to the next central conceptual structure to be described, it is worth speculating for a moment on what happens to the central numerical structure at the next stage transition (i.e. at the major shift that is presumed to occur around eleven years of age). Using the theoretical formulations described in this chapter, we can predict that two fully developed central numerical structures will be integrated, creating a super-ordinate structure that underlies children's ability to handle mathematical knowledge that requires this form of complexity. An obvious candidate for what this knowledge might look like can be found in the domain of rational numbers, fractions in particular, which, by their very nature, describe relationships that obtain between two quantities and/or two whole numbers. Work in this area has already begun and research efforts to identify these structures and to foster their development are described in Moss and Case 1999, and Moss 2003.

The central spatial structure

The cognitive sequence that has been identified in this domain can be presented most clearly by describing the manner in which children respond, at four age

Table 8.2. *Number knowledge test.*

Level 0 (4-year old level): go to Level 1 if 3 or more correct

1.   Can you count these chips and tell me how many there are? (Place 3 counting chips in front of child in a row)

2a.   (Show stacks of chips, 5 vs. 2, same colour). Which pile has more?

2b.   (Show stacks of chips, 3 vs. 7, same colour). Which pile has more?

3a.   This time I'm going to ask you which pile has less. (Show stacks of chips, 2 vs. 6, same colour). Which pile has less?

3b.   (Show stacks of chips, 8 vs. 3, same colour). Which pile has less?

4.   I'm going to show you some counting chips (Show a line of 3 red and 4 yellow chips in a row, as follows: R Y R Y R Y Y). Count just the yellow chips and tell me how many there are.

5.   Pick up all chips from the previous question. Then say: Here are some more counting chips (Show mixed array [not in a row] of 7 yellow and 8 red chips). Count just the red chips and tell me how many there are.

Level 1 (6-year-old level): go to Level 2 if 5 or more correct

1.   If you had 4 chocolates and someone gave you 3 more, how many chocolates would you have altogether?

2.   What number comes right after 7?

3.   What number comes two numbers after 7?

4a.   Which is bigger: 5 or 4?

4b.   Which is bigger: 7 or 9?

5a.   This time, I'm going to ask you about smaller numbers.
      Which is smaller: 8 or 6?

5b.   Which is smaller: 5 or 7?

6a.   Which number is closer to 5: 6 or 2? (Show visual array after asking question)

6b.   Which number is closer to 7: 4 or 9? (Show visual array after asking question)

7.   How much is 2 + 4? (OK to use fingers for counting)

8.   How much is 8 take away 6? (OK to use fingers for counting)

9a.   (Show visual array – 8 5 2 6 – and ask child to point to and name each numeral). When you are counting, which of these numbers do you say first?

9b.   When you are counting, which of these numbers do you say last?

Level 2 (8-year-old level): go to Level 3 if 5 or more correct

1.   What number comes 5 numbers after 49?

2.   What number comes 4 numbers before 60?

3a.   Which is bigger: 69 or 71?

3b.   Which is bigger: 32 or 28?

4a.   This time I'm going to ask you about smaller numbers.
      Which is smaller: 27 or 32?

4b.   Which is smaller: 51 or 39?

5a.   Which number is closer to 21: 25 or 18? (Show visual array after asking the question).

5b.   Which number is closer to 28: 31 or 24? (Show visual array after asking the question).

6.   How many numbers are there in between 2 and 6? (Accept either 3 or 4).

7.   How many numbers are there in between 7 and 9? (Accept either 1 or 2).

8.   (Show card 12 54) How much is 12 + 54?

9.   (Show card 47 21) How much is 47 take away 21?

Table 8.2. *(cont.)*

Level 3 (10-year-old level):

1. What number comes 10 numbers after 99?
2. What number comes 9 numbers after 999?
3a. Which difference is bigger: the difference between 9 and 6 or the difference between 8 and 3?
3b. Which difference is bigger: the difference between 6 and 2 or the difference between 8 and 5?
4a. Which difference is smaller: the difference between 99 and 92 or the difference between 25 and 11?
4b. Which difference is smaller: the difference between 48 and 36 or the difference between 84 and 73?
5. (Show card, '13, 39') How much is $13 + 39$?
6. (Show card, '36, 18') How much is $36 - 18$?
7. How much is 301 take away 7?

levels, to a task Dennis (1992) developed to assess spatial-artistic understanding across this age range. By presenting the same task (i.e. 'Draw a picture of a little boy or girl your age doing something they like outside in the grass') to all children between the ages of three and eleven years, Dennis (1992) was able to identify the following sequence. Note that the drawings that are reproduced here to illustrate age level performance are drawn from the present author's research with this task.

At four years, children typically produce a human figure that is recognizable as such, even if it is minimally articulated, and that appears to be floating on the page. Context elements (e.g. grass) that would ground the figure in space are noticeably absent or, if present, are not connected to the figure. The drawing shown in the upper left quadrant of Figure 8.2 is typical for this age level and it provides evidence that four-year-olds are able to conceptualize and represent the interrelationships among the parts of a human figure (knowledge that has been identified as a precursor structure for the central spatial structure). Although children at this age can also represent context elements such as a ground line, a sky line, a tree or a sun with reasonable accuracy (knowledge that is hypothesized to provide a second precursor structure for the central spatial structure) they rarely do so on this task, in spite of the explicit task instructions.

At six years, children typically produce a human figure that is located in a foreground setting, either by its location on the bottom of the page to suggest a ground line or with a richer elaboration of the setting (e.g. a grass line, a sky line, a sun). As illustrated in the drawing in the upper right quadrant of Figure 8.2, at this age the human figure and the context elements are not only

Figure 8.2. Children's drawings: a typical 4-year-old (upper left), 6-year-old (upper right), and 8-year-old (bottom left) product and an atypical 4-year-old (bottom right) response.

represented, they are also sufficiently coordinated on the page to root the figure in space and to provide an impression of a flat, unidimensional 'scene'. The higher-order knowledge structure that is presumed to underlie this level of competence, enabling children to integrate two sets of elements on the page (i.e. to keep one set of elements in mind while producing the second so both are well connected) has been labelled the *central spatial structure*.

At eight years, children typically produce one or more human figures that are located in a setting in which two spatial axes (i.e. foreground and background elements) are differentiated but not yet inter-linked. As illustrated in the drawing in the bottom left quadrant of Figure 8.2, indications of depth are present in the use of occlusion (e.g. overlapping clouds), side perspective of objects (e.g. the figure), and background elements (e.g. the bouquet of flowers the figure is holding) that are clearly behind foreground elements. A bidimensional central spatial structure is seen to underlie this level of competence, prompting children spontaneously to differentiate foreground and background elements in their response to the task directions.

At ten years, children typically produce one or more human figures located in a setting in which foreground, middle ground and background are differentiated and interconnected by a continuous ground space. A fully developed 'scene with depth' is apparent. The more complex conceptual structure that is hypothesized to underlie this level of competence is referred to, in the theory, as the elaborated-bidimensional central spatial structure.

Although the cognitive sequence that has just been described is robust (see Dennis 1992; Case et al. 1992) and is nicely illustrated in children's drawings, there are, of course, exceptions to this pattern. By examining these exceptions, we can obtain insight into the cognitive factors that underlie this progression. One such exception is illustrated in the bottom right quadrant of Figure 8.2. In this drawing, which can perhaps be captioned, 'A 4-year-old trying to be a 6-year-old', the 4-year-old artist attempted to ground the figure in a grass line (atypical for this age-level) and, in the process, was unable to produce an integrated human figure (also atypical for this age level). When asked what the forms outside the figure's head were, she replied, 'These are her cheeks and these are her ears.'

Because I had evidence that this child was perfectly capable of drawing an integrated human figure under other circumstances and because I knew she had more exposure to the domain of art than most children her age (because her mother was an artist), the interpretation that seems to provide the best fit for the present drawing is the following. Unlike most four-year-olds, this child knew that an appropriate response to the task required that some ground element (e.g. grass) be included in her drawing and that this element should be coordinated with the figure. However, her four-year-old working-memory capacity was insufficient to allow her to render both elements in a coordinated fashion. In her attempt to do so, one element (the figure) literally fell apart. Support for this interpretation is available to all who have experienced occasions when our competence has been reduced by excessive task demands and/or excessive loading of our working-memory capacity. If this interpretation is reasonable, then this drawing can serve as a graphic illustration of this process and, in so doing, illustrate the mechanism (i.e. growth in working-memory capacity) that was proposed, in the previous section, to explain system-wide constraints on the rate of cognitive change.

What happens to the central spatial structure change as children progress across the next major stage transition? Using postulates of the theory, we can predict that two fully developed central spatial structures will be integrated, producing a new higher-order structure and ushering in a level of competence that was not possible before. In this domain, one such competence may be the ability to draw a picture in which two distinct scenes are integrated. To create a measure for this level of functioning and to see whether it really was beyond the capability of most six to ten-year-olds, Dennis (1992) devised a second art task which required children to 'draw a picture of a mother looking out the window of her house to see where her son is playing. She only sees her son's face because he is peeking out from behind a tree.' In her findings, Dennis found that no six-year-olds, few eight-year-olds (7 per cent), and a small proportion of ten-year-olds (20 per cent) were able to achieve a minimum level of success on this task. By contrast, when the present author used this task with older children in several informal studies, the available evidence suggests that: (1) the majority of twelve-year-olds are able to depict two scenes in a loosely coordinated fashion, and (2) the ability to integrate crucial aspects of these scenes (i.e. the alignment between house and yard; the alignment between the mother's gaze and the son's face) increases systematically over the teenage years, in the manner predicted by the theory.

The central narrative structure

The cognitive sequence that has been identified in this domain can be presented most clearly by describing the manner in which children respond, at four age levels, to a task McKeough (1992) developed to assess narrative understanding across the middle childhood years. By presenting the same task (i.e. 'Tell me a story about a little boy or girl your age who has a problem and what they did to fix it') to all children between the ages of three and eleven years, McKeough (1992) was able to identify the following sequence. The examples provided are drawn from the present author's research with this task.

At four years, children typically describe a single event sequence, either a problem that isn't resolved (e.g. 'Tommy pushed me and I was crying') or, much less frequently, a resolution without a problem (e.g. 'Put a band-aid on it'). Although children at this age level can sometimes produce the other half of the story if their performance is scaffolded with explicit prompts, they rarely do so on their own. An event sequence schema (also called a script schema) is seen to underlie performance at this level and to provide one precursor structure for the central narrative structure.

At six years, children typically describe two coordinated event sequences – a problem and a resolution – in a bare-bones fashion (e.g. 'My bike broke and I told my Dad and he fixed it'). Although these stories are sometimes shorter than the ones produced at the previous level, their structure is much more sophisticated. By producing a story in which a problem is set up in the first episode and is resolved in the second, children create a narrative that has a 'plot', even if the plot is minimally articulated. In so doing, they demonstrate an understanding of the central feature of all stories in Western cultures. The cognitive structure that is hypothesized to underlie this level of performance is called the *central narrative structure*.

At eight years, children's stories typically include a problem, a sub-problem that creates a dramatic climax (either a failed attempt at a solution or an impediment to a solution), and a resolution that solves one of the problems presented in the story. A plot structure with some sort of dramatic climax is present, as illustrated in the following example: 'My bike broke and I asked my Dad to fix it but he was too busy. So I asked my Mom and she said she didn't know how. So I thought maybe I could fix it myself but I couldn't find what I needed. I was rummaging around in the basement looking for it and my Dad came down and said "O.K. I can fix it now." And he did.' Because stories at this level include a plot (e.g. bike is broken – bike gets fixed) and a subplot (e.g. failed attempts to solve the problem), they are more complex than stories produced at the previous level. A bidimensional central narrative structure is hypothesized to underlie them.

At ten years, children's stories typically include a problem, a subproblem, and a resolution that ties together all the elements of the story so it has a 'well-developed' or 'carefully planned' feeling as a consequence. The plot structure has dramatic tension and a well-developed resolution. An elaborated-bidimensional central narrative structure is proposed to account for performance at this level.

Again, we can ask: What happens to this conceptual structure when children progress into the next developmental stage? Using postulates of the theory, we can make the same predictions we made earlier for the central numerical structure and the central spatial structure and suggest that the capacity to integrate two fully developed central narrative structures into a higher-order structure will usher in a new level of narrative competence that is qualitatively distinct from the competence demonstrated in the previous stage. To test this hypothesis, Salter (1992) developed a second story task that asked subjects to tell a family story and to describe the meaning this story has for their present life. In essence, this task requires subjects to produce and to coordinate two well-developed stories – a story from the past and a story from the present – and research conducted with this task supports the progression predicted in the theory. The findings suggest that: (1) success on this task is not achieved by the majority of children until the age of twelve years, and (2) the connections that are constructed and/or derived between the past and the present increase

Table 8.3. *Progression in children's conceptual structures between 4 and 10 years of age.*

Age	Domain of number	Domain of space	Domain of narrative
4	A. Counting B. Global quantity	A. Object location B. Object shape	A. Event sequence B. Inner state
6	Mental number line (Number magnitude)	Mental reference line (Scene)	Mental story line (Plot)
8	Two number lines differentiated (tens and ones)	Two spatial reference axes differentiated (scene with depth)	Two story lines differentiated (plot and subplot)
10	Two number lines well integrated (tradeoffs between tens and ones)	Two spatial reference axes well integrated (scene with continuous depth: 3-dimensional)	Two story lines well integrated (plot, subplot, and integrated conclusion)

Level 0 (4-year-old): Two sets of relations, one linear (A) and one less so (B), can be conceptualized and assigned appropriate symbols.
Level 1 (6-year-old): Merging of two schemas into super-ordinate unit, often with a 'line-like' character.
Level 2 (8-year-old): Two super-ordinate (often 'line-like') structures differentiated and tentatively related.
Level 3 (10-year-old): Two super-ordinate (often 'line-like') structures differentiated and well integrated, giving child a good understanding of: the whole number system in the domain of numbers, a well-developed scene in the domain of art, and a well-developed story in the narrative domain.

systematically in complexity as children progress through the adolescent years.

A summary of the cognitive sequences that have just been described for three domains of mental functioning is provided in Table 8.3. By highlighting the manner in which children's conceptual structures are hypothesized to change across 4 age levels and across 3 domains of mental functioning, the table also illustrates four major postulates of the theory. These can be summarized as follows: (1) the form of children's conceptual structures remains constant across domains, unless modulated by extenuating circumstances (described further below); (2) the content of children's thought differs across domains; (3) a major change in children's thought occurs across the 4- to 6-year-old transition when two schemas that were previously independent are merged into a single, super-ordinate structure; (4) less major changes in children's thought occur across the 6- to 8-year-old and the 8- to 10-year-old transitions when the super-ordinate structure that was created in the previous sub-stage is progressively differentiated and elaborated.

On the basis of the information presented in Table 8.3, we can predict that children's performance will be reasonably consistent across content domains. More specifically, we can predict that children will perform at the same level on the number task, the art task and the story task unless there are reasons to explain why performance in one of these domains might be elevated or depressed (e.g. because of a special talent or disability; because of above-average or below-average exposure to experiences in that domain). A third factor that might affect consistency across domains is interest/disinterest in the content of a particular domain, which might be shaped by temperament factors or previous (affective) experience, and which might influence the subject's response to the task and the level of effort put into its completion.

In research conducted by Case et al. (1992) to test this hypothesis, the general pattern that emerged was one of consistency across domains, with the majority of children (e.g. 69 per cent) performing at the same level (or within $\frac{1}{2}$ substage) on tasks drawn from three separate domains, and with the minority of children (e.g. 29 per cent) showing a difference of $\frac{1}{2}$ to 1 substage across these tasks. On the basis of this evidence, as well as factor analysis studies conducted by Case and Okamoto (1996), we can conclude that the theoretical postulates described in this section have received a reasonable level of support.

How does change occur?

In central conceptual structure theory, the mechanisms that are seen to underlie the emergence of new conceptual structures from previous ones are identical to the mechanisms Piaget proposed to account for cognitive change; namely: equilibration, differentiation and hierarchic integration. The role these mechanisms play in the present theory has been amply illustrated in the foregoing discussion and needs no further elaboration here. To explain the common form that children's thought is believed to assume across content domains – a component of Piaget's theory that was never adequately addressed – central conceptual structure theory has proposed an additional mechanism that is largely, but not wholly, biologically based; namely: growth in working-memory capacity. As described in a previous section, this mechanism is believed to exert system-wide constraints on children's mental functioning and to influence the rate of cognitive change.

Why does change occur?

The factors that are seen to activate change in central conceptual structure theory are, once again, similar to the factors Piaget proposed; namely: maturation, exploration, social interaction and disequilibrium. However, the new constructs that have been proposed in central conceptual structure theory (e.g. growth in working-memory capacity; domain-specific central conceptual structures) make it possible to specify each of these factors more precisely. For example, the new constructs suggest that cognitive change is activated, not only by general biological growth, but also by growth in a specific component of our neurological apparatus (i.e. working-memory). To provide a second example, the new constructs suggest that cognitive change is activated, not only by general experience and exploration, but also, and possibly primarily, by particular sets of domain-specific experiences (e.g. ones that will enable children to acquire the knowledge specified in the conceptual structures). To provide a third and final example, the new constructs suggest that cognitive change is activated, not only by general social interaction, but also, and perhaps primarily, by specific sorts of social interaction (e.g. ones that will enable children to master the forms of discourse used in particular content domains to describe the experiences the domain presents).

Educational implications

The advantages the new constructs have for educational practice are apparent in the foregoing discussion. They suggest a range of particular experiences that may be more useful in promoting cognitive growth than the general sorts of experience Piaget proposed. Four additional implications for education can be derived from the domain-specific cognitive sequences that have been proposed and articulated in central conceptual structure theory. First, these sequences define knowledge structures that are believed to be central to competent performance in particular domains. For this reason, this knowledge can and should be taught, especially to children who may not have opportunities to acquire it on their own. Second, these sequences identify the manner in which this knowledge is typically constructed by children and the forms it typically assumes at various age/grade levels. In so doing, they provide a framework teachers can use to assess students' current level of understanding in particular domains and to identify the knowledge that should be taught at the next level up. Third, measures to assess this knowledge in three content domains have already been developed. They are available to teachers and they are relatively easy to use.

Fourth and finally, the cognitive sequences that have already been identified provide examples that can be used to implement the first three steps of a more general model for instructional design that is implicit in the broader theory (see Table 8.4) and that represents an advance over an earlier model that was proposed by Case and Bereiter (1982), using postulates of neo-Piagetian theory. Note that these steps are exceedingly difficult if not impossible to accomplish using Piaget's theory as a heuristic. The more specific formulations that are

Table 8.4. *Cognitive developmental model for instructional design.*

1. Identify the knowledge that is central to competent performance within a domain of experience.
2. Identify the manner in which this knowledge is constructed and the (precursor) forms of understanding students typically demonstrate at earlier age-levels.
3. Develop a measure for assessing students' beginning knowledge as well as their progression through this pathway.
4. Create a set of activities that recapitulates the natural developmental progression, and that enables students to build on their current knowledge and to gradually construct the knowledge specified in the objective.
5. Use learning and design principles from cognitive science to ensure that the activities are maximally effective in achieving this goal.

provided in central conceptual structure theory, coupled with the examples that have already been provided in three content domains, make this a manageable task. The fourth and fifth steps in the model have been implemented in all the instructional applications that have been developed to date and these steps are described further in the following section.

Educational applications

Although the developmental model for instructional design that is presented in Table 8.4 was not formulated explicitly until 1997 (see Griffin and Case 1997), this model was implicit in the broader theory and was used by several investigators to develop instructional programs to teach central conceptual structures in different content domains. The programs this author is familiar with are listed below and are described as a group in the remainder of this section.

In the domain of mathematics, a program to teach the six-year-old central numerical structure was developed by Griffin and Case in 1988. This program (originally called *Rightstart* and described in Griffin et al. 1994) was modified, expanded and renamed in 1995; the new program *Number Worlds* (Griffin and Case 1996) is described in several recent publications (see Griffin and Case 1997; Griffin 2002; Griffin 2003b). Programs to teach the eight-year-old central numerical structure and the four-year-old precursor structures were subsequently developed (see Griffin 1997; 1998; 2000). To teach higher-order central numerical structures, Moss and Case (1999) developed a program to teach rational number knowledge (also described in Moss 2003) and Kalchman (2001) developed a program to teach knowledge of functions.

In the domain of social-linguistic understanding, a program to teach the six-year-old central narrative structure was developed by McKeough (described in Case and McKeough 1990). Although no formal programs have been developed to teach the central spatial structures that were described earlier in this chapter, instructional units to teach each level in this progression (i.e. the four-year-old structure, the six-year-old structure and the eight-year-old structure) have been created and tested by students of the present author as part of their course assignments. To provide a flavour of these programs, the features that distinguish this set of programs from other educational programs are described in the following section.

Distinctive features

It is difficult to provide a summary overview of the range of programs that have just been listed, which span three content domains and several developmental levels within each domain. This can perhaps best be achieved by describing a core set of features that this group of programs shares and that distinguishes them from other programs that have been developed to teach the same general content (e.g. commercial curriculums). It should be noted here that each program has several distinctive features and these features don't always overlap across programs. Thus, in the present effort to abstract commonalities across programs, features that are important to particular programs may be lost. Five distinctive features are summarized below.

Detailed specification of objectives

The first step in the development of any program is a careful analysis and a detailed specification of the full network of knowledge (including all concepts, subconcepts, and skills) implied in the central conceptual structure to be taught. The knowledge network that is articulated in this process is often modelled in the form of a network of nodes and relations (see Griffin and Case 1997, for an example) so that the concepts to be taught, and the ways these are connected, can be precisely specified and used to guide instructional planning. The research base is usually consulted for this purpose and additional research is often conducted (usually in the form of interviews) to see whether the knowledge network that has been created captures all salient aspects of children's thought for that particular age level.

Developmental sequencing

Using the cognitive sequences that have been identified in the theory, a sequence of knowledge objectives that provides a good fit for children's spontaneous development is specified. The sequence is usually refined and elaborated on the basis of two additional sets of findings that are generated: (1) in the research conducted to complete step 1 (above) and (2) in the assessments conducted to identify children's entering knowledge. Activities to teach each step in the resulting sequence are created, providing a seamless set of activities that 'recapitulates the natural developmental progression' and that allows children to enter the program at their current level of functioning, and to progress through the sequence at a rate that is comfortable for them.

Use of current knowledge

In the programs that have been developed, children's current knowledge is not only used as a base to build *on*, it is also used as base to build *with*, as a knowledge structure that can be actively employed to help children construct new knowledge. This is illustrated in two sets of activities developed for the *Number Worlds* kindergarten program (designed to teach the six-year-old central numerical structure). First, because it is known that four and five-year-old children prefer base-five representations (e.g. the fingers on one hand) to base-ten representations in their effort to solve number problems, all the dot-set cards developed for this level of the program to teach number concepts, such as cardinality, display quantities in a base-five format (e.g. 7 is depicted as 5 dots arranged in a dice display on the top half of the card, with 2 additional dots displayed on the bottom half of the card). This allows children to use a form of representation that is natural for them to make sense of quantities larger than five. Second, because four-year-olds are known to love rhyming songs and stories and to remember information presented in this format, two characters called 'Plus Pup' and 'Minus Mouse' were created for the program to introduce children to addition and subtraction operations.

Conceptual bridging

Although this feature is closely related to the previous one, it goes beyond it by employing devices that will help children bridge concepts that are presently unrelated in their minds, and ultimately integrate these concepts into a higher-order structure. The Plus Pup and Minus Mouse characters that were mentioned above also serve this function. Because each character displays a symbol on its chest that corresponds to its name (e.g. +1), these characters provide a meaningful link between the world of real quantities and the world of formal symbols when they are used in activities where real quantities are incremented or decremented and children are required to predict the results. When children are required to work with formal symbols at the next grade level, Plus Pup and Minus Mouse will imbue these symbols with meaning. These activities are described more fully in Griffin (2003a).

Environmental supports

A range of sophisticated learning tools and environmental supports are always provided in these programs. To illustrate this range, each program includes: (a) opportunities to solve problems the domain presents, to interact with others (e.g. a more knowledgeable expert as well as peers), to explain their reasoning, and to communicate with peers; (b) exposure to the various ways that the knowledge to be constructed is represented and talked about in our culture; and (c) the provision of specific representational devices (e.g. board games in the math programs; cartoon strips in the narrative program) that allow children to enter worlds where the concepts to be acquired are physically represented, and which provide multiple opportunities for children to encounter and/or to work with these concepts as they move through these worlds (see Case and McKeough 1990; Griffin 2003b, for more detailed descriptions of these features).

As these brief summaries illustrate, the programs that have been informed by central conceptual structure theory have a much clearer and better-developed set of knowledge objectives than most other programs this author is familiar with. They are also, not surprisingly, much more finely attuned to children's natural developmental progression. To a greater extent than other programs, they use children's current knowledge, not only as a base to build on, but as a resource to build with, and they employ a variety of devices (e.g. conceptual bridging; representational devices that embody the concepts to be taught) to scaffold cognitive growth. The questions that naturally arise are: do these programs work? What are their effects? This is the subject of the final section in this chapter.

Program effects

The programs that have just been described have all been tested with children who had not yet acquired the central conceptual knowledge they were designed to teach, either because they were too young (i.e. they were 1–2 years below the age at which this knowledge is typically acquired) or because their general experience had not provided opportunities for them to acquire it (e.g. at-risk children living in poverty). In all cases, these programs were effective in enabling the majority of children who were exposed to them to acquire this knowledge in a relatively short period of time (see Griffin and Case 1997, for effects of the Number Worlds program; Moss and Case 1999, for effects of the rational number program; Case and McKeough 1990, for effects of the narrative program).

To provide but one example from the variety of research designs that were used across these studies to measure direct effects, I draw from the Number Worlds evaluation studies. In a series of studies conducted with children from low-income communities (and known to be at-risk for school failure), children who received the Number Worlds kindergarten program made significant gains in conceptual knowledge of number (assessed with the Number Knowledge test) and in number sense, when compared to matched-control groups who received readiness training of a different sort. These gains enabled them to start their formal schooling in grade one on an equal footing with their more advantaged peers (Griffin et al. 1994; Griffin et al. 1995; Griffin and Case 1996).

Although the effects mentioned above are impressive when compared to the intervention effects that have been documented in the instruction literature over the past century, the crucial question for the theory is: Is the knowledge that is acquired *central* to children's performance on a broad range of quantitative tasks? This question can be answered in at least two ways: (1) by considering the transfer effects and (2) by assessing children's subsequent learning in the domain. Both questions were examined in the series of studies, just mentioned, that were conducted to test the Number Worlds kindergarten program. To address the first question, a battery of developmental transfer tests (e.g. a science task, a time knowledge test, a money knowledge test) for which no training had been provided was administered to all children in the samples, before and after training. On the post-test administration, children who received the Number Worlds program consistently outperformed those in the control groups (Griffin et al. 1994; Griffin et al. 1995). To address the second question, children who received the Number Worlds program in their kindergarten year (and who graduated into a variety of more traditional first grade classrooms) were followed up one year later and evaluated on an assortment of mathematical tests (e.g. an oral arithmetic test, a written arithmetic test, a word problems test), using a double-blind procedure. Once again, those who had received the Number Worlds program in kindergarten were found to be superior to the control groups on virtually all measures, including teacher evaluations of 'general number sense' (Griffin et al. 1994; Griffin and Case 1996).

The expansion of the Number Worlds program to include curricula for grades one and two permitted a third form of evaluation: a longitudinal study in which children were tracked over a three-year period. At the beginning of the study and at the end of each year, children who received the Number Worlds program were compared with two other groups: (1) a second low-SES group who were originally tested as having superior achievement in mathematics, and (2) a mixed (largely middle-class) SES group who also showed a higher level of performance at the outset and who attended an acclaimed magnet school with a special mathematics coordinator and an enriched mathematics program. Over the course of this study, which extended from the beginning of kindergarten to the end of grade two, children who received the Number Worlds program gradually outstripped both other groups on the major measure used throughout this study (i.e. the Number Knowledge Test). On this measure, as well as on a variety of other mathematics tests (e.g. measures of number sense), the Number Worlds group outperformed the second low-SES group from the end of kindergarten onwards (Griffin and Case 1997).

Table 8.5. *Performance of number worlds group and two comparison groups on selected items from three transfer tests at the end of grade two (percentage passing).*

Test items	Number worlds Group (n = 28)	Low-SES Group (n = 21)	Mixed-SES Group (n = 31)
Time test			
Which is longer: 1 hr and 50 minutes or 2 hrs and 1 minute?	93	48	83
If I wait 30 min. and another 30 min., how long altogether (in hrs)?	93	43	70
It's 3 o'clock now. What time will it be in 2 hours?	85	33	68
Money test			
Show a dime plus 6 cents: how much do I have altogether?	96	52	67
Which is closer to 19 cents: a quarter or a dime?	93	43	63
This candy costs 7 cents. If I give 10 cents, how much do I get back?	85	38	60
Formal notation test			
23 + 36 (displayed in vertical format)	86	48	81
87 − 54 (displayed in vertical format)	86	24	58
$3 \times 5 =$	71	0	35

On tests of procedural knowledge (i.e. the Computation Test; see Stigler, Lee and Stevenson 1990) administered at the end of grade one, they also compared very favourably with groups from China and Japan that were tested on the same measures (Griffin and Case 1997). Finally, on a battery of transfer tests administered at the end of grade two (i.e. a time knowledge test, a money knowledge test, a formal notation test) the Number Worlds group outperformed the second low-SES group on all measures. As illustrated in Table 8.5, they also compared favourably to the mixed (largely middle class) SES group on all measures and, on two of these tests (i.e. the Money Test and the Formal Notation test), the Number Worlds group outperformed the mixed SES group as well.

Considered in conjunction, these findings provide strong evidence that the knowledge that was acquired is, indeed, central to children's performance.

More specifically, they suggest that the central conceptual knowledge that was specified in the theory and that was taught in the Number Worlds program has the properties suggested by the theory: (a) it underpins children's performance on a range of tasks in that domain and (b) it scaffolds higher-level functioning in that domain.

In addition to providing support for the theory that spawned these educational applications, the applied research has also contributed to the development of the theory. Once again, a single example is offered to illustrate this point. Consider Step 5 in the model for instructional design that is outlined in Table 8.4. Because this step (i.e. Use learning and design principles from cognitive science to ensure that the activities are maximally effective) was not well specified in the theory, a range of principles from cognitive science was used by the designers of each educational application to create learning tasks and learning environments that each investigator believed would be maximally effective. In the program evaluations that were conducted, two design principles proved to be crucial for this purpose and they were not ones that were salient in the theory. These were: (1) Provide ample opportunity for children to communicate, using the language of the domain and (2) Employ representational devices that are common in the culture and that embody major concepts in the domain. Both of these factors are highly salient in social-cultural explanations of cognitive change and this finding prompted us to add these factors to our design principles and to describe central conceptual structural theory within this broader context; for example, by including these factors among the experiences proposed to activate cognitive change (see Case et al. 2001).

Conclusion

It was suggested earlier that a major motivation for the development of central conceptual structure theory was a desire to preserve the strengths of Piaget's theory and to overcome its weaknesses. The extent to which this has been accomplished to date can be reviewed by considering the aspects of Piaget's theory that have been retained in the new theory, the new elements that have been added (i.e. to address limitations in Piaget's theory), and the advantage these combined theoretical formulations might have for education.

In the answers that have been provided in this chapter for the three guiding questions, it is apparent that much of Piaget's theory has been preserved in central conceptual structure theory. So much has been preserved, in fact, that the set of constructivist principles that were proposed earlier in this chapter to summarize Piaget's theory (e.g. the notions that knowledge is constructed by the individual through exploration and active participation; that development proceeds in an invariant sequence by a process of differentiation and hierarchic integration; that individuals use their current form of thought to make sense of the world) apply equally well to central conceptual structure theory. While these principles and the instructional implications that were derived from them (described earlier in this chapter) were seen to be strengths of Piaget's theory, in that they highlighted important principles of instructional design and pointed teachers in the right direction, the theory was also seen to have limited value in helping teachers put these principles into practice in particular school-based content domains.

The new element that was added in central conceptual structure theory – the articulation of domain-specific cognitive progressions that describe the content, as well as the form, of children's thought and the manner in which this content changes across the school-age years – provides much more specific guidance for teachers. It enables them to identify knowledge networks that underlie competent performance in particular content domains and that should be taught. It also enables them to determine the forms of this knowledge (i.e. the developmental milestones) that most children in their classrooms can be expected to have and the forms of this knowledge that are typically constructed at the next level up. Using this knowledge, they can establish learning objectives for their students that are finely attuned to children's developmental capacities. Finally, in the work that was conducted to articulate the new theoretical postulates, to integrate them with postulates retained from Piaget's theory and to test the validity of the new formulations, central conceptual structure theory has given educators three sets of tools that have already proven useful in enhancing learning and fostering cognitive change. These are: (1) tests to assess central conceptual understandings in three domains; (2) programs to teach these understandings in three domains and at several levels; and (3) a developmental model for instructional design that educators can use to create 'developmentally appropriate' learning sequences in domains that have not yet been charted. Considered in conjunction, these products suggest that central conceptual structure theory has considerable heuristic power.

In a series of articles produced shortly before his premature death in May 2000, Case (1996) and Case et al. (2001) marshalled evidence to suggest that central conceptual structure theory is 'progressive' (in terms of Lakatos's 1974 demarcation criteria) in two respects: (1) it provides a framework for integrating several dominant intellectual traditions, and (2) it provides a framework for integrating much current cognitive developmental research, conducted within different theoretical paradigms. In this chapter, I have attempted to show that central conceptual structure theory is progressive, as well, in a third, more applied, arena. It provides a framework that is capable of shaping educational practice much more precisely than was possible within Piaget's framework, of fostering learning toward desired end-points and of scaffolding both subject-matter mastery and developmental competence in the process.

REFERENCES

Adey, P. (this volume). Accelerating the development of general cognitive processing.

Bransford, J., Brown, A. and Cocking, R. (1999). *How people learn*. Washington, DC: National Academy Press.

Case, R. (1992). *The mind's staircase: exploring the conceptual underpinnings of children's thought and knowledge*. Hillsdale, NJ: Erlbaum.

(1996). Re-conceptualizing the nature of children's conceptual structures and their development in middle childhood. *Monographs of the Society for Research in Child Development, 61*, serial no. 246, 1–24.

Case, R. and Bereiter, C. (1982). From behaviourism to cognitive behaviourism to cognitive developmental theory: steps in the evolution of instructional design. Paper presented at the Conference for Educational Technology in the 1980s, Caracas, Venezuela, June 1982.

Case, R. and Griffin, S. (1990). Child cognitive development: the role of central conceptual structures in the development of scientific and social thought. In E. A. Hauert (ed.) *Developmental psychology: cognitive, perceptuo-motor, and neurological perspectives* (pp. 193–230). North-Holland: Elsevier.

Case, R. and McKeough, A. (1990). Schooling and the development of central conceptual structures: an example from the domain of children's narrative. *International Journal of Educational Psychology, 8*, 835–55.

Case, R. and Okamoto, Y. (1996). The role of central conceptual structures in the development of children's thought. *Monographs of the Society for Research in Child Development, 61*, serial no. 246.

Case, R., Griffin, S., McKeough, A. and Okamoto, Y. (1992). Parallels in the development of children's social, numerical, and spatial thought. In R. Case (ed.) *The mind's staircase: exploring the conceptual underpinnings of children's thought and knowledge* (pp. 69–284). Hillsdale, NJ: Erlbaum.

Case, R., Griffin, S. and Kelley, W. (2001). Socioeconomic differences in children's early cognitive development and their readiness for schooling. In S. Golbeck (ed.) *Psychological perspectives on early childhood education: reframing dilemmas in research and practice* (pp. 37–63). Mahwah, NJ: Erlbaum.

Dennis, S. (1992). Stage and structure in the development of children's spatial representations. In R. Case (ed.) *The mind's staircase: exploring the conceptual underpinnings of children's thought and knowledge* (pp. 229–45). Hillsdale, NJ: Erlbaum.

Fischer, K. (1980). A theory of cognitive development: the control and construction of hierarchies of skills. *Psychological Review, 87*, 477–531.

(this volume). Building general knowledge and skill.

Griffin, S. (1997). *Number worlds: grade one level*. Durham, NH: Number Worlds Alliance Inc.

(1998). *Number worlds: grade two level*. Durham, NH: Number Worlds Alliance Inc.

(2000). *Number worlds: preschool level*. Durham, NH: Number Worlds Alliance Inc.

(2002). The development of math competence in the preschool and early school years: cognitive foundations and instructional strategies. In J. M. Royer (ed.) *Mathematical cognition: current perspectives on cognition, learning, and instruction* (pp. 1–32). Greenwich, CT: Information Age Publishing.

(2003a). Laying the foundation for computational fluency in early childhood. *Teaching Children Mathematics, 6*, 306–9.

(2003b). Number Worlds: A research-based program for young children. In D. H. Clements, J. Sarama and A. M. DiBiase (eds.) *Engaging young children in mathematics: standards for early childhood mathematics education* (pp. 325–42). Hillsdale, NJ: Lawrence Erlbaum Associates, Inc.

Griffin, S. and Case, R. (1995). *Number worlds: kindergarten level.* Durham, NH: Number Worlds Alliance Inc.

(1996). Evaluating the breadth and depth of training effects when central conceptual structures are taught. *Society for Research in Child Development Monographs, 59*, 90–113.

(1997). Re-thinking the primary school math curriculum: an approach based on cognitive science. *Issues in Education, 3*, no. 1, 1–49.

Griffin, S., Case, R. and Sandieson, R. (1992). Synchrony and asynchrony in the acquisition of children's everyday mathematical knowledge. In R. Case (ed.) *The mind's staircase: exploring the conceptual underpinnings of children's thought and knowledge* (pp. 75–97). Hillsdale, NJ: Erlbaum.

Griffin, S., Case, R. and Siegler, R. (1994). Rightstart: providing the central conceptual prerequisites for first formal learning of arithmetic to students at-risk for school failure. In K. McGilly (ed.) *Classroom lessons: integrating cognitive theory and classroom practice* (pp. 24–49). Cambridge, MA: Bradford Books MIT Press.

Griffin, S., Case, R. and Capodilupo, A. (1995). Teaching for understanding: the importance of central conceptual structures in the elementary mathematics curriculum. In A. McKeough, I. Lupert and A. Marini (eds.) *Teaching for transfer: fostering generalization in learning* (pp. 121–51). Hillsdale, NJ: Erlbaum.

Hiebert, J. (1997). *Making sense: teaching and learning mathematics with understanding.* Portsmouth, NH: Heinemann Press.

Kalchman, M. (2001). Using a neo-Piagetian framework for learning and teaching mathematical functions. Unpublished doctoral dissertation, University of Toronto.

Lakatos, I. (1974). The role of crucial experiments in science. *Studies in History and Philosophy of Science, 4*, 309–25.

McKeough, A. (1992). Testing for the presence of a central social structure: use of the transfer paradigm. In R. Case (ed.) *The mind's staircase: exploring the conceptual underpinnings of children's thought and knowledge* (pp. 207–25). Hillsdale, NJ: Erlbaum.

Minstrell, J. (1989). Teaching science for understanding. In L. B. Resnick and L. E. Klopfer (eds.) *Towards the thinking curriculum: current cognitive research* (pp. 129–49). Alexandria, VA: Association for Supervision and Curriculum Development.

Moss, J. (2003). Introducing percents in linear measurement to foster an understanding of rational-number operations. *Teaching Children Mathematics, 9*, no. 6, 335–9.

Moss, J. and Case, R. (1999). Developing children's understanding of the rational numbers: a new model and an experimental curriculum. *Journal for Research in Mathematics Education, 30*, 122–47.

Pascual-Leone, J. (1969). Cognitive development and style: a general theoretical integration. Unpublished doctoral dissertation. University of Geneva.

(1970). A mathematical model for the transition rule in Piaget's developmental stages. *Acta Psychologica, 32*, 301–45.

Pascual-Leone, J. and Goodman, D. (1979). Intelligence and experience: a neo-Piagetian approach. *Instructional Science, 8*, 301–67.

Phillips, D. and Soltis, J. (1998). *Perspectives on learning.* New York: Teacher's College Press.

Salter, D. (1992). A cognitive developmental analysis of the interpretation of family stories by adolescents and pre-adolescents. Master's Thesis, Department of Educational Psychology, University of Calgary, Calgary, Alberta.

Siegler, R. (1976). Three aspects of cognitive development. *Cognitive Psychology, 8*, 481–520.

Siegler, R. S. and Robinson, M. (1982). The development of numerical understanding. In H. W. Reese and L. P. Lipsitt (eds.) *Advances in child development and behavior* (pp. 241–312). New York: Academic Press.

Stigler, J. W., Lee, S. Y. and Stevenson, H. W. (1990). *Mathematical knowledge of Japanese, Chinese, and American elementary school children.* Reston, VA: National Council of Teachers of Mathematics.

Wadsworth, B. (1996). *Piaget's theory of cognitive and affective development.* New York: Longman.

9   Accelerating the development of general cognitive processing

Philip Adey

The problem space

I should preface this chapter by making the context of our work clear. Our main aim over twenty years of working on 'cognitive acceleration' has been an educational one, to improve the life chances of large numbers of students in the education system by increasing their ability to think effectively and so increase their general problem-solving ability and their academic achievement. To be sure, in order to achieve this aim we have had to consider in some detail theoretical models of cognition and of cognitive development, and it may be that the empirical results we have obtained will throw some light on these theoretical models, but the development of theory has not been our primary purpose. It follows that this chapter will be somewhat pragmatic and will take an eclectic view of models of cognition, drawing ideas from a number of sources as they appear to offer fruitful avenues towards our goal of devising educational methods for the acceleration of cognitive development.

Furthermore, I should clarify the particular aspects of 'cognition' and of 'acceleration' which will be addressed. Cognition will be used here quite specifically to refer to *general* processing capability, that is, a function of the mind which can be applied across all contexts. While it would be difficult to deny the predictive validity of multilevel models of the mind which include context-specific abilities and domain-specific talents as well as a general processing mechanism, it is the last of these which is the particular concern of our cognitive acceleration programmes. As for 'acceleration', the focus will be on individual characteristics of cognitive acceleration. Although there are normative aspects related to the extent to which an individual shows development in advance of his peers, at the individual level what we are concerned with is the way in which a child's cognition develops throughout the school years under the influence of standard educational practices, and then with an increase in this rate of development in each individual. There is, of course, a wide range of rates (and endpoints) in cognitive development in any sample of humans.

It follows from these two delineations of the area to be explored that we perceive cognition to be both general and amenable to acceleration. So, how can this notion of the stimulation of the development of a central processor best be modelled, bearing in mind our need for a model which can inform educational practice?

Modelling cognitive acceleration

Here I will outline the approach we have taken to the problem of describing a plastic central processor, and the ways in which it could be stimulated, developed over the years from an originally Piagetian perspective.

In the 1970s Michael Shayer had successfully applied Inhelder and Piaget's (1958) account of the development of the schemata of formal operations both to the analysis of curricula (especially science curricula) in terms of the cognitive demand that was made by different topics, and to the development of 'Piagetian Reasoning Tasks', assessment instruments which allowed us to conduct a very large scale survey of norms of levels of cognitive development in the English school population (Shayer, Küchemann and Wylam 1976; Shayer and Wylam 1978). When in the early 1980s he turned his attention to the question of cognitive acceleration, it was natural to look again at Piaget's ideas about how cognition develops and to wonder whether this mechanism could be manipulated to the advantage of the students within the educational system. Foremost among these ideas are those of maturing cognitive structures which act as gatekeepers to perception, and of equilibration – the process by which existing structures must accommodate in the face of cognitive conflict. Piaget (1977) describes equilibration as the two way process between the mind and the environment. Faced with a cognitive task set by the environment, the mind must accommodate its mental structures to meet the task, in order to be able to assimilate the information. If the demand is low, accommodation will be minimal, and if it is very high, accommodation will not be possible. On this reading it seemed that a promising approach to cognitive acceleration would be to provide students with activities which generated cognitive conflict, challenges which were carefully pitched at a demand level appropriate to the child's ages. It was clear from the start that this was not a straightforward matter. For one thing, there was the issue of the contexts in which the activities should be set, and for another the question of the distance beyond the students' current capability that would be optimal for inducing cognitive re-structuring.

As for context, our own backgrounds and the perceived national need both drove us towards embedding the activities within the domain of science in the secondary school curriculum. But how do we analyse the science curriculum in such a way that opportunities for cognitive conflict are clearly revealed? Enumerating topics such as 'energy', 'chemical reactions' or 'photosynthesis' does not itself tell us much about the types of cognitive processing that each requires. This is where the Inhelder descriptions of each of the schemata of formal operations come into their own since they are well defined with clear levels of expression and are, moreover, easily seen as underpinning all higher level school science. These schemata include the control and exclusion of variables, ratio and proportionality, compensation and equilibrium, combinatorial and probabilistic thinking, and formal modelling. Each of these is a general way of thinking which can be applied in many different contexts. For example, the general schema of proportionality may be applied in studies of velocity, of solution concentration, and of the surface area to weight ratio of animals. Once the schema has been constructed in the mind it can be brought to bear on a wide range of problems. These schemata of formal operations became the 'content matter' of the intervention activities, although they offered a very different sort of content from the standard school science curriculum with which teachers were familiar. It is important to understand that there was never any supposition that these schemata could be taught directly by a process of instruction. Rather, they provided the structuring principle of each of the intervention activities and an ultimate, if sometimes distant, goal towards which the accelerated development was supposed to be heading.

Turning now to the question of the level of cognitive dissonance which creates productive cognitive conflict, we recognized from the start that existing cognitive structures do not make radical changes in response to demands which lie far beyond their capabilities. This is where Vygotsky's (1978) notion of a Zone of Proximal Development offered a powerful accessory to the simple idea of cognitive conflict. Here we have an idea which allows us to conceptualize the range of levels of demand from that which an individual can meet without difficulty, and which therefore causes no conflict, to that which is beyond his capability under even the most favourable conditions of support. The ZPD actually defines a range within which cognitive conflict can be productive, but with a critical proviso: the cognitive conflict has to be positively and efficiently managed by the teacher. The provision of a cognitive challenge by itself cannot be expected to provoke accommodation and cognitive growth. It is just as likely, in the absence of support and what Bruner calls 'scaffolding' by the teacher, to lead to rejection and a sense of helplessness in the student. The danger here of the development of 'learned helplessness' will be clear, but outside the scope of a book whose main focus is cognitive structures. The lesson that does emerge is that intervention programs for cognitive acceleration always depend critically on the skill of the teacher, and can never be delivered by inanimate materials alone. Again, the issue of the professional development of teachers for cognitive acceleration is beyond the scope of this book. See Adey, Hewitt, Hewitt and Landau (2004) for a full account of teacher professional development related to cognitive acceleration.

So far we have seen how Piaget's idea of equilibration modulated by Vygotsky's ZPD placed well-managed cognitive conflict as the first characteristic of effective cognitive acceleration activities, but it must be recognized that the actual activities were being developed in real classroom situations, not in psychology laboratories, and furthermore that the developers were experienced teachers who could draw on years of successful practice in a variety of school situations. In watching the early cognitive acceleration activities in action, they could draw on this intuitive (experience-based if not yet fully explicated) knowledge together with their readings of Piaget, Vygotsky, Feuerstein, and others to recognize new features of the intervention which seemed likely to be stimulating. For example, faced with a cognitive problem and in a supportive classroom atmosphere, students want to talk with one another and to share their difficulties and their attempts at solutions. This was then recognized as the social construction described by Vygotsky as being, in his opinion, the main driver of cognitive development. Thus the explicit promotion of social construction, students working together and with their teacher with a common purpose, was early added as the second main 'pillar' of cognitive acceleration.

By the same process of iteration between observation, experience and the literature a third pillar was soon added: metacognition. Making explicit their thinking, re-visiting a problem-solving procedure and inspecting the difficulties and false trails encountered were seen as important elements in the process of maximizing cognitive development and subsequently, as with social construction, activities and pedagogic procedures were designed to maximize opportunities for metacognition. Much more will be said about metacognition below.

Two further 'pillars' were added from a more pragmatic perspective. 'Concrete preparation' was established as a necessary introductory phase to a cognitive acceleration activity since it was clear that one could not simply present students with a problem without establishing first the context in which the problem was to be set and introducing new words and any apparatus that was to be used. A final act, 'bridging', was established as the process of taking the thinking established within the cognitive acceleration activity and showing how the same thinking could be used in other contexts. Bridging was a term introduced by Feuerstein, but it also recognizes the old literature on transfer which established that transfer could only occur if a specific effort was made to highlight the general elements of a learning situation and how they could be used in other contexts. The way we use the term 'bridging' is actually quite specific. It means that the teacher draws students' attention to the schema they are developing – for example, control of variables – and then elicits from the students other examples, drawn from science, other school subjects, or from outside school of where this schema is useful. Bridging can also happen in the other direction, when the teacher in a regular science lesson asks students to recall a particular cognitive acceleration lesson, in order to show how the schema introduced there will be useful in the present context.

On the basis of this model, we have designed sets of teaching activities together with programs of professional development for teachers. This type of teaching can never be defined by print or software materials alone, but must involve also a significant change in teacher's beliefs about the nature of teaching and learning which underpins the change in pedagogy they are required to make. The 'pillars' are articulated together like this: the core of an activity is designed which provides cognitive conflict. A short sequence of concrete preparation is written which allows the teacher to introduce the terms and apparatus to be used in the challenging task. The teacher now has to manage the conflict in such a way as to encourage students to consult with one another, that is to engage in social construction. The conflict encourages social construction, and the views of others maintain the conflict. Possibly at any time during the lesson, but especially towards the end, the teacher invites students to reflect on their own thinking and learning, what difficulties they encountered, what wrong turns they took, and how their thinking has changed. This is the metacognition which explicates the type of thinking they have been using implicitly. Finally, in the bridging phase, the teacher draws attention to other contexts in which the same type of thinking may be useful. In the next section, examples of activities will be given to show the use of these pillars.

In summary, we have a five-pillar model of cognitive acceleration: cognitive conflict and social construction together play a central role in the process of maximizing the development of schemata as general ways of thinking which can later be applied to a wide range of problems. Metacognition provides an opportunity to explicate and consolidate this schema-formation. In their seminal paper on the transfer problem, Perkins and Saloman (1989) distinguish the 'high road' to transfer, which involves deep-level changes in the mind's general processing capability which have very general application, from the more concrete 'low road' to transfer, which is more specific and relies on the conscious application of a strategy to a new problem. In our model, it is bridging which offers this 'low-road' route to transfer. The schemata of formal operations provide the target content matter of the activities. It is important to note that while the origin and nature of each of the pillars may be theoretically distinguished, in practice they cannot be separated. Cognitive conflict, for example, leads people to talk with one another and thus to social construction. The social interaction of listening to others' points of view, in turn, often generates new cognitive conflict. From an educational point of view this merging of the pillars is not a problem, but in terms of psychological models it does make it difficult, if not impossible, to validate separately the roles played by each of the pillars.

Some of the problems around the notions of metacognition and schemata will be discussed later, but here I should offer some specific examples of how the 'pillars' are operationalized in cognitive acceleration activities.

Practical expression of the model

In the original Cognitive Acceleration through Science Education (CASE) project (1982–7) a set of thirty activities were developed based on this five-pillar model. These were introduced into science classes of students aged twelve to fourteen years (Years 7 and 8 in England, Grades 6 and 7 in the United States), to be used instead of regular science lessons at the rate of one every two weeks over two years. The expression of the five pillars can be illustrated with one activity from *Thinking Science* (Adey, Shayer and Yates 2001) the printed materials of the project:

Activity 3, *Tubes*, is based on the schema of control of variables and exclusion of irrelevant variables. Students are given small tubes which vary in length, width, and material. They are asked to find out what factors affect the note made when one blows across the tube. Initially they play with the tubes more or less at random – this is the concrete preparation phase as they become familiar with the variables of length, width, material of the tubes and the pitch of the note produced by blowing. They are now encouraged to test the tubes just two at a time. Typically 11 and 12 year old students do not perceive any great difficulty with this, but actually they tend to choose their pairs at random, without any specific strategy for testing one variable at a time. The cognitive conflict must be induced by the teacher circulating around the class, asking groups what they can conclude from any pair of tubes they have tested, challenging them to explain how a particular difference in note can be attributed to a change in width, when both width and length have been changed, but never giving specific instructions to 'vary only one thing at a time'. Groups will be set tasks to explain their reasoning to each other, so any one can be called to explain it to the whole class. At certain times, the teacher may call the whole class's attention and ask different groups what they have found, how they can justify their conclusion, and ask other groups to say whether they agree with the reasoning being put forward. Here we have social construction in action, which does require that the students have to learn how to question one another, and even disagree with one another, in a polite manner. Generally towards the end of the lesson (although this may occur at any time) the teacher invites students to reflect on what they have learnt, how they have learnt it, what problems they encountered and how they tried to overcome these problems. This is the metacognitive phase of the activity. Frequently, no clear conclusion is reached. It is not expected that at the end of every such activity all students will have fully constructed the control of variables schema for themselves. One of the many things that teachers have to learn is that such construction is a very slow process and that in a cognitive acceleration lesson there need be no immediately observable content objectives attained. Rather, they are in for the long term, with a series of such activities spread over two years providing repeated exposure to well managed cognitive conflict and social construction.

More recently, we have been applying the same model to much younger children, aged five and six years old, in Year 1 in the English school system. The five pillars of cognitive acceleration remain the same, but with these young children the 'content' is provided by the schemata of concrete operations such as seriation, simple classification and points of view. There are also a number of practical differences associated with the fact that cognitive acceleration at Year 1 depends on primary class teachers, rather than on secondary subject teachers. The Year 1 cognitive acceleration activities are published as *Let's Think!* (Adey, Robertson and Venville 2001) and are used with just six children at a time. The teacher supports this group while other children get on with their own work (sometimes with a classroom assistant). Each day of the week another group gets the *Let's Think!* activity so that the whole class is covered in a week. The thirty activities are delivered at the rate of one a week for one year. As an example, we will consider one of the later activities, concerned with the schema of 'points of view' (spatial perception).

Crossroads: The teacher sits at one side of a table, with two children at each of the other three sides. On the table is a model of a city crossroads, with various buildings, vehicles, a bus stop, a tree, a horse, and a duck. From any one side of the table it is not possible to see all of the objects since some are hidden by buildings. Concrete preparation consists of naming all of the objects and ensuring that phrases such as 'in front of' 'behind' and 'beside' are understood by all. Then each pair of children is given a set of picture cards, and asked to choose the card which represents the scene *as they see it*. Often they will choose a card which shows an object they cannot actually see, although they know it is there. This leads to some discussion until they understand that the picture they choose must show just what they can actually see. So far this is not too demanding for most six year olds. Now they are asked to *imagine* themselves to be sitting at a different side of the table and to choose the picture which represents what they would see from there. They have mentally to place themselves in a different position and 'decentre' from their actual seating position. Each pair chooses their pictures, discussing it between them and arguing for their choice so that the cognitive conflict entrained with thinking themselves in another position leads to active social construction of an agreed image of what would be seen from that position. The teacher encourages each pair to share their choice together with their reasoning and this can be challenged by the other pairs. Toward the end, teacher asks the children to reflect on what they did, how they did it, what difficulties they encountered, and any strategies they may have discovered for solving the problem. This is the metacognitive phase. Typically these activities last about 30 minutes, by which time both teacher and children are quite exhausted – an effect we have repeatedly noticed from productive cognitive acceleration activities.

Effects in brief

All cognitive acceleration work has been subject to intense evaluation which has been widely reported (e.g. Adey, Robertson and Venville 2002; Adey and Shayer 1993, 1994; Shayer 1996; Shayer and Adey 2002). In brief, from the

Table 9.1. *Effect sizes from the original CASE experiment: CASE over controls.*

		Immediate post '87		Delayed post '88		GCSE[2], '89 or '90	
		Cognitive. development	Science	Science	Science	Maths	English
Year 7	Girls	−[1]	−	0.60	0.67	0.72	0.69
start	Boys	−	−	−	−	−	−
Year 8	Girls	−	−	−	−	−	0.44
start	Boys	0.75	−	0.72	0.96	0.50	0.32

[1] Only significant (p < .01) effects sizes are shown. All effects are of CASE classes >non-CASE control classes
[2] General Certificate of Secondary Education, the national public examination taken at 16+ years.

work with adolescents it has been shown that students who participate in cognitive acceleration programs when they are aged twelve to fourteen years go on to show significantly higher levels of cognitive development at the end of the program, and significantly higher grades in academic achievement, compared with controls, up to three years after the program in subject areas far removed from science. Table 9.1 summarizes the data from the original 1984–87 experiment. The effect sizes here are derived from residualized gain scores, that is, the gains made by experimental groups over and above that which would be expected on the basis of the control groups' 'normal' development over the same period. Thus each effect size is the mean residualized gain score of the experimental group divided by the pooled standard deviation of the gain scores of experimental and control groups.

As a general rule, effect sizes of 0.3 are considered respectable, 0.5 as large. Although not all subgroups' effects reached statistical significance in the early experiment, there is clear evidence of a substantial long-term far-transfer effect. An intervention set in a science context produced gains in national public examinations taken two or three years later, in English and mathematics as well as in science. Figure 9.1 shows some more recent data. Here, each point represents one school, the x-axis is the mean cognitive developmental level of the students entering the school aged eleven, and the y axis is the mean grade obtained in that school in the GCSE examination taken five years later. Unsurprisingly there is a strong relationship between the ability intake of the school and its mean performance. What is clear is that schools which have used CASE show significant gains in GCSE grades compared with non-CASE schools, whatever their intake. Data for English are shown, but similar effects were obtained for science and mathematics.

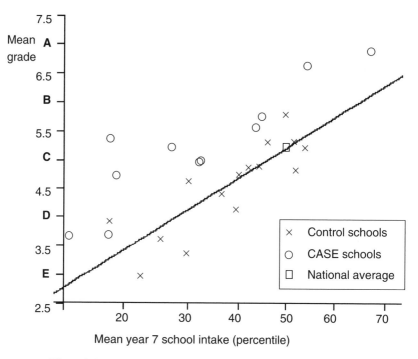

Figure 9.1. Value-added effect of CASE on GCSE English.

Table 9.2. *Effect sizes of the* Let's Think! *intervention on cognitive gain.*

| | Immediate post tests 2000 | |
	Drawing	Conservation
Boys	0.35	–
Girls	0.59	0.55

Work with the younger students, aged five to six, is more recent and we do not yet have any long-term effects to show, but Table 9.2 shows the immediate post-test effects.

For the purpose of this chapter, the most interesting issue is what valid conclusions can be drawn from the results about the model of cognitive acceleration outlined above, and what light the results throw on the three questions about cognition which this book is addressing. I will turn now to these questions.

What develops?

To describe the entity in the mind that develops as a 'cognitive structure' or even as a 'central cognitive processor' is clearly inadequate as such labels provide us with no features of the model on which we can build hypotheses about the macro characteristics which we might expect to observe, and possibly to manipulate. So, we must find more comprehensive and more complex ways of modelling whatever it is in the mind that develops with age and appropriate stimulation. This question can be approached at three main levels: the psychometric, the cognitive and the neurophysiological.

Starting with the last, our understanding of brain functioning is currently growing exponentially as tools such as positron emission tomography (PET scanning), functional magnetic resonance imaging (fMRI), and event-related potential (ERP) are providing increasingly sophisticated ways of tracking which parts of the brain are responsible for each type of response. An enormous amount is known about the development of the brain from the first differentiation in the human embryo about twelve days after conception of a set of neurones which are destined to become the brain and spinal column, through the explosive growth of neurones and their strange migratory habits over the next nine months, and then immediately after birth a second type of explosion, no longer growth in the number of neurones but rather in the connections between them (Johnson 1993). It seems that as soon as the infant enters the outside world and becomes subject to a bombardment of signals from the sense organs, the brain goes into a frenzy of building connections between neurones and also losing connections that are not used. The implication here is that the brain develops in part in response to stimulation, a proposition confirmed by Greenhough, Black and Wallace (1987) with their work on rats. There is, however, a difficulty with thinking about cognitive development only in terms of brain physiology: we just don't know anything like enough about the relationship between neuronal structure and function on the one hand and the way people actually process information on the other. I have to agree with John Bruer (1997) when he talks of 'a bridge too far' and warns against promoting any educational practice at all on the evidence of what we know about brain development and function.

At the other end of the spectrum of levels of describing cognitive processing, we have psychometric approaches. At their best (for example Carroll 1993) psychometrics offer powerful evidence for the structure of intelligence and thus form an important part of the armoury of those who seek to understand what it is in the mind that develops. What psychometric methods by themselves find difficult to deliver, however, are adequate explanatory models of the nature of intellectual functioning and development. There is also a problem that the word 'intelligence' has fallen into some disrepute, as it was appropriated by a group of psychometricians from Burt (1927) through to Herrnstein and Murray (1994) and Jensen (1973), who saw it as a more-or-less fixed capability of a child which could be reliably measured and then used to predict likely academic performance. This notion of intelligence held that it had a strong hereditary component and, allied to the belief in the reliability of IQ tests and observed differences in performances on these tests by different groups in society, led to a potentially explosive excuse for racism. This appropriation of the word made it rather unpalatable for cognitive psychologists to use, which is a pity because it seems silly to have to invent a new word for the central cognitive processing mechanism of the mind when 'intelligence' was designed to do the job. There are signs now that the word is being reclaimed and imbued with a more sophisticated and justifiable understanding of the meaning of intelligence.

Interestingly, teachers do have a rather sound intuitive idea of the nature of intelligence, and I would like to describe this as a precursor to addressing the middle, and most profitable, level of describing mind functions, that of cognitive models. I have been asking teachers for many years what counts, in their view and experience, as intelligent behaviour. When one of their students says something, or writes something, or does something which makes them say 'Yes! that is smart!', what sort of thing has the student said or written or done? The answers I get are remarkably consistent. They always include things about seeing patterns in data, about anticipating what the teacher is going to do next, about asking probing questions, and above all about applying knowledge from one context to a different context altogether. All of these features require that the students have made some sort of connection in their mind. So the professionals who are in the business of teaching and learning see connectivity as a central characteristic of intelligent behaviour. 'Connectivity' here is used here in the simple sense of the conscious or unconscious making of connections in the mind between one idea and another. In this sense, making comparisons, relating causes to effects, or the elucidation of any relationship between variables all involve connectivity.

How does this idea of connectivity relate to more formal ideas of 'intelligence' in the psychological literature? We might start by going back to Binet (1909), who more or less invented the modern idea of intelligence. Binet devised a wide range of types of questions, including executing three commands given simultaneously, comparing two objects from memory, or arranging five blocks in order of weight. (He did also use some rather different types of item, such as distinguishing an ugly from a pretty face, which we might now think to be somewhat culturally biased!) One of Binet's students was a young Swiss called Jean Piaget who with Bärbel Inhelder described the highest (formal) level of intellectual performance as the ability to, for example, operate on many variables in mind at once, use abstract ideas in conjunction with one another, and see actual events as a subset of many possible events (Inhelder and Piaget 1964; Smith 1992). From both Binet and from Inhelder and Piaget we again see the connectivity idea very clearly, so teachers' intuitive ideas of intelligence turn out to tally very closely with that held by the original analysts of the nature of intelligence. It is worth noting that although the psychometric approach whose origins are attributed to Binet and the cognitive-developmentalist approach which stems from the work of Piaget are sometimes seen as incompatible, Styles and Andrich (1997) have used Rasch scaling of a standard intelligence test (Raven's Progressive Matrices) and Piagetian measures together to show that both form a unidimensional scale on a single latent trait, which is postulated to be that of abstract reasoning.

If this 'connectivity' feature of intelligence has general validity – and I believe that it does – then whatever cognitive model of the central processing mechanism is proposed, it must afford connectivity a major role. This is precisely what the information processing models of Case (1985) and Pascual-Leone (1976) offer. They link the development of cognition described by Piaget to growth in working memory capacity, with increasing capacity allowing for increasing numbers of bits of information to be processed in parallel. The idea of working memory as a key element in the mechanism by which information from the outside world becomes constructed in long-term memory is now a well-established element in cognitive psychology (Baddeley 1990; Logie 1999). It is also an idea which we find to be readily accessible to teachers. Having told us that 'intelligence' to them means connectivity, a description of working memory as a notional space in the mind which can only hold a limited number of bits of information at one time, and which passes those bits of information through in less than a second, immediately offers an explanatory model which fits their daily experience of working with students of widely varying abilities.

Of course, the idea of working memory can explain only a limited range of the observations we make about how minds work, and no claim is being made that an adequate account of cognition can be provided by a model consisting only of sensing, working memory, and long-term memory. To account also for Chomskyan language-learning mechanisms, for example, one may need to posit one or more in-built 'modules' which are part of humans' evolutionary inheritance, but this is a hotly debated topic for which no clear resolution has yet been reached (see Karmiloff and Karmiloff-Smith 2001, for a recent analysis of rival models of language acquisition). Anderson (1992) would distinguish modules for syntactical parsing from phonological encoding, and would add modules for perception of three-dimensional space and for theory of mind. Baddeley (1990) proposes a pair of slave systems to working memory – the articulatory loop and the visuo-spatial scratchpad – as short term buffers for verbal and spatial information respectively, and Kintsch (1998) adds many more buffers. Furthermore, recent work (e.g. Demetriou, Christou, Spanoudis and Platsidou 2002; Kyllonen 2002) suggests that selective attention and inhibition processes act as gatekeepers to working memory, but this still leaves working memory as the workspace of thinking.

While recognizing that the elaboration and justification of such models is the stuff of cognitive psychology, for our purposes – that is to understand cognitive acceleration and to justify our methods to teachers – we do not need such sophisticated mind models. We ask, rather, what is the minimum architecture of the mind that we do need? Sensing, working memory, and long-term memory are accepted. If working memory is seen as increasing with age, then this very simple model is sufficient to account for the development of processing ability from birth to maturity. Further, by putting a little detail into the long-term memory idea we can account also for knowledge acquisition using a Hebbian (Hebb 1949) mechanism of strengthening neural networks by repeated use, concepts as higher-level organizations of knowledge within long-term memory, and conceptual change as the (sometimes sudden) re-structuring of such organization. On the other hand there are important facets of the observed mind which this model is too simple to explain. For example, without buying into Gardner's (1993) notion of multiple 'intelligences' (the absence of any general factor from which makes it suspect), there is no doubt – again from Carroll's (1993) factor analytical work – that in addition to a general processing mechanism the mind has abilities which are specialized within domains. Anderson (1992) argues that there must be at least two such specialized systems, but Carroll's factor analysis suggests many more. The model of specialized structural systems proposed by Demetriou, Gustafsson, Efklides and Plastidou (1992) offers a comprehensive account of such specialized and somewhat independent abilities. However, since in cognitive acceleration we are concerned with the general rather than the specialized abilities, we do not strictly need to address this aspect of the model of cognition.

A more serious flaw in the simple model from our point of view is that it tells us nothing about how the process of development might be accelerated. This is the question to be addressed in the next section.

How does it develop?

The 'it' in this question is, for us, the central cognitive processing mechanism and our interest in how it develops is directly related to our intention to manipulate that development. That, after all, is what cognitive acceleration claims to do.

If working memory capacity lies at the centre of the central processing mechanism, then one way in which intelligence develops must be by an increase in working memory capacity. However if, following Pascual-Leone (1976) and

Case's (1974) early work,[1] we accept that the number of bits of information that can be independently managed by working memory grows gradually from 0 at birth to about 7 at maturity, that suggests a rather slow rate of development expressed as bits per year – something less than one bit every two years on average. While it is perfectly possible (and I would say likely) that working memory capacity does increase under the influence of both maturation of the central nervous system and of cognitive stimulation, the potential of even the most successful of stimulation programs must be constrained by the normal range of the rate of growth of working memory available. Thus, while accepting the probability that well-managed cognitive conflict, as described in the first section of this chapter, will have some effect on the growth of working memory, it seems unlikely that this mechanism alone could account for the large effect sizes we have obtained in the cognitive acceleration projects. We therefore need to seek additional ways in which central processing can be enhanced, or made more efficient.

There seem to be two possible mechanisms by which a given w.m. capacity could be used more efficiently: the use of 'chunking', and the use of schemata. These are related but distinct, and may act separately or together. Chunking means the linking together of two or more variables as a compound variable which, as long as it is not deconstructed again, can be treated as a single variable and so dealt with in one working memory space instead of two or three. An example would be the conception of 'density'. Although the Piagetian account and the science misconceptions literature – e.g. Driver, Squires, Rushworth and Wood-Robinson (1994), Novak (1977), Pfundt and Duit (1988) – normally make uneasy bedfellows, from them together we can extract a rough chronology of the development of the density concept.

For preoperational children, up to about four years of age, no coherent account of even 'heaviness' as a global concept is available. The development of early concrete operations brings with it the ability to differentiate the 'heaviness' of different objects in terms which implicitly, but not explicitly, include the idea of 'heavy for a given size'. Thus a small lead ball will be described as 'heavy' while a large piece of Styrofoam will be described as 'light', even though the latter may be the heavier. We may imagine that this involves the integrated processing of perceptual signals of both absolute weight (pressure on the hand) and of size (from visual inputs). This is not a conscious process of integration and cannot be mentally or verbally deconstructed. After some further years of development and instruction in science, the twelve to fourteen-year-old may have encountered and learned to deal with density as a

[1] In a later formulation, Case (1984) suggests that total working memory space remains constant, but more sophisticated and efficient operational capability means that less space needs to be devoted to operations, leaving more space for storage of bits of information. The practical outcome from our point of view is not very different.

concept in physics. Here density is understood as the mass of one gram of a substance and at the stage of concrete generalization the student is able to solve density problems that require no more than the application of a learned formula in contexts which have become familiar through practice. Such problems as 'Calculate the density of a block of volume 200 cm^3 which has a mass of 250 g' demand no more than four or five spaces in working memory and are solved in a series of well-defined steps, fitting numbers into a formula. In the same way predicting whether a solid will float in a liquid, given a value of the density of each, requires no more than the calling up of a learned rule and the comparison of two numbers. Here the individual variables of mass and volume have been lost, chunked into the compound variable density. Only when the student is capable of using formal operations is she able at the same time to conceive of density as a property of a material (not an object) and to deconstruct this flexibly to a sense of mass for a given volume. Only at this stage, which requires six or seven spaces in working memory, can density be fully understood as professional physicists understand it, and can problems be solved even when presented in a form that is not readily recognized. In this example we can see the value of chunking as making available to individuals using concrete operations a limited, but still useful, version of the formal understanding of density.

A schema is a general way of thinking about the ordering and organization of variables encountered in the world. If we did not have schemata available to us then we would have to treat each problem completely anew and could transfer no processing from one context to another. To our five-year-olds, the practical problem of placing ten sticks in order of length is not a trivial one. The schema of seriation is not well established and they have to apply their early concrete operations to the single variable, length, successively with each overlapping set of three sticks. Their tendency is to attend to only two sticks at a time, which means that they establish that, say, A is longer than B, then that A is longer than C, and then they order them A, C, B without thinking of the possibility that B may be longer than C. They do not have a general schema of seriation. While still a few years short of fully developing formal operations, the twelve-year-olds we work with have significant difficulty in seeing the need to test just one variable at a time in the tubes activity outlined earlier in this chapter. To see at one time the independent variables of tube length, width and material, to hold two constant while trying two values of the third, and at the same time to relate each value of the varying independent variable to a corresponding value of the dependent variable (pitch of note), demands at least six spaces in working memory. I believe that it is unrealistic to claim that the effect of perhaps four control-of-variables activities within a cognitive acceleration program over some two months could, by themselves, expand students' w.m. capacity from four to six. Nor do the activities and methods of cognitive acceleration encourage the learning of rules ('only change one variable at a time') since such rules are almost inevitably misapplied without the formal understanding of why it matters. (My colleague Tony Hamaker was once forbidden by a class of twelve-year-olds to take off his sweater while conducting an experiment rolling balls of various masses and materials down a runway, because he 'had to keep everything the same except for the mass of the ball'.) I suggest that the cognitive construction during this eight-week period is no more than the beginning of the schema of control of variables, together with an awareness that these experiments are not as simple as they look, require more attention to the variables than one might think, and so that continued help will be required from the teacher and from more able peers. In other words, an element of uncertainty is introduced which operates as an internal mechanism for creating cognitive conflict whenever that type of problem is encountered.

Before elaborating on the distinction between chunking strategies and schemata and considering their places in a mind model, we need to consider the role that consciousness plays in the process. This may seem a rather immodest essay since the nature of consciousness is a problem which has dogged philosophers and psychologists since ancient times, and it is not a concept which is much explicated within the literature of cognitive psychology. However, no attempt will be made here to define the nature of consciousness nor to try to locate it in some particular part of the brain. Susan Greenfield (1995) has made a brave attempt at these conundra from a neurophysiological perspective. Consciousness is important in consideration of the 'what develops' question in two ways: its use of working memory capacity, and its centrality in metacognition.

My colleague Michael Shayer (Adey and Shayer 1994) makes an important distinction in the process of cognitive acceleration between 'going beyond' and 'going above'. The 'going beyond' is the process of pushing one's thinking on further than usual, of stretching one's capabilities as a result of cognitive conflict and social construction. At this point the student has experienced the conflict and with the help of well structured discussion may be achieving some partial, and still implicit, understanding of the problem and the embryonic development of a schema. Now, the 'going above' is the process of going back over what has been achieved, and how it has been achieved. In other words, this is the metacognitive phase, when what has been implicit so far is now brought into consciousness. Whatever arguments there may be about the nature of metacognition (Antonietti, Ignazi and Perego 2000; Brown 1987; Sánchez 1998), what is agreed in all understandings of the term is that it involves consciousness. The central meaning of metacognition is becoming conscious of one's own thinking. Our evidence (Larkin 1999, 2001) suggests that the ability to be metacognitive develops in line with the development of theory of mind, generally between four and six years of age.

That metacognition appears not to be available to very young children and also that it is necessary to 'go above' one's reasoning to inspect it and make it conscious are both consistent with the idea that being conscious of something itself must demand some working memory capacity. It is not possible, at the time that working memory is being used to its full capacity to deal with a challenging problem, also to be conscious of how one is solving the problem. Thus metacognition – at least related to demanding problems – must necessarily be one of reflection back and, with the help of the teacher or others, of revisiting the problem-solving process to expose it to inspection. In practice, it is neither necessary nor desirable to make metacognition a defined phase of a lesson which always comes near the end. Rather, one can at any time in the cognitive construction process interrupt and ask children to reflect on where they are, how they have got there, and where they have to go now in the process of solving the complete problem. But it is a separate process, and it is necessary to signal it clearly as such to students during a cognitive acceleration lesson.

Returning now to the cognitively economical processes of chunking and of schemata, the two may be distinguished partly by the sort of entities which they are, and partly by the role played in them by consciousness. A chunked concept is a concept, that is, it is a mental object which can be treated as a whole in various operations. A schema on the other hand is an executive process, an operation which acts on concepts and other mental objects. At least in their formation, chunking strategies are developed consciously, generally under the explicit direction of a teacher. It is true that after sufficient practice such strategies become automated – indeed that is the nature of their efficiency – but the recognition of appropriate contexts and the selection of the correct automatic chunking procedure to run remain essentially conscious processes. The development of schemata, however, I suggest is a predominantly unconscious process. After all, a stage of cognitive development is effectively defined by the schemata that are available at that stage, and cognitive development is an unconscious process. My proposal is that the schemata develop as automatic ways of processing information in response to the continued experience of trying to solve problems of different types, with constraint provided by maturation. Although formal schemata cannot be run fluently until formal operations (and the working memory capacity characteristic of that stage) are available, there is a pre-formal phase where the schemata may be partially formed when they can start to run, albeit uncertainly and with frequent errors and 'crashes'. Perhaps the occurrence of these crashes provides the internal cognitive conflict which spurs on the longer term cognitive developmental process. Even the process of selecting and running such procedures can be unconscious if they are automatically triggered by certain features in the problem.

To conclude this section, what is being claimed is that what develops is (a) working memory capacity and (b) strategies for more effectively using what working memory capacity is available. The former is very slow while the latter can be faster although even strategy and schema development takes many months. Consciousness requires working memory capacity, and is implicated in chunking strategies but not directly in schemata formation.

Why does it develop?

One plausible answer to the 'Why?' question is an evolutionary one: humans have become such a successful species because we have used challenge to develop higher orders of intelligence, which allow us to survive in a remarkable range of physical environments and to dominate other animals which have far greater physical prowess than we do. The key to the success of *homo sapiens* lies in our adaptability to variations in climate, in diet, and in social structures and much of this adaptability arises not so much from physical hardiness, as from intelligence. We adapt to cold climates by making clothes, to the availability of different foodstuffs by developing agriculture and using fire in cooking, and we adapt to social living from rural communities to cities and nations by formalizing complex social structures with governments and the specialization of roles within society. All of these means of adaptation arise directly from the capability of our large and complex brains which permit us to develop abstract ideas and language. Byrne (1995) and Nelson (1996) show how brain size and language developed together as *homo sapiens* evolved from a line of apes. Larger and more complex brain structure allowed for primitive language to develop (and with it the beginnings of abstract ideas) and in turn the manipulation of ideas demanded more language power which stimulated brain growth and selectively gave advantage to larger brains.

It is tempting to draw the parallel between this evolutionary (phylogenetic) process of brain stimulation and growth and our developmental (ontogenetic) process of cognitive acceleration but it would be disingenuous to claim very much for a simple 'recapitulation' theory, that individual development follows the path of the species' evolutionary development. There are, nevertheless, some parallels in the processes which are worth attending to, as long as we do not take them too literally. For example, in both cases there is two-way interaction between the developing brain and the environment, with the extent, and maybe even the course, of development depending on the extent and nature of stimulation received. In evolution this is a very long-term process, while in individual development one hopes that it is completed within about eighteen years. The active role of the child in his own cognitive development is apparent from the observed, apparently innate, tendency in humans to seek intellectual challenge. Case (1992) talks about higher-order structures being

... activated by the universal human experience of trying to make sense of, and abstract invariants from, the normal flux of human experience (p. 59)

Children in school are as likely to be 'bored' by undemanding work as by work which makes demands too great for their current cognitive capability.

There is plasticity of the central cognitive processor, such that while it develops 'naturally' in response to 'normal' environmental (including importantly social) stimuli, it can be permanently damaged by pathological under-stimulation, and can be significantly enhanced by a program of cognitive stimulation such as that described in the first part of this chapter. Thus, whilst the question 'why does cognition develop' seemingly must have an evolutionary answer, this answer does lead us to the idea that individual cognitive development within a social context must have a possible range, from under-stimulation, through a mean or 'normal' value, towards some maximum attainable.

What sets this maximum? The first answer, at any particular age, must be the complexity of the central nervous system which in humans appears to be programmed to develop from some twelve days after conception to some fifteen to eighteen years after birth. To be sure, even that physiological development is influenced by cognitive stimulation, but there is a limit to this process, again best perhaps conceptualized in terms of the Zone of Proximal Development, that penumbra whose horizon continually recedes as one works along it. Of relevance here is the uneven rate of growth of the brain from birth to maturity, with spurts in growth which accord quite well with the main stages of cognitive development described by Piaget (Epstein 1986; Epstein 1990, Styles 1995). The limits to the rate of cognitive growth set by physiological factors relate especially to the development of the general central processing mechanism which I have associated particularly in this chapter with working memory capacity. There is a more complex story to be told about conceptual development, about which science educators have had much to write over the past twenty years, but that would be to go beyond the brief of this chapter. Suffice it to say that cognitive development sets a limit on the development of concepts, but that full maturity of cognition does not, by itself, bring in train a sophisticated level of conceptual development. That requires also instruction, specific experiences, and probably the independent development of specialized structural systems.

Conclusion

In this chapter, some key ideas derived from empirical work and from theoretical model-building in developmental psychology have been drawn on in an attempt to design an educational program which is cognitively stimulating. The program is based on the principles that there is some general processing mechanism of the brain which accounts, at least partially, for common notions of intelligence, and that this general processor is sufficiently plastic to be amenable to stimulation. Evidence from long-term effects of 'cognitive acceleration' supports the notion of plasticity, and that from transfer of effects supports the claim of generality. The idea of working memory has played a central role in the model, with 'acceleration' being based on the influence of stimulation on the development of working memory capacity, and on the more efficient use of existing working memory through schemata and chunking. Metacognition has been presented as a central pillar of effective cognitive stimulation, but one which is still dogged by outstanding questions.

REFERENCES

Adey, P., Hewitt, G., Hewitt, J., and Landau, N. (2004). *The professional development of teachers: practice and theory*. Dordrecht: Kluwer Academic.
Adey, P., Robertson, A. and Venville, G. (2001). *Let's Think!* Slough, UK: NFER-Nelson.
  (2002). Effects of a cognitive stimulation programme on Year 1 pupils. *British Journal of Educational Psychology, 72*, 1–25.
Adey, P. and Shayer, M. (1993). An exploration of long-term far-transfer effects following an extended intervention programme in the high school science curriculum. *Cognition and Instruction, 11*(1), 1–29.
  (1994). *Really raising standards: cognitive intervention and academic achievement*. London: Routledge.
Adey, P., Shayer, M. and Yates, C. (2001). *Thinking science: the curriculum materials of the CASE project* (3rd edn). London: Nelson Thornes.
Anderson, M. (1992). *Intelligence and development: a cognitive theory*. London: Blackwell.
Antonietti, A., Ignazi, S. and Perego, P. (2000). Metacognitive knowledge about problem-solving methods. *British Journal of Educational Psychology, 70*, 1–16.
Baddeley, A. (1990). *Human memory: theory and practice*. London: Lawrence Erlbaum.
Binet, A. (1909). *Les idées modernes sur les enfants*. Paris: Ernest Flammarion.
Brown, A. L. (1987). Metacognition, executive control, self-regulation and other more mysterious mechanisms. In R. Kluwe and F. Weinert (eds.) *Metacognition, motivation and understanding* (pp. 65–116). London: Lawrence Erlbaum.
Bruer, J. T. (1997). Education and the brain: a bridge too far? *Educational Researcher, 26*(8), 4–16.
Burt, C. (1927). *The measurement of individual capacities: a review of the psychology of individual differences*. London: Oliver and Boyd.
Byrne, R. (1995). *The thinking ape: evoloutionary origins of intelligence*. Oxford: Oxford University Press.
Carroll, J. B. (1993). *Human cognitive abilities*. Cambridge: Cambridge University Press.
Case, R. (1974). Structures and strictures: some functional limits to cognitive growth. *Cognitive Psychology, 6*, 544–74.
  (1984). The process of stage transition – a neo-Piagetian view. In R. J. Sternberg and W. H. Freeman (eds.) *Mechanisms of cognitive development*. New York.
  (1985). *Intellectual development: birth to adulthood*. New York: Academic Press.
  (1992). The role of central conceptual structures in the development of children's scientific and mathematical thought. In A. Demetriou, M. Shayer and A. Efklides (eds.) *Neo-Piagetian theories of cognitive development*. London: Routledge.

Demetriou, A., Christou, C., Spanoudis, G., and Platsidou, M. (2002). The development of mental processing: efficiency, working memory, and thinking. *Monographs of the Society for Research in Child Development, 67.*

Demetriou, A., Gustafsson, J.-E., Efklides, A. and Plastidou, M. (1992). Structural systems in developing cognition, science, and education. In A. Demetriou and M. Shayer and A. Efklides (eds.) *Neo-Piagetian theories of cognitive development.* London: Routledge.

Driver, R., Squires, A., Rushworth, P. and Wood-Robinson, V. (1994). *Making sense of secondary science.* London: Routledge.

Epstein, H. T. (1986). Stages in human brain development. *Developmental Brain Research, 30,* 114–19.

    (1990). Stages in human mental growth. *Journal of Educational Psychology, 82,* 876–80.

Gardner, H. (1993). *Frames of mind* (2nd edn). New York: Basic Books.

Greenfield, S. (1995). *Journey to the centers of the mind.* New York: W. H. Freeman.

Greenhough, W. T., Black, J. E. and Wallace, C. S. (1987). Experience and brain development. *Child Development, 58,* 539–59.

Hebb, D. O. (1949). *The organization of behavior.* New York: John Wiley.

Herrnstein, R. and Murray, C. (1994). *The Bell curve: intelligence and class structure in American life.* New York: Free Press.

Inhelder, B. and Piaget, J. (1958). *The growth of logical thinking.* London: Routledge and Kegan Paul.

    (1964). *The early growth of logic in the child: a classification and seriation.* London: Routledge and Kegan Paul.

Jensen, A. (1973). *Educability and group differences.* London: Methuen.

Johnson, M. H. (1993). *Brain development and cognition.* Oxford: Blackwell.

Karmiloff, K. and Karmiloff-Smith, A. (2001). *Pathways to language; from fetus to adolescent.* Cambridge, MA: Harvard University Press.

Kintsch, W. (1998). *Comprehension: a paradigm for cognition.* Cambridge: Cambridge University Press.

Kyllonen, P. (2002). 'g': Knowledge, speed, strategies, or working memory capacity? A systems perspective. In R. Sternberg and E. L. Grigorenko (eds.) *The general factor in intelligence: how general is it?* Mahwah, NJ: Lawrence Erlbaum Associates.

Larkin, S. (1999). An exploration of metacognition in five- and six-year-olds. London: British Psychological Society.

    (2001). Creating metacognitive experiences for 5- and 6-year old children. In M. Shayer and P. S. Adey (eds.) *Learning intelligence.* Buckingham: Open University Presss.

Logie, R. H. (1999). Working memory. *The Psychologist, 12*(4), 174–8.

Nelson, K. (1996). *Language in cognitive development.* Cambridge: Cambridge University Press.

Novak, J. (1977). *A theory of education.* Ithaca: Cornell University Press.

Pascual-Leone, J. (1976). On learning and development, Piagetian style. *Canadian Psychological Review, 17*(4), 270–97.

Perkins, D. N. and Saloman, G. (1989). Are cognitive skills context bound? *Educational Researcher, 18*(1), 16–25.

Pfundt, H. and Duit, R. (1988). *Bibliography: students' alternative frameworks and science education* (5th edn). Kiel: IPN.

Piaget, J. (1977). *The development of thought: equilibration of cognitive structures*. Oxford: Blackwell.

Sánchez, J. M. (1998). Nature and modes of metacognition. In J. M. Martínez, J. Lebeer and R. Garbo (eds.) *Is intelligence modifiable?* (pp. 23–48). Madrid: Bruño.

Shayer, M. (1996). *Long term effects of cognitive acceleration through science education on achievement: November 1996*. Centre for the Advancement of Thinking.

Shayer, M. and Adey, P. (eds.) (2002). *Learning intelligence: cognitive acceleration across the curriculum from 5 to 15 years*. Milton Keynes: Open University Press.

Shayer, M., Küchemann, D. and Wylam, H. (1976). The distribution of Piagetian stages of thinking in British middle and secondary school children. *British Journal of Educational Psychology, 46*, 164–73.

Shayer, M. and Wylam, H. (1978). The distribution of Piagetian stages of thinking in British middle and secondary school children. II – 14- to 16-year olds and sex differentials. *British Journal of Educational Psychology, 48*, 62–70.

Smith, L. (1992). *Necessary knowledge: Piagetian perspectives on constructivism*. London: Lawrence Erlbaum.

Styles, I. (1995). *Evidence of phrenoblysis*. Perth, WA: Murdoch University.

Styles, I. and Andrich, D. (1997). Faire le lien entre variables psychométriques et variables cognitivo-développementales régissant le fonctionnement intellectuel. *Psychologie et Psychométrie, 18*(2/3).

Vygotsky, L. S. (1978). *Mind in society*. Cambridge, MA: Harvard University Press.

10   Dealing with change: manifestations, measurements and methods

Elena L. Grigorenko and Paul A. O'Keefe

The main purpose of this chapter is to discuss briefly major methodologies used for the analysis of change. Throughout the development and maturation of approaches to measuring change, different types of change have been recognized and different methods of quantifying change have been developed (e.g., Collins and Horn 1991; Harris 1963). There is a colloquial reference to so-called old and new approaches to measuring change. 'Old' approaches refer to such conventional indicators of change as the differences between measures in a given time point and a subsequent time point. 'New' approaches refer to ever more complex methodologies for describing and quantifying development, whether spontaneous or occurring in response to intervention.

Clearly, the amount of information on a subject studied by many outstanding scientists that can be introduced in a single chapter is limited. Moreover, a single chapter cannot compete with the comprehensive volumes that have recently been written on the same topic (e.g. Collins and Sayer 2001; Gottman 1995; Moskowitz and Hershberger 2002; von Eye and Niedermeier 1999). Therefore, the strategy selected in this chapter for material presentation is to introduce briefly selected methodological approaches, illustrate them with specific examples, and provide the reader with a wealth of relevant references.

We decided to illustrate various change-related methodologies by reviewing a limited content area – the field of studies related to acquisition, both natural and in response to targeted intervention, of oral and written language. Such a decision is not random, of course. The selection was driven by two considerations. First, the processes of oral and written language acquisition are fundamentally developmental because they (a) mark the emergence of something new (skill, function, or level); (b) assume both procedural continuity and

This research was supported by Grant R206R50001 from the Institute of Educational Sciences (formerly the Office of Educational Research and Improvement), US Department of Education. Preparation of this report was supported by Grant R206R00001 from the same organization. Grantees undertaking such projects are encouraged to express freely their professional judgment. This article, therefore, does not necessarily represent the position or policies of the US Department of Education, and no official endorsement should be inferred. Correspondence should be sent to Elena L. Grigorenko, PACE Center, Yale University, Box 208358, New Haven, CT 06520-8358.

discontinuity; and (c) presume directionality (Pascual-Leone 1995; van Geert 1995; Vygotsky 1982). Second, these acquisitions embody change in its purest form. Both speaking and reading, from a developmental point of view, are characterized by (1) the existence of a zero point (i.e. there are developmental stages that do not include these processes – pre-linguistic and pre-reading stages), (2) unfolding developmental trajectories (i.e. both oral and written languages have to be mastered so that the child's performance meets certain criteria at different stages of development), and (3) their modifiable nature (i.e. speaking and reading interventions can improve the child's performance).

The following procedure was employed in the search for the original publications to be discussed in the present chapter. The article search was conducted using three different databases: PsycInfo, ERIC, and Medline. The terms *development*, *intervention*, *treatment* and *teaching* were identified as major methods of change. Each of these key words was independently cross-searched with the terms *language* and *reading*. Similarly, the four key words signifying change were cross-referenced with the terms *dyslexia*, *developmental dyslexia* and *specific language impairment*. The search was limited to articles that were written in English and published between 1993 and May of 2003. Any articles mentioning such conditions as mental retardation, autism, Turner's, Down's or any other developmental syndrome were omitted. The search resulted in 392 returns, of which sixty-five articles turned out to be review articles and, therefore, were not evaluated. In addition, from the remaining publications reporting empirical data, we excluded all articles that did not contain any reference to change occurring as an outcome of developmental processes or in response to an intervention. Specifically, 138 publications used cross-sectional rather than longitudinal analyses. Although cross-sectional methodologies are informative for understanding development, they are not, strictly speaking, designed to quantify change and, thus, are not in the focus of this chapter. Therefore, cross-sectional articles were excluded from the analysis. These elimination procedures limited the collection of articles for analyses to 189. Of these publications, thirty were deleted from our evaluation due to lack of clarity in describing the methodological procedures applied.

The purpose of this literature evaluation was two-fold. First, we wanted to survey the field in order to provide an adequate review of the methodologies of quantifying change. Second, we wanted to have at least an estimate – even if such an estimate might be biased, since we did not screen book chapters and dissertations – of the 'popularity', as defined by frequency of use, of different methodologies by simply establishing the percentage of usage of a given methodology. A review of methodologies used in the final set of 159 articles resulted in clustering the publications in five major groups of studies utilizing (1) difference scores; (2) techniques describing unsolicited change; (3) growth curves; (4) case analyses; and (5) dynamic systems methodologies. Figure 10.1

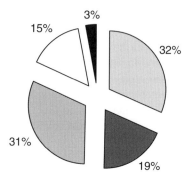

□Case methodologies ■Unsolicited change □Intervention-based change
□Growth curves   ■Dynamic systems

Figure 10.1. Proportional representation of dominant analysis types in the surveyed publications (1993–2003).

illustrates the proportions of these methodologies in the surveyed literature. Consequently, we structured our review around these methodologies. We start, however, with a brief account of the types of change identified in the literature.

Types of change

The concept of *change* is as old as or older than psychology itself. The first debates on the nature and importance of change for understanding humans and the world around them can be traced to the Ancient Greeks Heraklitos and Parmenides. Whereas Heraklitos viewed change as a ubiquitous phenomenon and held that nothing is ever the same (stable), Parmenides argued that stability is the foundation of the world and that change is only perceived, and therefore an illusion. Remarkably, although many theories of change and stability have been developed since, the bottom line of the argument is still not resolved, with the distinction between change and stability being one of the fundamental puzzles of human development (Oyama 2000).

Although no classification of change is universally accepted, many researchers have attempted to describe systematically different types of change. For example, in his work on linear syllogistic reasoning, van Geert (1995) has discussed three parameters characterizing the general growth model of a skill. Specifically, he talks about (a) a growth parameter (i.e. the changing process); (b) the current state of the changing process (i.e. the at-the-moment degree of

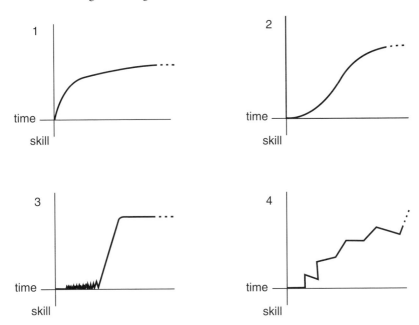

Figure 10.2. Types of change. Drawing by J. O'Keefe.

familiarity or mastery of the skill being acquired); and (c) a set of scaffolding factors immediately available to the child (i.e. motivational and instrumental factors the child has available to him or her in the process of the skill acquisition). Van Geert (1995) stated that various types of growth or change can be represented by combinations of these parameters. Here, following van Geert, we selectively present four types of growth that can be, at least in first approximation, captured by the parameters mentioned above – linear/nonlinear learning curves, S-shaped learning curves, saltatory growth, and stepwise growth (see Figure 10.2, 1–4).

The main assumption of the *linear/non-linear learning curve* is that of continuity of skill acquisition. The essence of this type of growth is that any future state of the skill is a function of the current state of the skill; thus, most skills improve with practice, along the dimension of acquiring competence in a domain (Figure 10.2, 1). Although this general assertion is preserved, what is really remarkable about this type of learning curve is that the initial pattern of rapid improvement is typically followed by lesser improvement with further practice. These curves are referred to as negatively accelerated learning curves; they are typically described by power functions. Based on the omnipresence of this type of learning in human development, 'the power law of practice' is said to be a ubiquitous characteristic of learning. The general learning curve is well described. The following parameters are referred to typically in specifications of learning curves: the range of learning (i.e. how far the initial performance is removed from the individual maximum), the trial number, and individual-specific learning rate parameters. It is fairly easy to see how these parameters map on the (a)–(c) parameters of van Geert. What is important for our discussion here is the statement that the change described by the linear/curvilinear learning curve is continuous. In this sense, it is not essential whether the change is linear (of which there are no examples in lifespan development) or non-linear; what is important is that the change is continuous and can be systematically described by a function depicting the rate of change depending on a given point on the change trajectory.

S-shaped learning curves, also referred to as logistic growth model curves, are, in a certain sense, derivatives of the learning curves described above and are also considered to be quite characteristic of a number of learning and developmental processes (Fischer and Rose 1994). The modification of the learning curve into the S-shaped curve results from the realization that the beginning stages of learning or trait acquisition might also occur at a rate different from the middle portion of the curve (see Figure 10.2, 2). Thus, S-shaped curves describe situations in which the learning in the middle of the process occurs at a much higher speed than at either the beginning or the end of the process.

Saltatory learning curves (see Figure 10.2, 3) depict situations when, after a prolonged beginning period of limited change, a rapid and substantial gain of skill occurs (e.g. van der Maas and Molenaar 1992). Saltatory curves are also characterized by a halt at some level of development, which is then specified as the maximum possible level of development for a given individual (or group). A well-studied example of saltatory growth is the mastery of the alphabet. Although there is a lot of intra-individual variation on how the alphabet is acquired by children, once it is mastered the maximum level of possible performance is reached.

Finally, *stepwise curves* assume the presence of random fluctuations in skill during skill acquisition (see Figure 10.2, 4). In other words, although there is a general tendency to excel developmentally, at any given time the curve can represent progress, regress, or halt in the mastery of a skill.

Clearly, although metaphorically these four types of changes can be described with the set of parameters presented by van Geert, each more complex curve requires more parameters to represent the curve. Moreover, if, as indicated above, the first type of curve, the linear/nonlinear curve, assumes continuity of development, the fourth type of curve allows for discontinuity. The more complex the shape of the curve, the harder it is to describe and, consequently, to quantify the change. What are the methods available to researchers interested in quantifying change?

Difference scores: old and new issues

The absolute majority of the publications that appeared in our search – less than 50 per cent – utilized different variants of the difference-scores methodologies, capturing solicited (i.e. provoked by intervention) and unsolicited (i.e. occurring in the course of typical development) change. Thus, here we review the description of this methodology and quantifying changes.

Conventional approaches to measuring change utilized primarily simple change scores, quantified as the difference between raw or standardized scores on pre- and post-tests. In other words, this type of change quantification is based on evaluating the differences across two or more occasions between measures obtained for one variable on a sample of individuals. Thus, the basic questions here are whether there is a change in the mean of the variable and, if so, whether the change is worthy of noting. To address these questions, roughly speaking, two general types of methodologies have been developed. One approach involves a situation where differences between two time measurements are calculated, in raw or standardized form; the magnitude of the difference is referred to as *gain score*. The second approach involves a collection of methodologies that takes into account multiple time measures, considering simultaneously in the analyses the initial and consequent points of measurement. This set of methodologies typically includes various types of analysis of variance and covariance. It is important to note that difference-score approaches are applied in two general contexts – when change is viewed as a result of deliberate intervention (i.e. a program that was designed to trigger a change) and when change is expected as an outcome of normally unfolding developmental processes (i.e. unsolicited change). Below we discuss a number of points relevant to conducting the difference-scores analyses in contexts of investigating both triggered and unsolicited change.

Simple difference scores

Multiple problems arise with the use of simple change scores (e.g. Bereiter 1963; Lord 1952; Schmitz 2001). These problems are due to (1) the apparent lack of reliability of gain scores as compared to reliability levels of the original variables; (2) the presence of ceiling effects in subgroups of a sample; (3) the disturbance of the equal-interval scale assumption encountered at the higher and lower ends of ability distributions with regard to the quantification of gain (e.g. high initial values tend to demonstrate little differences between multiple measurement occasions, thus producing negative correlations between initial status and change); and (4) regression to the mean (i.e. systematic biases originated by the tendency of extreme values for the first occasion to be followed by more average values for the second occasion.

The first and most apparent problem with gain scores is their lack of reliability. This conclusion was initially made by Lord (1952), based on the assumptions of classical test theory. Lord stated that when two imperfect scores are subtracted from each other, the resulting indicators would be even more imperfect. Even when the reliabilities of the first and second measures are medium or high, the reliability of the difference is low! Furthermore, the reliability of a gain score is substantially impacted by the relative standard deviations of the test in a given sample, the placement of the test on the ability distribution, the distribution of item difficulty in the test, and a number of other factors.

The second weakness of the gain scores is the presence of a ceiling effect due to learning that occurs between the two occasions of test administration. Clearly, when the test is administered for the first time, it is often more difficult because of its novelty than during its second administration, when it is more familiar. Thus, it is not unusual that the variation at the second testing occasion is suppressed. This suppression creates a number of problems for interpreting the meaning of gain scores. Thus, if a researcher is interested in working with gain scores, he or she would do well to insure that the pre-test is easy enough for lower-ability students to be differentiated (rather than to floor) and hard enough for the high-ability students not to be differentiated at the post-test (rather than to ceiling).

Third, the nature of the scale on which change is measured is not well understood. What has been clearly demonstrated, however, is that the units of change are not independent of the initial level of performance (i.e. measurement at first occasion). For example, it is a well-known observation that highly able individuals tend to demonstrate smaller gains. A quantitative interpretation of this observation refers to the introduction of a negative bias to the analyses of gain scores. By itself, this is not good, but it can be dealt with statistically. A qualitative interpretation of this observation, however, is more troublesome, because more than one explanation can account for the negative correlation between initial status and change for highly able individuals. The first possibility is that, given the initially high level of performance of highly able individuals at the pre-test, these individuals do not benefit from the intervention administered to the group in between pre-test and post-test. The second possibility is, however, that as a result of training, high-ability individuals tinker with their strategies, demonstrating more efficient and possibly quicker solutions. The third possibility is that high-ability individuals, by the time of the second testing, demonstrate lowered motivation or are bored with the test, which results in their lowered performance. Unfortunately, these three possibilities cannot be distinguished within the simple arithmetic gain-score paradigm of group data analyses. Of

the three problems discussed above, the third appears to be the most fundamental one. Apparently, this problem cannot be compensated for by means of
the classical test theory approach, but it can be addressed by means of modern
psychometric theories, specifically item response theory (IRT, Embretson and
Reise 2000; Hambleton, Swaminathan, and Rogers 1991; Hambleton and Slater
1997). IRT is a rapidly developing field of research, introduced to the field of
measurement in the early 1950s (Lord 1952), which initially gained popularity
in the 1960s, 1970s and 1980s (e.g. Lord 1980; Wright and Stone 1979), and
today is the major tool in test development (e.g. Embretson and Reise 2000;
Hambleton, Swaminathan, and Rogers 1991). There are also applications of
IRT developed for quantifying change (e.g. Embretson 1991).

Finally, another major factor to consider while working with gain scores is
the detrimental impact on regression to the mean on their interpretation and
understanding (e.g. Campbell and Kenny 1999). The problem is that, in order to
establish the presence and to quantify the impact of regression to the mean, one
usually needs to have more than two time points observing the performance
in the sample on a particular test. Clearly, the need to have more than two
time points challenges the very reason for using gain scores – they are easy
to compute and understand because they are based on only two observations,
and, if more than two observations are available, other methodologies can be
used that quantify change more reliably!

Much professional attention has been devoted to ways of compensating for
these weaknesses in change scores (e.g. Cohen and Cohen 1975; Cronbach and
Furby 1970; Rasch 1980), but none of the procedures that have been developed
have been universally accepted (e.g. Campbell and Kenny 1999; Embretson
1994, 1996; Rogosa 1995). Yet, it has been stated that gain scores can be used
to characterize differences in performance on two occasions (Schmitz 2001).
But in using gain scores, it is necessary to be aware of the criticisms of this
methodology.

Due, in part, to multiple warnings in the literature with regard to simple
difference scores, researchers today rarely use this methodology. In fact, in our
search of the literature, we have not observed a single publication that used
simple difference scores. Yet, given the purpose of this chapter, we thought that
the discussion of simple difference scores was warranted. Having done that,
we can move on to the discussion of the results of our literature search.

Quantifying triggered change: how do we know that an intervention worked?

As indicated above, a set of methodologies has been developed to take into
account simultaneously pre- and post-intervention scores (note that post-
intervention scores can be obtained more than once, right after the intervention).

A number of recent volumes offer excellent treatment of families of relevant methodologies (Campbell and Kenny 1999; Cohen, Cohen, West and Aiken 2003; Moskowitz and Hershberger 2002; Reise and Duan 2003), so here we limit our discussion only to the summary of our literature search.

In the reviewed publications, we encountered a number of methodologies used to quantify the change occurring as a result of an intervention of some kind. The majority of the studies (Benson et al. 1997; Blachman et al. 1999; Berninger et al. 1999, 2000; Chambers et al. 1998; Chera and Wood 2003; Churches et al. 2002; Das et al. 1995; Dryer et al. 1993; Elkind et al. 1993; Facoetti et al. 2003; Gillon 2000, 2002; Goldstein and Obrzut 2001; Greaney et al. 1997; Greenway 2002; Guyer et al. 1993; Habib et al. 2002; Hart et al. 1997; Hatcher 2000; Hatcher, Hulme and Ellis 1994; Hecht and Close 2002; Ho et al. 2001; Lovett and Steinbach 1997; Lovett et al. 2000; Lundberg 1995; McCarthy et al. 1995; Morris et al. 2000; Nelson et al. 1996; Oakland et al. 1998; O'Shaughnessy and Swanson 2000; Pogorzelski and Wheldall 2002; Poskiparta et al. 1999; Post et al. 2001; Schneider et al. 1997, 1999, 2000; Uhry and Shepherd 1997; Vadasy et al. 2002; van Daal and Reitsma 1999; Wheldall 2000) used the traditional pre-/post-test intervention design, with some studies reporting multiple follow-up points and both immediate and delayed effects of intervention (e.g. Blachman et al. 1999; Gillon 2002; McCarthy et al. 1995; Schneider et al. 1997, 1999, 2000) and performance on transfer tasks (e.g. Benson et al. 1997).

With regard to incorporating both pre- and post-test data, three approaches were dominant – one using repeated analysis of variance including time and group variables as factors in the analysis (e.g. O'Shaughnessy and Swanson 2000; Uhry and Shepherd 1997), one covarying the pre-test scores using analysis of variance for group comparison (e.g. Chambers et al. 1998), and one using paired t-tests (e.g. Bouldoukian et al. 2002). There also were studies in which, although reported, the performance at the baseline was not controlled for (e.g. Churches et al. 2002). The majority of the studies contained a no-treatment control group, but there were studies comparing effectiveness of various treatments (e.g. Berninger et al. 1999, 2000; Dryer et al. 1993; Goldstein and Obrzut 2001; Graham and Wong 1993; Greaney et al. 1997; Hatcher, Hulme, and Ellis 1994; Lovett and Steinbach 1997; Lovett et al. 2000; Nelson et al. 1996; Post et al. 2001; Schneider et al. 2000; van Strien et al. 1995), effectiveness of the same treatment for various groups (e.g. Hatcher 2000; Schneider et al. 1999; van Daal and Reitsma 1999), or added effectiveness of programs administered consecutively (e.g. Vadasy et al. 2002). Some studies reported only pre- to post-test differences, without using control groups (e.g. Greenway 2002; Uhry and Shepherd 1997).

In addition, a number of researchers used the criterion-based approach, where training was administered until the a-priori criterion was reached (in such cases the change was quantified as the number of sessions necessary to master the criterion – e.g. Camarata, Nelson and Camarata 1994) or training was administered for a certain duration and the percentage of responses or participants reaching the criterion was presented (e.g. Stone and Connell 1993; Swisher et al. 1995).

Finally, a number of publications, in addition to tracking change, explored physiological correlates/causes of the observed psychological change (e.g. Richards et al. 2000, 2002; Simos et al. 2002; Stein, Richardson and Fowler 2000).

Clearly, a variety of methodologies are used to quantify change in response to an intervention or multiple interventions. In completing this section on the analysis of change scores in response to intervention, we want to comment on issues of summative interpretations of indicators of change. Since we systematically reviewed the literature in two developmental domains, language and reading, we encountered a number of studies in which the same outcome variables (e.g. reading comprehension) were targeted through a variety of interventions (e.g. word-level versus sub-word-level interventions). Not surprisingly, the reports presented a variety of outcomes. In the context of interpreting and discussing difference-scores techniques, we would like to mention the methodology of meta-analysis – a way to summarize data from a number of diverse intervention studies in an attempt to describe a 'meta-change'. Here we provide a brief illustration of meta-analyses using a portion of the data we encountered in our literature search. Again, there are a number of recent publications presenting technical foundations (Arthur, Bennet and Huffcutt 2001; Lipsey and Wilson 2001) and illustrations (e.g. Swanson 1999) of meta-analysis.

In our illustrative mini-meta-analysis, we identified all publications that used educational interventions in an attempt to enhance reading comprehension. The data in these publications were reported in a variety of ways ranging from means and standard deviations at pre- and post-tests (a number of publications presented delayed follow-up evaluations as well) to inferential statistics (e.g. t- and F-tests). The data were uniformly converted into d-statistics (standard difference). In addition, the studies were coded for the following variables: (1) type of target population (typically developing children, children at-risk for academic failure, and children with special academic needs); (2) type of study (studies registering comparative gains in the intervention and control groups or studies registering change from pre- to post-test); and (3) type of outcome (immediate versus delayed). The combined sample included thirteen studies and 1086 participants (Chambers et al. 1998; Dryer et al. 1993; Elkind et al. 1993; Gillon 2000; Goldstein and Obrzut 2001; Graham and Wong 1993; Greenway 2002; Hatcher et al. 1994; Lovett et al. 2000; Morris 2000; O'Shaughnessy et al. 2000; Schneider et al. 2000; Wheldall 2000). The outcomes of the studies were not uniform with standardized differences ranging from −0.083 to 1.60.

In conducting these summary analyses, we wanted to ask three questions. First, we wanted to estimate the degree of modifiability of comprehension skills in response to *any* kind of intervention. Second, we were interested in a comparison of the effect size of change across different groups of participants involved in the reviewed intervention studies. Finally, we were interested in the impact of intervention on the immediate versus delayed performance. Correspondingly, three types of meta-analyses were carried out. First, we explored the effects of targeted intervention on reading comprehension. Whether quantified in a controlled experimental design involving multiple intervention groups or in a quasi-experimental pre-/post-test design, the triggered change was statistically significant ($d = 0.362$, $Z = 4.704$, $p < 0.001$ and $d = 0.808$, $Z = 4.81$, $p < 0.001$) for controlled and quasi-experiments, respectively). However, interesting moderator effects were identified in this meta-analysis. Apparently, the interventions were much more effective for children with special needs and at-risk children than for typical readers. Finally, the effect size estimated immediately after the intervention was substantial and greatly exceeded the effect size estimated with a time delay ($d = 0.439$, $Z = 6.28$, $p < 0.001$ and $d = 0.038$, $Z = 0.502$, $p > 0.1$ for immediate and delayed outcomes, respectively). Thus, meta-analytic approaches are extremely helpful in deriving summative estimates of change from a number of studies and stratifying these estimates for subsamples and subconditions in which the change occurs.

Quantifying unsolicited change: observing natural development

A large portion (24) of the screened papers reported unsolicited developmental changes (i.e. changes not caused by experimental manipulations originated by the experimenter) in various language- and reading-related psychological processes. Methodology-wise, these articles were heterogeneous, not illustrating, in particular, any specific statistical approach, but providing a glance at the types and distributions of the techniques utilized in the attempt to describe and quantify self-occurring developmental changes.

The champion analytical methodology is that of analysis of variance, both univariate and multivariate. These techniques were employed in thirteen publications surveyed (Fazio, Naremore and Connell 1996; Hadley 1998; Hadley and Rice 1996; Johnston et al. 2001; Joseph et al. 2002; Lyytinen et al. 2001, 2003; Manis et al. 1993; Pennington and Lefly 2001; Snowling et al. 1996; 2000; Sprenger-Charolles et al. 2000; Viholainen et al. 2002), with the majority of publications employing the repeated measures analysis of variance (Fazio, Naremore and Connell 1996; Hadley 1998; Hadley and Rice 1996; Johnston et al. 2001; Joseph et al. 2002; Lyytinen et al. 2001, 2003; Manis et al. 1993; Pennington and Lefly 2001; Snowling et al. 1996; Viholainen et al. 2002).

In addition, there were applications where the follow-up performance was evaluated with other techniques suitable for analysis of change (e.g. Mann-Whitney test, Korhonen 1995; paired t-test, Boulet et al. 1998; Pharr et al. 2000; Rescorla and Roberts 2002; Rescorla 2000, 2002).

One of the most commonly encountered methodological tasks in this set of publications is that of predicting the future status of the variable of interest based on the same outcome variable as measured at the baseline (e.g. predicting reading comprehension in Grade 5 based on reading comprehension in Grade 2) or on a set of related variables, which themselves predict the outcome variable both concurrently and longitudinally. There, if the outcome variable was continuous, the analytical technique used the most for this type of task was that of linear regression. In studying the relevant literature we found both use of theory-driven, hierarchical regression (e.g. Gallagher, Frith and Snowling 2000; Lyytinen et al. 2001; Manis and Custodio 1993; McGee et al. 2002; Mirak and Rescorla 1998; Rescorla 2002; Wessling and Reitsma 2001) and data-driven, stepwise regression (e.g. Fazio, Naremore and Connell 1996) approaches. We also found examples of simultaneous regression (Lewis et al. 2000; Olofsson and Niedersoe 1999). A number of studies utilized methodologies of path analyses (Olofsson and Niedersoe 1999) and structural equation modelling (Laakso et al. 1999). If the outcome variable was categorical (e.g. whether the child is diagnosable with developmental dyslexia in Grade 2 based on some measure collected in kindergarten), then authors used logistic regression (e.g. Gallagher, Frith and Snowling 2000).

Another oft-observed application, which, in essence, is an extension of the prediction application above, was that of prediction of group membership (i.e. whether the child is diagnosable with the same condition, non-condition, or some other condition) at the follow-up, given the membership in a certain group at baseline (e.g. being diagnosed with Specific Language Impairment, SLI). Two preferred techniques are used in establishing group membership based on developmental data – logistic regression and discriminant analyses (e.g. Hurford et al. 1993, 1994, 2002; Pennington and Lefly 2001). These applications included both predicting membership at follow-up time(s) based on relevant indicators at baseline (e.g. Hurford et al. 1993, 1994, 2002; Pennington and Lefly 2001; Snowling et al. 2000), and predicting change in the group membership from baseline to follow-up (Manis et al. 1999).

Finally, we encountered a number of studies that used developmental frequency analyses (e.g. changes in percentage of certain types of linguistic errors over time). The majority of these publications presented the data in forms of percentages and frequencies and carried out qualitative analyses of these data (Hadley and Rice 1996; Joseph et al. 2002; Rescorla and Roberts 2002).

In addition to the articles mentioned above, yet another good source of examples of capturing change in the context of unsolicited (e.g. normal) development is a collection of essays describing major longitudinal studies in the United States (Phelps, Furstenberg and Colby 2002).

Case studies

A substantial number of articles (50) reported change data from individual cases; these data were collected either in the process of unfolding developmental change (e.g. Anderson 1999; Cipriani et al. 1998; Eyer and Leonard 1995) or as an outcome of intervention (e.g. Berninger 2000; Brooks 1995; Brunsdon et al. 2002; Butler et al. 2000; Daly and Martens 1994; Hillis 1993; Louis et al. 2001; Miller and Felton 2001; Ottem 2001; Peach 2002; Silliman et al. 2000; Yampolsky and Waters 2002). Not surprisingly, a variety of analytical approaches were used to summarize and present these data. Arguably, all modes of quantifying change described in this chapter can be applied to analysing case study data; what matters for the choice of an analytical approach is the number and frequency of measurements. Among the evaluated publications, many researchers used presentation of assessment data before, during and after the intervention (Butler et al. 2000; Daly and Martens 1994; Daly et al. 2002; Miller and Felton 2001; Ottem 2001; Yampolsky and Waters 2002) or at various stages of longitudinal evaluation (e.g. Cipriani et al. 1998), and graphical representations of change in time (e.g. Anderson 1999; Brooks 1995; Daly and Martens 1994; Daly et al. 2002; Hillis 1993; Louis et al. 2001; Peach 2002; Yampolsky and Waters 2002). Furthermore, in a number of publications, the change was captured through tracking performance on individual items (i.e. treating items as observational units). In this regard, a number of analytic techniques assessing change categorically are relevant; specifically, logistic regression (e.g. Brunsdon et al. 2002), contingency tables analyses (e.g. Brunsdon et al. 2002; Louis et al. 2001; Yampolsky and Waters 2002) and repeated measures analysis of variance (Louis et al. 2001) can be utilized for the analysis of change. Researchers also analyse differences in quality and quantity of errors prior to and after intervention (e.g. Brunsdon et al. 2002; Hillis 1993). Finally, much attention is given to qualitative analyses of change (e.g. Anderson 1999; Berninger 2000; Eyer and Leonard 1995; Silliman et al. 2000).

Although we have not encountered a realization of the so-called person-oriented longitudinal statistical analysis in our review, we find it necessary to mention this approach here. This type of analysis addresses changes at the individual level by using configural statistical analyses and latent transition analyses, especially relevant to applications dealing with individual and small-group data and for studying short-term development (for review, see Bergman, Magnusson and El-Khouri 2003).

As apparent from this brief summary, a variety of methodologies are used for quantifying change, both solicited (arising in response to intervention), and unsolicited (attributable to the normal course of development). What is characteristic of the studies described above is that the majority of them used a two-timepoint design; some of the presented studies dealt with more than two points, but treated these additional time points as delayed outcomes rather than points on time trajectories. Below we present a number of methodologies utilized for analyses of change through multiple time points.

Growth curves

When there are more than two points in a timeframe within which change is evaluated, growth-curve analyses are often utilized. The logic of growth-curve modelling is, maybe surprisingly so, quite similar to that of the difference scores. Although, initially, the term *growth curve* simply referred to a graphical representation of change over time (e.g. changes in height across years from birth in an individual as compared to the group mean, Scammon 1927), now, commonly, growth curve models are referred to as slopes-as-outcomes models, and this reference reveals the meaning of these models. In other words, growth curve models are designed to measure the rate of change, just as the difference-scores approaches are, but they do so much more reliably than the gain-scores models because they are able to incorporate multiple repeated measures minimizing the measurement error. It is fair to say that growth curves, within the last 20 to 30 years, have gained sufficient popularity and now appear to be one of the most widely studied and applied analytical techniques (McArdle 2001).

However, this popularity of the growth curve methodologies creates a certain terminological confusion. Specifically, in this chapter, when we presented theoretical models of change, we also used the term *growth curves*. Just in the paragraph above, we implied that any graphical representation of the change in a trait over time could be considered a growth curve. Finally, below, we briefly summarize various statistical methodologies referred to as growth curve analyses. This multiplicity of the meaning of the term *growth curve*, although unfortunate, is inevitable. Thus, it is important to keep the context of the discussion in mind when talking about growth curves.

In addition to the brief summary of types of theoretical growth curves developed to capture different types of change, one more piece of theory needs to be introduced prior to the following discussion of growth curve methodologies of statistical analyses. This piece of theory relates to two fundamental concepts of change – absolute and normative change and/or stability (Baltes et al. 1977). Normative stability or change is defined exclusively at the group level and relates to the concept of developmental stage. Here what matter are the milestones of development established for humanity as a whole or its particular subgroup (culture, nation, tribe and so on). Absolute stability or change can be defined at both the individual and group levels. In its limit, absolute stability at the individual level assumes a lack of any fluctuation on a trait between different occasions of the trait measurement. Absolute stability at the group level assumes a lack of fluctuation of the group mean between different measurement occasions. To appreciate the relevance of this theoretical distinction to our discussion, consider the graphical representation of growth curves produced by Scammon (1927) – he plotted absolute change at the individual level against normative change at the group level.

In the majority of studies of change (especially in developmental psychology), it is typically assumed that all members in a sample of interest change in correspondence with some underlying common trajectory (i.e. in reference to normative change or stability), but each participant might follow this trajectory with specific deviations. For example, for a typical sample of seven-year-olds, during the period of reading acquisition it is assumed that reading will be mastered; what is of interest is individual variation in the mastery of the skill.

Following McArdle (2001), in this brief review of relevant issues in growth curve analyses, we structure the discussion below along the following three types of growth curves: (1) linear models, (2) non-linear models, and (3) multivariate growth curves.

Linear models

The essence of these types of models is in the assumption that a simple straight line can be fitted into a set of measurements. If, however, various nonlinear curvatures occur, then a small set of power polynomials could be used to describe them. Under this type of modelling, each individual is assumed to demonstrate the trajectory of the skill acquisition that resembles a straight line, which can be characterized by the intercept and slope. These individual growth curves can be averaged to represent the group growth curve. If curvatures are observed, then they can be characterized by higher-order parameters (e.g. acceleration), and these parameters can also be characterized at individual and group levels. The main idea here is that, for individual differences in growth to be captured and characterized accurately, individual data should be collected within some normative samples (e.g. a bunch of seven-year-olds mastering reading). An example of differentiating individual and group data comes from the work on the vocabulary growth in a normative sample of two-year-olds: the individual growth curves in this study inexorably demonstrated upward curvature (acceleration), but showed many individual differences in the rate of change (velocity) (Huttenlocher, Haight, Bryk and Seltzer 1991).

The relevant simplicity of this approach resulted in its widespread applications. However, like any approach, this approach has a number of weak points. Among these are difficulties associated with (1) estimations of individual parameters, especially for higher-order terms and incomplete data; (2) inability of even higher-order polynomials to capture complex developmental shifts; (3) lack of interpretability of many individual parameters; and (4) instability of meaning of individual parameters (McArdle 2001). There are a number of attempts in the field to respond to these criticisms and yet preserve the simplicity of linear modelling. Such attempts refer to ideas of dividing the development into phases or stages connected by critical points, where the dynamics of development changes its course (e.g. Bryk and Raudenbush 1992), or whether introducing a way to reorganize the observed data through finding some 'latent curves' driving the measurements (e.g. Meredith and Tisak 1990).

Nonlinear models

The psychological literature contains many examples of nonlinear growth (e.g. Bock and Thissen 1980; Seber and Wild 1989; Zeger and Harlow 1987). The main thrust behind nonlinear application of growth curve modelling is the attempt to model observations over a wide range of normative groups (e.g. different ages or different life periods), minimizing the number of parameters in the model. These types of models are referred to as composite models because they are based on multiple functions, each of which describes a specific part of the modelled growth process (e.g. Bock and Thissen 1980; Hauspie et al. 1991; Preece and Baines 1978). However, the interpretation of the fits of alternative models and individual parameters still remains a challenge (e.g. Browne and du Toit 1991).

Multivariate models

Relatively few applications illustrating analysis of multiple variables using growth curves are available in developmental psychology. However, a number of recent examples are of great importance to this emerging field. For example, McArdle and Woodcock (1997) demonstrated, using data on multiple cognitive abilities, that a model conceptualized as a latent growth model of a single factor provides a poor fit for the data. To develop a methodology allowing developmental explorations of a multivariate system, McArdle (2001) suggested an application of structural equation modelling. Muthén et al. (2003) provide yet another example illustrating how sets of reading-development-related variables can be modelled by means of growth mixture modelling. What is especially interesting in this application is the capacity of the model to handle different observed variables collected at different times by linking them to sequential pathways of reading development; specifically, in this application, multiple measures of word recognition in Grade 1 are predicted by multiple measures of phonemic awareness in kindergarten.

Current methodological work is resulting in the development of increasingly sophisticated growth curves, encompassing both the models' general (Seber and Wild 1989) and specific (e.g. Sayer and Cumsille 2001) aspects. The sophistication relates to multiple levels of hierarchy (Raudenbush 2001), dealing with unbalanced, incomplete or missing data (Bryk and Raudenbush 1992; Pinherio and Bates 2000; Verbeke and Molenberghs 2000), and attempting to capture the possible discontinuity of growth (Osgood 2001; Rovine and Molenaar 2001). Thus, growth curve modelling approaches have strong representation in theoretical literature. What about empirical literature?

Our literature search resulted in identifying twenty-four studies using growth curve approaches. Two of these studies (Aro et al. 1999; Hick et al. 2002) used the graphical variant of growth curve approaches, meaning that they graphed individual trajectories on children across time. Twenty-two articles utilized different statistical approaches to growth curve analyses; the majority of these models were univariate growth curve models; both linear (e.g. Tressoldi et al. 2001) and non-linear (e.g. Kemper, Rice and Chen 1995) models were fitted. All articles presented group data, with the exception of one that analysed changes in performance of a single boy (Robinson and Mervis 1999). Based on the research questions answering which growth curve analyses were implemented, these publications can be divided into three groups.

The first group of papers ($N = 6$) used growth curve analyses for the purposes of determining the impact of a given intervention. The central question here is whether, in response to intervention, children show more growth than is expected by chance (e.g. Abbott et al. 1997; Campbell et al. 2001; Stage et al. 2003). Similarly, often the question of interest is the one comparing the growth in different groups subjected to different interventions (Abbott and Berninger 1999; Foorman et al. 1997; Kappers 1997). To obtain answers to these questions, group statistics (e.g. the slope of the group curve) are analysed. Moreover, the analyses of group curves are helpful in understanding the role of other mediating or moderating variables (Foorman et al. 1997). In addition, a number of other conclusions can be derived from the analyses of individual curves. For example, in analysing slopes of individual growth curves, authors engaged in the discussion of who did and did not gain from the intervention and why (Abbott et al. 1997; Abbott and Berninger 1999; Kappers 1997) and what third factors, other than baseline performance and the type of intervention, influence the gain (Foorman et al. 1997; Kappers 1997). A number of researchers reported that the best fits were the models obtained when higher-order polynomial terms were included (e.g. Campbell et al. 2001). Some researchers found that the linear models were not adequate for the representation of growth rate across larger chunks of lifespan; multiple curves needed to be fitted to accommodate the data (e.g. Campbell et al. 2001).

The second group of articles ($N = 10$) employed growth curve analyses to investigate unsolicited changes across time (Burchinal et al. 2002; Flowers et al. 2000; Francis et al. 1996; Jacobson 1999; Landry et al. 1997; Meyer et al. 1998; Rescorla, Mirak and Singh 2000; Rice et al. 1998, 2000; Shaywitz et al. 1999) or for program evaluation, where all students were provided with a curriculum (e.g. Stage 2001). Typical research questions in these studies had to do with identification of third variables (demographic-, ability-, personality-based) that somehow impacted or differentiated developmental pathways of interest. Similarly to the group of papers above, group and individual growth curves were analysed. A number of studies (e.g. Burchinal et al. 2002; Flowers et al. 2000; Francis et al. 1996; Landry et al. 1997; Meyer et al. 1998) utilized multi-level models, investigating associations between variables collected within nested designs. Similarly, a number of papers included higher-order polynomial terms (Burchinal et al. 2002; Francis et al. 1996; Landry et al. 1997; Rescorla, Mirak and Singh 2000; Rice et al. 1998, 2000; Shaywitz et al. 1999). Some researchers used growth curve modelling to verify various theoretical developmental models (Francis et al. 1996; Jacobson 1999).

We found only one study (Compton 2000) that combined the first and second types of growth curve modelling by using the data obtained from modelling unsolicited change to divide the sample of children into subgroups so that the outcome of intervention was maximized; consequently, the interventions themselves were modelled with growth curve approaches.

In sum, growth curves are well represented in both theoretical and empirical literature dealing with change.

Time series

Collectively, approaches utilizing many measurement points distributed in time are referred to as time-series approaches. But how many is enough? The rule of thumb is at least twenty. Fifty is better. Whereas fifty and more time measures are typical for specific branches in psychology (e.g. psychophysiology), they are not seen as often in developmental psychology. Clearly, both difference-scores approaches (when only two points in time are used) and growth curve methodologies are variants of time series with a limited number of observations.

Time-series approaches exist in an overwhelming variety of shapes and forms (Brillinger 2001). They are used for purposes of describing sequential data, estimating various parameters with the goal of generating a stochastic model capturing the dynamic of the time series, and identifying the system behind the sequential data. One other special case of general time-series approaches is chaos modelling (e.g. Alligood et al. 1997). The distinct feature of chaos models is their sensitive dependence upon initial condition, but the dependence is such that the generated time paths appear to be random (Brock 2001). If all parameters of the system are within their pre-determined limits, the system converges to homeostasis. However, a slight violation of parameter limitations can result in the system's manifestation of chaotic behaviours.

Time-series models constructed for a single variable are characterized by trend and rhythm. The indicator of trend shows the nature of change of quantity associated with the variable of interest across time (e.g. a variable demonstrates a linear trend if the increase from one measurement occasion to the next is constant). The indicators of rhythm capture the periodicity of the change in the variable (e.g. the amount of office noise is usually higher during work days and lower during weekends). If models contain more than one variable changing in time, these time series can be characterized by synchronicity of the relationships between variables (e.g. typically the development of reading skill and vocabulary are synchronous, but in cases of specific reading disabilities, the development of these skills is desynchronized). The majority of time-series applications deal with data stretched in time on the same scale structured by a time-like parameter (for a review, see Brillinger 2001). However, the assumption of interval is not crucial for time series. For example, Markov approaches allow the modelling of data in which the assumptions of interval data are not realized (e.g. Gottman and Roy 1990).

Like other sciences dealing with issues of change over time, developmental and education psychology are gradually incorporating various ideas generated by theories addressing sequential data (for a review, see Collins and Sayer 2001). In the context of this chapter, we will review briefly only one general methodological approach encountered in our literature search – that of dynamic systems.

Boker (2001) distinguishes growth curve models and dynamic systems models by stating that the former models generate predictions regarding a single trajectory of central tendency (referred to as the attractor, a single point) whereas the latter models generate predictions regarding multiple trajectories (referred to as a basin of attraction, a vector field plot). If the growth curve models use multiple measurements as a way to characterize the entire curve, the dynamic systems models use multiple measurements to hypothesize and verify hidden patterns characteristic of a system changing in time. In doing so, the dynamic systems models rely on the current value at any particular point in the curve and its first derivative (the rate of change or the velocity) to predict the second derivative of any particular point (the acceleration) (Piccinin 2001).

The technique used for these types of analyses is referred to as differential structural equation modelling (Boker 2001; Piccinin 2001). Although a new and exciting direction, differential structural equation modelling (dSEM) has some theoretical and practical problems that need to be addressed both theoretically and empirically (Piccinin 2001). Specifically, little is known about the validity of assumptions central to dSEM, such as the homogeneity of shape of attractor basin across individuals and variability in the estimates of first- and second-order derivatives within and across individuals. Similarly, there are no certain answers to questions such as how many measurement points are needed, how they should be spaced in time, and for what psychological processes these models are of use.

Although the dynamic system theory (also referred to as systems theory) is gaining popularity in the developmental literature, very few studies have utilized the applied methodologies developed on this theory's basis (e.g. Gogate and Walker-Andrews 2001; Thelen 1989; Thelen and Smith 1994). A special interest in the dynamic systems approaches in psychology is attributable, in part, to the realization made in a large body of developmental literature that states that development, largely, is discontinuous (e.g. van Geert 1997; Pascual-Leone and Baillargeon 1994) and includes abrupt changes, stabilizations and non-linear and linear gains and losses (e.g. Wimmers, Beek, Savelsbergh and Hopkins 1998). Yet, the demands of data collection (many data points are needed) and data analyses (rather sophisticated data-analytical approaches are utilized) prevent, at this point, these methodologies from wide-scale adoption.

Dynamic systems models operate under the general assumption that under what are mostly stable pressures of independent variables, including biological foundations such as genetic makeup, or environmental context such as educational patterns or SES, dependent variables (cognitive, behavioural, and social–emotional variables) can attain relatively stable states (attractors). Attractors can change suddenly, however, with changes to independent variables. For our purposes, that is to say, if the relative stability of reading-acquisition skill is challenged by an appropriate intervention, the reading-acquisition skill could fall apart, or be transformed into a different (higher-order) skill in a discontinuous manner. Methodologies based on nonlinear dynamic systems claim well-defined ways to establish linkages between changes in independent variables and changes in attractors.

Let us return to van Geert (1997) for an illustration. In syllogistic reasoning there supposedly exists a method of constructing syllogisms that combines previous outputs of reasoning development (a child's ability to form a conjunction with the logical operator *and*) with an external intervention (instruction on how to solve linear syllogisms). An adequate intervention would transfer the first stage of reasoning development into a new stage of reasoning development (knowing how to solve linear syllogisms). According to the dynamic systems approach, such a transformation could be of a discontinuous nature. After the skill has been mastered, however, each subsequent intervention would strengthen the reasoning but would keep it within the attractor stage, thus safeguarding the principle of finding the solution to a syllogism task. Van Geert provides yet another example of a dynamic systems model, the so-called Verhulst model (van Geert 1991, 1993, 1994), which has been explored primarily in the domain of language development (Ruhland and van Geert 1998). In this model, a variable called the 'grower' (whose change in time can be observed) departs from an arbitrary level (or 'seed'), and grows (increases or decreases) to reach a state of equilibrium (which in turn can change as an outcome of some disturbance).

While the dynamic systems approach continues to gain a modicum of popularity, it is still a minor player in the developmental psychology literature. One such example of a dynamic model is Thelen and Smith's dynamic model of motor development (1994, 1997). Another example of a dynamic systems approach is linked to the model of transition in catastrophe theory (Thom 1975), the mathematical theory that allows the detection of phase shifts in dynamic systems (i.e. a system in which time-based change is inherent). Eight mathematically defined indicators define the catastrophe (or transformation) stage of a dynamic system (Gilmore 1981; van der Maas and Molenaar 1992). Certain of these indicators (bimodality of the trait distribution, inaccessibility of the skill, sudden jump, anomalous variance, and critical slowing down) have been studied in the context of developmental research (e.g. the development of analogical reasoning, Hosenfeld, van der Maas and van den Boom 1997b and the conservation research, Hartelman et al. 1998).

Although the number of specific applications of the models described above is somewhat limited in psychological literature, researchers (Hosenfeld, van der Maas and van den Boom 1997a; Thomas 1989; Thomas and Lohaus 1993; Thomas and Turner 1991) have had success in locating several indicators of bimodality (separating those who have and have not mastered the skills) in developmental data in performance on tasks such as conservation, classification, the understanding of horizontality and verticality, and analogical reasoning. The presence of bimodality stresses the importance of taking non-linearity of development into account.

Currently, assumptions of linearity form the basis of most testing models (and corresponding data-analytic procedures) – that is, most models suppose that any effect is proportional to the magnitude of the input of some controlling variables (the better the intervention, the better the outcome). However, numerous reported observations have shown that interventions lead to proportional effects only up to a certain point (or starting from a certain point). When (or before) a certain threshold is reached, however, the impact of the intervention may change both qualitatively and quantitatively. And here is the point most relevant to our discussion: non-linear effects of intervention and the nonlinear nature of parameters are often ignored in the context of traditional group-difference-based approaches to quantifying change. For example, van der Maas and Molenaar (1992) discuss the possibility that the impact of standardized training might be especially substantial for those children who are close to the acquisition of the skill, but very small for those children who are far away from mastery of the skill. Specifically, if the distance to the 'mastery point' is short, it is possible for interventions to successfully introduce the necessary dynamics into the system (instability, expressed as increased variability in performance, in terms of van der Maas and Molenaar 1992) to insure transition to mastery.

Moreover, non-linear dynamic systems can be used to model the impact of an intervention where complex dynamic forms can be realized from relatively simple equations (Glass and Mackey 1988; Newell and Molenaar 1998; Robinson and Mervis 1998). Here, the identification of relevant developmental variables that might act as critical variables in the shaping of system dynamics over time is a primary goal. Two assumptions underlie these analyses: (1) the mastery of a skill is the product of the coalescence of numerous constraints to action imposed by critical variables (e.g. Newell and Molenaar 1998); (2) large-scale qualitative changes in emerging skills can result from small qualitative changes in critical variables; and (3) the stability-transformation dynamics of the emergence and the transformation of skills are linked to the interplay between sets of cooperating and competing critical variables. Researchers constantly work on the development, realization and application of newly developed methodologies (e.g. van Geert and van Dijk 2002).

Concluding thoughts

In this chapter, we briefly reviewed major methodologies currently applied in the fields of developmental and educational psychology for the quantification of change. We started by describing types of change distinguishable theoretically and proceeded with providing illustrations for methodologies available for quantification of change. Four different types of change were described; each type of change can be characterized by a different parameter set addressing the change's continuity–discontinuity, linearity–non-linearity, and rhythm of change. We stated that simpler models of change require fewer time points and use less sophisticated analytical procedures; the demand for great detail of measurement in time and the complexity of the analytic technique used correspondingly increases with the complexity of the modelled change. To illustrate this assertion, we structured the review with an empirical analysis of the citations generated in a systematic literature search within two domains of development – the acquisition of language and reading. The frequency analysis of the dominant methodologies in the encountered citations indicates that the most popular type of analysis is that of difference scores, followed by growth curves. The dynamic-system methodologies are still relatively infrequent in studies of change. Simpler analytical approaches are linked to more global interpretations of the data (e.g. whether the change occurred), whereas more sophisticated approaches are linked to the generation of complex models of development (e.g. what kind of change and under what conditions it occurred).

The main objective of this chapter was to evaluate the degree of 'penetration' of the methodological developments regarding measurements of change into the domain of presentation of empirical results obtained in educational and developmental psychology. As it appears from the observations described above, there are a limited number of applications of complex methodologies. There are multiple reasons for this situation. First, complex methodologies are designed to meet the needs of complex datasets. Such complex datasets are difficult to collect and require much time and personnel commitment; therefore, the number of illustrations of applications of such methodologies is limited by the lack of complex datasets suitable for these methodologies. In other words, the introduction of change from utilization of conventional data analytic strategies to capitalizing on novel analytic strategies requires a systemic change, allowing for time and effort in collecting the data structures suitable for novel methodologies.

Second, there are certain areas of developmental and educational psychology in which the 'call for' methodologies of dealing with change is comparatively greater than in others. Often, however, these areas are somewhat remote from mainstream fashionable areas of psychology. One such area is that of dynamic testing and assessment. The dynamic assessment approach, by its very meaning, implies quantification of change: in this paradigm what is typically looked at is the modification in performance between first and second administration of a test (or a testing item) occurring in response to an intervention. Yet, at this stage of its existence, dynamic testing is a methodology utilized primarily in clinical settings and with relatively small sample sizes (for a review, see Sternberg and Grigorenko 2002). There appears to be a disconnect between the theoretical thought on developing complex methods of quantification of change and the applied development of the field in which precise methods of quantification of change are most needed.

Third, we limited our review to publications on reading and language. Clearly, this is a limited selection of domains of development; as we pointed out earlier, the literature on motor development has more examples of the utilization of complex methodologies of change quantification. Thus, it is possible that the distribution of frequencies of different methodologies illustrated in Figure 10.1 will be different if other developmental domains are surveyed.

Finally, the reality of empirical research in the fields of developmental and educational psychology is such that it calls for a variety of methodologies applicable to different tasks, datasets, and contexts. In this chapter we attempted to illustrate how different methods of quantifying change can be applied in a variety of different situations and how and why it is important to take into consideration their respective strengths and weaknesses.

REFERENCES

Abbott, S. P. and Berninger, V. W. (1999). It's never too late to remediate: teaching word recognition to students with reading disabilities in grades 4–7. *Annals of Dyslexia, 49*, 223–50.

Abbott, S. P., Reed, E., Abbott, R. D. and Berninger, V. W. (1997). Year-long balanced reading/writing tutorial: a design experiment used for dynamic assessment. *Learning Disability Quarterly, 20*(3), 249–63.

Alligood, K. T., Sauer, T. D. and Yorke, J. A. (1997). *Chaos. An introduction to dynamic systems.* New York: Springer.

Anderson, R. (1999). Impact of first language loss on grammar in a bilingual child. *Communication Disorders Quarterly, 21*(1), 4–16.

Aro, M., Aro, T., Ahonen, T., Raesaenen, T., Hietala, A. and Lyytinen, H. (1999). The development of phonological abilities and their relation to reading acquisition: case studies of six Finnish children. *Journal of Learning Disabilities, 32*(5), 457–63, 478.

Arthur, W., Jr, Bennett, W., Jr and Huffcutt, A. I. (2001). *Conducting meta-analysis using SAS.* Mahwah, NJ: Erlbaum.

Baltes, P. B., Reese, H. W. and Nesselrode, J. R. (1997). *Life-span developmental psychology: introduction to research methods.* Monterey, CA: Brooks/Cole.

Benson, N. J., Lovett, M. W. and Kroeber, C. L. (1997). Training and transfer-of-learning effects in disabled and normal readers: evidence of specific deficits. *Journal of Experimental Child Psychology, 64*(3), 343–66.

Bereiter, C. (1963). Some persisting dilemmas in the measurement of change. In C. W. Harris (ed.) *Problems in measuring change* (pp. 3–20). Madison: University of Wisconsin Press.

Bergman, L. R., Magnusson, D. and El-Khouri, B. M. (2003). *Studying individual development in an interindividual context.* Mahwah, NJ: Erlbaum.

Berninger, V. W. (2000). Dyslexia the invisible, treatable disorder: the story of Enstein's ninja turtles. *Learning Disability Quarterly, 23*(3), 175–95.

Berninger, V. W., Abbott, R. D., Brooksher, R., Lemos, Z., Ogier, S., Zook, D. et al. (2000). A connectionist approach to making the predictability of English orthography explicit to at-risk beginning readers: evidence for alternative, effective strategies. *Developmental Neuropsychology, 17*(2), 241–71.

Berninger, V. W., Abbott, R. D., Zook, D., Ogier, S., Lemos-Britton, Z. and Brooksher, R. (1999). Early intervention for reading disabilities: teaching the alphabet principle in a connectionist framework. *Journal of Learning Disabilities, 32*(6), 491–503.

Blachman, B. A., Tangel, D. M., Ball, E. W., Black, R. and McGraw, C. K. (1999). Developing phonological awareness and word recognition skills: a two-year intervention with low-income, inner-city children. *Reading and Writing, 11*(3), 239–73.

Bock, R. D. and Thissen, D. (1980). Statistical problems of fitting individual growth curves. In F. E. Johnston, A. F. Roche, C. Susanne (eds.) *Human physical growth and maturation: methodologies and factors* (pp. 265–90). New York, NY: Plenum.

Boker, S. M. (2001). Differential structural equation modelling of intraindividual variability. In L. M. Collins and A. G. Sayer (eds.) *New methods for the analysis of change* (pp. 3–27). Washington, DC: APA.

Bouldoukian, J., Wilkins, A. J. and Evans, B. J. (2002). Randomised controlled trial of the effect of coloured overlays on the rate of reading of people with specific learning difficulties. *Ophthalmic and Physiological Optics, 22*(1), 55–60.

Boulet, D., Bryce, S., Bliss, L. S. and Linebaugh, C. (1998). Listener judgments of impaired narration at two age levels. *Journal of Children's Communication Development, 20*(1), 1–8.

Brillinger, D. R. (2001). Time series: general. In N. J. Smelser and P. B. Baltes (eds.) *Social and behavioral sciences* (vol. 23, pp. 15724–31). Amsterdam, Holland: Elsevier.

Brock, W. A. (2001). *Chaos theory*. In N. J. Smelser & P. B. Baltes (eds.) *International encyclopedia of the social and behavioral sciences* (pp. 1643–6). Amsterdam, Holland: Elsevier.

Brooks, P. (1995). A comparison of the effectiveness of different teaching strategies in teaching spelling to a student with severe specific difficulties/dyslexia. *Educational and Child Psychology, 12*(1), 80–8.

Browne, M. W. and Du Toit, S. H. C. (1991). Models for learning data. In L. M. Collins and J. L. Horn (eds.) *Best methods for the analysis of change* (pp. 47–68). Washington: American Psychological Association.

Brunsdon, R. K., Hannan, T. J., Coltheart, M. and Nickels, L. (2002). Treatment of lexical processing in mixed dyslexia: a case study. *Neuropsychological Rehabilitation, 12*(5), 385–418.

Bryk, A. and Raudenbush, S. (1992). *Hierarchical linear models in social and behavioral research: applications and data analysis methods*. Newbury Park, CA: Sage.

Burchinal, M. R., Peisner-Feinberg, E., Pianta, R. and Howes, C. (2002). Development of academic skills from preschool through second grade: family and classroom predictors of developmental trajectories. *Journal of School Psychology, 40*(5), 415–36.

Butler, D. L., Elaschuk, C. L. and Poole, S. (2000). Promoting strategic writing by postsecondary students with learning disabilities: a report of three case studies. *Learning Disability Quarterly, 23*(3), 196–213.

Camarata, S. M., Nelson, K. E. and Camarata, M. N. (1994). Comparison of conversational-recasting and imitative procedures for training grammatical structures in children with specific language impairment. *Journal of Speech and Hearing Research, 37*(6), 1414–23.

Campbell, D. T. and Kenny, D. A. (1999). *A primer on regression artifacts*. New York: Guilford Press.

Campbell, F. A., Pungello, E. P., Miller-Johnson, S., Burchinal, M. and Ramey, C. T. (2001). The development of cognitive and academic abilities: growth curves from an early childhood educational experiment. *Developmental Psychology, 37*(2), 231–42.

Chambers, B., Abrami, P. C., Massue, F. M. and Morrison, S. (1998). Success for all: evaluating an early-intervention program for children at risk of school failure. *Canadian Journal of Education, 23*(4), 357–72.

Chera, P. and Wood, C. (2003). Animated multimedia 'talking books' can promote phonological awareness in children beginning to read. *Learning and Instruction, 13*(1), 33–52.

Churches, M., Skuy, M. and Das, J. P. (2002). Identification and remediation of reading difficulties based on successive processing deficits and delay in general reading. *Psychological Reports, 91*(3, pt. 1), 813–24.

Cipriani, P., Bottari, P., Chilosi, A. M. and Pfanner, L. (1998). A longitudinal perspective on the study of specific language impairment: the long-term follow-up of an Italian child. *International Journal of Language and Communication Disorders, 33*(3), 245–80.

Cohen, J. and Cohen, P. (1975). *Applied multiple regression/correlation analysis for the behavioral sciences.* Hillsdale, NJ: Lawrence Erlbaum.

Cohen, J., Cohen, P., West, S. G. and Aiken, L. S. (2003). *Applied multiple regression/correlation analysis for the behavioral sciences.* Mahwah, NJ: Lawrence Erlbaum.

Collins, L. M. and Horn, J. L. (eds.) (1991). *Best methods for the analysis of change.* Washington, DC: American Psychological Association.

  (2001). *Best methods for the analysis of change.* Washington, DC: APA.

Collins, L. M. and Sayer, A. G. (eds.) (2001). *New methods for analysis of change.* Washington, DC: APA.

Compton, D. L. (2000). Modeling the response of normally achieving and at-risk first grade children to word reading instruction. *Annals of Dyslexia, 50,* 53–84.

Cronbach, L. and Furby, L. (1970). How should we measure change – or should we? *Psychological Bulletin, 74,* 68–70.

Daly, E. J. and Martens, B. K. (1994). A comparison of three interventions for increasing oral reading performance: application of the instructional hierarchy. *Journal of Applied Behavior Analysis, 27*(3), 459–69.

Daly, E. J., Murdoch, A., Lillenstein, L., Webber, L. and Lentz, F. E. (2002). An examination of methods for testing treatments: conducting brief experimental analyses of the effects of instructional components on oral reading fluency. *Education and Treatment of Children, 25*(3), 288–316.

Das, J. P., Mishra, R. K. and Pool, J. E. (1995). An experiment on cognitive remediation of word-reading difficulty. *Journal of Learning Disabilities, 28*(2), 66–79.

Dryer, R., Beale, I. L. and Lambert, A. J. (1993). The balance model of dyslexia and remedial training: an evaluative study. *Journal of Learning Disabilities, 32*(2), 174–86.

Elkind, J., Cohen, K. and Murray, C. (1993). Using computer-based readers to improve reading comprehension of students with dyslexia. *Annals of Dyslexia, 43,* 238–59.

Embretson, S. E. (1991). A multidimensional latent trait model for measuring learning and change. *Psychometrika, 56,* 495–516.

  (1994). Comparing changes between groups: Some perplexities arising from psychometrics. In D. Laveault, B. D. Zumbo, M. E. Gessaroli and M. W. Boss (eds.) *Modern theories of measurement: problems and issues.* Ottawa: Edumetric Research Group, University of Ottawa.

  (1996). Item response theory models and inferential bias in multiple group comparisons. *Applied Psychological Measurement, 20,* 201–12.

Embretson, S. E. and Reise, S. R. (2000). *Item response theory for psychologists.* Mahwah, NJ: Erlbaum Lawrence.

Eyer, J. A. and Leonard, L. B. (1995). Functional categories and specific language impairment: a case study. *Language Acquisition: A Journal of Developmental Linguistics, 4*(3), 177–203.

Facoetti, A., Lorusso, M. L., Paganoni, P., Umilta, C. and Mascetti, G. G. (2003). The role of visuospatial attention in developmental dyslexia: evidence from a rehabilitation study. *Cognitive Brain Research, 15*(2), 154–64.

Fazio, B. B., Naremore, R. C. and Connell, P. J. (1996). Tracking children from poverty at risk for specific language impairment: a three-year longitudinal study. *Journal of Speech and Hearing Research, 39*(3), 611–24.

Fischer, K. W. and Rose, S. P. (1994). Development of coordination of components in brain and behavior: a framework for theory and research. In G. Dawson and K. W. Fisher (eds.) *Human behavior and the developing brain* (pp. 3–66). New York: Guilford.

Flowers, L., Meyer, M., Lovato, J., Wood, F. and Felton, R. (2000). Does third grade discrepancy status predict the course of reading development? *Annals of Dyslexia, 51*, 49–74.

Foorman, B. R., Francis, D. J., Winikates, D., Mehta, P., Schatschneider, C. and Fletcher, J. M. (1997). Early interventions for children with reading disabilities. *Scientific Studies of Reading, 1*(3), 255–76.

Francis, D. J., Shaywitz, S. E., Stuebing, K. K., Shaywitz, B. A. and Fletcher, J. M. (1996). Developmental lag versus deficit models of reading disability: a longitudinal, individual growth curves analysis. *Journal of Educational Psychology, 88*(1), 3–17.

Gallagher, A., Frith, U. and Snowling, M. J. (2000). Precursors of literacy delay among children at genetic risk of dyslexia. *Journal of Child Psychology and Psychiatry and Allied Disciplines, 41*(2), 202–13.

Gillon, Gail T. (2000). The efficacy of phonological awareness intervention for children with spoken language impairment. *Language, Speech and Hearing Services in the Schools, 31*(2), 126–41.

(2002). Follow-up study investigating the benefits of phonological awareness intervention for children with spoken language impairment. *International Journal of Language and Communication Disorders, 37*(4), 381–400.

Gilmore, R. (1981). *Catastrophe theory for scientists and engineers.* New York: Wiley.

Glass, L. and Mackey, M. (1988). *From clocks to chaos.* Princeton, NJ: Princeton University Press.

Gogate, L. J. and Walker-Andrews, A. (2001). The intersensory origins of word comprehension: an ecological-dynamic systems view. *Developmental Science, 4*, 1–37.

Goldstein, B. H. and Obrzut, J. E. (2001). Neuropsychological treatment of dyslexia in the classroom setting. *Journal of Learning Disabilities, 34*(3), 276–85.

Gottman, J. M. (ed.) (1995). *The analysis of change.* Mahwah, NJ: Erlbaum.

Gottman, J. M. and Roy, A. K. (1990). *Sequential analysis: a guide for behavioral researchers.* Cambridge: Cambridge University Press.

Graham, L. and Wong, B. Y. (1993). Comparing two modes of teaching a question-answering strategy for enhancing reading comprehension: didactic and self-instructional training. *Journal of Learning Disabilities, 26*(4), 270–9.

Greaney, K. T., Tunmer, W. E. and Chapman, J. W. (1997). Effects of rime-based orthographic analogy training on the word recognition skills of children with reading disability. *Journal of Educational Psychology, 89*(4), 645–51.

Greenway, C. (2002). The process, pitfalls and benefits of implementing a reciprocal teaching intervention to improve the reading comprehension of a group of year 6 pupils. *Educational Psychology in Practice, 18*(2), 113–37.

Guyer, B. P., Banks, S. R. and Guyer, K. E. (1993). Spelling improvement for college students who are dyslexic. *Annals of Dyslexia*, 43, 186–93.

Habib, M., Rey, V., Daffaure, V., Camps, R., Espesser, R., Joly-Pottuz, B. et al. (2002). Phonological training in children with dyslexia using temporally modified speech: a three-step pilot investigation. *International Journal of Language and Communication Disorders, 37*(3), 289–308.

Hadley, P. A. (1998). Early verb-related vulnerability among children with specific language impairment. *Journal of Speech Language and Hearing Research, 41*(6), 1384–97.

Hadley, P. A. and Rice, M. L. (1996). Emergent uses of BE and DO: evidence from children with specific language impairment. *Language Acquisition: A Journal of Developmental Linguistics, 5*(3), 209–43.

Hambleton, R. K. and Slater, S. C. (1997). Item response theory models and testing practices: current international status and future directions. *European Journal of Psychological Assessment, 13*, 21–8.

Hambleton, R. K., Swaminathan, H. and Rogers, H. J. (1991). *Fundamentals of item response theory.* Newbury Park, CA: Sage.

Harris, C. W. (ed.) (1963). *Problems in measuring change.* Madison; University of Wisconsin Press.

Hart, T. M., Berninger, V. M. and Abbott, R. D. (1997). Comparison of teaching single or multiple orthographic-phonological connections for word recognition and spelling: implications for instructional consultation. *School Psychology Review, 26*(2), 279–97.

Hartelman, P. A. I., van der Maas, H. L. J. and Molenaar, P. C. M. (1998). Detecting and modelling developmental transitions. *The Journal of Developmental Psychology, 16*, 97–122.

Hatcher, P. J. (2000). Sound links in reading and spelling with discrepancy-defined dyslexics and children with moderate learning difficulties. *Reading and Writing, 13*(3–4), 257–72.

Hatcher, P. J., Hulme, C. and Ellis, A. W. (1994). Ameliorating early reading failure by integrating the teaching of reading and phonological skills: the phonological linkage hypothesis. *Child Development, 65*(1), 41–57.

Hecht, S. A., and Close, L. (2002). Emergent literary skills and training time uniquely predict variability in responses to phonemic awareness training in disadvantaged kindergarteners. *Journal of Experimental Child Psychology, 82*(2), 93–115.

Hick, R. F., Joseph, K. L., Conti-Ramsden, G., Serratrice, L. and Faragher, B. (2002). Vocabulary profiles of children with specific language impairment. *Child Language Teaching and Therapy, 18*(2), 165–80.

Hillis, A. E. (1993). The role of models of language processing in rehabilitation of language impairments. *Aphasiology, 7*(1), 5–26.

Ho, C. S., Lam, E. Y. and Au, A. (2001). The effectiveness of multisensory training in improving reading and writing skills of Chinese dyslexic children. *Psychologia, 44*(4), 269–80.

Hosenfeld, B., van der Maas, H. L. J. and van den Boom, D. C. (1997a). Detecting bimodality in the analogical reasoning performance of elementary schoolchildren. *International Journal of Behavioral Development, 20*, 529–47.

(1997b). Indicators of discontinuous change in the development of analogical reasoning. *Journal of Experimental Child Psychology, 64*, 367–95.

Hurford, D. P., Darrow, L. J., Edwards, T., Howerton, C. J., Mote, C. R., Schauf, J. D. et al. (1993). An examination of phonemic processing abilities in children during their first-grade year. *Journal of Learning Disabilities, 26*(3), 167–77.

Hurford, D. P., Potter, T. S. and Hart, G. S. (2002). Examination of three techniques for identifying first-grade children at risk for difficulty in word identification with an emphasis on reducing the false negative error rate. *Reading Psychology, 23*(3) 2, 159–80.

Hurford, D. P., Schauf, J. D., Blaich, T., Bunce, L. and Moore, K. (1994). Early identification of children at risk for reading disabilities. *Journal of Learning Disabilities, 27*, 371–82.

Huttenlocher, J., Haight, W., Bryk, A. and Seltzer, M. (1991). Early vocabulary growth: relation to language input and gender. *Developmental Psychology, 27*, 236–49.

Jacobson, C. (1999). How persistent is reading disability? Individual growth curves in reading. *Dyslexia: The Journal of the British Dyslexia Association. 5*(2), 78–93.

Johnston, J. R., Miller, J. and Tallal, P. (2001). Use of cognitive state predicates by language-impaired children. *International Journal of Language and Communication Disorders, 36*(3), 349–70.

Joseph, K. L., Serratrice, L. and Conti-Ramsden, G. (2002). Development of copula and auxiliary BE in children with specific language impairment and younger unaffected controls. *First Language, 22*(65, pt. 2), 137–72.

Kappers, E. J. (1997). Outpatient treatment of dyslexia through stimulation of the cerebral hemispheres. *Journal of Learning Disabilities, 30*(1), 100–24.

Kemper, S., Rice, K. and Chen, Y. (1995). Complexity metrics and growth curves for measuring grammatical development from five to ten. *First Language, 15*(44, pt. 2), 151–66.

Korhonen, T. T. (1995). The persistence of rapid naming problems in children with reading disabilities: a nine-year follow-up. *Journal of Learning Disabilities, 28*(4), 232–9.

Laakso, M., Poikkeus, A. and Lyytinen, P. (1999). Shared reading interaction in families with and without genetic risk for dyslexia: implications for toddlers' language development. *Infant and Child Development, 8*(4), 179–95.

Landry, S. H., Smith, K. E., Miller-Loncar, C. L. and Swank, P. R. (1997). Predicting cognitive-language and social growth curves from early maternal behaviors in children at varying degrees of biological risk. *Developmental Psychology, 33*(6), 1040–53.

Lewis, B. A., Freebairn, L. A. and Taylor, H. G. (2000). Academic outcomes in children with histories of speech sound disorders. *Journal of Communication Disorders, 33*(1), 11–30.

Lipsey, M. W. and Wilson, D. B. (2001). *Practical meta-analysis.* Thousand Oaks, CA: Sage.

Lord, F. M. (1952). A theory of mental test scores. *Psychometric Monograph No 7.*
(1980). *Applications of item response theory to practical testing problems.* Hillsdale, NJ: Lawrence Erlbaum.

Louis, M., Espesser, R., Rey, V., Daffaure, V., Di Cristo, A. and Habib, M. (2001). Intensive training of phonological skills in progressive aphasia: a model of brain plasticity in neurodegenerative disease. *Brain and Cognition, 46*(1–2), 197–201.

Lovett, M. W. and Steinbach, K. A. (1997). The effectiveness of remedial programs for reading disabled children of different ages: does the benefit decrease for older children? *Learning Disability Quarterly, 20*(3), 189–210.

Lovett, M. W., Lacerenza, L., Borden, S. L., Frijters, J. C., Steinbach, K. A. and De Palma, M. (2000). Components of effective remediation for developmental reading disabilities: combining phonological and strategy-based instruction to improve outcomes. *Journal of Educational Psychology, 92*(2), 263–83.

Lundberg, I. (1995). The computer as a tool of remediation in the education of students with reading disabilities: a theory-based approach. *Learning Disability Quarterly, 18*(2), 89–99.

Lyytinen, P., Eklund, K. and Lyytinen, H. (2003). The play and language behavior of mothers with and without dyslexia and its association to their toddlers' language development. *Journal of Learning Disabilities, 36*(1), 74–86.

Lyytinen, P., Poikkeus, A., Laakso, M., Eklund, K. and Lyytinen, H. (2001). Language development and symbolic play in children with and without familial risk for dyslexia. *Journal of Speech Language and Hearing Research, 44*(4), 873–85.

Manis, F. R., Custodio, R. and Szeszulski, P. A. (1993). Development of phonological and orthographic skill: a two-year longitudinal study of dyslexic children. *Journal of Experimental Child Psychology, 56*(1), 64–86.

Manis, F. R., Seidenberg, M. S., Stallings, L., Joanisse, M., Bailey, C., Freedman, L. et al. (1999). Development of dyslexic subgroups: a one-year follow up. *Annals of Dyslexia, 49*, 105–34.

McArdle, J. (2001). Growth curve analysis. In N. J. Smelser and P. B. Baltes (eds.) *Social and behavioral sciences* (vol. 9, pp. 6439–45). Amsterdam, Holland: Elsevier.

McArdle, J. and Woodcock, J. (1997). Expanding test-retest designs to include developmental time-lag components. *Psychological Methods, 2*, 403–35.

McCarthy, P., Newby, R. F. and Recht, D. R. (1995). Results of an early intervention program for first grade children at risk for reading disability. *Reading Research and Instruction, 34*(4), 273–94.

McGee, R., Prior, M., Williams, S., Smart, D. and Sanson, A. (2002). The long-term significance of teacher-rated hyperactivity and reading ability in childhood: findings from two longitudinal studies. *Journal of Child Psychology and Psychiatry and Allied Disciplines, 43*(8), 1004–16.

Meredith, W. and Tisak, J. (1990). Latent curve analysis. *Psychometrika, 55*, 107–22.

Meyer, M. S., Wood, F. B., Hart, L. A. and Felton, R. H. (1998). Longitudinal course of rapid naming in disabled and nondisabled readers. *Annals of Dyslexia, 48*, 91–114.

Miller, L. L. and Felton, R. H. (2001). 'It's one of them . . . I don't know': case study of a student with phonological, rapid naming, and word-finding deficits. *Journal of Special Education, 35*(3), 125–33.

Mirak, J., and Rescorla, L. (1998). Phonetic skills and vocabulary size in late talkers: concurrent and predictive relationships. *Applied Psycholinguistics, 19*(1), 1–17.

Morris, D., Tyner, B., and Perney, J. (2000). Early steps: replicating the effects of a first-grade reading intervention program. *Journal of Educational Psychology, 92*(4), 681–93.

Moskowitz, D. S. and Hershberger, S. L. (eds.) (2002). *Modeling intraindividaul variability with repeated measures data: methods and applications.* Mahwah, NJ: Erlbaum.

Muthén, B., Khoo, S.-T., Francis, D. J. and Boscardin, C. K. (2003). Analysis of reading skills development from kindergarten through first grade: an application of growth mixture modeling to sequential process. In S. P. Reise and N. Duan (eds.) *Multilevel modeling.* Mahwah, NJ: Erlbaum.

Nelson, K. E., Camarata, S. M., Welsh, J., Butkovsky, L. and Camarata, M. (1996). Effects of imitative and conversational recasting treatment on the acquisition of grammar in children with Specific Language Impairment and younger language-normal children. *Journal of Speech and Hearing Research, 39,* 850–9.

Newell, K. M., and Molenaar, P. C. M. (1998). *Applications of nonlinear dynamics to developmental process modeling.* Mahwah, NJ: Lawrence Erlbaum.

Oakland, T., Black, J. L., Stanford, G., Nussbaum, N. L. and Balise, R. R. (1998). An evaluation of the dyslexia training program: a multisensory method for promoting reading in students with reading disabilities. *Journal of Learning Disabilities, 31*(2), 140–7.

Olofsson, A. and Niedersoe, J. (1999). Early language development and kindergarten phonological awareness as predictors of reading problems: from 3 to 11 years of age. *Journal of Learning Disabilities, 32*(5), 464–72.

Osgood, D. W. (2001). Application of multilevel models to the analysis of change. In L. M. Collins and A. G. Sayer (eds.) *New methods for the analysis of change* (pp. 97–104). Washington, DC: APA.

O'Shaughnessy, T. E. and Swanson, H. L. (2000). A comparison of two reading interventions for children with reading disabilities. *Journal of Learning Disabilities, 33*(3), 257–77.

Ottem, E. (2001). Use of pictographic-articulatory symbols to promote alphabetic reading in a language-impaired boy: case study. *AAC: Augmentative and Alternative Communication, 17*(1), 52–60.

Oyama, S. (2000). *The ontogeny of information: developmental systems and evolution.* Durham, NC: Duke University Press.

Pascual-Leone, J. (1995). Learning and development as dialectical factors in cognitive growth. *Human Development, 38,* 338–48.

Pascual-Leone, J. and Baillargeon, R. (1994). Developmental measurement of mental attention. *International Journal of Behavioral Development, 17,* 161–200.

Peach, R. K. (2002). Treatment for phonological dyslexia targeting regularity effects. *Aphasiology, 16*(8), 779–89.

Pennington, B. F. and Lefly, D. L. (2001). Early reading development in children at family risk for dyslexia. *Child Development, 72*(3), 816–33.

Pharr, A. B., Ratner, N. B. and Rescorla, L. (2000). Syllable structure development of toddlers with expressive specific language impairment. *Applied Psycholinguistics, 21*(4), 429–49.

Phelps, E., Furstenberg, F. F. and Colby, A. (eds.) (2002). *Looking at lives: American longitudinal studies of the twentieth century.* New York: Russell Sage Foundation.

Piccinin, A. M. (2001). Differential structural equation modeling of intraindividual variability. In L. M. Collins and A. G. Sayer (eds.) *New methods for the analysis of change* (pp. 29–32). Washington, DC: APA.

Pinherio, J. C. and Bates, D. M. (2000). *Mixed-effect models in S and S-PLUS.* New York, NY: Springer.

Pogorzelski, S., and Wheldall, K. (2002). Do differences in phonological processing performance predict gains made by older low-progress readers following intensive literacy intervention? *Educational Psychology, 22*(4), 413–27.

Poskiparta, E., Niemi, P. and Vauras, M. (1999). Who benefits from training in linguistic awareness in the first grade, and what components show training effects? *Journal of Learning Disabilities, 32*(5), 437–46, 456.

Post, Y. V., Carreker, S. and Holland, G. (2001). The spelling of final letter patterns: a comparison of instruction at the phoneme and the rime. *Annals of Dyslexia, 51*, 121–46.

Preece, M. A. and Baines, M. K. (1978). A new family of mathematical models describing the human growth curve. *Ann. Hum. Biol., 7*, 507–28.

Rasch, G. (1980). *Probabilistic models for some intelligence and attainment tests.* Chicago: University of Chicago Press (original work published in 1960: Rasch, G. *Probabilistic models for some intelligence and attainment tests.* Copenhagen: Danmarks Paedagogiske Institut).

Raudenbush, S. W. (2001). Toward a coherent framework for comparing trajectories of individual change. In L. M. Collins and A. G. Sayer (eds.) *New methods for the analysis of change* (pp. 33–64). Washington, DC: APA.

Reise, S. P. and Duan, N. (2003). *Multilevel modeling.* Mahwah, NJ: Lawrence Erlbaum.

Rescorla, L. (2000). Do late-talking toddlers turn out to have reading difficulties a decade later? *Annals of Dyslexia, 50*, 87–102.

(2002). Language and reading outcomes to age nine in late-talking toddlers. *Journal of Speech Language and Hearing Research. 45*(2), 360–71.

Rescorla, L. and Roberts, J. (2002). Nominal versus verbal morpheme use in late talkers at ages three and four. *Journal of Speech Language and Hearing Research, 45*(6), 1219–31.

Rescorla, L., Mirak, J. and Singh, L. (2000). Vocabulary growth in late talkers: lexical development from 2;0 to 3;0. *Journal of Child Language, 27*(2), 293–311.

Rice, M. L., Wexler, K. and Hershberger, S. (1998). Tense over time: the longitudinal course of tense acquisition in children with specific language impairment. *Journal of Speech Language and Hearing Research, 41*(6), 1412–31.

Rice, M. L., Wexler, K., Marquis, J. and Hershberger, S. (2000). Acquisition of irregular past tense by children with specific language impairment. *Journal of Speech Language and Hearing Research, 43*(5), 1126–45.

Richards, T. L., Berninger, V. W., Aylward, E. H., Richards, A. L., Thomson, J. B., Nagy, W. E. et al. (2002). Reproducibility of proton MR spectroscopic imaging (PEPSI): comparison of dyslexic and normal-reading children and effects of treatment on brain lactate levels during language tasks. *American Journal of Neuroradiology, 23*(10), 1678–85.

Richards, T. L., Corina, D., Serafini, S., Steury, K., Echelard, D. R., Dager, S. R. et al. (2000). Effects of a phonologically driven treatment for dyslexia on lactate levels measured by proton MR spectroscopic imaging. *American Journal of Neuroradiology, 21*(5), 916–22.

Robinson, B. F. and Mervis, C. B. (1998). Disentangling early language development: modeling lexical and grammatical acquisition using an extension of case-study methodology. *Developmental Psychology, 34*, 363–75.

  (1999). Comparing productive vocabulary measures from the CDI and a systematic diary study. *Journal of Child Language, 26*(1), 177–85.

Rogosa, D. R. (1995). Myths and methods: 'myth about longitudinal research' plus supplemental questions. In J. M. Gottman (ed.) *The analysis of change* (pp. 3–66). Mahwah, NJ: Erlbaum.

Rogosa, D., Brandt, D. and Zimowskyk, M. (1982). A growth curve approach to the measurement of change. *Psychological Bulletin, 92*, 726–48.

Rovine, M. J. and Molenaar, P. C. M. (2001). A structural equations modeling approach to the general linear mixed model. In L. M. Collins and A. G. Sayer (eds.) *New methods for the analysis of change* (pp. 65–96). Washington, DC: APA.

Ruhland, R. and van Geert, P. (1998). Jumping into syntax: transitions in the development of closed class words. *British Journal of Developmental Psychology, 16*, 65–95.

Sayer, A. G. and Cumsille, P. R. (2001). Second-order latent growth models. In L. M. Collins and A. G. Sayer (eds.) *New methods for the analysis of change* (pp. 177–200). Washington, DC: APA.

Scammon, R. E. (1927). The first seriatim study of human growth. *American Journal of Physical Anthropology, 10*, 329–36.

Seber, G. A. F. and Wild, C. J. (1989). *Nonlinear models.* New York, NY; Wiley.

Schmitz, B. (2001). Change: methods of studying. In N. J. Smelser and P. B. Baltes (eds.) *International encyclopedia of the social and behavioral sciences, vol. 3* (pp. 1640–3). Amsterdam, Holland: Elsevier.

Schneider, W., Ennemoser, M., Roth, E. and Kuespert, P. (1999). Kindergarten prevention of dyslexia: does training in phonological awareness work for everybody? *Journal of Learning Disabilities, 32*(5), 429–36.

Schneider, W., Kuespert, P., Roth, E., and Vise, M. (1997). Short- and long-term effects of training phonological awareness in kindergarten: evidence from two German studies. *Journal of Experimental Child Psychology, 66*(3), 311–40.

Schneider, W., Roth, E. and Ennemoser, M. (2000). Training phonological skills and letter knowledge in children at risk for dyslexia: a comparison of three kindergarten intervention programs. *Journal of Educational Psychology, 92*(2), 284–95.

Shaywitz, S., Fletcher, E., Holahan, J. M., Shneider, A. E., Marchione, K. E., Stuebing, K. K. et al. (1999). Persistence of dyslexia: the Connecticut Longitudinal Study at adolescence. *Pediatrics, 104*, 1351–9.

Silliman, E. R., Jimerson, T. L. and Wilkinson, L. C. (2000). A dynamic systems approach to writing assessment in students with language learning problems. *Topics in Language Disorders, 20*(4), 45–64.

Simos, P. G., Fletcher, J. M., Bergman, E., Breier, J. I., Foorman, B. R., Castillo, E. M. et al. (2002). Dyslexia-specific brain activation profile becomes normal following successful remedial training. *Neurology, 58*(8), 1203–13.

Snowling, M. J., Bishop, D. V. M. and Stothard, S. E. (2000). Is preschool language impairment a risk factor for dyslexia in adolescence? *Journal of Child Psychology and Psychiatry and Allied Disciplines, 41*(5), 587–600.

Snowling, M. J., Goulandris, N. and Defty, N. (1996). A longitudinal study of reading development in dyslexic children. *Journal of Educational Psychology, 88*(4), 653–69.

Sprenger-Charolles, L., Cole, P., Lacert, P. and Serniclaes, W. (2000). On subtypes of developmental dyslexia: evidence from processing time and accuracy scores. *Canadian Journal of Experimental Psychology, 54*(2), 87–104.

Stage, S. A. (2001). Program evaluation using hierarchical linear modeling with curriculum-based measurement reading probes. *School Psychology Quarterly, 16*(1), 91–112.

Stage, S. A., Abbott, R. D., Jenkins, J. R., and Berninger, V. W. (2003). Predicting response to early reading intervention from verbal IQ, reading-related language abilities, attention ratings, and verbal IQ-word readings discrepancy: failure to validate discrepancy method. *Journal of Learning Disabilities, 36*(1), 24–33.

Stein, J. F., Richardson, A. J. and Fowler, M. S. (2000). Monocular occlusion can improve binocular control and reading in dyslexics. *Brain, 123*, 164–70.

Sternberg, R. J. and Grigorenko, E. L. (2002). *Dynamic testing.* New York, NY: Cambridge University Press.

Stone, C. A. and Connell, P. J. (1993). Induction of a visual symbolic rule in children with specific language impairment. *Journal of Speech and Hearing Research, 36*(3), 599–608.

Swanson, H. L. (1999). Reading research for students with LD: a meta-analysis of intervention outcomes. *Journal of Learning Disabilities, 32*, 504–32.

Swisher, L., Restrepo, M. A., Plante, E. and Lowell, S. (1995). Effect of implicit and explicit 'rule' presentation on bound-morpheme generalization in specific language impairment. *Journal of Speech and Hearing Research, 38*(1), 168–73.

Thelen, E. (1989). Self-organization in developmental process: can systems approaches work? In M. Gunnar and E. Thelen (eds.) *Systems and development. The Minnesota Symposium on Child Psychology, 22* (pp. 77–117). Mahwah, NJ: Erlbaum.

Thelen, E. and Smith, L. B. (1994). *A dynamic systems approach to the development of cognitions and action.* Cambridge, MA: Bradford Books, MIT.

  (1997). Dynamic systems theories. In W. Damon (series ed.) and R. M. Lerner (vol. ed.), *Handbook of child psychology, vol. 1: theoretical models of human development* (5th edn, pp. 563–634). New York, NY: Wiley.

Thom, R. (1975). *Structural stability and morphogenesis.* Reading, MA; Benjamin.

Thomas, H. (1989). A binomial mixture model for classification performance: a commentary on Waxman, Chambers, Yntema, and Gelman. *Journal of Experimental Child Psychology, 48*, 423–30.

Thomas, H. and Lohaus, A. (1993). Modeling growth and individual differences in spatial tasks. *Monographs of the Society for Research in Child Development, 58*, (9, serial no. 237).

Thomas, H. and Turner, G. F. W. (1991). Individual differences and development in water-level task performance. *Journal of Experimental Child Psychology, 51*, 171–94.

Tressoldi, P. E., Stella, G. and Faggella, M. (2001). The development of reading speed in Italians with dyslexia: a longitudinal study. *Journal of Learning Disabilities, 34*(5), 414–17.

Uhry, J. K. and Shepherd, M. J. (1997). Teaching phonological recoding to young children with phonological processing deficits: the effect on sight-vocabulary acquisition. *Learning Disability Quarterly, 20*(2), 104–25.

Vadasy, P. F., Sanders, E. A., Peyton, J. A. and Jenkins, J. R. (2002). Timing and intensity of tutoring: a closer look at the conditions for effective early literacy tutoring. *Learning Disabilities Research and Practice, 17*(4), 227–41.

van Daal, V. H. P. and Reitsma, P. (1999). Effects of outpatient treatment of dyslexia. *Journal of Learning Disabilities, 32*(5), 447–56.

van der Maas, H. L. J. and Molenaar, P. M. C. (1992). Stagewise cognitive development: an application of catastrophe theory. *Psychological Review, 99*, 395–417.

van Geert, P. (1991). A dynamic systems model of cognitive and language growth. *Psychological Review, 98*, 3–53.

   (1993). A dynamic systems model of cognitive growth: competition and support under limited resource conditions. In L. B. Smith and E. Thelen (eds.) *A dynamic systems approach to development: applications.* (pp. 265–331). Cambridge, MA: MIT Press.

   (1994). *Dynamic systems of development: change between complexity and chaos.* New York: Prentice Hall/Harvester Wheatsheaf.

   (1995). Dimensions of change: a semantic and mathematical analysis of learning and development. *Human Development, 38*, 322–31.

   (1997). Variability and fluctuation: a dynamic view. In E. Amsel and K. A. Renninger (eds.) *Changes and development: issues of theory, method, and application* (pp. 193–212). Mahwah, NJ: Erlbaum.

van Geert, P. and van Dijk, M. (2002). Focus on variability: new tools to study intra-individual variability in developmental data. *Infant Behavior and Development, 25*, 340–74.

van Strien, J. W., Stolk, B. D. and Zuiker, S. (1995). Hemisphere-specific treatment of dyslexia subtypes: better reading with anxiety-laden words? *Journal of Learning Disabilities, 28*(1), 30–4.

Verbeke, G. and Molenberghs, G. (2000). *Linear mixed models for longitudinal data.* New York, NY: Springer.

Viholainen, H., Ahonen, T., Cantell, M., Lyytinen, P. and Lyytinen, H. (2002). Development of early motor skills and language in children at risk for familial dyslexia. *Developmental Medicine and Child Neurology, 44*(11), 761–9.

Von Eye, A. and Niedermeier, K. E. (1999). *Statistical analysis of longitudinal categorical data in the social and behavioral sciences.* Mahwah, NJ: Lawrence Erlbaum.

Vygotsky, L. S. (1982). *Myshlenie i rech'* [Thought and language]. Moskva: Pedagogika.

Wessling, R. and Reitsma, P. (2001). Preschool phonological representations and development of reading skills. *Annals of Dyslexia, 51*, 203–29.

Wheldall, K. (2000). Does Rainbow Repeated Reading add value to an intensive literacy intervention program for low-progress readers? An experimental evaluation. *Educational Review, 52*(1), 29–36.

Wimmers, R. H., Beek, P. J., Savelsbergh, G. J. P. and Hopkins, B. (1998). Developmental changes in action: theoretical and methodological issues. *British Journal of Developmental Psychology, 16*, 45–63.

Wright, B. D. and Stone, M. H. (1979). *Best test design.* Chicago: MESA.

Yampolsky, S. and Waters, G. (2002). Treatment of single word oral reading in an individual with deep dyslexia. *Aphasiology, 16*(4–6), 455–71.

Zeger, S. L. and Harlow, S. D. (1987). Mathematical models from laws of growth to tools for biological analysis: fifty years of growth. *Growth, 51*, 1–21.

11 Dynamic modelling of cognitive development: time, situatedness and variability

Paul van Geert

Modelling and the representation of phenomena

In her book *Life with Picasso*, Françoise Gilot recalls a discussion about the portrait that Picasso painted of Gertrude Stein in 1906 (Gilot and Lake 1964). Many people first found that the portrait was not a very good likeness. Later, however, many began to think that, over the course of the years, Gertrude Stein had come to resemble the portrait. Picasso had predicted that although the portrait was not a very good likeness, Stein herself would become a good likeness of the portrait.

Gertrude Stein's portrait reminds us of a basic feature of what a model should be, namely the representation of what the modeller sees as the *essence* of the modelled phenomenon (Casti 1997). However, it also reminds us of the fact that resemblance runs both ways. If the model is powerful enough, it will come to dictate what the essence of the modelled phenomenon should be.

A model leaves out those aspects that are not considered essential or important and it exaggerates or idealizes what it considers characteristic. In that sense, what a model does not show, what it considers not characteristic, is about as interesting as what the model does show. The dictum that what must be left out of representation is more fundamental than what is actually displayed is probably more characteristic of traditional Japanese than of Western art, but it is nevertheless applicable to all forms of art, including the art of modelling. In this chapter, I shall try to explain that the way we model our data on cognitive development – both in the form of statistical and conceptual models – has a great effect on what we think cognitive development and development in general actually are. I shall discuss alternative ways of representing and modelling based on a dynamic systems view of the nature of psychological variables and their development.

Differences and similarities as starting point of models

A classical distinction in psychology concerns the differences between models that generalize and average over individuals (psychonomic models) and those that capitalize on differences between individuals (mostly the psycho-metric models). In the introduction I referred to modelling as the representation of what one considers the essence of a phenomenon. The existence of these two kinds of models clearly demonstrates that there are two widely accepted visions of the essence of psychological phenomena, namely what people have in common and what distinguishes people from each other (the differential approach in general). In addition to the differences between people, there are also meaningful differences within people. The most salient dimension of difference within people is that of development: fundamental changes within the person over time. Developmental models have often combined the focus on differences within the individual over time with the generalizing approach, thus specifying developmental changes as phenomena that are uniform across subjects. Piaget's theory is an example of this kind of theory.

The neo-Piagetian approach, on the other hand, has combined the developmental with the differential approach, emphasizing the importance of differences in developmental trajectories, for instance by means of the notion of developmental webs (Bidell and Fischer 2003; Fischer and Bidell 1998). Recently, Demetriou et al. (2002) have combined an information processing with a developmental and differential approach in their modelling of cognitive development. In a recent special issue of *Infant Behaviour and Development* on variability in infancy, various existing cross-sectional data sets were re-analysed with a particular focus on inter-individual variability. The conclusions were that aggregating over individuals leads to the description of a developmental path that does not represent any of the individual paths in particular (see for instance Yonas, Elieff and Arterberry 2002).

In addition to the within-person differences that encompass major changes in the person's functioning and that require relatively long periods of time, there is also another form of within-person difference that is almost by definition left out of the modelling endeavour, namely the short-term fluctuation of performance and behaviour.

Short-term fluctuation and variability

True scores and error variability

Irrespective of whether models generalize over individuals, focus on the differences between people or focus on the differences within people across development, they usually omit short-term fluctuation or variability. In fact, a considerable part of statistical modelling is aimed at estimating how much of the variability, for instance across people, is due to measurement error, which, by definition, bears no information on the phenomenon under scrutiny. In classical reliability theory (Traub 1994) and classical true score theory (Lord and Novick

1968), differences between a person's levels of performance (for instance expressed in the form of a test score) over short time intervals (for instance a week or a month) reflect the effect of errors in the measurement. The true score or true level is assumed to have remained identical over such short stretches of time.

Our standard statistical methods imply a number of highly specific assumptions about the nature or essence of psychological phenomena. These assumptions are clearly and explicitly represented by what is left out from our models – and what is in fact painstakingly removed from those models – namely (short-term) fluctuation. The characteristic assumption is that a person 'has' a true score on a variable. This true score can be approached by taking an infinite number of tests and averaging over the results. Although this infinite repetition cannot be anything else than a thought experiment, the fact that this thought experiment is taken seriously means that the taking of a test is, in essence, considered not to affect the probed phenomenon (intelligence, for instance). All these assumptions are related to another fundamental assumption, namely that, for all intents and purposes, the individual and the environment or context are independent constituents, that interact with one another but meanwhile retain their independence.

Variability in dynamic systems and situated approaches

The situated nature of psychological phenomena

In dynamic systems theory (see for instance Thelen and Smith 1994) and contextual or situated cognition theory (Clark and Chalmers 1998; Clark 1997), the latter assumption has been radically altered. Organism and environment are seen as intimately intertwined. What we call a psychological variable, such as a concept or an ability, consists in fact of a temporal cooperation between properties of the organism and properties of the adapted environment. According to Thelen and Smith, for instance, a one-year-old baby does not 'have' an object concept. The object concept is the (transient) result of a temporal and local soft-assembly process. The baby does not carry an object concept in his head that acts as a little machine that allows him to solve the A-not-B problem, for instance (see Thelen and Smith 1994, Smith et al. 1999). The same logic applies to all other psychological variables: they are not properties of the subject per se, but are local and temporal constellations of abilities of the person and affordances of the environment.

What the dynamic systems and contextualist, or, more precisely, situated approach have done is to replace the notion of a concept or psychological variable as an isolated, static object in the mind or in the brain, by the notion of a concept or psychological variable as a *process*. It is a kind of process that occurs over relatively short time spans (e.g. during the baby's solving the A-not-B problem) and that involves a continuous loop or interplay between the properties of the subject and the properties of the context or environment.

Starting with the assumption that a concept or psychological variable in general is not a property of the person but a property of the person–context system, we can now assert that the person and the context are not independent of one another. The context is the result not only of its own intrinsic properties but also of the selections and transformations that the person makes on this context. The properties of the person during his or her interaction with the context are determined by the possibilities, support and means that the context provides.

Variability: a key property

If a concept or psychological variable is a process and not a static property, and moreover, if it is a process that is assembled on the basis of components that are themselves stochastically distributed (contextual and organismic components), the concept or psychological variable must, by necessity, be characterized by a certain variation, by a certain reaction norm. This variation can be great or small. It is not a contingent property of the concept or variable, but a characteristic property, because it is characteristic of the way the process – and thus the concept or variable – is assembled.

The way performance, action or skill varies over the short term can be indicative of ongoing developmental processes, such as a rapid change. Researchers of cognitive development who have based their work on catastrophe theory have shown that increased variability is an indicator of a discontinuous change in a developmental variable (see for instance van der Maas and Molenaar 1992; van der Maas 1993; Hosenfeld, van der Maas and van den Boom 1997a,b; Wimmers 1996; Ruhland and van Geert 1998). On the other hand, variation and fluctuation also provide opportunities for exploration and selection of better-adapted forms of thinking and acting (see van Geert, Savelsbergh and van der Maas 1999, for a further discussion). For instance, during the first year of life, many behavioural and physiological modes of activity are considerably more variable than, for instance, after the first birthday (de Weerth and van Geert 2000, 2002a, 2002b, de Weerth, Hoijtink and van Geert 1999). This high initial variability allows the developing system to tune in on a smaller range that is optimally adapted to the range of contexts that are characteristic of the infant in question.

In summary, if concepts and psychological variables in general are in fact processes and not static phenomena, they are characterized by a specific level of variability. This variability is in itself a developmental phenomenon. It will change in the course of development and it has specific functions for development, such as offering a range of selection and optimalization.

Time, conditional dependence and characteristic frequency

Time and conditional dependence

In dynamic systems theory, time is an intrinsic property of the phenomena under study. The temporal dimension functions at various levels: the microgenetic level of the processes as such and the macrogenetic level of developmental change, which involves, among others, changes in the nature of the short term variability. With time being so important, another interesting consequence of dynamic systems theory in particular is that it no longer endorses the assumption of conditional independence that is almost an axiom in most of our statistical modelling. Most measurement in developmental psychology is done on individuals that are members of particular groups, e.g. a group of five-year-olds. In the group, the subjects are completely independent of one another, and so is the variation in the measured variable.

It is important to note that the outcomes of structural statistical models, such as factor models, can be radically different, depending on whether they are based on intra-individual data or, what is most common, inter-individual data (Molenaar 2004; Molenaar, Huizenga and Nesselroade 2002). Nevertheless, the outcomes of inter-individual variability (the standard cross-sectional and group design) are almost always used as structural models that implicitly pertain to individuals.

By focusing on sequences of actions, which are conditionally coupled, the dynamic systems approach endorses the view that the temporal context of an event is just as important as the spatial and material context (the environment). Human beings are characterized by the fact that they adapt and learn, and many psychological variables, especially those that are measured in the context of developmental studies, refer to this ability of learning, change and adaptation. Thus, if a learning and developing person is concerned, the idea of a true score as the average of many (imaginary) independent repetitions of the test must fail in light of the fact that any repetition will carry the effect of the preceding test administration. All testing, as Grigorenko and Sternberg (1998) have claimed, is dynamic testing. We expect that a person will learn from a first test administration and apply this information to a second. The notion of conditional dependence of actions and events is intimately related to learning and the effect of experiences, i.e. changes in and development of the capacities and abilities of the person. A person's learning or developmental history is literally a history, with events and actions that took place at particular times and, equally important, with particular frequencies.

Time and the characteristic frequency of a phenomenon

In a developmental context, events have a characteristic frequency. For instance, how often does an infant experiment with hiding objects, how often does a child have to solve addition problems in the class, with which frequency does an adolescent experiment with friendship relations, and so forth. This characteristic frequency is important both from the viewpoint of development and from the viewpoint of measurement. It is conventional wisdom that practice makes perfect, i.e. that the frequency with which activities are carried out matters, and this is so because the next event depends on the preceding ones. However, the relation between frequency and change is highly nonlinear, as many of the classical experiments on training Piagetian concepts, such as conservation, have convincingly shown.

The notion of characteristic frequency has also implications for measurement. A researcher who studies the growth of addition skills, for instance, can measure his subjects many times and easily collect dense time-serial data. The reason is that, in the context of schooling, children are doing additions frequently and regularly, simply because that is the way in which they improve their skill. A student of identity development, for instance, is faced with an entirely different problem. The number of occasions in which a person is actually confronted with identity issues is, in most cases, very small (van Halen 2002). An identity test, if the subject is taking it seriously, is such an occasion. It is very difficult, if not impossible, to repeat such a test many times, because such repetition is itself not consistent with the characteristic frequency of processes that explicitly involve identity issues (given that identity, just like any other psychological variable, is also considered a 'soft-assembled' process; note, however, that this characteristic frequency is itself subject to developmental change and may increase sharply in times of crisis, for instance). The frequent repetition of such tests (provided a person would be willing to cooperate with it) would soon interfere with the processes that we call identity and lead to something that is a function of the repeated testing itself. The point is that a test of a person's identity (whatever that means) consists of an event (the test) that has – eventually – a major impact on the phenomenon itself and thus becomes a crucial cause or condition in the development of the measured phenomenon. This is very different from a test of a pupil's subtraction skills, or the observation of a child's language production.

In summary, in a dynamic systems perspective, time plays an essential role. The phenomena of interest are processes that are conditionally dependent on one another and occur with characteristic frequencies. This has important consequences for the way we measure such phenomena. If we leave the conditional dependence and the characteristic frequency out of our measurement – which is in fact the common practice – we lose an essential feature of what characterizes those measured phenomena as having a developmental and time-dependent nature.

Does a child 'have' a concept?

Does a child, or a person in general, 'have' a concept or psychological property, for that matter? If the concept is a situated phenomenon, i.e. if it exists in the form of the interplay between the person and the context, the concept cannot be a property of the person alone, and in that sense, people 'have' no concepts. This is basically the answer of Thelen and Smith (1994, Smith et al. 1999). However, pursuing our example of the A-not-B error in infants, one can ask what it is, then, that distinguishes an infant who makes the A-not-B error from a slightly older infant who does not. The answer, consistent with Thelen and Smith's theory, is that the difference consists of a whole range of organismic and contextual differences between these two infants. These organismic differences pertain to things such as memory, perceptual strategies, motor patterns and so forth. If the infant is put in an A-not-B situation, these elements, in interaction with a context, give rise to an action pattern that we refer to as an understanding of the object concept (or not).

In a neural network model, the organismic component of a concept is in the constellation of weights between the neurons (Clark and Chalmers 1998). However, saying that the concept is in the constellation of the brain or physical neural network is not satisfactory. The particular constellation of the brain or neural network as such is not specific to the object concept, or any other concept for that matter. It is a constellation that fulfils a multitude of functions, dependent on the actual physical contexts in which it is put to work.

The difference between an infant that makes the A-not-B error and one that does not can also consist of contextual differences between the two. If we change the context, e.g. make the time interval between showing the two locations shorter, an infant can solve the problem without making the error. In this case, the crucial difference between having the concept or not lies in the context. This view is also endorsed by the viewpoint of distributed cognition or situated cognition in educational contexts (Greeno et al. 1998), that assigns a crucial importance to the context as bearer (or co-bearer, if one may say so) of knowledge.

However, we still have not answered the question whether a particular person 'has' a particular concept (or psychological property or variable, for that matter). If the concept is a temporally and spatially bound process and if the process itself is crucially dependent both on the person and on the context, it is difficult to imagine how we could see the concept as something that is present 'in' the subject. The first part of the solution to this problem is to contend that the notion of a person as an isolated entity, with internal properties that have intrinsic referential meanings outside any particular context in which they could eventually function, makes no sense under a dynamic systems view. The word 'person' refers to a dynamic unity of a person in a characteristic range of contexts. In that sense, person and context (the characteristic contexts) form a unity of description, although it is a unity similar to the proverbial coin: it has two sides.

The second part of the solution is to specify the meaning of an assertion such as 'the person has an object concept' or 'the person has a score of seven on a conservation test'. In order to do so, I shall introduce a distinction between determinate and indeterminate properties. This distinction will bring us to the second part of this chapter, which deals with the issue of the measurement of psychological variables, in particular in a developmental context.

Models of measurement and description

Determinacy of properties and the notion of characteristicness

Determinate and indeterminate properties

Suppose that someone wishes to know how much coffee I drank yesterday. The amount of coffee I drank yesterday is a *determinate property* (for all intents and purposes, that is), which can be expressed in the form of a specific volume (e.g. 68 centilitres). Since no one has made an exact note of how much coffee I drank yesterday, the only way to measure, in fact estimate, this amount is by indirect means. The coffee researcher could present me with a questionnaire, or could ask me to measure off an amount of liquid equal to the amount of coffee I drank yesterday. The point is that the estimated amount and the real amount are of the same kind: they are both determinate amounts of liquid. The difference between the true amount and the estimated amount boils down to measurement (or estimation) error. Suppose now that someone else wishes to specify *today* how much coffee I shall drink *tomorrow*. Today, the amount of coffee that I shall drink tomorrow is an *indeterminate* property. It is indeterminate in a trivial sense: that is, the amount I shall drink tomorrow will be determined tomorrow, and will depend, among others, on the contingencies that the day of tomorrow will bring along. The description of the indeterminate amount takes an entirely different form from the description of the determinate amount of coffee. It will probably consist of a specification of a range (between 50 and 100 centilitres) and will probably also involve conditional statements such as 'if the canteen is not closed' or 'if he does not have a headache', etc. More precisely, the description of an indeterminate property amounts to a description of a structure of degrees of freedom, namely the degrees of freedom that constrain and determine the amount of coffee I drink, given that this amount depends on so many factors. In fact, what I describe if I describe the amount of coffee

I shall drink tomorrow is the dynamics of my coffee drinking, and this dynamics is characterized, among others, by a structure of conditions and degrees of freedom (degrees of possible and characteristic variation).

The notion of characteristicness

If someone asks me how much coffee I drink, that person is probably not interested in how much coffee I shall drink tomorrow and only tomorrow. He is interested in what he might call a characteristic property of mine, namely how much coffee I drink 'in general' or 'habitually'. That is, the researcher is interested in something that is characteristic of me. His question pertains both to my past record and to my future. This past record and future are bound by fuzzy time limits, since the person who wants to know how much coffee I drink also knows that my habits may change; more precisely, that there may be a (developmental) evolution in my coffee drinking. If the question refers to a fixed past record, let us say the past three months, the amount of coffee I drank is a determinate property, which can be estimated and which involves measurement error. However, since the amount of coffee I drink depends both on personal and contextual factors, the *exact* amount that I drank the last three months is as such of no great interest. That is, this true coffee drinking score is only of interest insofar as it tells something about what is characteristic of me, but this exact amount as such is not characteristic. What is characteristic is my range of coffee drinking, its form of dependence on contextual factors, its effect on the contexts that I shall select and the actions that I shall perform in order to get my daily coffee, and so forth.

Let us now apply this reasoning to the question of whether a person, a baby for instance, 'has' an object concept. In a dynamic systems framework, this object concept is instantiated in the form of an actual process that has, in principle, occurred n times in the past. This n times is a determinate property, but it is crucially dependent on contextual factors, just as my coffee drinking, and its exact frequency, is as such not very interesting. In fact, if we ask about the child's object concept, we wish to know something that is characteristic of the child and that is in itself an indeterminate property. More precisely, we refer to something that is a mixture of a determinate property (the past) and an indeterminate property (the future). Thus, we describe the child's object concept as a mixture of a *history* (which we estimate and approximate and confine by means of fuzzy boundaries) and a *dynamics*, namely the dynamics of the object concept as it pertains to this baby in particular.

Usually, the dynamics of something like an object concept, let alone that of verbally signified, 'abstract' concepts, is extremely complicated. However, we can approximate the description of the dynamics of the object concept by describing a number of essential features of that dynamics: a characteristic range of performance, likelihood of success, conditions on successful solutions of object concept problems and so forth. In this sense, the child's 'having' an object concept is a fuzzy property, because the history of object concept action and the applicability of the dynamics of object concept action to the child-context system does not amount to a simple, well-defined property. Statements about psychological properties, such as the presence of concepts, and the measurement of psychological variables are in fact deeply concerned with the problem of the description and measurement of dynamic, time-dependent complexity.

In a developmental context, it is our aim to make statements about a developmental time frame, in which we can capture developmental changes in the concepts and variables at issue. I have argued that the description of a psychological variable boils down to a description of a history and a description of a dynamics. Development thus pertains to developments or changes in that history and changes in the dynamics. The question is, how are we going to specify such histories and how will we specify the dynamics that are characteristic of the phenomenon in which we are interested? I shall first concentrate on the issue of how developmental histories can be described.

Measurement frequency and methods for describing developmental histories

Measurement frequency

If developing and having a concept, the object concept, for instance, amounts to the occurrence of processes – actions more precisely – in which that concept is instantiated or locally assembled, tapping the history of the object concept in a particular child would ideally amount to describing how often and in which conditions this object concept qua process has occurred in the past record of the child. In principle, this problem is similar to describing the history of preposition use in a child, for instance. A student of language acquisition is interested, for instance, in the question of the development of prepositions. In language acquisition studies, such a question is habitually answered by regularly observing spontaneous language production in the child and by counting the frequency with which such prepositions occur. This is of course a lot easier than observing spontaneous occurrences of the object concept, but the formal aspects of the problem are similar. The first issue one should address in pursuing the description of the history of a variable – the preposition, the object concept, . . . – is concerned with the frequency of observation or measurement. In a study of the growth of spatial prepositions in young children (van Geert and van Dijk 2002; van Dijk and van Geert, submitted), we applied a mixed design. A standard longitudinal language observation design with observations made every two weeks was supplemented with six intensive observation periods, in which observations were made every other day.

In this way, we obtained an impression of the relationship between the long- and short-term fluctuations and change. The frequency of observation tried to capture the natural, or characteristic, fluctuations of the phenomenon at issue. The total length of the study, which covered about a year, is also consistent with the characteristic rate of development of a linguistic category such as a preposition.

Our study resulted in a description of the 'history' of spatial preposition use in four children. The description is limited, in that it captures only a fragment of the total production of prepositions in the children (our observations lasted about an hour, were two-weekly and sometimes every other day, but they were of course not continuously tapping the child's ongoing language production).

Describing a developmental history

The question is, how does one describe such history? The standard tendency is to see the fluctuations as error fluctuation and to estimate the 'true' level by averaging over various measurements. This is of course inconsistent with the dynamic model, which views every frequency as 'historically true' in its own right. There is measurement error, of course, but that error concerns our eventual mistakes of mishearing a word, not understanding words due to environmental noise and so forth (I shall later deal with the issue of ambiguity). The history of the child's use of spatial prepositions is captured by various properties, and first of all by the *range* of frequencies and by the changes in the range. There are various simple methods for specifying changes in the variability of a developmental phenomenon (van Geert and van Dijk 2002).

The change and evolution of the characteristic range can be specified by simply plotting the maximum and minimum values of the variable over a moving time window. In addition to plotting the extreme values, one can also plot a moving percentile value, e.g. the 90 percentile of the values of a moving window with a length of a month or two months (the window size or period depends on the total number of observations and the characteristic rate of change of the observed phenomenon). Still another technique is to smooth the maximum and minimum plot by means of a technique that resembles a so-called Loess smoothing procedure[1] (locally weighted least squares smoothing, Simonoff 1996). By inspecting these 'envelopes' (lines that contain the data rather than follow a central tendency), both the general developmental trend and the changes in the variability become obvious (see Figure 11.1).

---

[1] This smoothing procedure is based on a preset window, e.g. a window covering 20 per cent of the observed data. The data in the window are used to estimate a linear or quadratic model for that particular window. In estimating this model, the data have different weights: the closer the data are to the centre of the window, the more important their effect on the estimated model. By shifting this window across the whole data set, one obtains a smoothed line that follows the local distributions of the data quite faithfully.

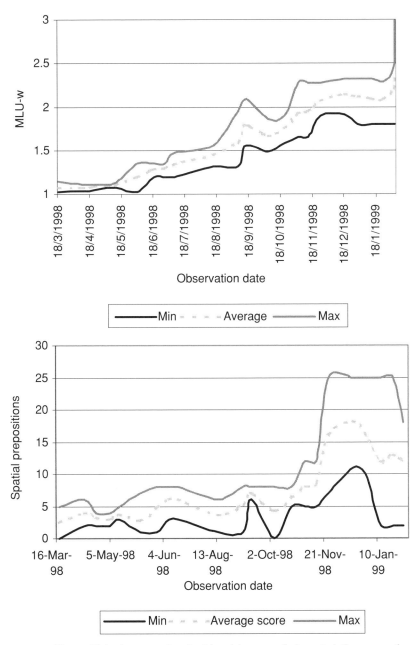

Figure 11.1. An example of a bimodal range of characteristic scores; the vertical axis represents the degree of characteristicness of each of the scores specified by the horizontal (score) dimension.

In addition to plotting the envelope covering the extreme values, it is also informative to plot the central tendency, i.e. the local average of the data, which can be done by means of the aforementioned Loess smoothing. The resulting moving average, however, is not seen as an estimation of the 'true' level, which would be inconsistent with our dynamic view on the nature of change and development. Instead, this central tendency is seen as an addition to marking the course of the extremes.

Variability as a source of information about development
By using the actual variability in the spatial prepositions, instead of reducing the data to their average and smoothing away the so-called outliers, we were able to show that spatial prepositions develop along a discontinuous path, with a sharp rise in variability at the time of the discontinuity (van Dijk and van Geert, submitted). Such discontinuities are predicted, among others, by catastrophe studies: see van Geert, Savelsbergh and van der Maas 1999. Our finding of a discontinuity by taking account of the local extreme values is in line with Fischer's assertion that stage-transitions are observable on the level of optimal performance (peak level) and cannot be observed on the level of functional performance.

In our study of the differences between Mean Length of Utterance on the one hand and spatial prepositions on the other hand we found a radically different pattern of change in variability (van Geert and van Dijk 2002; van Dijk et al. 2000, van Dijk and van Geert, submitted). A closer inspection of the variability in MLU, for instance, revealed that children tend to show fluctuations in MLU that would put them in three distinct MLU stages if each of the observations was taken separately. Variability in MLU changed more or less linearly with age, different from the variability in the spatial prepositions, which changed in a non-linear fashion and which is indicative of a discontinuous change.

Measurement contexts and conditions
If one aims at describing the history and the dynamics of a developmental phenomenon – for instance the development of prepositions or of the object concept – one must reckon with the range of characteristic contexts in which such a phenomenon occurs and by which it is crucially influenced. That is, if cognition is a situated phenomenon, its situatedness is part of its very nature, and in diagnosing cognitive levels we should also aim at diagnosing the contexts in which this particular level of cognition is supposed to function. The competing belief that a psychological variable such as a developmental level exists in the form of a true level, a true property of the person, leads to the search for a single best measurement condition, which usually takes the form of a standardized

test. However, there is absolutely no compelling reason why the *Tertium non datur* principle should hold in the case of measurable developmental levels. According to that principle, either a person *is* at developmental level *n* or he *is not* at level *n*. Given the way brains and bodies are organized and the way they function in adapted contexts, it is possible that a person is *both* at level *n* and at level *m*, even if, under any *specific* condition or context of activity, a person is either at *n* or at *m* (or eventually something in between, or eventually at both levels to a certain extent).

The bimodal specification of developmental levels finds its roots in Vygotsky's distinction between the child's actual developmental level and the child's developmental level under educational help. The distance between those two marks the zone of proximal development and constitutes an important dynamic factor in development. A similar distinction has been made by Fischer, in the form of the functional level of development versus the optimal level of development (Fischer and Rose 1994; Fischer and Yan 2002). The person is not so much characterized by some ephemeral 'average' level as by his range of levels, which crucially depend on the conditions of testing. Similar pleas for a fundamentally multi-modal structure of the developmental level have been made by Alibali and Goldin-Meadow (1993), Goldin-Meadow, Alibali and Church (1993) and Goldin-Meadow and Alibali (2002). Accepting the fact that a cognitive developmental level means in fact a *range* of characteristic levels that need not be unimodal implies that the measurement of cognitive levels must take place under conditions that can capture this range; for instance, a combination of conditions of unsupported and supported testing (Fischer and Rose 1994).

A major objection against such practice could be that by doing so one introduces contextual variation into the measurement of a person's characteristics qua person and thus introduces a source of variability that does not depend on the person himself. However, this objection is based on the assumption that the person and the context are independent phenomena. This assumption has been criticized by advocates of contextualist and situated theory, ranging from Vygotsky (1978) to Clark (1997). They claim that organisms and their environments are closely adapted to one another, and thus that person and context are not independent. Persons select and create their environments and the environment modifies and shapes the person. Cognitive development, for instance, takes place in a cultural context that carefully monitors the child's growing abilities and that continues to adapt the micro-contexts in which children are active. In addition, the cultural context itself is the historical product of cognition and human labour aimed at creating better adapted contexts for human life (see for instance Valsiner 1987). Put differently, the characteristic developmental levels of a person are closely related to that person's characteristic contexts. Thus, if measurement implies that a person be characterized by his or her cognitive level, the measurement must both address the characteristic range of the person's performance and the characteristic contexts in which this performance occurs. Since learning and support from others are highly characteristic of the developmental process in children, measurement should include the effect of learning and the effect of supportive contexts.

Characteristic ranges and intrinsic ambiguity

If we accept that intra-individual variability is an essential feature of a developing system, we must represent the level in that system by means of a range. In statistics, we are used to the notion of confidence ranges, which is the range within which we assume the true value lies, with a confidence of, for instance, 95 per cent. In the range of characteristic levels, however, any level is as true as any other. The range specifies the extension of what the observer considers the child's *characteristic* range. Elsewhere I have suggested the use of fuzzy logic principles to specify characteristic ranges (van Geert 2002). For instance, suppose that we have a 'ruler' that measures cognitive development in some particular domain (see Fischer and Dawson 2002). There is a range projected onto that ruler that covers the characteristic levels of performance of a particular child. The range need not be continuous. For instance, if the characteristic range under support differs from the no-support condition, there are in fact two characteristic ranges, each linked with a characteristic context (namely the characteristic context of functioning on one's own and the characteristic context of functioning under educational guidance and support). In addition to the characteristic levels, there are levels that are not characteristic of the child. That is, they might occur, but they will occur under conditions that are highly uncharacteristic of the child's functioning (e.g. under high pressure, serious illness, etc.). The characteristic and non-characteristic ranges need not be contingent (see Figure 11.2).

Context dependency and variability are closely related to the fact that developing phenomena – the prepositions or the object concept that featured in our examples – can go through a stage in which their nature is intrinsically ambiguous or fuzzy. For instance, a particular word produced by a child at an early stage of language acquisition need not be categorically specific, for instance either a preposition or not a preposition. Early words may be essentially ambiguous, i.e. both preposition and not a preposition. This – transient – fuzziness is a characteristic feature of the development of such categories (see van Geert and van Dijk 2003, for a discussion of how such ambiguity can be quantified). A word produced by a child in a particular context has a degree-of-membership in a particular linguistic category, for instance the category 'preposition'. In fuzzy logic, this degree of membership is a continuous variable. On the other hand, the standard approach is to treat class membership as a discontinuous

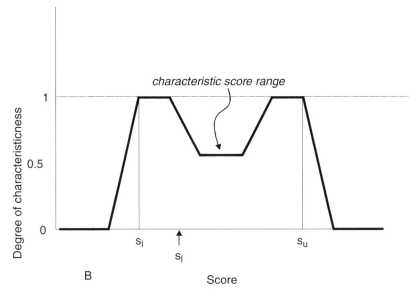

Figure 11.2. Moving min-max graph of Heleen's Mean Length of Utterance (left) and spatial prepositions (right) (time frame 18 days, last window 15 days).

variable, i.e. a word is either a preposition (100 per cent membership) or it is not (0 per cent membership). In a developmental context, a word may have properties of a preposition and properties of some other category, verbs for instance. Development in that case amounts to a change in the membership function. That change can be smooth or discontinuous. Smooth, i.e. gradual, changes need not be linear. They can follow the form of a transition function, for instance an S-shaped function, which specifies that the 'fuzzy' stage is short and intermediary (see Steenbeek and van Geert, submitted, for an application to the stability of sociometric choices in children).

Dynamic modelling of cognitive development

Dynamic growth models

So far I have mainly discussed the statistical modelling of cognitive developmental levels, with a strong emphasis on the exploratory and descriptive statistical methods, based on the belief that the way we describe things is a direct expression of what we see as the essence of the described phenomenon. Let me now turn to a different form of modelling, which starts with the theoretical concepts in order to deductively infer (potential) data. By way of example, I shall discuss dynamic growth modelling of developmental data.

In principle, a dynamic growth model describes the change in a variable as a function of its preceding state in time, a structure of resources and relationships with other variables. The relationships with other variables can be conditional, competitive or supportive (see van Geert 1991; van Geert 1994). Dynamic growth models are particularly suitable for modelling inter-individual variability. Inter-individual variability can be introduced by altering the values of the model's parameters. The linear differences in the parameters are transformed into non-linear qualitative differences in the resulting growth patterns.

However, growth models mostly produce smooth continuous growth curves, reminiscent of the notion of an underlying true score or level. Non-smooth fluctuations can result from chaotic oscillations in the modelled data. These are often the consequence of delays in the effects of the variables on each other. A disadvantage of these chaotic oscillations is that they only occur if the rates of change exceed certain thresholds in proportion to the speed with which variables can actually affect other variables (or the variable itself). Such high rates are often empirically unlikely. Another disadvantage is that such chaotic oscillations easily lead to instability of the entire system. A better solution than the chaotic processes is to conceive of a growth model as a simplification of the actual process of variable performance, which specifies only some central value of that performance.

Accounting for intra-individual variation in growth models
Instead of modelling growth as the change in a single value on a variable, it can also be modelled as a change in a vector of such variables. The person's current state, as far as that variable is concerned, is represented by a range of values with different weights, corresponding with the differences in characteristicness of these values, as discussed earlier in this chapter (see van Geert 1998, 2000, for an application of this principle to the theories of Vygotsky and Piaget). Thus, growth should be modelled for a continuous array of values instead of a single value. The set of values can be imagined in the form of a 'wave' with a particular distribution, specified for a specific dimension or variable (e.g. a cognitive developmental variable). The wave travels across the dimension or variable with a characteristic speed. In the course of its displacement, the wave undergoes certain contractions or expansions, which correspond with decreases and increases of variability (see Figure 11.3 for an example). This kind of model is not a growth model any more, strictly speaking, but a diffusion model. Technically, growth and diffusion models are closely related to one another (Banks 2003).

An interesting property of growth models that are specified over ranges or arrays instead of single values is that they can display patterns of change that

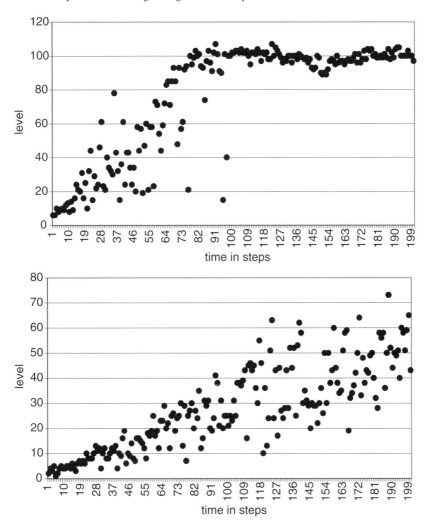

Figure 11.3. Two examples of a single-variable dynamic growth model based on a characteristic score range.

are difficult to obtain with the single-value models. One property is multi-modality: the simultaneous existence of more than one characteristic level (which, in practice, means the existence of more than one continuous range of values). Multi-modality is characteristic of transitory stages, when one mode of cognitive function gets replaced by another. It is also characteristic of the use of cognitive strategies that can be used as alternative ways of solving roughly similar kinds of problems (see for instance Siegler's wave model, Siegler 2002). In some cases, the distinct modes (i.e. simultaneous cognitive levels) are expressed in the form of distinct performance modalities, e.g. either by non-verbal pointing and gesture or by verbal explanation (Goldin-Meadow and Alibali 2002). Another interesting phenomenon that a range model can simulate quite easily is the occurrence of discontinuities in development. Discontinuities have been found in various domains of development, for instance in the form of sudden changes in cognitive level (see for instance van der Maas and Molenaar 1992; van der Maas 1993; Hosenfeld, van der Maas and van den Boom 1997a,b; Wimmers 1998; Ruhland and van Geert 1998; van Dijk and van Geert, submitted).

The major issues

This volume addresses three major issues: What changes in development, how does it change, why does it change? In this chapter, I have worked from a dynamic systems perspective and have strongly emphasized the issues of measurement and description. Which answers does the perspective discussed in the current chapter give to these questions?

What changes in development?

The answer to the question as to what changes in development depends on the phenomenon in which one is interested. Some phenomena are of course more fundamental and interesting than others, but I have not dealt with the question of which contents – which concepts, which skills, which structures – should be taken as the major focus of developmental research. That is an issue that I leave to other authors. What I have tried to emphasize is that, as soon as a topic or a phenomenon has been chosen, one should not try to find its true level or true presence, because such true level is an illusion. Development is concerned with different time scales, short and long term. Over the short term, phenomena have a characteristic variability, which will change over the course of development. Variability can be described by specifying the extremes of a phenomenon, that is, the limits within which it moves, and by specifying central tendencies. This variability, including the way a phenomenon depends on contexts – and contexts depend on the phenomenon – can be used to describe the intrinsic dynamics of the phenomenon in question, i.e. the process that shapes and moves it. It often takes great investments to unravel the dynamics of a phenomenon, such as the acquisition of the object concept or of prepositions, or for that matter, the structure of the cognitive system as a whole. However, the dynamics can be approached by focusing on the variability of the phenomenon, on its extreme values, its sensitivity to contextual variation and its influence on contextual variation, and the degrees of freedom within which it moves. All these phenomena are part of the natural history of the phenomenon in question, i.e. of its actual course of change, which one should try to capture by observing the phenomenon by means of time-serial studies, among others.

How and why does development occur?

A better understanding of the dynamics of a phenomenon – for instance of the way variables affect one another over time – suggests an answer to the second and third questions, namely how does a phenomenon change and why. In my view, dynamic modelling is an indispensable tool in developmental research. Almost any developmental theory or model contains a number of causal and conditional principles of change that, if put on the long-term temporal scale of developmental time, can give rise to non-linear and in general quite complicated effects. Modelling is about the only way to find out what a theory potentially predicts, given its basic assumptions and a variety of conditions. Unfortunately, the dynamics is often taken out of the model by linearizing the phenomena by means of averaging over groups and by employing other statistical techniques that make use of differences between individuals instead of differences and changes over real time. The point that I want to make is that most of the existing developmental theories and models contain the elements of a dynamic system in the broad sense of the word, in the form of the causal, conditional, sometimes reciprocal, relations between variables that they postulate, but that they seldom, if ever, put these dynamic principles together and check, by means of modelling, what kind of developmental patterns they potentially generate. The neo-Piagetian theories are an exception. Various researchers have used dynamic modelling based on the causal principles distinguished in their theories to come to a better understanding and explanation of the predicted or empirically observed patterns (see Fischer and Rose 1994, Case and Okamoto 1996; Demetriou et al. 2002). In summary, the question of how and why things develop can be answered by putting the implicit dynamics that many developmental theories already encompass into a coherent framework, based on real-time relations between the variables or phenomena of interest.

The place of dynamic systems theory among the major theories of development

The latter point brings me to a final question, namely that of the relationship between the dynamic viewpoint discussed in this chapter, and the major theories of cognitive development. The relationship – how could it be else – is a little complex. On the one hand, I believe the dynamic viewpoint is perfectly compatible with a great variety of developmental theories, simply because they entail many principles of change that are intrinsically dynamic. In that case, the dynamic viewpoint is almost like a methodological addition to those theories, providing them with tools that help them turn their conceptual statements into mathematically formulated, deductive models. In my own work, for instance, I have shown various ways in which classical theories, such as that of Piaget and Vygotsky, can be transformed into dynamic systems models that operate on the basis of the developmental principles that these classical theories have put forward (see for instance van Geert 1994b, 1998, 2000). The neo-Piagetian dynamic models discussed earlier are another example of the compatibility with a dynamic framework.

In spite of the potential similarities, there may also exist crucial differences. The dynamic approach not only applies to the long-term interactions between macroscopic developmental variables (for instance, the child's lexicon, or the level of understanding of arithmetical operations) but also applies to the short-term dynamics of the variables themselves. Earlier in this chapter, I argued that a concept, or any other psychological variable for that matter, should be conceived of as a process, not as a more or less static internal structure. That is, the dynamic viewpoint has major consequences for the way we conceptualize the nature of our basic theoretical notions, which are the content of the developmental process. The dynamic systems approach entails a contextualist, i.e. situated, and time-bound view on the nature of basic psychological phenomena. It focuses on variability, ambiguity and fuzziness as intrinsic aspects of those phenomena and challenges the existence of true scores and 'crisp' categories. This view on the nature of concepts, skills and abilities need not be shared by researchers who would otherwise nevertheless adhere to a dynamic view on the level of the long-term developmental interactions between the variables discerned by their theories. The contextualist and situated view comes in gradations, of course. Some theorists are quite radical in their rejection of notions such as 'concept' or 'knowledge' qua descriptive and explanatory terms (see for instance Thelen and Smith 1994 and Smith et al. 1999). Others take a considerably more moderate stance, accepting a contextualist and situated view without discarding notions like concept and knowledge as useful theoretical terms (see for instance Fischer and Bidell 1998). In summary, a dynamic view on development is compatible with many existing theories to the extent that those theories already contain dynamic notions and relationships. In that case the dynamic model may function as a useful addition to those theories. On the other hand, dynamic theories of cognition may entail a view on the nature of theoretical notions that is not compatible with the way they are conceptualized in the theories at issue.

REFERENCES

Alibali, M. W. and Goldin-Meadow, S. (1993). Gesture–speech mismatch and mechanisms of learning. What the hands reveal about a child's state of mind. *Cognitive Psychology, 25*, 4, 468–523.

Banks, R. B. (2003). *Growth and diffusion phenomena: mathematical frameworks and applications.* Berlin: Springer-Verlag.

Bidell, Th. R. and Fischer, K. W. (2003). Beyond the stage debate: action, structure and variability in Piagetian theory and research. In R. J. Sternberg and C. A. Berg (eds.) *Intellectual development* (pp. 100–40). Cambridge: Cambridge University Press.

Carroll, J. B. (1993). *Human cognitive abilities: a survey of factor-analytic studies.* New York: Cambridge University Press.

Case, R. (1985). *Intellectual development. Birth to adulthood.* New York: Academic Press.

(1992). *The mind's staircase: exploring the conceptual underpinnings of children's thought and knowledge.* Hillsdale, NJ: Erlbaum.

Case, R. and Okamoto, Y. (1996). The role of central conceptual structures in the development of children's thought. *Monographs of the Society for Research in Child Development.* 1996; vol. 61 (1–2): v–265.

Casti, J. L. (1997). *Would-be worlds: how simulation is changing the frontiers of science.* New York: John Wiley and Sons.

Clark, A. (1997). *Being there: putting brain, body and world together again.* Cambridge, MA: MIT Press.

Clark, A. and Chalmers, D. (1998). The extended mind. *Analysis, 58*, 7–19.

De Weerth, C. and van Geert, P. L. C. (2000). The dynamics of emotion-related behaviors in infancy. In M. Lewis and I. Granic (eds.) *Emotion, development and self-organization. Dynamic systems approaches to emotional development* (pp. 324–48). Cambridge: Cambridge University Press.

(2002a), A longitudinal study of basal cortisol in infants: intra-individual variability, circadian rhythm and developmental trends. *Infant Behaviour and Development, 25*, 2002, 340–74.

(2002b), Changing patterns of infant behaviour and mother-infant interaction: intra- and interindividual variability. *Infant Behaviour and Development, 24*(4), 2002, 347–71.

De Weerth, C., van Geert, P. and Hoijtink, H. (1999). Intraindividual variability in infant behaviour. *Developmental Psychology, 35*, 4, 1102–12.

Demetriou, A., Christou, C. Spanoudis, G. and Platsidou, M. (2002). The development of mental processing: efficiency, working memory, and thinking. *Monographs of the Society for Research in Child Development.* 2002; vol. 67(1) 268: vii–154.

Demetriou, A., Efklides, A. and Platsidou, M. (1993). The architecture and dynamics of developing mind: experiential structuralism as a frame for unifying cognitive developmental theories. *Monographs of the Society for Research in Child Development*, 58 (5–6, serial no. 234).

Elman, J. L., Bates, E. A., Johnson, M. H. and Karmiloff-Smith, A. (1996). *Rethinking innateness: a connectionist perspective on development.* Cambridge, MA: MIT Press.

Fischer, K. W. (1980). A theory of cognitive development: the control and construction of hierarchies of skills. *Psychological Review, 87*, 477–531.

Fischer, K. W. and Bidell, T. R. (1998). Dynamic development of psychological structures in action and thought. In R. M. Lerner (ed.) and W. Damon (series ed.), *Handbook of child psychology: vol. 1. Theoretical models of human development* (5th edn, pp. 467–561). New York: Wiley.

Fisher, K. W. and Dawson, Th. L. (2002). A new kind of developmental science: using models to integrate theory and research. *Monographs of the Society for Research in Child Development.* 2002; vol. 67(1), 156–67.

Fischer, K. W. and Rose, S. P. (1994). Dynamic development of coordination of components in brain and behaviour: a framework for theory and research. In G. Dawson and K. W. Fischer (eds.) *Human behaviour and the developing brain* (pp. 3–66). New York: Guilford.

Fischer, K. W. and Yan, Z. (2002). Darwin's construction of the theory of evolution: microdevelopment and explanations of variation and change in species. In N. Granott and J. Parziale (eds.) *Microdevelopment: transition processes in learning and development* (pp. 294–318). Cambridge: Cambridge University Press.

Gardner, M. K. and Clark, E. (1992). The psychometric perspective on intellectual development in childhood and adolescence. In R. J. Sternberg and C. A. Berg (eds.) *Intellectual development* (pp. 16–43). Cambridge: Cambridge University Press.

Gilob, F. and Lake, C. (1964). *Life with Picasso*. New York: McGraw Hill.

Goldin-Meadow, S. and Alibali, M. W. (2002). Looking at the hands through time: a micro-genetic perspective on learning and instruction. In N. Granott and J. Parziale (eds.) *Microdevelopment: transition processes in development and learning* (pp. 80–108). Cambridge: Cambridge University Press.

Goldin-Meadow, S., Alibali, M. W. and Church, R. B. (1993). Transitions in concept acquisition: using the hand to read the mind. *Psychological Review, 100*, 279–97.

Greeno, J. G. and Middle School Mathematics Through Applications Project Group. (1998). The situativity of knowing, learning, and research. *American Psychologist, 53*, 5–26.

Grigorenko, E. L. and Sternberg R. J. (1998). Dynamic testing. *Psychological Bulletin, 124* (1), 75–111.

Hartelman, P. A., van der Maas, H. L. J. and Molenaar, P. C. M. (1998). Detecting and modelling developmental transitions. *British Journal of Developmental Psychology, 16*, 97–122.

Hosenfeld, B., van der Maas, H. L. J. and van den Boom, D. C. (1997a). Detecting bimodality in the analogical reasoning performance of elementary schoolchildren. *International Journal of Behavioral Development, 20*(3), 529–47.

(1997b). Indicators of discontinuous change in the development of analogical reasoning. *Journal of Experimental Child Psychology, 64*(3), 367–95.

Kail, R. and Bisanz, J. (2003). The information processing perspective on cognitive development in childhood and adolescence. In R. J. Sternberg and C. A. Berg (eds.) *Intellectual development* (pp. 229–60). Cambridge: Cambridge University Press.

Lord, F. M. and Novick, M. R. (1968). *Statistical theories of mental test scores*. Reading, MA: Addison-Wesley.

Molenaar, P. (2004). A manifesto on psychology as idiographic science: bringing the person back into scientific psychology – this time forever. Measurement. *Interdisciplinary Research and Perspectives, 2* (in press).

Molenaar, P. C. M., Huizenga, H. M. and Nesselroade, J. R. (2002). The relationship between the structure of intra-individual and inter-individual variability: a theoretical and empirical vindication of developmental systems theory. In U. Staudinger and U. Lindenberger (eds.) *Understanding human development.* Dordrecht: Kluwer.

Ruhland, R. and van Geert, P. (1998). Jumping into syntax: transitions in the development of closed class words. *British Journal of Developmental Psychology, 16,* 65–95.

Siegler, R. S. (2002). Microgenetic studies of self-explanation. In N. Granott and J. Parziale (eds.) *Microdevelopment: transition processes in development and learning* (pp. 31–58). Cambridge: Cambridge University Press.

Simonoff, J. S. (1996). *Smoothing methods in statistics.* Springer: New York.

Smith, L. B., Thelen, E., Titzer, R. and McLin, D. (1999). Knowing in the context of acting: the task dynamics of the A-not-B error. *Psychological Review, 106,* 235–60.

Steenbeek, H. and van Geert, P. (submitted). 'Do you still like to play with him?' Variability and the dynamic nature of children's sociometric ratings.

Thelen, E. and Smith, L. B. (1994). *A dynamic systems approach to the development of cognitions and action,* Cambridge, MA: Bradford Books, MIT.

Traub, R. E. (1994). *Reliability for the social sciences: theory and applications.* Thousand Oaks, CA: Sage.

Valsiner, J. (1987). *Culture and the development of children's action.* Chichester: Wiley.

van der Maas, H. L. (1993). *Catastrophe analysis of stagewise cognitive development.* Amsterdam: Faculty of Psychology, University of Amsterdam (Academic dissertation).

van der Maas, H. L. and Molenaar, P. C. (1992). Stagewise cognitive development: an application of catastrophe theory. *Psychological Review, 99,* 395–417.

van Dijk, M. and van Geert, P. (submitted). Continuity and discontinuity in early language development: is the acquisition of prepositions continuous or discontinuous?

van Dijk, M., De Goede, D., Ruhland, R. and van Geert, P. (2000). Kindertaal met bokkensprongen/Child language cuts capers. *Nederlands Tijdschrift voor de Psychologie en haar Grensgebieden, 55,* 232–45.

van Geert, P. (1991). A dynamic systems model of cognitive and language growth. *Psychological Review, 98,* 3–53.

(1994). *Dynamic systems of development: change between complexity and chaos.* New York: Harvester Wheatsheaf.

(1994b). Vygotskian dynamics of development. *Human Development, 37,* 346–65.

(1998). A dynamic systems model of basic developmental mechanisms: Piaget, Vygotsky, and beyond. *Psychological Review, 105,* 634–77.

(2000). The dynamics of general developmental mechanisms: from Piaget and Vygotsky to dynamic systems models. *Current Directions in Psychological Science, 9*(2): 64–8.

(2002). Developmental dynamics, intentional action and fuzzy sets. In N. Granott and J. Parziale (eds.) *Microdevelopment: transition processes in development and learning* (pp. 319–43). Cambridge: Cambridge University Press.

van Geert, P. L. C., Savelsbergh, G. and van der Maas, H. (1999). Transitions and non-linear dynamics in developmental psychology. In G. Savelsbergh, H. van der Maas and P. L. C. van Geert (eds.) *Non-linear developmental processes.* (pp. 11–20). New York: Elsevier Science Publishers.

van Geert, P. L. C. and van Dijk, M. (2002). Focus on variability: new tools to study intra-individual variability in developmental data. *Infant Behaviour and Development, 25*, 2002, 340–74.

(2003). The problem of inter-observer reliability in ambiguous observation data. *First Language, 23*(3): 259–84.

van Halen, C. (2002). The uncertainties of self and identity. Groningen: doctoral dissertation.

Vygotsky, L. S. (1978). *Mind in society*. London: Harvard University Press.

Wimmers, R. H. (1996). Grasping developmental change: theory, methodology and data. Free University of Amsterdam: doctoral dissertation.

Wimmers, R. H., Savelsbergh, G. J. P., van der kamp, J. and Hartelman, P. (1996). A developmental transition in prehension modelled as a cusp catastrophe. *Developmental Psychobiology* (submitted).

12 Modelling individual differences in change through latent variable growth and mixture growth modelling: basic principles and empirical examples

Jan-Eric Gustafsson

Introduction

One of the most interesting and challenging tasks in the intersection of the fields of developmental psychology and differential psychology is the study of individual differences in development over time. To understand the nature of change during development, how change occurs, and what causes change it seems necessary not only to investigate general patterns, but also to take individual differences into account. There was, however, a time, not so long ago, when those with a focus on individual differences were reluctant to approach questions about change, because measurement of change was regarded as hopelessly difficult (e.g. Harris 1963). And those focusing on developmental problems have tended to neglect individual differences altogether.

During the last two decades the situation has changed dramatically for the better, however. One reason for this is the appearance of a new class of analytic techniques, namely growth curve models, or, for short, growth models. The basic idea of growth modelling is to describe developmental trajectories over time in terms of parsimonious models, the parameters of which may capture aspects such as initial level and rate of change. The analysis of growth curves was early identified as an important approach to research in developmental psychology (e.g. Bayley 1956). However, it was not until appropriate statistical techniques were developed in the 1980s that growth models were adopted on a wider scale in developmental psychology. Important contributions to the development and dissemination of this class of models were made by McArdle (1988), McArdle and Epstein (1987), Meredith and Tisak (1990), Rogosa, Brandt and Zimowski (1982), Rogosa and Willett (1985) and others.

Growth curve models are well suited for research on several of the fundamental questions which are investigated in developmental psychology. The basic reason for this is that most of the phenomena studied in developmental research concern change over time, and time is explicitly represented as a variable in growth models. Growth models do, furthermore, provide integrated structures for representing the correlations, variances and means of a set of repeatedly measured variables, and they can do so under a broad variety of assumptions about the nature of the developmental process, such as whether it is continuous or discontinuous, or if it is unidimensional or multidimensional. The growth curve techniques also allow flexible approaches for studying antecedents and consequences of individual development. These advantages, among others, were reasons for Fischer and Dawson (2002) to suggest that '[g]rowth analysis should be a basic part of developmental research' (p. 163).

The main purpose of the present chapter is to provide a simple and concrete introduction to these techniques. While the focus thus primarily is methodological, the discussion will address some of the issues that need to be solved to achieve a true integration of developmental and differential psychology.

Basic growth models

The simplest growth model is a linear model, which may be represented by a simple regression model with an intercept parameter which expresses initial level and a slope parameter which expresses linear change. This model may be thought of as a repeated measures model, in which measures of the same characteristic are regressed upon time. Typically, however, we have measurements at few time points, often no more than three to five, so when we try to estimate such models at the individual level the estimates of the slope and intercept parameters are swamped by noise. Thus, it is not a viable approach to use ordinary regression techniques on the data from one individual at a time, assemble the parameter estimates, and then relate these to other variables.

An alternative approach is to apply what is called 'random coefficients' modelling. In this approach the individual parameters are not estimated, but instead assumptions are made about their distribution (e.g. normal), and the estimation problem then is to determine the parameters of this distribution (i.e. mean and variance for a normal distribution). Such random coefficients models may be estimated with software for hierarchical linear modelling (see e.g. Goldstein 1985; Raudenbush and Chan 1992). Growth models may also be specified as structural equation models (SEM, see McArdle 1988; Muthén 1996, 1997; Muthén and Khoo 1998; Willet and Sayer 1994). In the SEM framework, latent variables are introduced which may be thought of as 'containers' for the random coefficients. In a linear growth model there is thus one latent variable which represents individual differences in intercept parameters, and another latent variable which represents individual differences in the slope parameters. These latent variables may then be used as dependent and as independent variables in extended SEM models, in which antecedents and consequences of change are studied. This is an extremely powerful framework for studying individual differences in development.

In the present chapter, application of this framework will be illustrated with a study of individual differences in change in achievement over time in higher education. In particular, I will analyse the achievement over four years of study of some 3,000 civil engineering students. Before going into this example there is reason, however, to bring up yet another complication. This has to do with the problem that it may not be possible to capture the full range of individual differences with the parameters of a more or less elaborate growth model. What if there are distinct subclasses of persons who develop along different trajectories, and which therefore need to be described by different models?

Such heterogeneity may, indeed, be dealt with in an approach that is called 'mixture growth modelling' and which owes its development to Muthén (2000, 2001a, 2001b; Muthén and Muthén 2000). The basic idea in mixture modelling is that a population may be regarded as being composed of two or more homogeneous subpopulations for which different models need to be fitted (Muthén 1989). This is thus like a multiple-group modelling situation, except that no explicit variable exists for identification of group membership. Instead separation of the different subpopulations (or latent classes) is one of the results of the analyses. Such latent variable mixture modelling may be performed with the Mplus program (Muthén and Muthén 2001), and it will be applied in our empirical study as well.

Development through the course of higher education

Quite a large proportion of a cohort spends at least a couple of years in tertiary level education in order to acquire vocational skills and/or a general education. For some students the years of higher education are characterized by sucessful studies and growth of competences, while for others the experience of higher education is not so positive.

Some quite interesting early qualitative studies of development and cognitive change in higher education have been reported by Heath (1978) and Perry (1970). In these studies, which were based on repeated interviews with rather small groups of students at Princeton and Harvard, different kinds of relations to studying and knowledge were identified among the students in a developmental framework.

Another area of research which is more directly related to the empirical work to be presented here concerns prediction of academic achievement. However, this research has almost exclusively focused on first-year achievement. Thus, there is almost no research available which concerns prediction of development of achievement over time. The reasons for this are probably to be found in technical difficulties which have to do with the fact that a smaller and smaller fraction of a group of students which started together one year will remain together in later years, because of planned and unplanned deviations from the normal course of study. This will cause similar problems of restriction of range as when prediction of achievement is only done among those admitted to an education, and not among those who apply for it. As has been demonstrated by Gustafsson and Reuterberg (2000) it is, however, possible to solve these problems by application of missing-data modelling (Muthén, Kaplan and Hollis 1987) and such an approach may solve the problem of attrition during the course of study as well.

There is thus a great need to understand individual differences in development over a full program of study, such as the civil engineer program which is under study here. In the empirical study it is shown how this may be done with growth modelling and mixture growth modelling techniques.

Method

The empirical study relies on data from a large-scale longitudinal project, in which there is information about everyone in Sweden born during the years 1972 to 1979 (for a short description in Swedish, see Gustafsson, Andersson and Hansen 2000). The variables represent background data (e.g. socioeconomic status, country of birth) and a wealth of information about educational achievements and choices from the last grade of compulsory school through tertiary education. Here a small subset of this information is used.

Most of the analyses have been conducted with Mplus Version 2 (Muthén and Muthén 2001), under the STREAMS 2.5 (Gustafsson and Stahl 2000, 2001) modelling environment.

The civil engineer program

Sweden has a system of Credit Points (CP), where one term of successful full-time studies with a workload of forty hours per week can yield twenty credit points, and one year can yield forty credit points. Grades are generally given on a three-level scale: pass with distinction, pass and fail ('väl godkänd, godkänd, underkänd'). A number of programs, however, use a two-level scale: pass and fail. Others, like law and engineering, use scales with several levels. In the official record keeping the credit points earned in successful examination are entered, but no information is available about which particular grade was achieved. Thus, the data available for analysis represent the number of credit points achieved, without any further information about the quality of the academic achievement.

A complete civil engineer (CE) education is in Sweden offered by seven universities or technical universities. In 1993 there were some 15 programs of study, with different specializations. The programs comprise a total of 180 credit points, which implies that the education normally is to be completed in four and a half years. However, few admitted students complete the programs according to these expectations. Less than two thirds of the students admitted to the CE programs in the late 1980s had completed their programs seven years later. The number of students experiencing failure in their studies thus is fairly large, but there also are other reasons why students don't complete their educations, such as getting a job, or starting another, and perhaps more attractive, program of study.

Subjects

In the Autumn term of 1993 a total of 5,579 students were admitted to the CE programs (Svensson, Gustafsson and Reuterberg 2001). The number of applicants was higher, however, there being 8,350 students who had chosen a CE program as their first choice. However, here we only have access to data for those born from 1972 and later, and some of the students admitted were born before 1972. The data set to be analysed comprises 471 students. Of these 21 per cent were born in 1972, which implies that they were twenty-one years old when they started their education. About 30 per cent were born in 1973 (i.e. twenty years old) and 48 per cent were born in 1974 (i.e. nineteen years old). Some 24 per cent of the admitted students are females.

We will study the achievement of these students during their first four years of study, i.e. from the academic year 1993/4 through the academic years 1996/7. This is how far in time the available data extend.

Predictors of achievement

In the Swedish system for admission to higher education, applicants are rank-ordered on the basis of their results on two selection instruments. One is grades from upper secondary education, and the other is the score on the Swedish Scholastic Achievement Test (SweSAT). The latter test is voluntary, but for a program with a highly competitive admission situation such as the CE program, most applicants take the test. To around 65 per cent of the study positions in the CE program admittance is based on grades, and admittance to the remaining study positions is based on the SweSAT score.

For the cohorts under study here the grades are assigned on a scale from 1 to 5 under a norm-referenced system. For purposes of selection to higher education a mean grade based on the grades achieved in the subjects included in the program of study is computed. Even though this variable (grade) is not of any particular theoretical interest in the present study it must be included in all analyses because selection is explicitly based on this variable.

The SweSAT consists of six subtests which measure both verbal and non-verbal abilities, the capacity to make use of information, and general

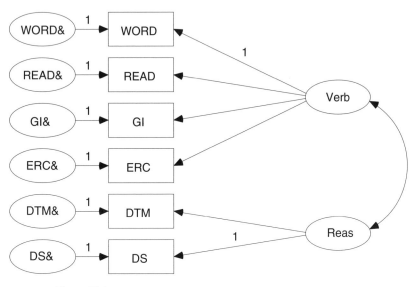

Figure 12.1.

knowledge. The following subtests are included in the SweSAT version (1993A) that will be analysed here:

- *Vocabulary* (WORD), which measures understanding of words and concepts.
- *Data sufficiency* (DS), which aims to measure numerical reasoning ability.
- *Reading comprehension* (READ), which measures reading comprehension in a wide sense.
- *Diagrams, tables and maps* (DTM) which is a problem-solving test with information presented in tables, graphs and/or maps.
- *General information* (GI) which measures knowledge and information from many different areas.
- *English reading comprehension* (ERC) which measures reading comprehension in English

In practical applications the six subtest scores are summed into a total raw score, which is transformed into a normed score, in such a way that variations in the difficulty of different versions of the test are taken into account.

It is known, however, that the test measures two major dimensions of ability (Gustafsson, Wedman and Westerlund 1992). An oblique confirmatory factor analytic model with one verbal (verb) and one non-verbal reasoning (reas) factor may thus be fitted to the test (see Figure 12.1). This two-factor model will be used in the analyses of antecedents of individual differences in change.

Table 12.1. *Credit points obtained over the four years of study.*

Year	N	Mean	Sd
Credit points 1993	3471	27.79	11.42
Credit points 1994	3002	30.24	13.17
Credit points 1995	2305	32.34	13.35
Credit points 1996	2349	33.45	12.28

Results

The presentation of the results will be done in three steps. First some descriptive results are presented. Then results from a regular growth model fitted to the CP obtained during the four years will be presented, and finally results from a mixture growth modelling approach are discussed.

Descriptive results

Table 12.1 presents descriptive data for the credit points obtained for each of the four academic years.

It may first of all be noted that there is an increase in the mean credit point score over the years, from 27.8 in 1993 to 33.5 in 1996. This would seem to suggest that achievement is improving over time. It must, however, be observed that there is also a considerable attrition over the years. The results for 1995 are thus computed on 2305 students only, or 66 per cent of the group that started in 1993. It is reasonable to assume that students with a poorer achievement are over-represented among the missing students in 1995, which may explain the increase in mean achievement among those who obtained a result in 1995.

A credit point is recorded for each of the four years for just 1635 students. This group of students obtained a mean credit point score of 31.5 during the first year of study, which is higher than the result obtained by all admitted students (27.8). If we were to evaluate the results over time by analysing only those students with a complete result we would thus face a similar problem as when prognostic validity is investigated: only a small group of positively selected students remain for analysis, which causes the familiar problem of restriction of range.

As has been shown by Gustafsson and Reuterberg (2000; see also Reuterberg 2002) the restriction of range problem may, however, be solved through use of missing data modelling (e.g. Muthén, Kaplan and Hollis 1987). With this technique all cases are included in the analysis through computation of one covariance matrix and mean vector for each combination of valid scores. In

Table 12.2. *Patterns of credit points obtained over the four years.*

Year	Comb 1	Comb 2	Comb 3	Comb 4	Comb 5	Comb 6	Comb 7	Comb 8
CP 1993	X	X	X	X	X	X	X	X
CP 1994	X	X	X	X				
CP 1995	X	X			X	X		
CP 1996	X		X		X		X	
N	1635	527	569	271	116	27	29	297

Table 12.3. *Correlations among credit points over the four years.*

	CP 1993	CP 1994	CP 1995	CP 1996
CP 1993	1			
CP 1994	0.57	1		
CP 1995	0.33	0.4	1	
CP 1996	0.22	0.21	0.2	1

the modelling these separate matrices are then in a sense weighed together into one matrix, which represents the matrix that would be observed if complete data had been available for all cases. This technique will be used here.

Table 12.2 presents the different combinations of scores obtained over the four years.

The different patterns of achievement over the years could of course be analysed with respect to both the meaning of each pattern, and possible predictors. Some combinations thus indicate failure and drop-out from the program (e.g. Comb 4 and 8), while others indicate successful studies (e.g. Comb 1, 2, 3), but possibly with a year off to do something else. Here, however, we will, initially at least, just regard these patterns of study activity as different patterns of missing data.

Before going into growth curve modelling of these data there is reason to take a further look at some descriptive statistics. Table 12.3 presents the correlations among the four achievement measures, which have been computed with pairwise deletion of missing data.

The correlations display the typical pattern of diminishing with an increasing time distance (see Humphreys 1968). It may be noted, however, that even adjacent measures towards the end of the period show low correlations. It is also of some interest to describe the total number of credit points earned during the four years. Figure 12.2 presents a histogram of the total scores.

The distribution has at least three distinguishable peaks. One is for a very low total of credit points (0–20). Another peak is at around 120 credit points,

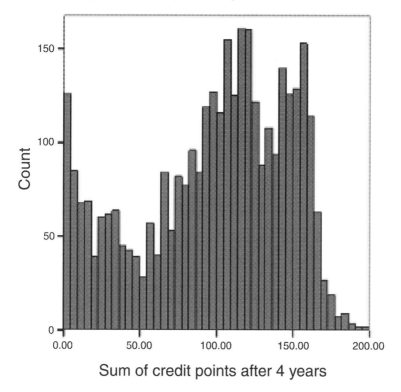

Figure 12.2.

and the third around 160 credit points. This distribution seems to reflect both the number of years of active study, and individual differences in achievement during each year of study.

Growth modelling of achievement

As has already been pointed out, growth models may be estimated in several different ways, but the most flexible and powerful approach seems to be through structural equation modelling. In the SEM approach to growth modelling a model is set up in which two or more latent variables are specified to represent individual differences in the parameters of the growth model. In Figure 12.3 a path diagram is shown for a linear growth model for the credit points measure over the four years.

The model includes two latent variables: *Int* and *Slope*. The *Int* variable represents initial individual differences in achievement, which here is achievement during the first year. This latent variable has a fixed relation of unity to all

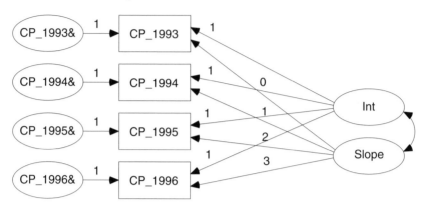

Figure 12.3. Path diagram for a linear growth model for the credit points earned over 4 years.

four manifest variables. The *Slope* variable represents individual differences in change over time. The *Slope* variable has a relation of 0 with the CP 1993 measure, a fixed relation of 1 with CP 1994, a fixed relation of 2 with CP 1995 and a fixed relation of 3 with CP 1996. This expresses the modelling assumption that change is a linear function of time. In this model the means of the manifest variables are constrained to 0. This, along with the fixed relations between the latent variables and the manifest variables, allows the latent variables to function as containers, as it were, of parameters of the random coefficients model. Thus, for the *Int* latent variable a mean and a variance are estimated, where the variance represents individual differences in the intercept of the growth model. For the *Slope* parameter too a mean and a variance are estimated, and here the variance parameter represents individual differences in linear change over time.

The SEM approach thus allows easy set-up, estimation and interpretation of the growth models. Missing data can be dealt with by at least some programs, as can ordinal data. It is, furthermore, possible to use a wide array of different estimators which are suitable for data with different distributional characteristics. What is even more important, however, is that the latent variables of the growth model may be used both as independent and dependent variables within larger SEM models, which also include measures of antecedents and consequences of change.

The model specified in Figure 12.3 has been estimated with the Mplus program (Muthén and Muthén 2001). The missing data modelling option has been used, so all available data are taken into account in the estimation of the model. According to the goodness-of-fit test this model does not fit so well (chi-square = 75.10, df = 5). However, the sample size is large so we should rely on other measures of fit to evaluate how well this model accounts for the observed data. The RMSEA measure is 0.064, with a 90 per cent confidence

Table 12.4. *Parameter estimates from the linear growth model.*

Variable	Mean	Variance
Intercept	27.74	100.73
Slope	1.45	7.39

interval between 0.051 and 0.077. These measures indicate acceptable fit, even though they also indicate that there is some room for improvement of the model. The CFI measure of 0.954 also indicates acceptable fit. This model may thus be accepted as a first approximation of the observed data. Table 12.4 presents some of the parameter estimates.

The estimate of the mean of the intercept parameter is 27.7, which comes close to the observed mean for CP 1993. The mean of the slope is 1.45, which estimate is significantly different from 0 ($t = 16.89$). Thus, this analysis too indicates that there is an increase in achievement over time. According to the growth model the mean credit point score in 1996 would be $27.74 + 3*1.45 = 32.09$. This estimate is somewhat lower than the observed value of 33.5, but it should be remembered that the observed measure is computed for those students remaining in the education.

The variance estimates of the intercept and slope are both highly significant ($t = 24.12$ and $t = 7.42$ respectively). For the intercept the standard deviation is around 10, and if a normal distribution is assumed, the mean of the intercept plus/minus two standard deviations would cover about 95 per cent of the observations. This would imply an estimated interval from around 8 to around 48 credit points. The observed interval is likely to have 0 as the lower end, however, which indicates that the distribution is not quite symmetric. For the slope parameter the standard deviation is 2.7. This implies that those with the lowest slope have an estimate of -4.0 (i.e. $1.45 - 2*2.7$) and those with the highest slope have an estimate of 6.9 (i.e. $1.45 + 2*2.7$). These examples show that some students develop favourably over time, while for others achievement gets successively worse. The slope parameter expresses the yearly change, so by the end of the period there are large individual differences in achievement as a function of differential change.

The slope and the intercept parameters correlate -0.65. This implies that those who start out at a high level of achievement improve less than those who start out at a low level of achievement. One of the reasons for this is that it is not possible, in principle at least, to obtain more than forty credit points during one year. Thus, those who achieve the credit points they are supposed to achieve during the first year of study cannot increase their achievement during the remaining years.

The next question to be addressed is if there are other variables that may account for the individual differences in slope and intercept parameters. In particular, it is of great interest to know if the instruments used for selection of students to the CE program are capable of predicting achievement level and changes in achievement level during the four years. As has already been mentioned, the Swedish system for selection of students uses grades from upper secondary school and the Swedish Scholastic Aptitude Test as selection instruments. We will now investigate how these measures relate to the parameters of the growth model.

It has already been established that performance on the six subtest scores of the SweSAT can be accounted for in terms of two latent variables (verb and reas). There thus are three correlated predictors (grades, verb and reas) which predict the int and slope latent variables. In order to obtain the correct estimates it is, however, not possible to restrict the analysis to those who have been admitted to the CE program. This is because there is restriction of range on the predictor variables for those admitted, and, more importantly, because in Sweden a disjunctive selection system is used, in which students may be admitted either because they have high grades, or because they have a high score on the SweSAT. This disjunctive selection system causes a negative correlation between grades and SweSAT score among those admitted, which in turn causes considerable bias in the estimation of the relations among the selection instruments and achievement among those admitted. There may, in fact, be a negative relation between SweSAT and achievement among those admitted, when in fact the true correlation is positive and quite high (Gustafsson and Reuterberg 2000; Reuterberg 2002). This problem may, however, be solved by adding information on the selection instruments for those who applied (or were eligible for applying) but were not admitted, and to estimate the model as a missing data model.

This model, which comprises eleven manifest variables and three latent variables, has been estimated from a dataset of 40,065 cases. The dataset includes those born during the years 1972 to 1974 who have completed a natural science or technology program of upper secondary school, and therefore are eligible to apply to the CE program. The standardized parameter estimates for the regression of the int and slope variables are presented in Table 12.5.

As may be seen in the table all the partial regression coefficients are highly significant. For the intercept variable the predictors account for no less than 45 per cent of the variance, which corresponds to a multiple R of 0.67. For the slope variable 28 per cent of the variance is accounted for (multiple R = 0.53). The best predictor for the intercept is grades (0.62) but the reas factor also contributes with a positive coefficient, while the verb factor has a negative relation with intercept. For the slope variable the pattern of prediction is reversed: here grades and reas have negative relations, while verb has a positive relation.

Table 12.5. *Coefficients for the regression of intercept and slope on selection instruments.*

	Intercept		Slope	
Variable	b	t	b	t
Grades	0.62	19.46	−0.26	−3.07
Reas	0.38	7.61	−0.55	−4.06
Verb	−0.41	−8.64	0.43	3.37

These results thus indicate that the cognitive requirements are quite different during the course of the CE program: during the initial year achievement is above all determined by grades and non-verbal reasoning abilities. It should be observed that the grades for this particular group of persons is more heavily weighted towards mathematics and science achievement than achievement in other areas, because maths and science form a heavy part of the curriculum of the science and technology programs. This pattern of relationships is easily understood, given that the first year of study in the CE programs has a heavy emphasis on mathematics and basic science courses. The pattern of relations with the slope factor indicates that a high level of performance on verb and a lower level of performance on reas and grades is associated with a positive development of achievement. One possible explanation for this pattern is that the later parts of the CE programs tend to be more applied, and involve more reading and writing.

These results show that it is possible to establish meaningful patterns of relationships between traditional measures of individual differences and parameters determined from a growth model for change in achievement over time. There is reason to believe, however, that the growth model fitted above may not fully capture the observed data. One problem with the model thus is that it does not take into account the fact that the credit points measure cannot become lower than 0, and that it cannot exceed 40 (at least not by much) at the same time as a credit points score of 40 is the ideal result. The distribution of the credit points measure is thus not well captured by a normal distribution. Below, alternative models will, therefore, be explored.

Mixture growth modelling

There are several statistical models which partition heterogeneous data sets into homogeneous populations. Latent class analysis is one example, and latent profile analysis is another. Muthén (e.g. 2001b) has recently extended the SEM framework to include categorical latent variables as well, thereby making it possible to specify a wide variety of models which involve partitioning of a

Table 12.6. *Statistics for models assuming a different number of latent classes.*

Number of classes	Model type	H0 Value	No Param	AIC	BIC	Entropy
1		−43111.1	9	86240.3	86295.6	NA
2	Constraints on parameters over classes	−42703.9	12	85431.7	85505.5	0.836
2	No constraints on parameters over classes	−42148.8	19	84335.6	84452.5	0.733
3	Constraints on parameters over classes	−42655.7	15	85341.5	85433.8	0.783

set of data into homogeneous subsets. This allows specification of latent class models and other classical mixture models as special cases of a more general model. This more general model includes both categorical and continuous latent variables and allows specification of models in which different SEM models are fitted for different latent classes.

It is, thus, possible to specify models in which one growth model applies to one subset of the data, and another growth model applies to another subset of the data. This approach will be used here, by simply testing hypotheses about an increasing number of latent classes. Such mixture growth models may be estimated with the Mplus program (Muthén and Muthén 2001), and particularly when used in combination with the STREAMS program (Gustafsson and Stahl 2001) they are fairly easy to estimate.

In the first step, the hypothesis that there are two latent classes was tested, and this model converged without any problems. In order to see if there is an improvement of fit, changes in the minimum of the loglikelihood function in relation to the number of parameters estimated may be investigated, and changes in information measures such as the AIC or BIC may also be investigated.

All these statistics give evidence of improvement when comparing the two-class model with the basic non-mixture growth model. In this two-class model all the parameters except the mean of the latent variables are, however, constrained to be equal over the two groups, so this is a very restrictive model. Relaxing the constraints of equality causes the fit of the two-class model to improve further, as is seen in Table 12.6.

Next, the hypothesis that there are three latent classes was tested. This model has a better fit than the constrained two-class model, but a worse fit than the unconstrained two-class model. However, when the equality constraints on the parameters of the three-class model were removed the model failed to converge. This suggests that the two-class model without constraints on the parameters

Table 12.7. *Parameter estimates
from the two-class mixture growth
model.*

Variable	Class 1	Class 2
Mean of intercept	23.2	37.3
Mean of slope	2.05	0.6
Var of intercept	74.9	2.3
Var of slope	9.4	0.1
Corr slope and intercept	−0.65	na
Error var CP 1993	51.6	9.5
Error var CP 1994	150.6	20.7
Error var CP 1995	176.8	45.4
Error var CP 1996	131.7	74.2
Number of cases	2271	1200

over classes is the model to be preferred. Table 12.7 presents estimates of parameters for the two classes.

This model identifies one class with a high mean intercept (37.3), a mean slope close to zero, and a very low variance in both intercept and slope. The error variances of the manifest variables also are low in this class. There are 1200 cases in this group, who thus may be said to be successful students. The other class, in which there are 2271 cases, represents more of a regular linear growth model, with considerable variance estimates for both slope and intercept. The mean of the intercept is 23.2, so the first-year achievement is only about half of what is expected. The large variance of the slope parameter shows, however, that some students develop favourably, while the achievement of other students drops even lower.

The mixture growth model thus separates the students into one consistently high-performing class, and one class for which achievement varies over time. This decomposition of the population also transforms the nature of the prediction problem. For class 2 the problem is one of predicting membership of this class; after that has been done there is no further variation to account for. For class 1, however, we are still faced with the same kind of prediction problem as we have already studied in our growth model.

It is, in principle, possible to extend the mixture growth model with independent variables, and to fit different models for the different classes. Here, however, we run into the problem that there are missing data on the manifest independent variables, which Mplus does not allow for mixture models. In order to analyse the two latent classes a simpler, two-step, approach has instead been used, in which the class belongingness of each individual case has

Table 12.8. *Coefficients for the regression of latent class belongingness on selection instruments.*

	Class 1			Class 2		
Variable	B	b	Wald	B	b	Wald
Grades	0.96	0.17	424.8	2.1	0.29	775.6
SweSAT	0.05	0.06	50.1	−0.03	−0.03	10.1

Table 12.9. *Unstandardized coefficients for the regression of intercept and slope on selection instruments.*

	Intercept		Slope	
Variable	Total	Class 1	Total	Class 1
Grades	9.55	8.14	−0.73	−0.93
Reas	1.92	1.66	−0.5	−0.41
Verb	−1	−1.03	0.19	0.19

been determined, and this information has then been used to perform separate analyses for the two classes.

First, an analysis has been performed in which class belongingness has been predicted in one ordinary logistic regression analysis (performed with SPSS) for each class, using the total SweSAT score and the grades as independent variables. These analyses have been conducted on the same set of some 40,000 cases as was used before. Table 12.8 presents the results.

The high-performing class 2 has a considerably higher regression coefficient for grades than has class 1, while for both classes SweSAT has low coefficients. Thus, the consistently high-performing CE students have higher grades than have those with a lower and more varying level of achievement.

For persons belonging to class 1 we can repeat the same regression analysis of the parameters of the growth model on the selection instruments. Table 12.9 presents the results, and for purposes of comparison the table also includes the results for the total group.

Here it is necessary to focus the comparison on the unstandardized regression coefficients, because these are not affected by differences in degree of selectivity among the two groups of subjects. The overall patterns of results are quite similar for class 1 and the total group. Thus, for verb, the unstandardized coefficients are identical with respect to both intercept and slope for the two groups. For the other two predictors there are some differences but these are quite small, and they do not indicate that the pattern of results obtained in the ordinary growth model is an artifact caused by the failure to distinguish the two classes in this analysis.

Discussion and conclusions

The main purpose of the present study has been to illustrate use of growth modelling for understanding general patterns and individual differences in change of academic achievement over extended periods of time in higher education. The study also is of interest from a substantive point of view, however. Thus, given that almost all previous prediction oriented studies have focused on first-year achievement, there is a great need for this kind of knowledge from both practical and theoretical points of view. The substantive aspects will be developed in greater detail elsewhere, but some results are briefly discussed below.

Substantive findings

A linear growth model over the four years fits the data reasonably well, and the results indicate substantial individual differences both in first-year achievement and in development over time. What is even more interesting is that the pattern of cognitive abilities required during the first year appears to be different from those in later parts of the program. Mathematical reasoning abilities, along with high performance from upper secondary education, are important for success during the first year of the CE program (see also Svensson et al. 2001). However, a positive development throughout the other three years of the program is associated with verbal ability. These results indicate that studies which investigate prediction of academic achievement only by investigating first-year achievement may be capturing only a limited aspect of a more complex reality.

The results also indicate that the CE program may, indeed, put too heavy an emphasis on mathematics and basic science during the first year of study. This emphasis is likely to put so heavy a strain on some students that they drop out of the education, even though they may have the abilities required for success in the other parts of the program, and may well be able to cope with the requirements of the current first-year program if given more time. It might, thus, be worthwhile to consider some changes of the structure of the CE program.

The mixture growth modelling revealed an interesting complication to the ordinary growth model, namely that there is a rather large group of consistently high-achieving students which is not well represented by the linear growth model. This pattern of achievement is, of course, the desired one, so optimally every student should belong to this class. Among the predictors investigated here, grades from upper secondary school predict membership in the class, but it does seem to be an important task for further research to investigate a broader range of characteristics of the consistently high-performing group.

The models fitted in this paper rely heavily on missing-data modelling. This approach yields unbiased estimates under the assumption that missingness is random given the information in the variables included in the model. One of the most powerful predictors of whether a person will remain in an education or not is previous achievement, and this information is included in the model. This suggests that the missing-data model should yield valid results. However, in future research the robustness of the results against violations of the assumptions of the missing-data modelling should be investigated more closely through extensions of the model to other independent variables, and also through further analyses of the different patterns of missingness. Here too a mixture modelling approach may prove fruitful.

Developmental and differential approaches to the study of change

Before concluding this chapter there is reason to address some more general theoretical and methodological issues in studying change, and particularly how developmental and differential approaches may be fruitfully combined in the study of change.

The example presented in the current study has been conducted within a differential tradition, and within this tradition the study yields meaningful results, both when it comes to describing change, and analysing correlates of change. From the point of view of developmental research the example may in itself seem somewhat lacking.

One of the characteristics of the differential, or psychometric, approach is that it is group-based rather than individual-based (Gustafsson 2002). Thus, the focus is on comparisons between individuals on a measure of some characteristic within a more or less clearly defined population. The measures employed in psychometric research also are more empirically based than theoretically based. An example which illustrates both the group-orientation and the empirical orientation of psychometric research is, of course, the IQ-test. Such tests express the relative standing of an individual within an age-group (or population for adults), on a measure which has well defined measurement properties, but for which the meaning of the scores is only poorly understood theoretically. The credit points measure studied in the present study has similar properties to the IQ-measure. Even though it seemingly has an absolute character it is defined in administrative terms (i.e. one point on the scale expresses one week's worth of study) rather than in psychological terms. Thus, the credit points measure may have a different meaning psychologically and educationally depending upon area and level of study.

To understand the nature of change from a developmental perspective, and in particular to be able to address the question what changes during development, it seems that a well-established understanding of the meaning of measure is a prerequisite. It is quite obvious that the traditional psychometric approach is fairly limited in its ability to provide deep answers to the more fundamental developmental questions.

This limitation certainly is a characteristic of the current study as well, which is because of the poorly understood properties of the credit points measure. As an example this measure of academic achievement may be contrasted with a more developmentally oriented scale, namely the scheme of intellectual and ethical development in the college years developed by Perry (1970). The Perry scheme was established on the basis of yearly interviews during the four years of college education at Harvard University. Several studies were conducted during the 1950s and 1960s which involved more than a hundred Harvard undergraduates.

The Perry scheme describes nine 'positions' which may be taken by a student with regard to knowledge and how to deal with the relative nature of knowledge. Position 1 is a dualistic position characterized by an absolute view of knowledge and a sharp distinction between right and wrong. Positions 2 and 3 modify the dualistic conception to allow for simple forms of pluralism. In positions 4, 5 and 6 successively more relativistic and contextual views of the nature of knowledge are established. In positions 7, 8 and 9 the student establishes modes of dealing with the relativistic world through choice and commitment. The Perry scheme describes the main line of development, but he also describes three positions of deflection (temporizing, escape and retreat), which explain why some students are halted in their development.

The Perry scale is a developmental scale which, in principle, could have been used as a dependent variable in the current study. Had data on the Perry scale been available (which, however, would have been an insurmountable task to accomplish) growth models certainly could have been fitted to this dependent variable as well. Because the results of these models would be interpretable in terms of a dimension with an intrinsic meaning they would, potentially at least, have much greater theoretical value from a developmental perspective than the analysis based on the credit points measure.

It should be added that developmental researchers too have come to realize that further progress within the developmental field may require more attention to basic measurement issues. Rose and Fischer (1998) argued that it is necessary to develop well-constructed rulers for measuring developmental constructs. Such rulers would provide a necessary conceptual and metric basis for application of quantitative modelling methods, such as growth modelling. While there is no universally accepted developmental measure, new methods of scaling and measurement will make it possible to develop such rulers (Fischer and Dawson, 2002), and there are indeed promising starts (e.g. Dawson 2002).

Integrating differential and developmental psychology

Given measures that actually reflect development, the full power of the growth modelling approach to describe individual differences in development, and to determine causes and consequences of development, would be available. There may be reason to end this chapter with a short description of a recently published study which in an interesting manner has used both growth modelling and mixture growth modelling to integrate psychometric and developmental models.

Demetriou, Christou, Spanoudis and Platsidou (2002) conducted a study of cognitive development, with the aim of investigating constructs from three traditions: information-processing, differential and developmental psychology. While these traditions can easily be recognized as distinct epistemological traditions, there also is considerable overlap in the phenomena investigated, and gains may be made if concepts from the different traditions are integrated. In the study three main constructs were focused upon, namely processing efficiency, working memory and problem solving.

A longitudinal study was conducted which involved subjects who were eight, ten, twelve and fourteen years old at the first measurement. Two more testings were done which were spaced one year apart. At each testing occasion participants were tested with a large test-battery designed to measure processing efficiency (i.e. speed of processing and inhibition), working memory capacity, and problem solving (quantitative, spatial and verbal reasoning).

In the first step of analysis, confirmatory factor analysis was used to fit a three-stratum hierarchical model. The first stratum represented the hypothesized dimensions within each of the three domains, and the second stratum represented the three dimensions processing efficiency, working memory and problem solving. At the third stratum a general factor was found with strong relations to all the second-stratum factors.

In a further step of analysis growth modelling was used to study patterns of change in the three dimensions processing efficiency, working memory, and problem solving. For each dimension a composite measure of performance in each domain at each occasion was included in the analysis, so the model comprised nine manifest variables. First a growth model assuming linear growth within each domain was specified. This model thus included an intercept and a slope parameter for each domain. These parameters were allowed to correlate freely. In order to specify linear growth, the slope parameter was fixed to have a relation of 0, 1 and 2 with the manifest variables at the three measurement occasions, respectively. However, this model did not fit the data, because the assumption of linear growth was not tenable. The relation of the slope variable and the manifest variable at the third measurement occasion therefore was allowed to be estimated as a free parameter. After this change the basic growth model fitted well.

The estimated parameters showed that the means of the slopes for all the variables were significant and positive when the effects of age at the first testing was not controlled for. However, controlling for age only the mean of the slope of processing efficiency was positive, indicating an increase in processing efficiency over time. The growth model also showed that the variance of the intercept parameters was significant for all the dimensions, indicating large individual differences in the initial states of processing. The three intercept parameters also were highly correlated. The variance of the slope parameters for speed of processing and for problem solving was significant, but not that for working memory. The slope parameters also were regressed onto the intercept parameters. While such regressions were found within abilities, no significant regressions were found across abilities, which shows that growth in an ability is not affected by the level of other abilities at a given point in time.

Demetriou et al. (2002) also used mixture growth modelling to investigate if there are different types of developers. They used the Mplus program to investigate a different number of hypothesized latent classes. Thus, the growth model described above was fitted under the assumption that there are two, three and four classes of subjects. The model with four classes was the best-fitting one. The four classes had different estimated mean and variance parameters for both slope and intercept for the three abilities.

Class 2 was the largest class and included 53 per cent of the total sample. The children in this class had the lowest mean of intercepts and the largest mean of slopes. They were thus the ones who showed the largest growth. The majority of the children belonged to the two youngest age groups. Class 1 included 11 per cent of the sample. Children in this class had high speed of processing and tended also to have relatively high levels in the other two abilities. Most of the children in this class were older, and the pattern of results suggests that they had already to a large extent developed their abilities. Class 3 comprised 16 per cent of the sample and in this class too the children tended to be older. Class 4, which comprised 11 per cent of the sample, also tended to represent older children. The children in these two classes were identical in level and growth of speed of processing, and their results for working memory also were similar. However, class 3 developed positively in problem solving, while class 4 developed negatively in this ability.

Demetriou et al. (2002) observed that there were systematic differences in processing efficiency both among the four classes and the four age cohorts, while for working memory there were large differences among classes but not among age cohorts. The effect of testing occasion was significant for both processing efficiency and working memory. Demetriou et al. (2002) interpreted this pattern of results as suggesting that processing efficiency was a developmental factor, and working memory was an individual differences factor. Thus, the main conclusion of the Demetriou et al. (2002) study, which also involved a large number of analyses not described here, is that differential and developmental psychology can be integrated into a unified model, through separating different aspects of change in information processing. Changes in efficiency in focusing and processing information explain developmental differences, while differences in working memory capacity explain individual differences.

REFERENCES

Bayley, N. (1956). Individual patterns of development. *Child Development, 27*, 45–74.
Dawson, T. L. (2002). New tools, new insights: Kohlberg's moral reasoning stages revisited. *International Journal of Behaviour Development, 26*, 154–66.
Demetriou, A., Christou, C., Spanoudis, G. and Platsidou, M. (2002). The development of mental processing: efficiency, working memory and thinking. *Monographs of the Society for Research in Child Development, serial no. 268, 67*(1).
Duncan, T. E., Duncan, S. C., Strycker, L. A. and Li, F. (1999). *An introduction to latent variable growth curve modelling. Concepts, issues, and applications.* Mahwah, NJ: Lawrence Erlbaum Associates.
Fischer, K. W. and Dawson, T. L. (2002). A new kind of developmental science: using models to integrate theory and research. Commentary in Demetriou, A., Christou, C., Spanoudis, G. and Platsidou, M. (2002). The development of mental processing: efficiency, working memory and thinking. *Monographs of the Society for Research in Child Development, serial no. 268, 67*(1), 156–67.
Goldstein, H. (1995). *Multilevel statistical models.* London: Edward Arnold.
Gustafsson, J. E. (2002). Measurement from a hierarchical point of view. In H. I. Braun, D. N. Jackson and D. E. Wiley (eds.) *The role of constructs in psychological and educational measurement* (pp. 73–95). Mahwah, NJ: Lawrence Erlbaum Associates.
Gustafsson, J.-E. and Reuterberg, S.-E. (2000). *Metodproblem vid studier av Högskoleprovets prognosförmåga – och deras lösning!* (Methodological problems in studies of the prognostic power of the SweSAT – and their solution). *Pedagogisk Forskning i Sverige, 5*(4), 273–83.
Gustafsson, J.-E. and Stahl, P. A. (2000). *STREAMS User's Guide. Version 2.5.* Molndal, Sweden: MultivariateWare.
    (2001). *Using Mplus under STREAMS 2.5.* Molndal, Sweden: MultivariateWare.
Gustafsson, J.-E., Andersson, A. and Hansen, M. (2000). *Prestationer och prestationsskillnader i 1990-talets skola.* (Achievement and achievement differences in school during the 1990s). SOU 2000: 39, pp. 135–211.
Gustafsson, J.-E., Wedman, I. and Westerlund, A. (1992). The dimensionality of the Swedish Scholastic Aptitude Test. *Scandinavian Journal of Educational Research, 36*, 21–39.
Harris, C. W. (1963). *Problems in measuring change.* Madison: University of Wisconsin Press.
Heath, R. (1978). Personality and the development of students in higher education. In Parker, C. A. (ed.) *Encouraging development in college students.* Minneapolis: University of Minnesota Press.
Humphreys, L. G. (1968). The fleeting nature of college academic success. *Journal of Educational Psychology, 59*, 375–80.

McArdle, J. J. (1988). Dynamic but structural equation modelling of repeated measures data. In R. B. Cattell and J. Nesselroade (eds.) *Handbook of multivariate experimental psychology* (2nd edn, pp. 561–614). New York: Plenum Press.

McArdle, J. J. and Epstein, D. (1987). Latent growth curves within developmental structural equation models. *Child Development*, 58, 110–33.

Meredith, W. and Tisak, J. (1990). Latent curve analysis. *Psychometrika*, 55, 107–22.

Muthén, B. (1989). Latent variable modelling in heterogeneous populations. *Psychometrika*, 54, 557–85.

   (1996). Growth modelling with binary responses. In A. V. Eye and C. Clogg (eds.) *Categorical variables in developmental research: methods of analysis* (pp. 37–54). San Diego, CA: Academic Press.

   (1997). Latent variable growth modelling with multilevel data. In M. Berkane (ed.) *Latent variable modelling with application to causality* (pp. 149–61). New York: Springer Verlag.

   (2000). Methodological issues in random coefficient growth modelling using a latent variable framework: applications to the development of heavy drinking. In J. Rose, L. Chassin, C. Presson and J. Sherman (eds.) *Multivariate applications in substance use research* (pp. 113–40). Hillsdale, NJ: Erlbaum.

   (2001a). Second-generation structural equation modelling with a combination of categorical and continuous latent variables: new opportunities for latent class/latent growth modelling. In Collins, L. M. and Sayer, A. (eds.) *New methods for the analysis of change* (pp. 291–322). Washington, DC: APA.

   (2001b). Latent variable mixture modelling. In G. A. Marcoulides and R. E. Schumacker (eds.) *New developments and techniques in structural equation modelling* (pp. 1–33). Lawrence Erlbaum Associates.

Muthén, B., Kaplan, D. and Hollis, M. (1987). On structural equation modelling with data that are not missing completely at random. *Psychometrika*, 42, 431–62.

Muthén, B. and Khoo, S. T. (1998). Longitudinal studies of achievement growth using latent variable modelling. *Learning and individual differences, special issue: latent growth curve analysis*, 10, 73–101.

Muthén, B. and Muthén, L. (2000). Integrating person-centered and variable-centered analysis: growth mixture modelling with latent trajectory classes. *Alcoholism: Clinical and Experimental Research*, 24, 882–91.

Muthén, L. K. and Muthén, B. O. (1998). *Mplus User's Guide*. Los Angeles, CA: Muthén and Muthén.

   (2001). *Mplus User's Guide* (2nd edn). Los Angeles, CA: Muthén and Muthén.

Perry, W. G. (1970). *Forms of intellectual and ethical development in the college years: a scheme*. New York: Holt, Rinehart and Winston.

Raudenbush, S. W. and Chan, W. (1992). Growth curve analysis in accelerated longitudinal designs. *Journal of Research in Crime and Delinquency*, 29, 387–411.

Reuterberg, S.-E. (2002). Correcting validity coefficients for restriction of range and disjunctive selection rules with missing-data modelling: a simulation study. Manuscript.

Rogosa, D. R., Brandt, D. and Zimowski, M. (1982). A growth curve approach to the measurement of change. *Psychological Bulletin*, 92, 726–48.

Rogosa, D. R. and Willett, J. B. (1985). Understanding correlates of change by modelling individual differences in growth. *Psychometrika*, 50, 203–28.

Rose, S. P. and Fischer, K. W. (1998). Models and rulers in dynamical development. *British Journal of Developmental Psychology, 16*, 123–31.

Svensson, A., Gustafsson, J.-E. and Reuterberg, S.-E. (2001). *Högskoleprovets prognosvärde. Samband mellan provresultat och framgång första studieåret för civilingenjörs-, jurist- och lärarutbildningarna.* (The prognostic power of the SweSAT. Relations between test performance and first year achievement for civil engineers, lawyers, and teachers). National Agency for Higher Education, Report 2001:19R.

Willett, J. B. and Sayer, A. G. (1994). Using covariance structure analysis to detect correlates and predictors of individual change over time. *Psychological Bulletin, 116*, 363–81.

Index

NOTE: page numbers in *italic type* refer to tables and figures.

absolute stability, 331
abstract understanding, 167, 178–9
academic achievement, 381
  Civil Engineer Program, 382–3,
    385–96
acceleration *see* cognitive acceleration
accommodation, 109
ACT-R model, 146–50, 152
action plans, 40
action understanding *see* sensorimotor
    understanding
activation space, 89
active experience, 268
adaptive networks, 86, 110
addition-rule, 122, 135
ambiguity, 368–9
amygdala, 226–7
analysis of variance, 328
anterior cingulate cortex, 227, 230
appraisals, 222, 223
art tasks, 277–80
assimilation, 109
associative knowledge, 189–90, 192, 209
attachment, 233–4
attention, 221, 222, 230
attractors, 88–91, 92, 93–4, 97, 99, 102, 104,
    222–3
autoassociator networks, 112

back-up strategies, 188, 193
Baddeley, A. D., 24, 35
balance scale task
  computational model, 146–50
  developmental model, 142–6
  LCA applied to, 126–32
  past research on, 118–24
  Rule Assessment Methodology, 120–2,
    124–32
  rules and response times, 132–7
  transition between rules, 137–41

Band, G., 37
basins of attraction, 88, 92, 93–4, 96, 97, 99,
    102, 105
bimodality, 137, 139, 141, 338, 367
Binet, A., 306
bottom-up dynamics, 54–8
brain
  and emotion, 223–30
  organization, 10, 223
  physiology, 305
  size, 313
brain stem, 224–5, 227
bridge building, 163–7
bridging, 13, 81, 92–6, 299–300
buggy-rule, 122, 128, 135
bulb task, 169–79
Butterfield, E. C., 124

candy sellers, 242–3, 244
candy selling
  as collective activity, 247
  social history of, 245
  use of price ratio, 244, 248–50
cascade correlation networks, 112
CASE (Cognitive Acceleration through
    Science Education), 301, *303*
Case, R., 264, 283, 313
case studies, 330–1
catastrophe theory, 137, 139, 357
categorical reasoning, 29–30, *42–4*, 45, 46,
    47, 48, 49, 50, *53*
causal reasoning, 31, *42–4*, 45, 46, 47, 49,
    50
central conceptual structure theory, 264, 270
  content of thought, 273–4
  educational applications, 285–91
  educational implications, 284–5
  factors activating change, 283–4
  form of thought, 271–3
  and Piaget's theory, 291–2

central conceptual structures, 273–4, 282–3, 284
  narrative, *282*, 280–2, 285
  numerical, 274–5, *282*, 285, 288–90
  spatial, 275–80, *282*
central executive system, 24, 35–6, 57
central narrative structure, *282*, 280–2, 285
central numerical structure, 274–5, *282*
  instructional programs, 285, 288–90
central spatial structure, 275–80, *282*
cerebral cortex, 221–3
change
  types of, 320–3
  see also cognitive change; conceptual
    change; measuring change;
    mechanisms of change
chaos models, 335
characteristic frequency, 359
characteristic ranges, 368–9
characteristicness, 362–3
Chen, Z., 197
Chi, M. T. H., 106
children
  content of thought, 273–4
  fair sharing among, 251–6
  form of thought, 271–3
  as subjects, 246, 247
  teaching fractions to, 251–9
  use of mathematics, 241
  see also candy sellers
choice/no-choice method, 196–7, 201–7, 211–12
chunking, 309–10, 312
Civil Engineer Program, 382–3
  research results, 385–96
classical approach, 2–3
cognition, impact of emotion on, 221–3
cognitive acceleration, 12–14, 62
  aim of, 296
  application of model, 301–2
  and central conceptual structures, 284–91
  and consciousness, 311, 312
  defining, 296
  effects of, 302–4
  and evolution, 313–14
  and metacognition, 311–12
  modelling, 297–301
  teaching, 300
  and working memory, 308–12
Cognitive Acceleration through Science
    Education (CASE), 301, *303*
cognitive change
  aspects of, 1
  as central to education, 264

  conceptions of, 2–4, 74, 75
  general models of, 4–10
  inducing and causing, 10–14
  measuring and modelling, 14–16
  modelling dynamics of, 91–103
  strong and weak, 104–7
  theory criteria, 76–7
  theory of, 111–12
  what, why and how, 16–19
  see also conceptual change; mechanisms of
    change
cognitive coherence, 224
cognitive conflict, 267, 297, 298, 300, 311
cognitive development
  accelerating *see* cognitive acceleration
  as continuous, 189, 209
  dynamic approach, 369–72, 373–4
  impact of emotion on, 230–5
  information-processing approach, 207–12, 307
  neurophysiological approach, 305
  Piaget's theory of, 265–70
  psychometric approach, 305–6
cognitive dissonance, 298
cognitive psychology, 21, 27, 65, 67
cognitive variability, 9, 207, 208
collective activities, 241, 247
  fair sharing, 251–6
combination, 80, 92–6, 109
compensation-rule, 124, 127, 128, 129, 135, 136
competencies, 159
complexity, and skill development, 162, 163, 165
computational estimation, 201–7
computer models, 187, 210–11
  proportional reasoning, 146–50, 151
  SCADS, 190–5, 201, 209, 210–11
concepts, 356, 357–8, 360
  object concept, 356, 360, 362–3
conceptual bridging, 287
conceptual change
  cognitive account of, 78–83
  dynamical account of, 83–4
  mechanisms of, 74–5, 78–83, 107–11
  modelling, 91–103
    neural networks, 84–91
  strong and weak, 104–7
  theoretical background, 76–8
conceptual structures *see* central conceptual
    structures
concrete operational stage, *267*
concrete preparation, 13, 299, 300, 301, 302
conditional dependence, 358
conflation, 79, 96

connectionist models, and rules, 124
connectivity, 305, 306, 307
consciousness, 25, 311, 312
conservation tasks, 246
constructivism, 268
constructivist principles, 268, 291
content of children's thought, 273–4
content-realizing points, 87, 92, 104
context
  concept dependent on, 360–1
  of measurement, 366–8
  and representation, 173
  of skill development, 165, 166, 168
context neurones, 84, 85
contextualist approach, 3, 356
continuous change, 189, 209, 322
  see also discontinuity
coordination of mappings, 175–6, 178
coordination of skills, 166–7
critical slowing down, 139, 141
Crowley, K., 195
cultural forms in quantification, 243–4
cultural-developmental approach, 247–8
cusp model, 137–9
cycle of levels in tiers, 166–7

DEF (directive-executive function), 23,
  36–41
Demetriou, A., 55, 76, 398
Dennis, S., 277, 280
density concept, 309–10
determinate properties, 361, 362
development
  and difference, 355
  of mind, 32
    general forms of, 32–3
    general processes, 33–41
    thought domains, 41–53
  quantifying, 328–30, 335
  variability as feature of, 357
  see also higher education;
    microdevelopment
developmental assessment tests, 275,
  277–82
developmental history, 364–6
developmental model for problem solving,
  142–6
developmental psychology, 22, 27, 65
  and differential approach, 396–400
developmental range, 166
developmental scale of skills, 160–1
developmental sequencing, 286–7
developmental stages, 265–6, 267, 272, 273
  and emotion, 231–3
  measuring, 366–8

developmental transitions see phase
  transitions
diencephalon, 225–6, 227
difference scores, 323–5
differential psychology, 21–2, 27, 65, 67
  and developmental approach, 396–400
differential structural equation modelling
  (dSEM), 336
differentiation, 82, 102–3, 267, 283
diffusion model, 370
dimensional-change card sort, 39
directive-executive control processes, 25–6
directive-executive function (DEF), 23,
  36–41
discontinuity, 137, 141, 144, 366, 372
  see also phase transitions
discovery heuristics, 194
disequilibrium, 268, 283
divergence, 139, 140, 141
domains of thought, 27–32, 260, 308
  criteria for, 26–7
  development of, 41–53, 67–8
  dynamic relations with processes, 53–9,
    60–5
  see also central conceptual structures
dual representations, 45–6
dynamic approach, 3–4
  to conceptual change, 83–4
    modelling, 91–103
    neural networks, 84–91
dynamic assessment approach, 340
dynamic connectionism, 5
dynamic growth models, 369–72
dynamic modelling, 58, 91–103, 336–9,
  369–72, 373
dynamic relations, 53–65
dynamic systems theory, 32, 217, 218–21,
  337, 356, 358, 373–4
dynamical neural networks, 84–91

Edelman, G. M., 84
education
  and central conceptual structures, 284–91
  and cognitive change, 264
  and constructivism, 269–70
  and Piaget's theory, 266
  and skill development, 179–80
  teaching fractions, 251–9
  see also higher education; science
    education
effortful control, 230–1
electrical circuit building, 169–79
electroencephalogram (EEG) techniques,
  234
Elman, J. L., 89

emotion, 10
    functionality of, 220
    impact on cognition, 221–3
    impact on cognitive development, 230–5
    intentionality of, 220
    and neural processes, 223–30
environmental supports *see* support
environmental variability, 18
episodic buffer, 24
epistemic subject, 246, 259
equilibration, 266, 283, 297
error variability, 355
event sequence schema, 280
evolution, and cognitive acceleration,
    313–14
experience
    impact on education, 268
    and strategy choice, 190
exploration, 268, 283
external dynamics, 87

fair sharing, 251–6, 258–9
false belief tasks, 39
feedback, 229
feedforward networks, 112
Ferretti, R. P., 124
fluctuation, 9, 355–6
Fodor, J., 106
foresighted representations, 48–9
form of children's thought, 271–3
form-function shifts, 249
formal operational stage, *267*
formal operations *see* schemata of formal
    operations
fractions, 251–9
frequency
    characteristic, 359
    of measurement, 335–9, 359, 363–4
frequency range, 364
Frye, D., 40
functional architecture level of change, 74
functional level, 166
functional shift model, 36
functionality, 219, 220
fusion, 81, 99–101, 109

gain scores, 323, 324–5
Gearhart, M., 257
general processes, 23–6, 33–41, 296
generalization, 157
generative networks, 86, 100
genetic method, 247–51, 256
goal sketch filters, 194, 201
goals, 244
groping, 157, 169

growth curve models, 331–5, 336, 379–81,
    387–91, 398–9
    see also dynamic growth models; mixture
    growth models

Heath, R., 381
hierarchical complexity, 51
hierarchical integration, 267, 283
hierarchy of intelligence, 22
higher education
    development during, 381–2
        research method, 382–4
        research results, 385–96
historical subject, 247, 261
hypothalamus, 225
hysteresis, 137, 139, 140–1, 149

identity tests, 359
implicit representations, 49
indeterminate properties, 361–2
individual activity, 247
individual differences, 21, 54, 55, 59–65,
    67–8, 233–4
    study of, 379–80
information-processing approach, 21, 307
    contribution to cognitive development,
        207–12
    methodological issues, 195–7
    theoretical issues, 186–95
    to computational estimation, 201–7
    to problem solving, 197–201
Inhelder, B., 306
inhibition of response, 36–7
inhibitory control, 230–1
instruction *see* education; teaching
instructional design model, 284, 285, *285*
instructional programs, 285–91
integrated representations, 46–7
integration, hierarchical, 267, 283
intelligence, 22, 27, 54, 55, 66–7, 305–7
    see also mind
intentionality, 220
internal dynamics, 87
interventions
    quantifying change, 325–8, 334
    see also cognitive acceleration
interweaving, 80, 81, 96
intra-individual variability, 370–2
item response theory (IRT), 325

Jansen, B. R. J., 129
juggling skills, 167–9

Kail, R., 34
knowledge, in instructional programs, 287

knowledge construction, 268
knowledge structures *see* central conceptual
    structures; operational structures

landscape, 90–1, 92, 105, 106
language, 313, 318–19
latent class analysis (LCA), 7, 125, 126, 150
    applied to balance scale task, 126–32
latent class model, 125, 126
latent variable modelling, 15
latent variables, 7, 125
learning curves, 321–3
Lecacheur, M., 202
Lemaire, P., 188, 196, 200, 202
limbic system, 226, 227
limited time mechanism, 54
linear growth models, 380
linear learning curve, 321–2
linear models of change, 332–3, 338
Loess smoothing procedure, 364
logistic growth, 32–3, 35, 62
long-term memory, 307, 308
Lord, F. M., 324

McClelland, J. L., 124
McKeough, A., 280
many-to-one correspondences, 249
mappings, 79, 80, 92–101
    of representations, 168, 173–6, 178
mark-up in candy selling, 242–3, 244, 248–50
Marr, D., 74
mathematical cognition
    Piaget's approach, 245–7
    see also central numerical structure
mathematical means, in quantification, 244
mathematical reasoning, 395
mathematical-state transitions, 83
mathematics
    in children's activities, 241
    instructional programs, 285, 288–90
    see also quantification practices
maturation, 268, 283, 297
measurement contexts and conditions, 366–8
measurement error, 355, 364
measurement frequency, 335–9, 359, 363–4
measurement models
    ambiguity, 368–9
    characteristic ranges, 368–9
    characteristicness, 362–3
    describing developmental history, 364–6
    determinate and indeterminate properties,
        361–2
measuring change, 318
    case studies, 330–1
    difference scores, 323–5

dynamic systems models, 336–9
growth curves, 331–5
methodological developments, 340–1
time series models, 335–9
triggered change, 325–8, 334
unsolicited change, 328–30, 335
mechanics of change, 17–18
mechanisms of change, 17–18, 67, 74–5,
        78–83, 107–11, 112
mental number line structure, 274–5
meta-analysis, 328
metacognition, 299, 300, 301, 302, 311–12
metacognitive knowledge, 190, 194,
        209–10
metaphors, 169, 174–5, 180
metarepresentation, 108
methods *see* research methods/methodology
microdevelopment, 8, 158, 161–3
    building bridges, 163–7
    building electrical circuits, 169–79
    juggling skills, 167–9
microgenetic analysis, 195–6, 198, 201, 211,
        247, 248–9, 253–5
mind
    approaches to, 21–3
    architecture of, 66
        general processes, 23–6
        specialized processes, 26–7
        thought domains, 27–32
    development of, 32
        general forms, 32–3
        general processes, 33–41
        thought domains, 41–53
    dynamic relations, 53–9
    individual differences, 59–65
misconceptions, 169
missing data models, 382, 385, 388, 390, 396
mixture growth models, 381, 391–5, 399–400
modelling
    dynamics of change, 91–103
    strong and weak change, 104–7
    see also dynamic modelling
models
    differences and similarities, 354–5
    nature of, 354
    see also computer models; growth curve
        models; measurement models
multi-modality, 371
multigroup analysis, 144
multivariate models, 333

narrative structure *see* central narrative
        structure
negative feedback, 229
neo-Piagetian theories, 259–60, 373

neural networks, 79, 84–91, 308, 360
neural processes, emotion in, 223–30
neuraxis, 224
neurophysiological approach, 305
non-linear dynamics, 86, 110
non-linear learning curve, 321–2
non-linear models of change, 333, 338
normative stability, 331
novel knowledge, 175
Number Knowledge test, 275
Number Worlds, 285, 287, 288–90
numerical structure *see* central numerical
　　structure

object concept, 356, 360, 362–3
ontogenetic analysis, 247, 249–50, 255–6
operational structures, 265, 267
opportunity to learn measure, 257, 258–9
optimal level, 162, 166
orbitofrontal cortex, 227, 233, 234
overlapping waves model, 7, 143–6, 151,
　　188–9, 208, 209

part–whole relations *see* fractions
Parziale, J., 163
Perkins, D. N., 300
Perry, W. G., 381, 397
Perry Scheme, 397
person-oriented longitudinal statistical
　　analysis, 330
phase changes, 105
phase transitions, 6, 99, 111, 137–41, 218, 232
phonological loop, 25
Piaget, J., 1, 109, 157, 306
　　and central conceptual structure theory,
　　　　291–2
　　structural developmental approach, 245–7,
　　　　259
　　theory of cognitive development, 265–70
　　see also balance scale task; neo-Piagetian
　　　　theories
planning, 40
positive feedback, 229
Posner, M. I., 230, 231
pre-operational stage, *267*
prefrontal cortex, 227
price ratio, 244, 248–50
Principal Component Analysis (PCA), 102
principled representations, 50
problem behaviour graph, 75
problem solving, 142–6, 197–201, 398–400
　　dynamic relations, *37, 38*, 58–9, 60–5
　　see also reasoning; skill development
processes
　　concepts as, 356

　　see also domains of thought; general
　　　　processes
processing capacity, 24–5, 35–6
processing efficiency, 23–4, 33–5, 398–400
　　dynamic relations, *37, 38*, 54, 57, 58–9,
　　　　60–5
production composition, 147
production rules, 146, 148
progression, 9–10
properties
　　determinate, 361, 362
　　indeterminate, 361–2
proportional reasoning
　　computational model of, 146–50, 151
　　see also balance scale task
propositional reasoning, 31–2, *42–4*, 45, 46,
　　47, 48, 49, 50
protorepresentations, 45
psychological subject, 260
psychometric approach, 305–6, 396
　　see also differential psychology

quantification practices
　　in candy selling, 242–3, 244
　　cultural forms in, 243–4
　　fair sharing, 251–6, 258–9
　　fractions, 251–9
　　mathematical means and goals, 244
　　presuppositions in, 244
　　and social history, 245
quantitative reasoning, 30, *42–4*, 45, 46, 47,
　　48, 49, *53*

Raftopoulos, A., 76
RAM *see* Rule Assessment Methodology
random coefficient models, 380
reading comprehension, 327–8
reasoning, 60–5, 395
　　see also domains of thought; problem
　　　　solving; proportional reasoning;
　　　　propositional reasoning
reentrant connections, 84, 85
refinement, 82, 103
regression, 8, 9–10, 329
regression analysis, 394
regression model, 380
regulation of emotion, 231
repeated measures model, 380
representation
　　development of, 50–3
　　metarepresentation, 108
　　and skill development, 165, 166, 167, 172–8
　　systems of, 47, 175–8
　　transition to, 170–2
　　types of, 41–50

representational change, 74, 75, 83, 84–91, 104, 108, 112
representational flexibility, 51–2
research methods/methodology, 210–12, 234–5
    case studies, 330–1
    choice/no-choice methods, 196–7, 201–7, 211–12
    developments, 340–1
    difference scores, 323–5
    genetic method, 247–51, 256
    growth curves, 331–5
    literature search, 319–20
    meta-analysis, 328
    quantifying triggered change, 325–8, 334
    quantifying unsolicited change, 328–30, 335
    time series models, 335–9
response times (RTs), 132–7
restriction of range, 382, 385
restructuring, 79, 96–9
retrieval strategy, 188, 193
rhythm, in time series models, 336
Rothbart, M. K., 230, 231
Rule Assessment Methodology (RAM), 7, 120–2, 124–32
rule hierarchies, 40
rules
    consistent use of, 142–3
    criteria for, 124
    overlapping waves model of, 143–6
    and response times, 132–7
    theoretical approaches to, 152
    transition between, 137–41

S-shaped learning curves, 322
Saloman, G., 300
saltatory learning curves, 322
Salter, D., 281
Salthouse, T. A., 54
Saxe, G. B., 257
SCADS (Strategy Choice and Discovery Simulation), 190–5, 201, 209, 210–11
scale of skills, 160–1
schemata, 169, 174–5, 180, 267
    and working memory, 310–11, 312
schemata of formal operations, 297, 298, 300
science education
    building bridges, 163–7
    building electrical circuits, 169–79
    cognitive acceleration in, 297–8, 301–4
    concept of skill in, 158
self-awareness, 41
self-evaluation, 40–1
self-organization, 217

self-organizing neural processes, 223–30
Seltzer, M., 257
sensorimotor stage, 267
sensorimotor (action) understanding, 163–4, 166, 169, 170–2, 177
Shayer, M., 297, 311
Shrager, J., 190
Shultz, T. R., 112
Siegler, R. S., 120, 143, 188, 190, 195, 196, 197, 200
simultaneity mechanism, 54
situated cognition theory, 3, 356
situatedness, 356–7, 360
skill development
    building bridges, 163–7
    building electrical circuits, 169–79
    educational implications, 179–80
    juggling, 167–9
skill theory, 159, 160–1
skills
    defining, 159
    framework for analysing, 158–63
Smith, L. B., 219, 356, 360
social construction, 299, 300, 301, 302, 311
social history, 245, 261
social interaction, 268, 283, 284
sociogenetic analysis, 248, 250, 255
solicited (triggered) change, 323
    quantifying, 325–8, 334
spatial reasoning, 30–1, 42–4, 45, 46, 47, 48, 49, 53
spatial structure see central spatial structure
spatial-artistic understanding, 277–80
specialized processes see domains of thought
speed of processing, 24, 34–5, 54, 57, 60–5, 112
staircase model, 143, 188
stepwise curves, 322
stop-signal procedure, 36
storage buffers, 35–6
strategies
    consistent use of, 142–3
    defining, 188
    overlapping waves model of, 143–6
    rules and response times, 132–7
    transition between, 137–41
strategy adaptiveness, 189
strategy change, 188–90
    choice/no choice approach, 196–7
    microgenetic approach, 195–6
    and toddlers' problem solving, 198–201
strategy choice, 189, 190, 192, 208–9
Strategy Choice and Discovery Simulation (SCADS), 190–5, 201, 209, 210–11
strategy competition, 188

strategy development
  in computational estimation, 201–7
  in toddlers' problem solving, 197–201
strategy discovery, 194–5
strategy distribution, 189, 199–200, 203, 208
strategy efficiency, 189, 203–4
strategy execution, 192–4
strategy repertoire, 189, 199, 208
strategy selection, 189, 204–5
strategy variability, 188, 199
strong cognitive change, 104–7
structural analogy, 80, 81
structural equation models (SEMs), 380, 387
structural-developmental approach, 245–7,
    251
subject
  epistemic, 246, 259
  historical, 247, 261
  psychological, 260
sudden jump, 139
sum strategy, 188, 193
support
  for cognitive acceleration, 298
  in instructional programs, 287–8
  in skill development, 162, 165, 166
Swedish Scholastic Achievement Test
    (SweSAT), 383, 390
syllogistic reasoning, 337
symbolic individuation, 108
symbols, 89–90
synaptic plasticity, 230
synaptic shaping, 227
synchronization, 217, 224, 228, 229
systems of representations, 47, 175–8
systems theory see dynamic systems theory

Tabor, W., 102
Tanenhaus, M. K., 102
teaching
  cognitive acceleration, 300
  and constructivism, 269–70
  fractions, 251–9
  instructional programs, 285–91
  and Piaget's theory, 266
temporal context, 358
thalamus, 225
Thelen, E., 219, 356, 360
theory of mind, 39–40
thinking
  dynamic relations, 54, 60
  see also domains of thought
time, 358, 359
time series models, 335–9

toddlers' problem solving, 197–201
tool strategy, 200
top-down dynamics, 58–9
transcendent representations, 47–8
transfer, 299, 300
transitions see phase transitions
trend, in time series models, 336
triggered change see solicited change
true scores, 355, 356
tuning, 80, 81–2, 102–3

unsolicited change, 323
  quantifying, 328–30, 335

van der Maas, H. L. J., 129
van Geert, P., 32, 320, 337
van Maanen, L., 126
van Rijn, H., 146, 147
variability, 218, 372
  as characteristic of concepts, 357–8
  environmental, 18
  error variability, 355–6
  importance of cognitive, 9, 207, 208
  as information source, 366
  intra-individual in growth models, 370–2
verbal ability, 395
verbal justification, 119–20
verbal (propositional) reasoning, 31–2, 42–4,
    45, 46, 47, 48, 49, 50
Verhulst model, 337
vertical integration, 228, 229, 232, 233
Visitation Set Gravitation (VSG) network, 102
visuo-spatial reasoning, 42–4, 45, 46, 47, 48,
    49, 53
visuo-spatial sketchpad, 25
Vygotsky, L. S., 247, 298

weak cognitive change, 104–7
Williams, B. R., 36
working memory, 24, 35–6, 398–400
  dynamic relations, 38, 54, 55, 57, 58–9,
    60–5
  of neural networks, 85
  and strategy, 205, 210
working memory capacity
  and central conceptual structure theory,
    271, 279, 283, 284
  efficient use of, 309–12
  growth of, 307–9

Zelazo, P. R., 39
Zone of Proximal Development (ZPD), 298,
    314, 367